I have a workroom in my home and at the studio. I pay attention to decorating my workroom at home, but I tend to neglect the one at the studio, so it's yucky. But I spend much more time at the studio, so today I just tried to make my room there a little cuter.

But it's still yucky.

—Katsura Hoshino

Shiga Prefecture native Katsura Hoshino's hit manga series *D.Gray-man* has been serialized in *Weekly Shonen Jump* since 2004. Katsura's debut manga, "Continue," appeared for the first time in *Weekly Shonen Jump* in 2003.

Katsura adores cats.

D.GRAY-MAN
VOL. 21
SHONEN JUMP ADVANCED
Manga Edition

STORY AND ART BY
KATSURA HOSHINO

English Adaptation/Lance Caselman
Translation/John Werry
Touch-up Art & Lettering/HudsonYards
Design/Matt Hinrichs
Editor/Gary Leach

D.GRAY-MAN © 2004 by Katsura Hoshino. All rights reserved.
First published in Japan in 2004 by SHUEISHA Inc., Tokyo. English translation rights arranged by
SHUEISHA Inc.

Printed in the U.S.A.

Published by VIZ Media, LLC
P.O. Box 77010
San Francisco, CA 94107

10 9 8 7 6 5 4 3 2 1
First printing, November 2011

www.viz.com

www.shonenjump.com

SHONEN JUMP ADVANCED MANGA EDITION

D.Gray-man

STORY & ART BY
Katsura Hoshino

vol. 21

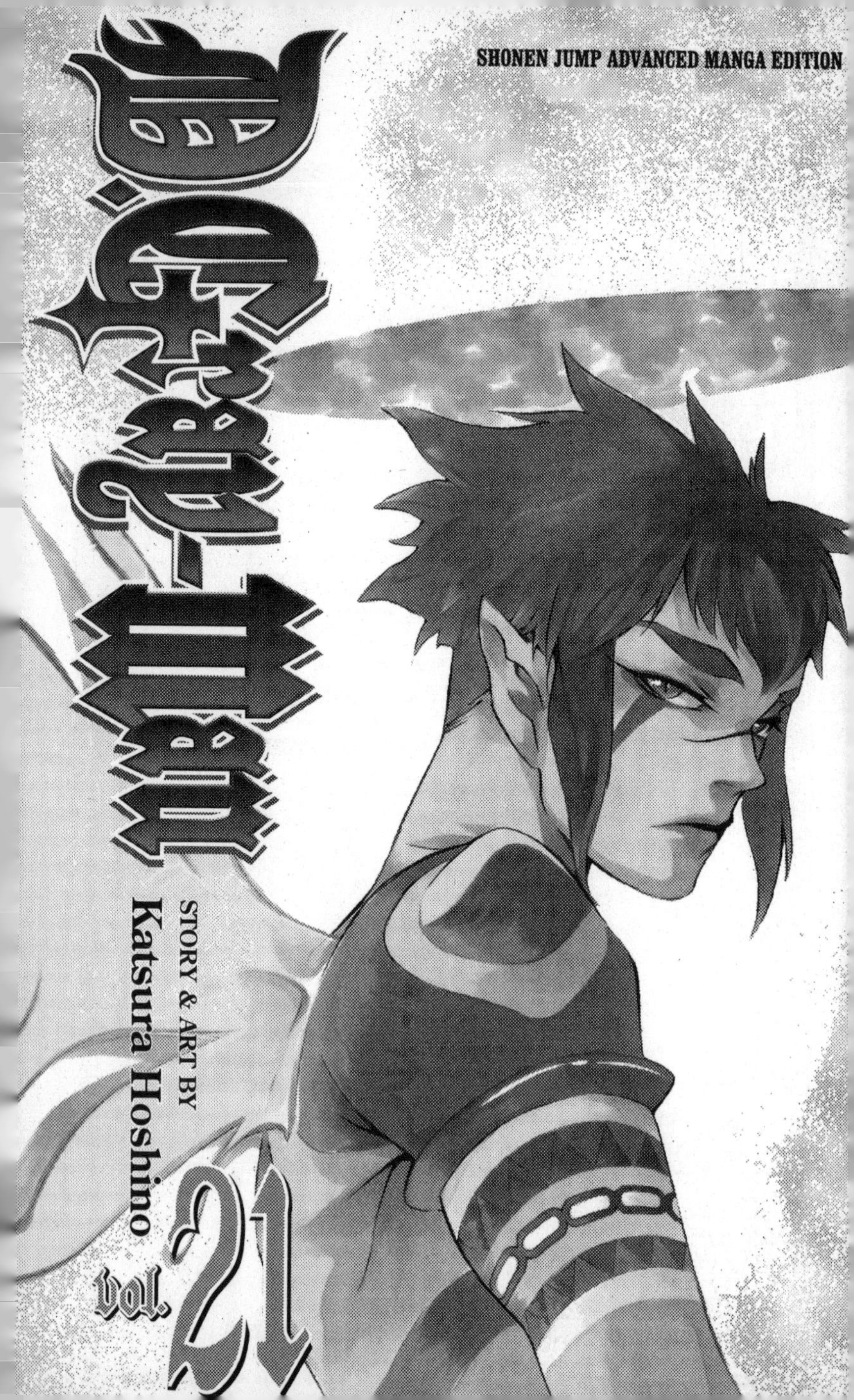

D.Gray-man

CHARACTERS

EXORCISTS

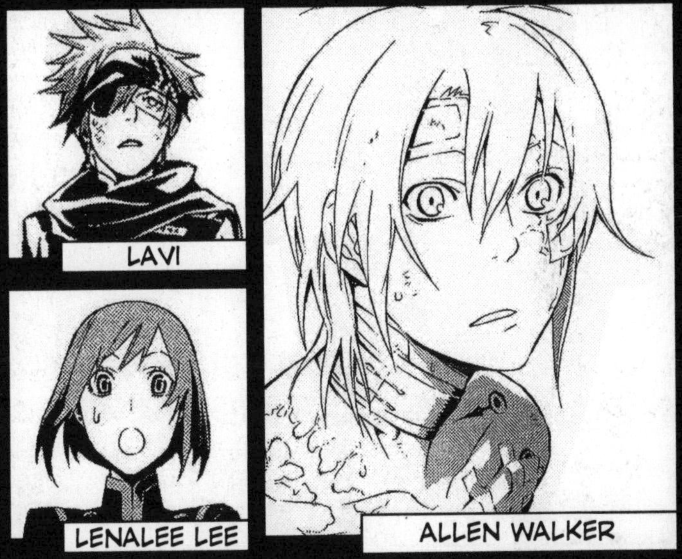

LAVI
LENALEE LEE
ALLEN WALKER

SECOND EXORCISTS

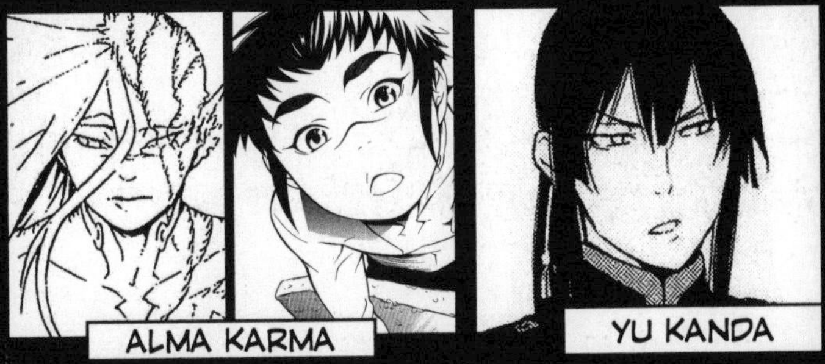

ALMA KARMA
YU KANDA

THIRD EXORCISTS

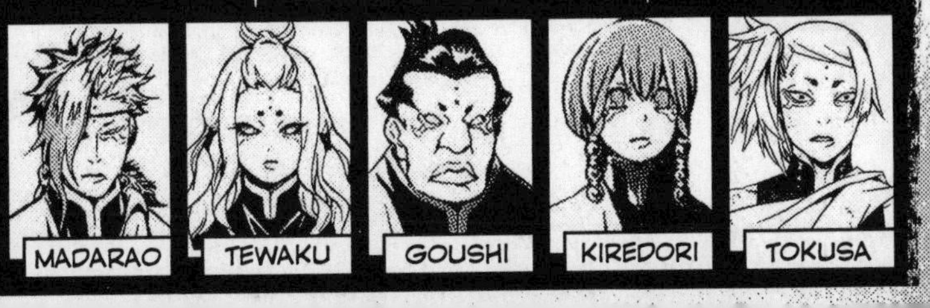

MADARAO
TEWAKU
GOUSHI
KIREDORI
TOKUSA

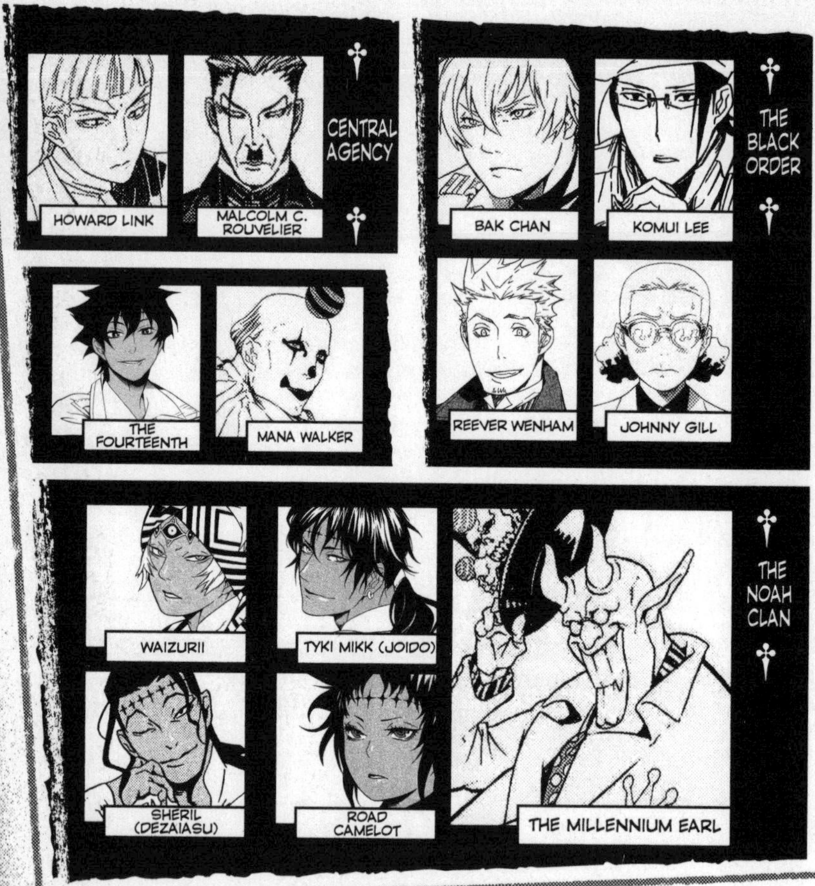
THE BLACK ORDER
KOMUI LEE
BAK CHAN
JOHNNY GILL
REEVER WENHAM
CENTRAL AGENCY
MALCOLM C. ROUVELIER
HOWARD LINK
MANA WALKER
THE FOURTEENTH
THE NOAH CLAN
THE MILLENNIUM EARL
TYKI MIKK (JOIDO)
WAIZURII
ROAD CAMELOT
SHERIL (DEZAIASU)

STORY

IT ALL BEGAN CENTURIES AGO WITH THE DISCOVERY OF A CUBE CONTAINING AN APOCALYPTIC PROPHECY FROM AN ANCIENT CIVILIZATION AND INSTRUCTIONS IN THE USE OF INNOCENCE, A CRYSTALLINE SUBSTANCE OF WONDROUS SUPERNATURAL POWER. THE CREATORS OF THE CUBE CLAIMED TO HAVE DEFEATED AN EVIL KNOWN AS THE MILLENNIUM EARL BY USING THE INNOCENCE. NEVERTHELESS, THE WORLD WAS DESTROYED BY THE GREAT FLOOD OF THE OLD TESTAMENT. NOW, TO AVERT A SECOND END OF THE WORLD, A GROUP OF EXORCISTS WIELDING WEAPONS MADE OF INNOCENCE MUST BATTLE THE MILLENNIUM EARL AND HIS TERRIBLE MINIONS, THE AKUMA.

THE MILLENNIUM EARL AND THE NOAH ATTACK THE NORTH AMERICA BRANCH OF THE ORDER IN AN ATTEMPT TO AWAKEN ALMA KARMA! DURING THE BATTLE, ALLEN SEES KANDA'S PAST AND LEARNS THAT KANDA AND ALMA WERE SECOND EXORCISTS, EXPERIMENTAL SUBJECTS IMPLANTED WITH THE BRAINS OF EXORCISTS WHO BECAME UNFIT FOR BATTLE AND USED TO DETERMINE WHETHER THE SYNCHRONIZATION FACTOR OF INNOCENCE CAN BE TRANSFERRED! BUT WHAT WILL ALLEN DO WITH THIS SHOCKING REVELATION?! AND WHAT DOES THE FUTURE HOLD FOR KANDA AND ALMA?!

D.GRAY-MAN
Vol. 21

CONTENTS

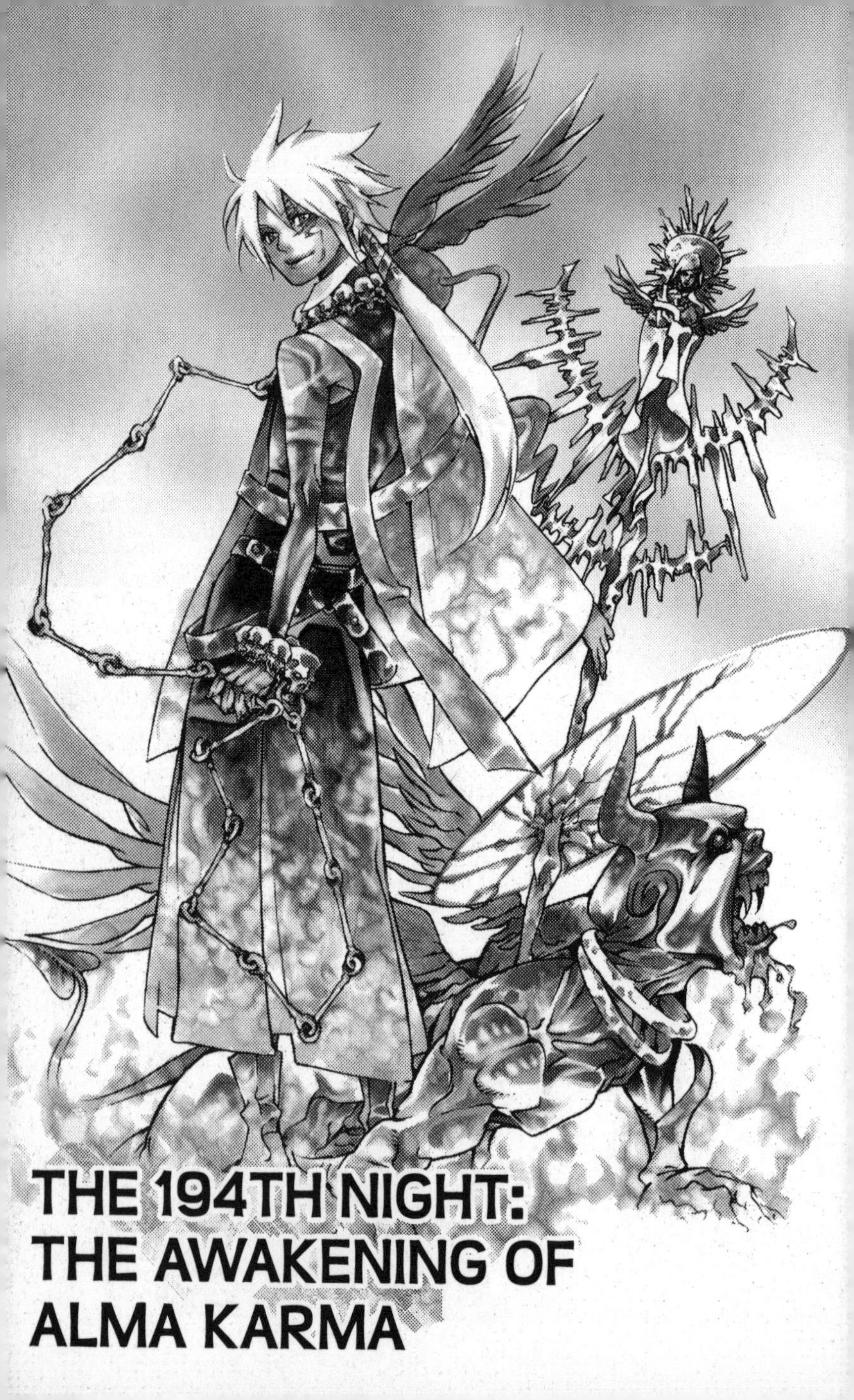

THE 194TH NIGHT: THE AWAKENING OF ALMA KARMA

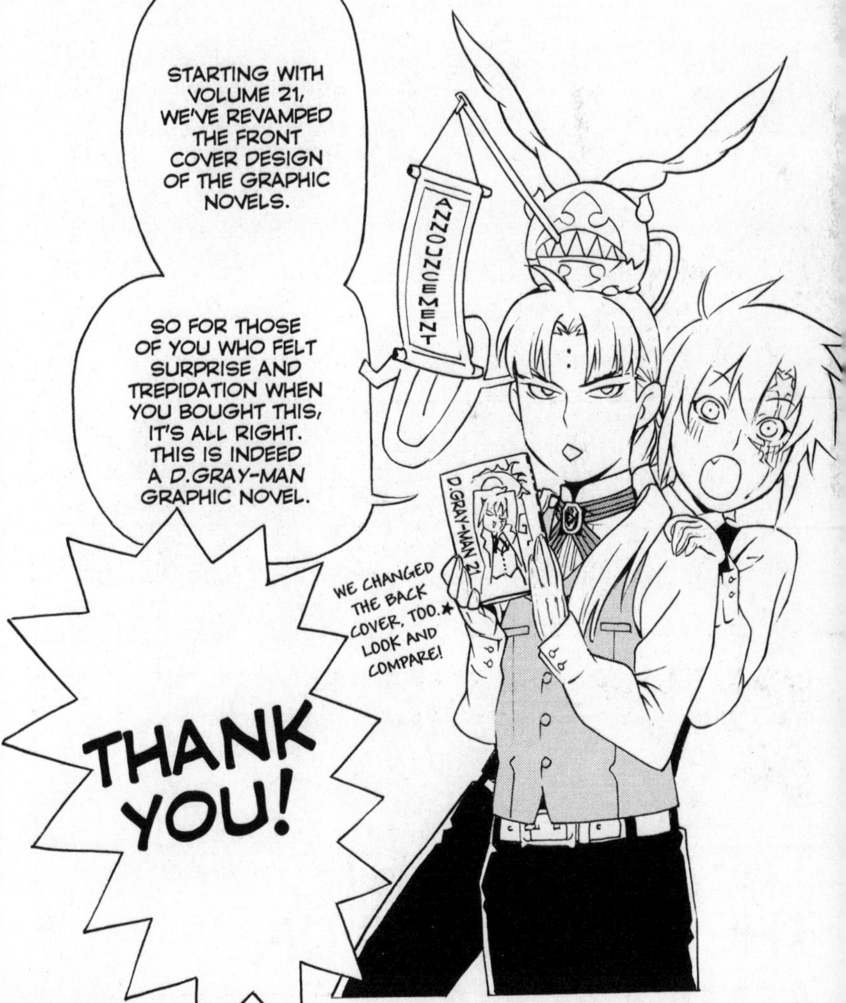

STARTING WITH VOLUME 21, WE'VE REVAMPED THE FRONT COVER DESIGN OF THE GRAPHIC NOVELS.
ANNOUNCEMENT
SO FOR THOSE OF YOU WHO FELT SURPRISE AND TREPIDATION WHEN YOU BOUGHT THIS, IT'S ALL RIGHT. THIS IS INDEED A *D.GRAY-MAN* GRAPHIC NOVEL.
D.GRAY-MAN 21
WE CHANGED THE BACK COVER, TOO.★ LOOK AND COMPARE!
THANK YOU!

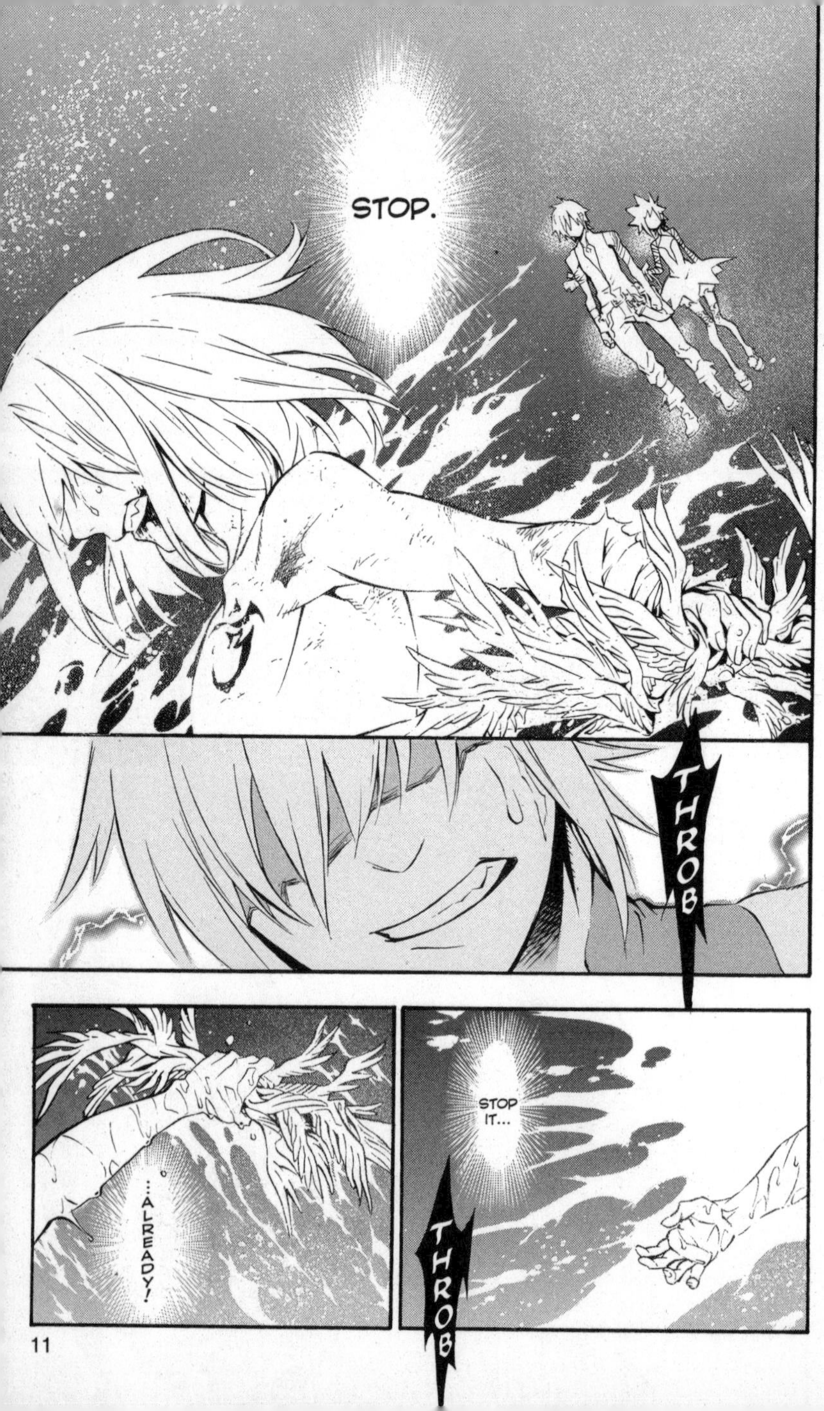
STOP.
THROB
STOP IT...
THROB
...ALREADY!

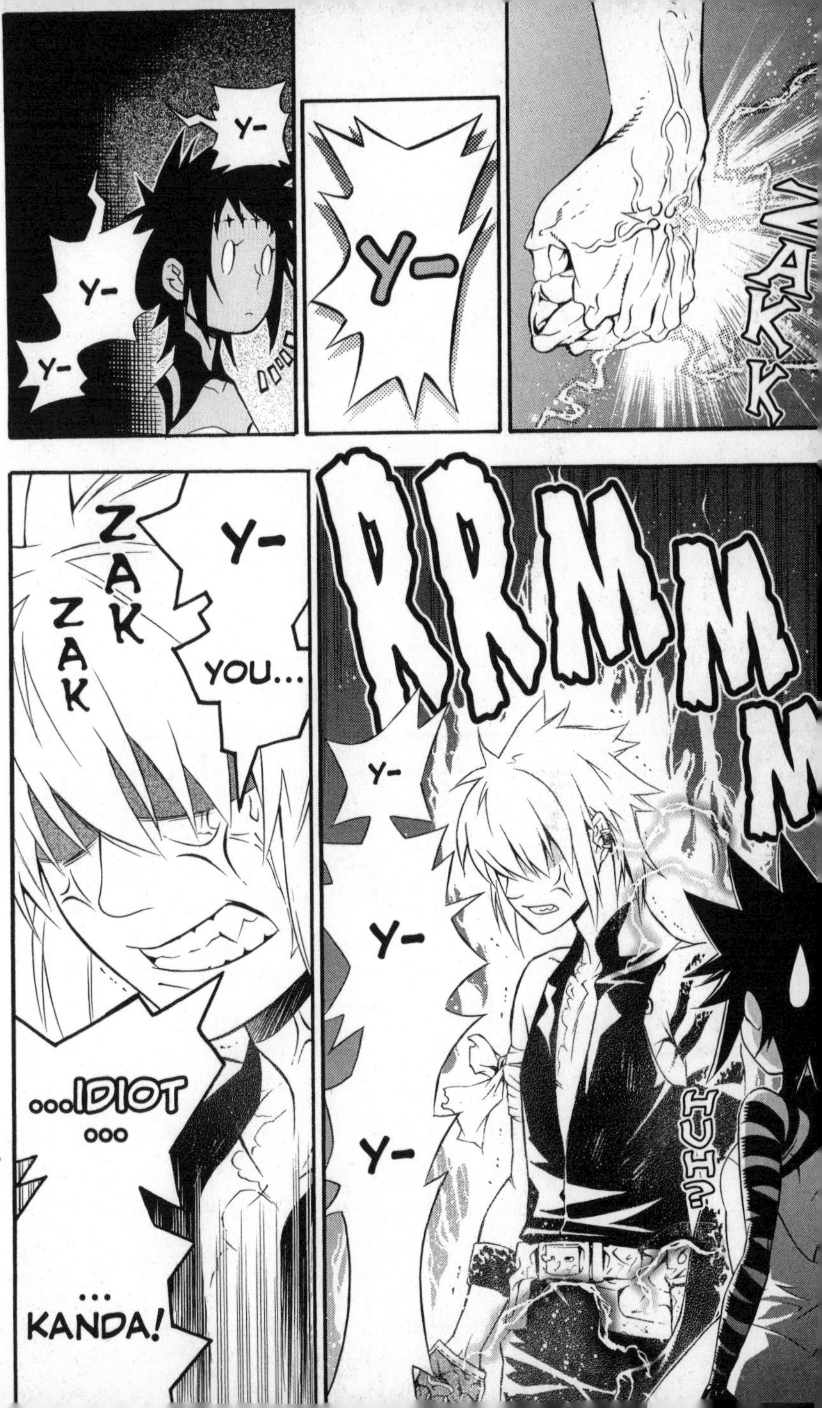
ZAKK
Y-
Y-
Y-
Y-
RRMMM
Y-
Y-
Y-
HUH?
Y-
ZAK
ZAK
YOU...
...IDIOT...
...KANDA!

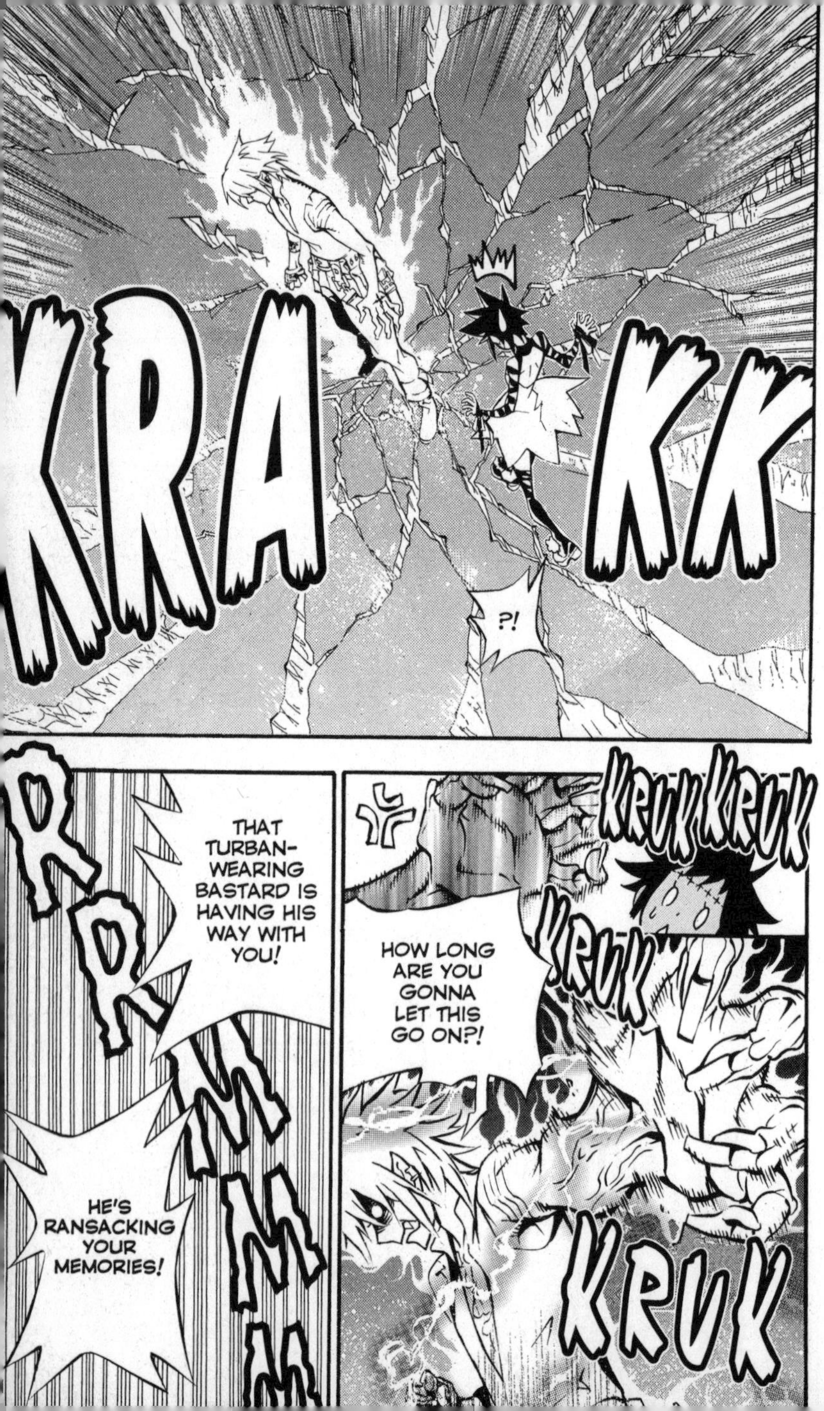
KRAKK
?!
KRUK KRUK
KRUK
HOW LONG ARE YOU GONNA LET THIS GO ON?!
KRUK
THAT TURBAN-WEARING BASTARD IS HAVING HIS WAY WITH YOU!
HE'S RANSACKING YOUR MEMORIES!

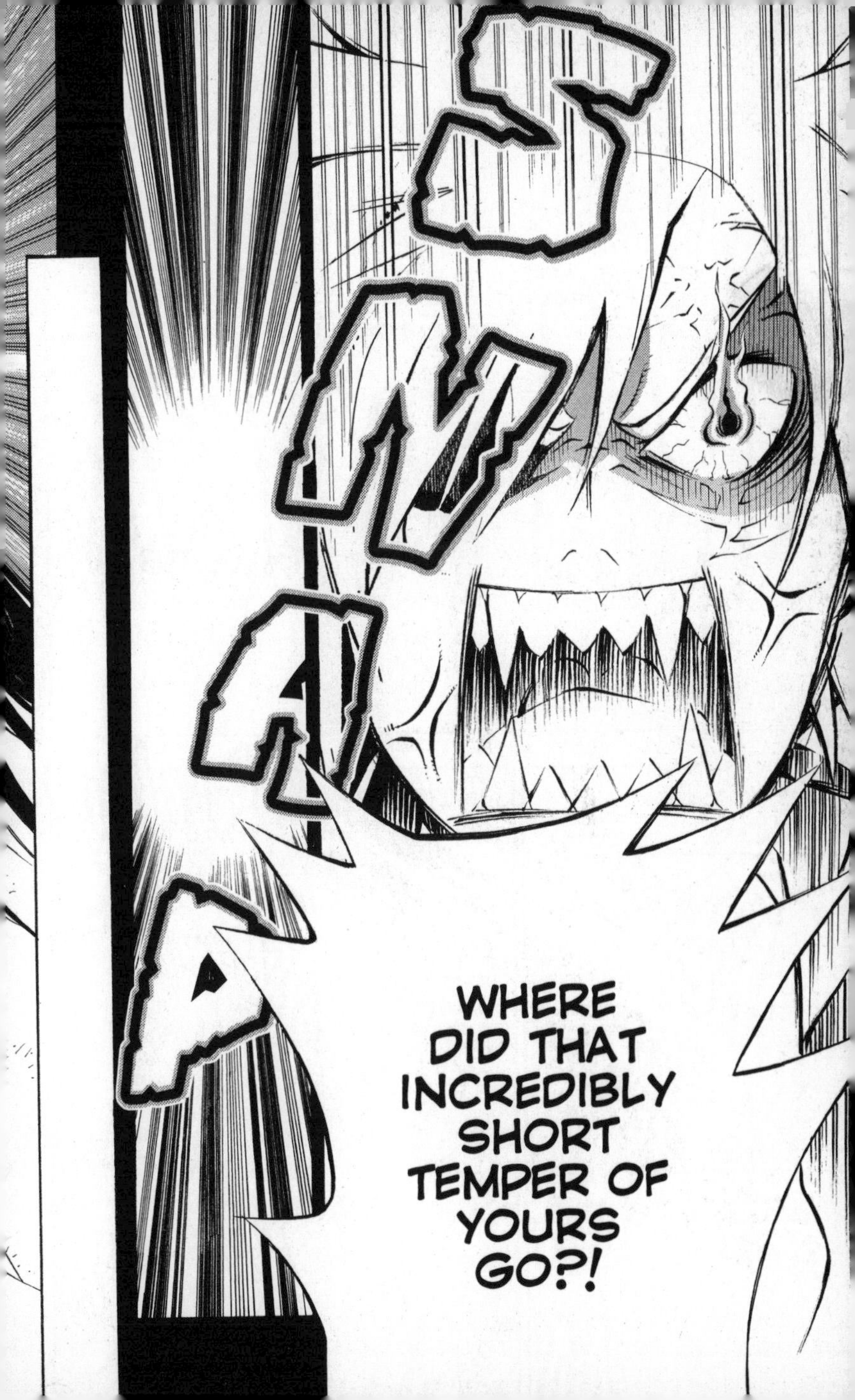
SNAP
WHERE DID THAT INCREDIBLY SHORT TEMPER OF YOURS GO?!

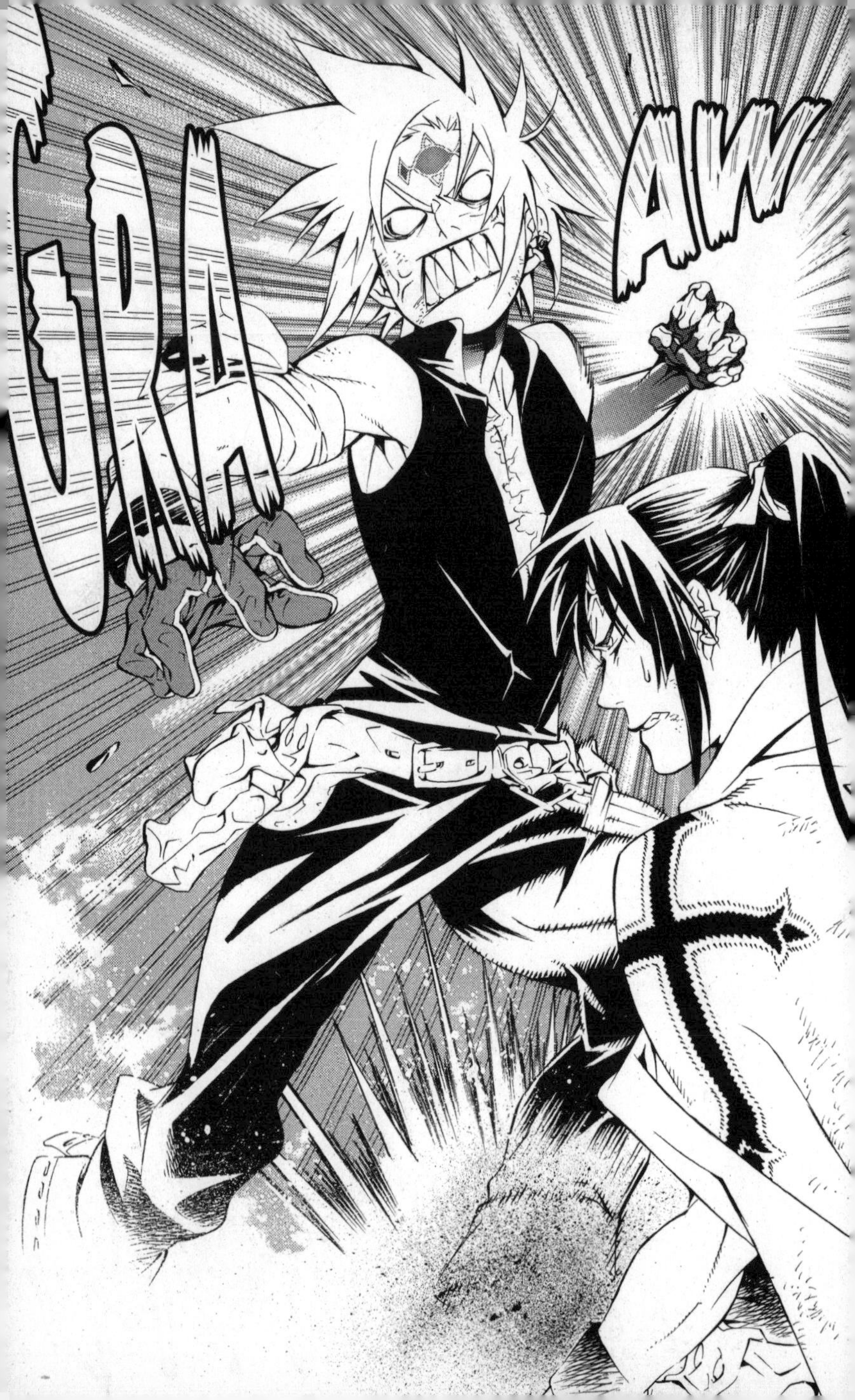
GRA
AW

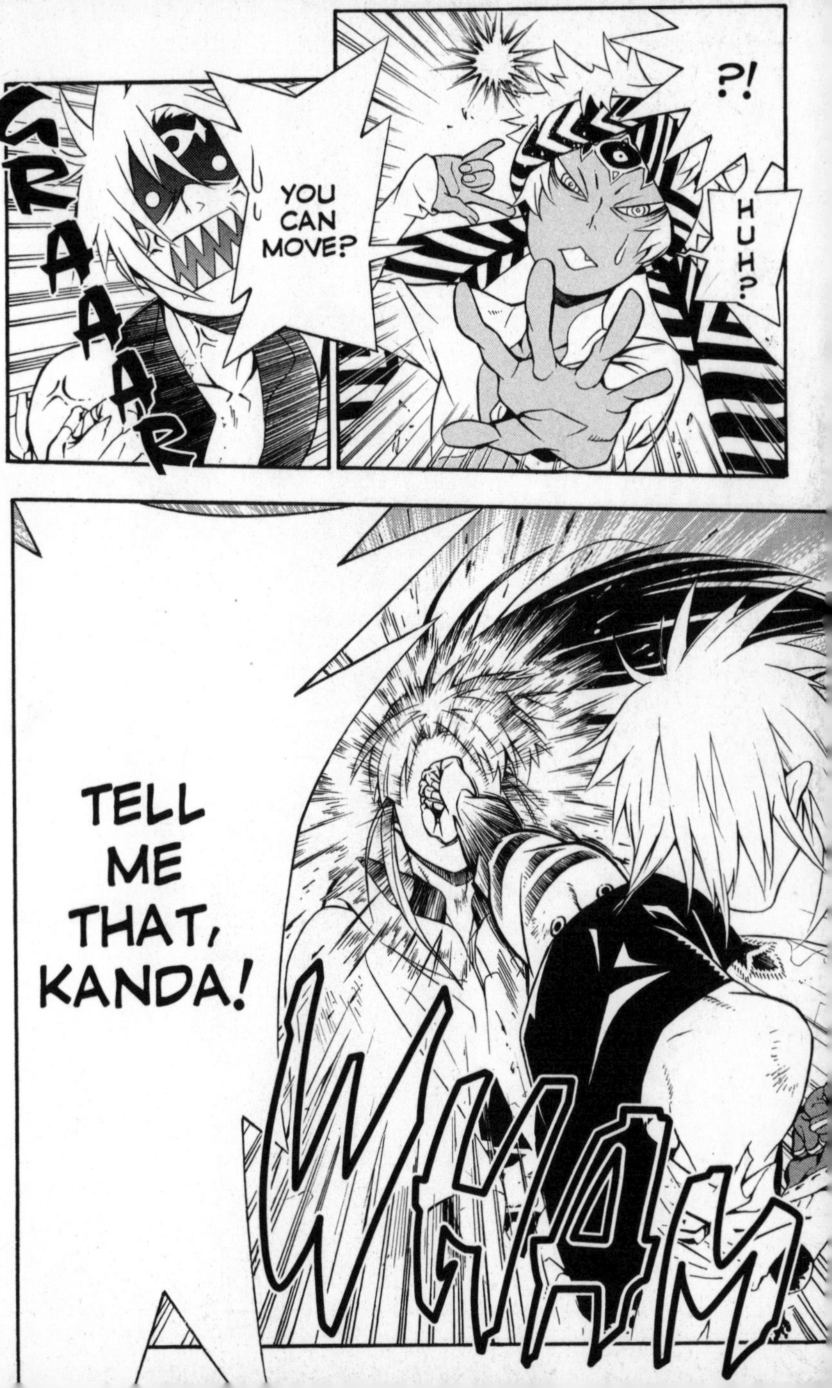
?!
HUH?
GRAAAAR
YOU CAN MOVE?
TELL ME THAT, KANDA!
WHAM

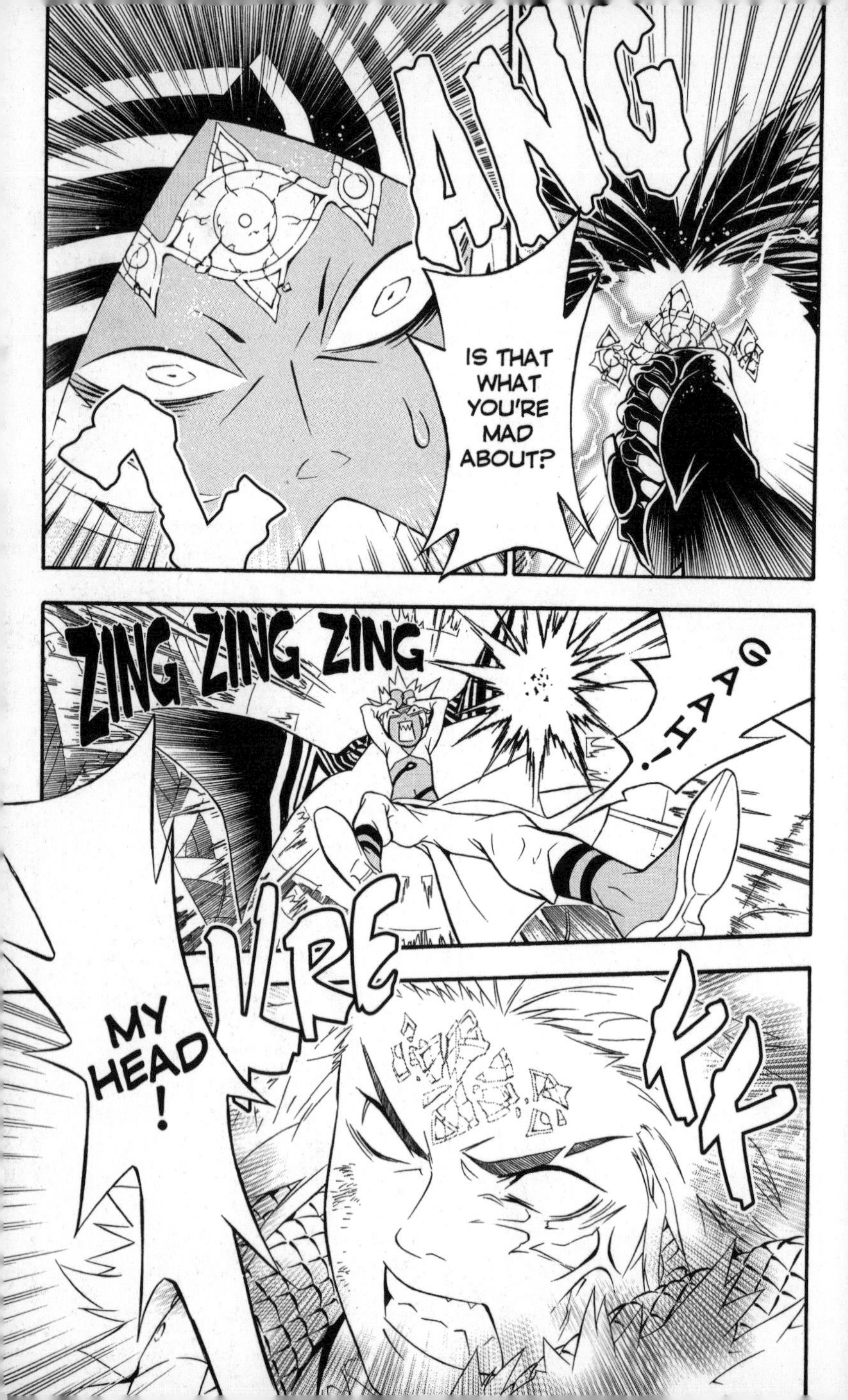
ANG
IS THAT WHAT YOU'RE MAD ABOUT?
GAAH!!
ZING ZING ZING
VREKK
MY HEAD!

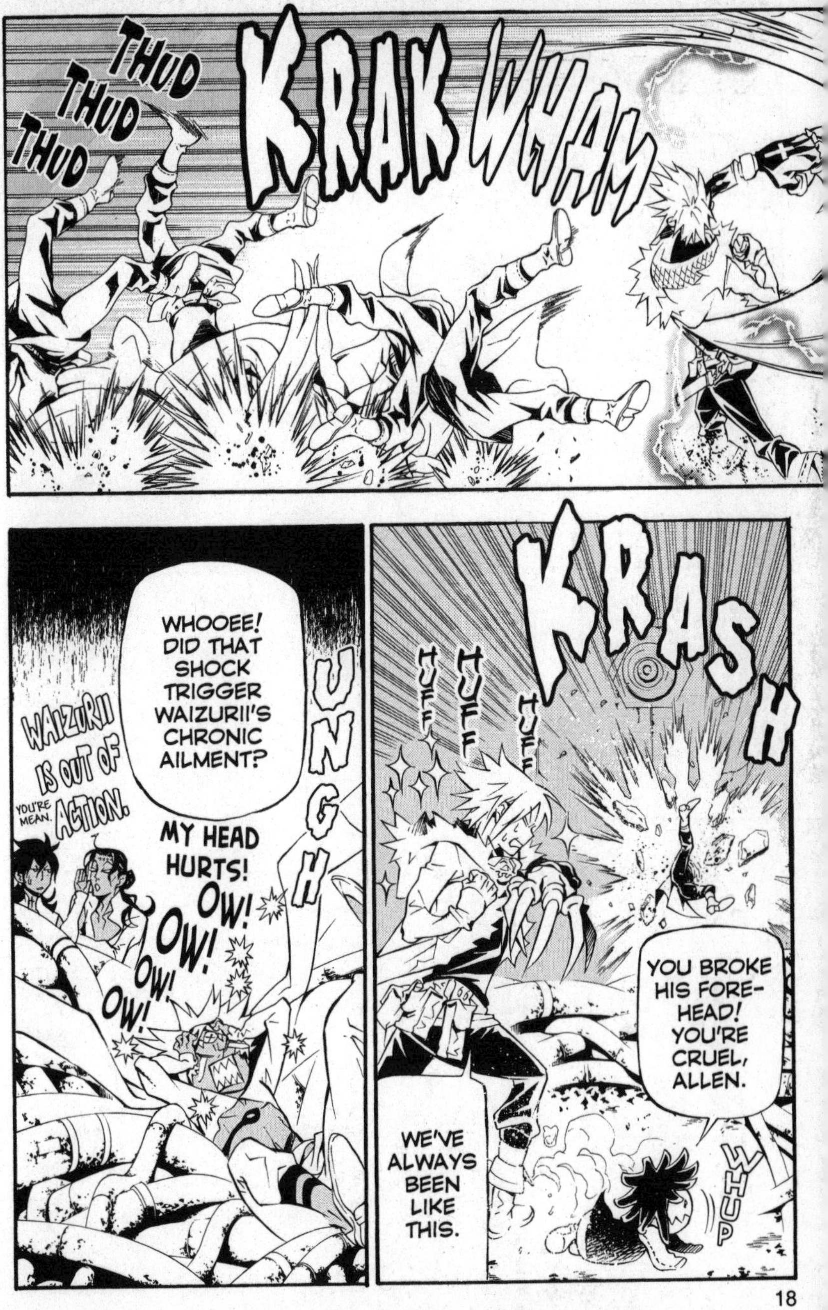
KRAK WHAM
THUD THUD THUD
KRASH
HUFF HUFF HUFF
YOU BROKE HIS FORE-HEAD! YOU'RE CRUEL, ALLEN.
WE'VE ALWAYS BEEN LIKE THIS.
WHUP
UNGH
WHOOEE! DID THAT SHOCK TRIGGER WAIZURII'S CHRONIC AILMENT?
WAIZURII IS OUT OF ACTION.
YOU'RE MEAN.
MY HEAD HURTS! OW! OW! OW! OW!

READ THIS WAY

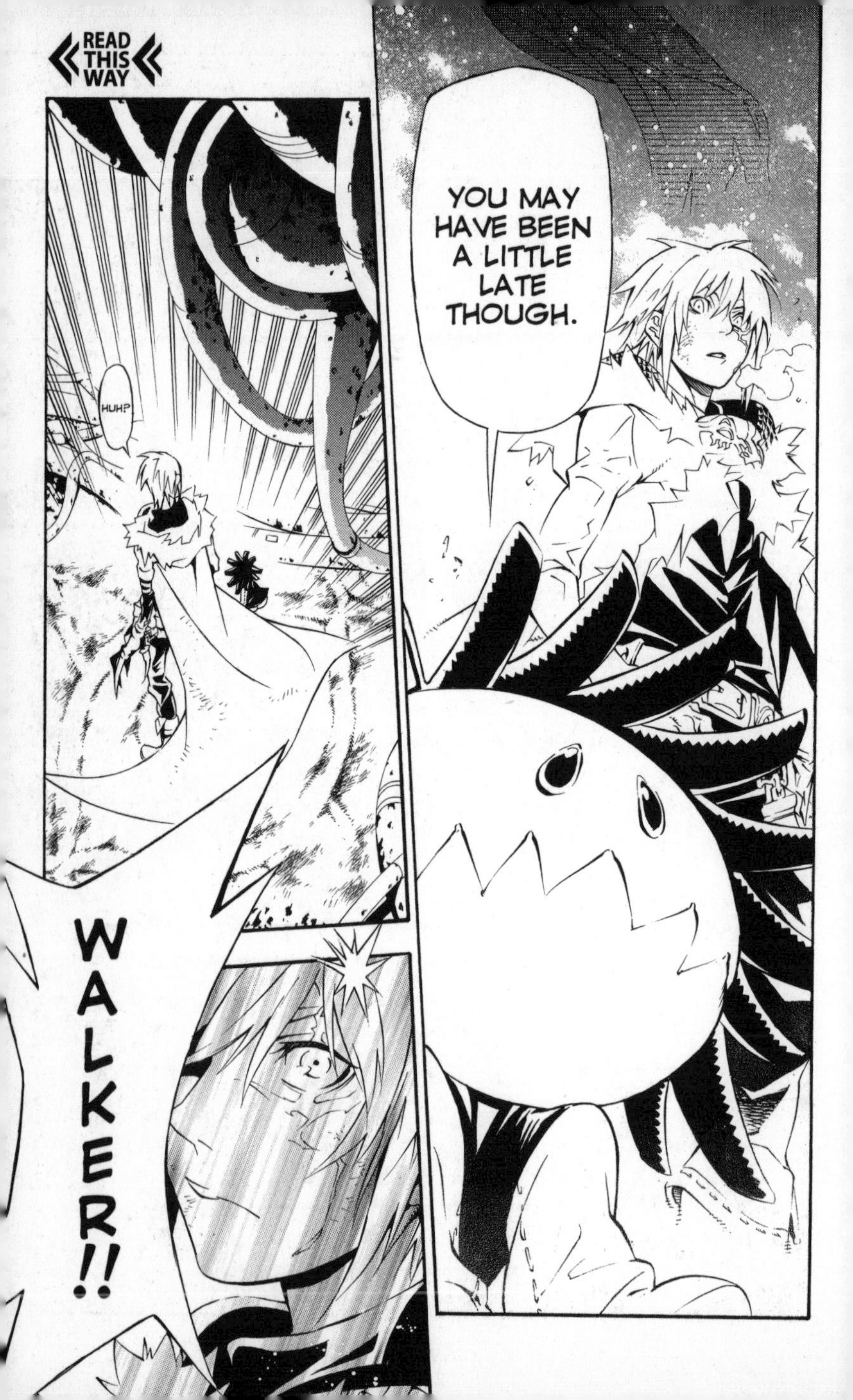
YOU MAY HAVE BEEN A LITTLE LATE THOUGH.
HUH?
WALKER!!

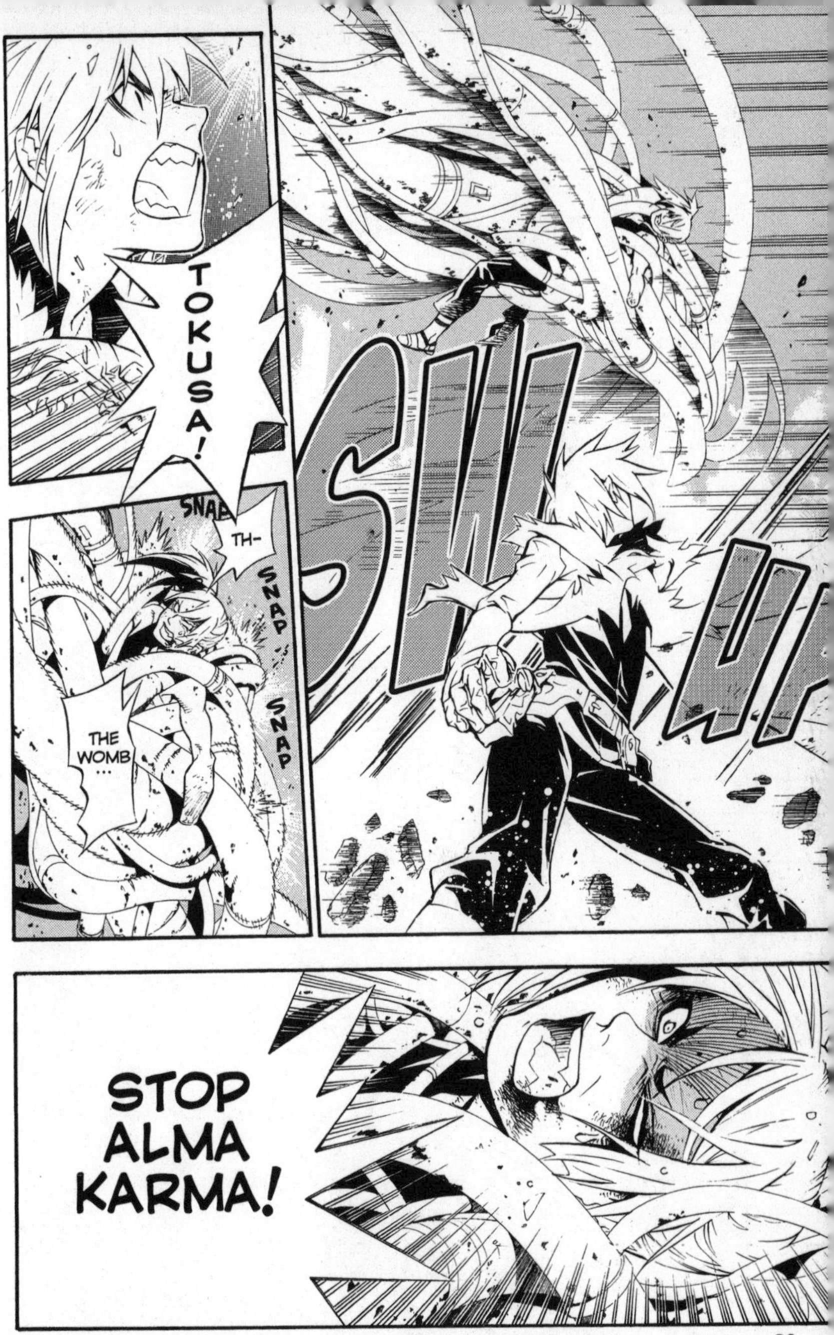
SHWU
TOKUSA!
SNAP
TH-
SNAP
SNAP
THE WOMB...
STOP ALMA KARMA!

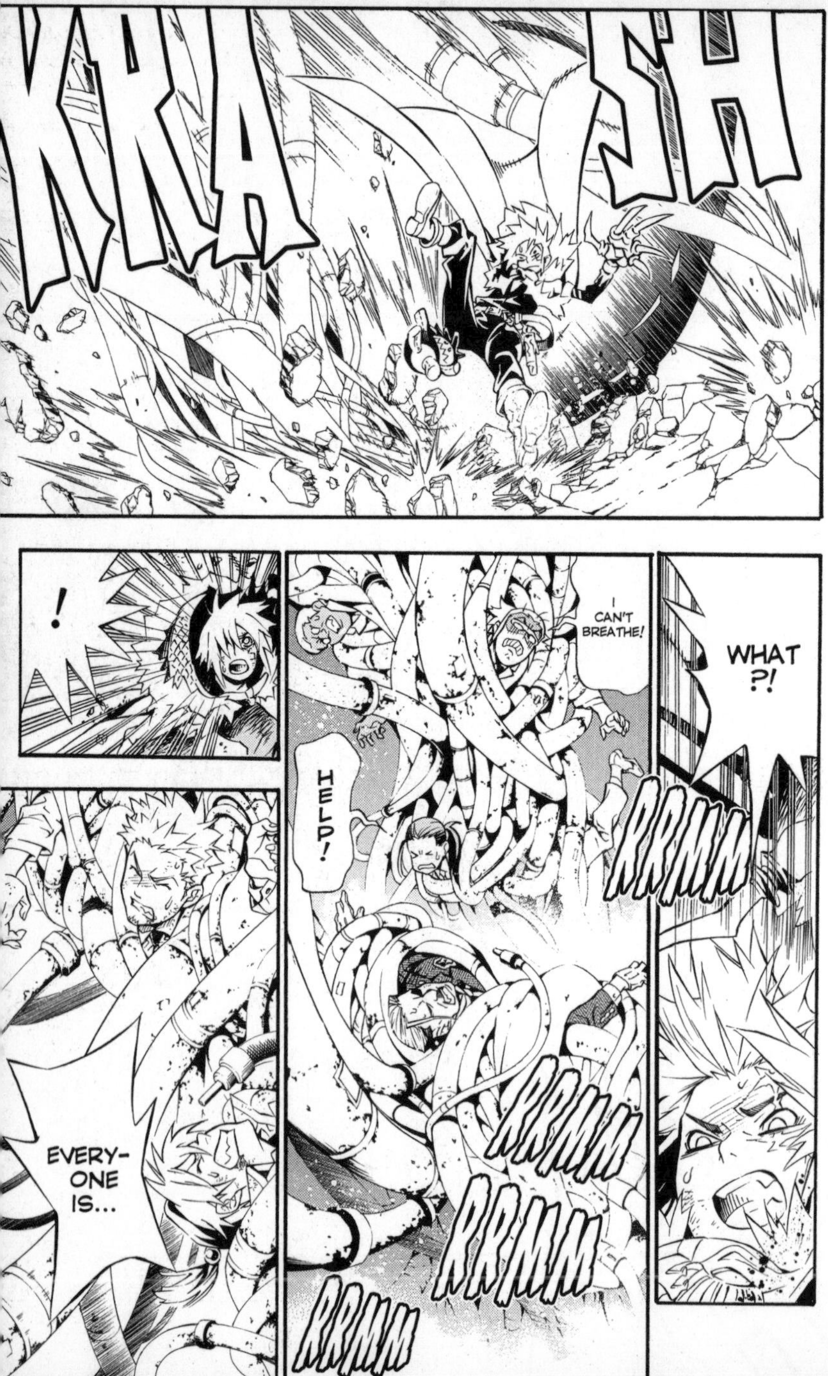
KRASH
WHAT ?!
RRMM
I CAN'T BREATHE!
HELP!
RRMM
RRMM
RRMM
!
EVERY-ONE IS...

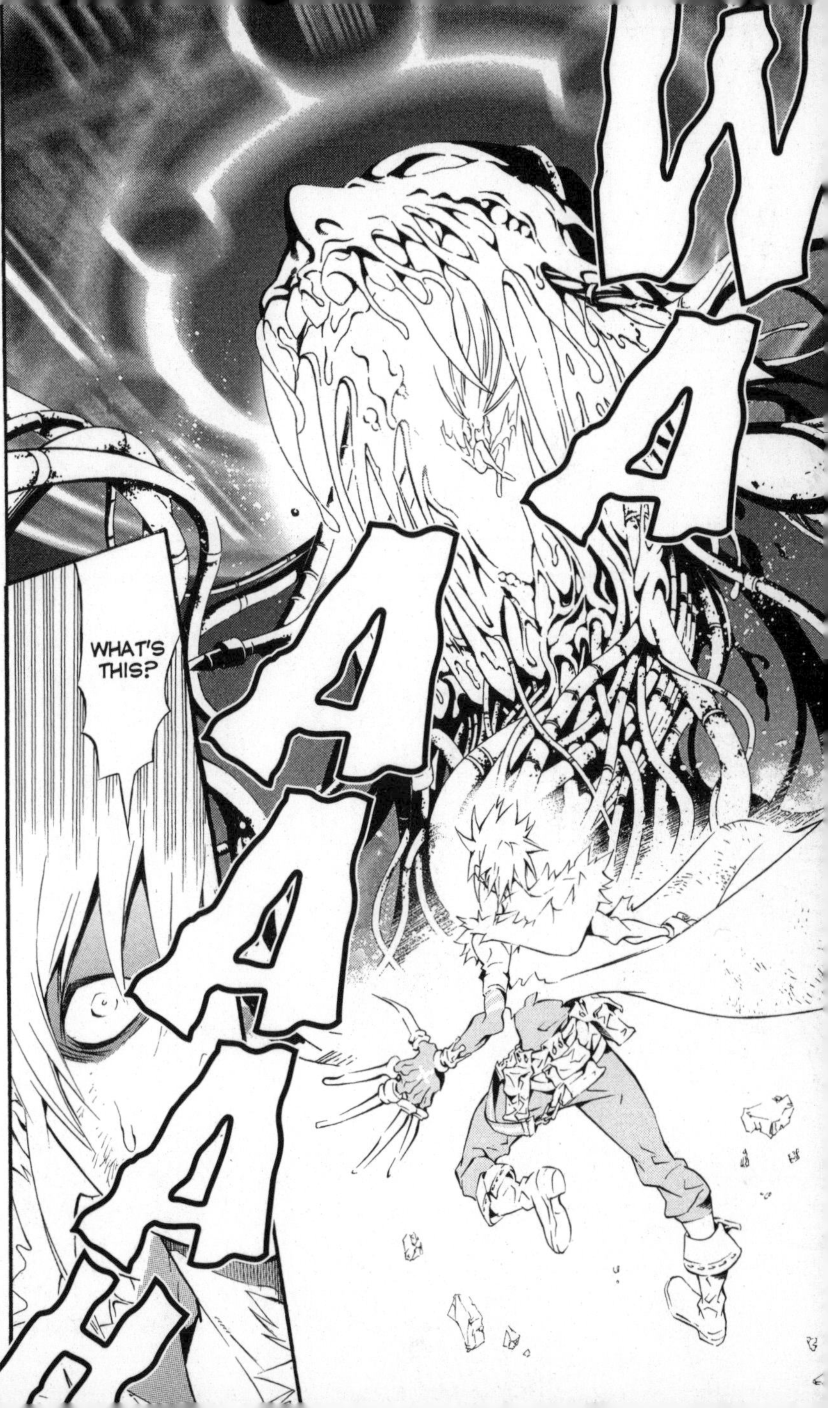
WAAAAAH
WHAT'S THIS?

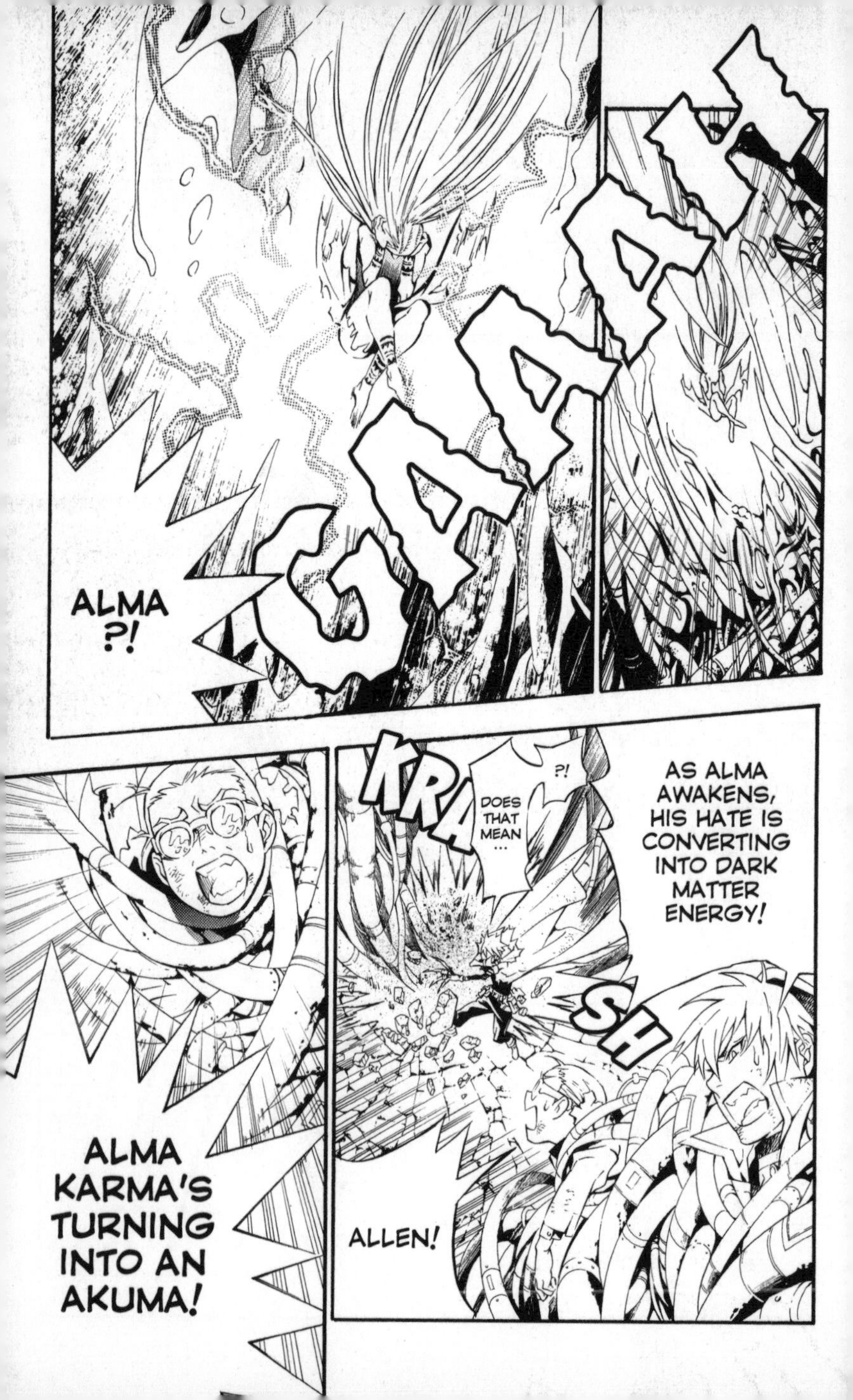
GAAA
ALMA ?!
AS ALMA AWAKENS, HIS HATE IS CONVERTING INTO DARK MATTER ENERGY!
?!
DOES THAT MEAN ...
KRASH
ALLEN!
ALMA KARMA'S TURNING INTO AN AKUMA!

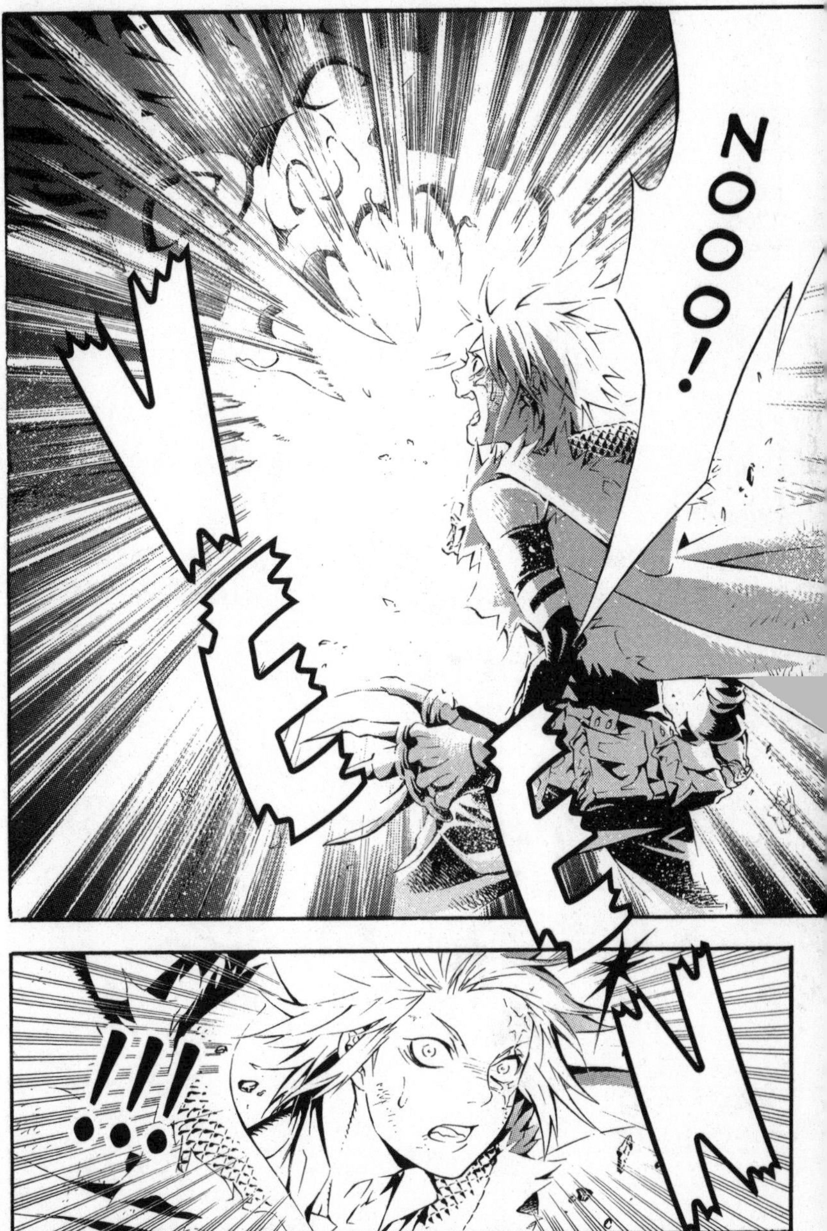
NOOOO!

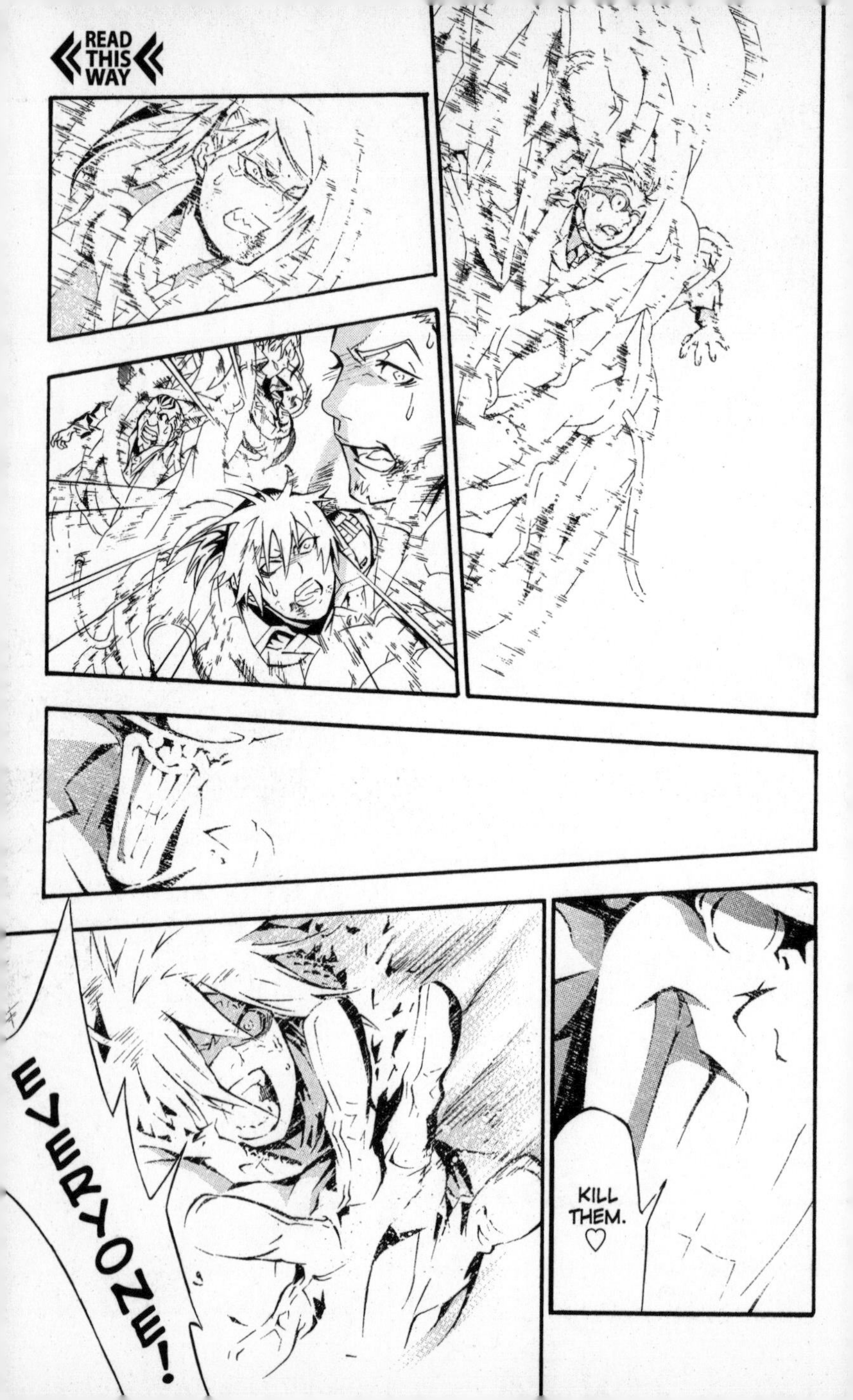
READ THIS WAY
KILL THEM. ♡
EVERYONE!

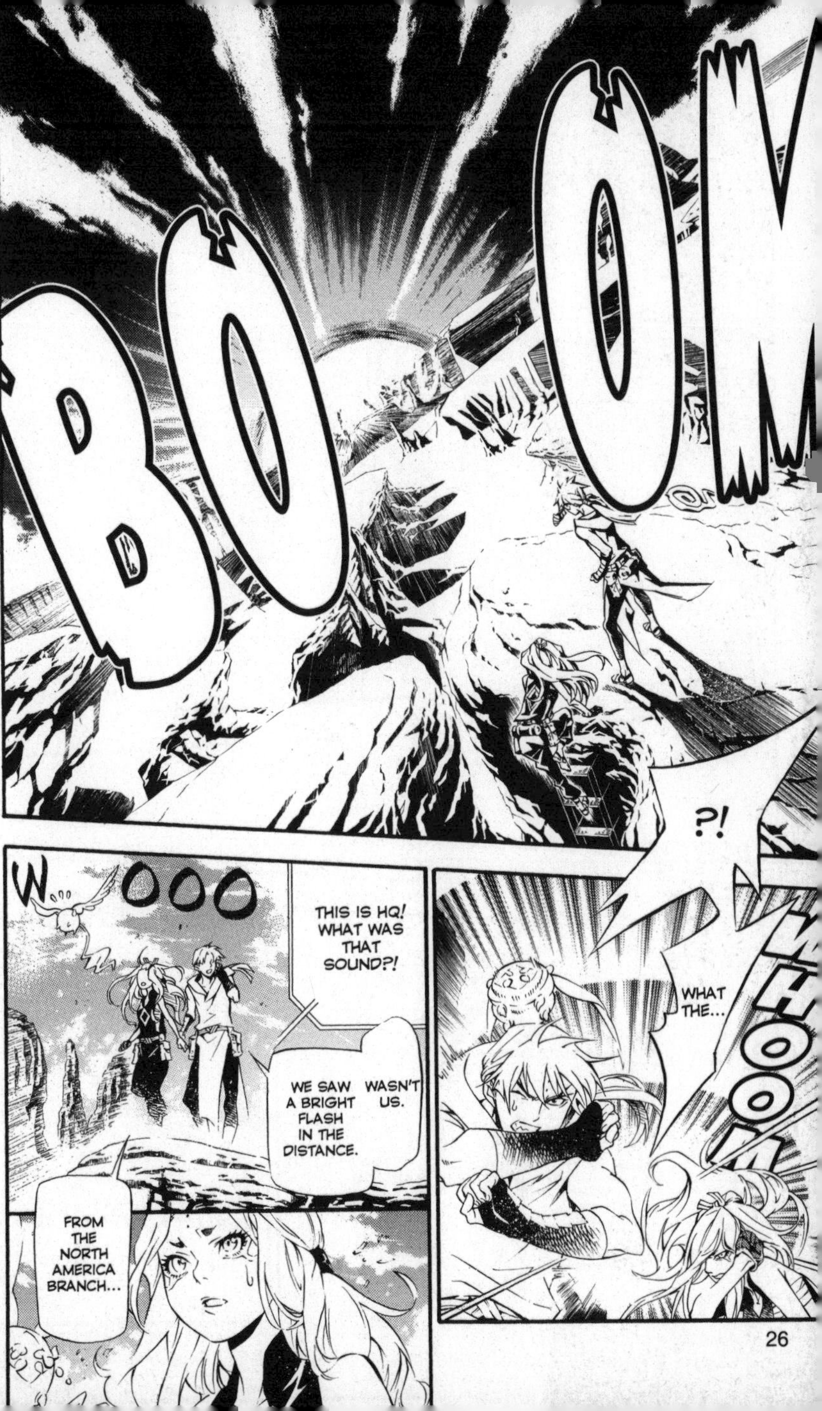
BOOOM
?!
WHOOM
WHAT THE...
THIS IS HQ! WHAT WAS THAT SOUND?!
WOOO
WASN'T US.
WE SAW A BRIGHT FLASH IN THE DISTANCE.
FROM THE NORTH AMERICA BRANCH...

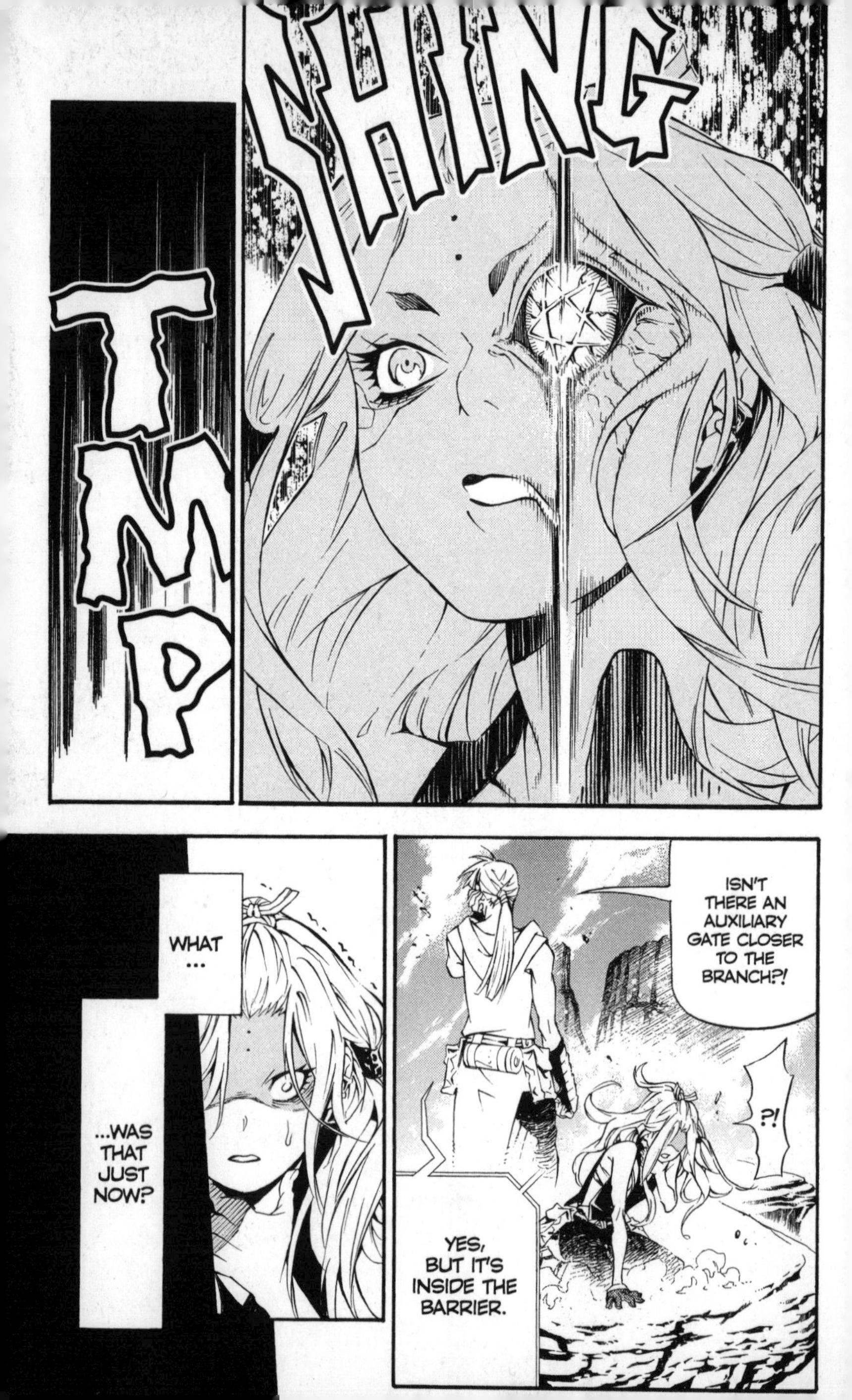
SHING
TMP
ISN'T THERE AN AUXILIARY GATE CLOSER TO THE BRANCH?!
?!
YES, BUT IT'S INSIDE THE BARRIER.
WHAT ...
...WAS THAT JUST NOW?

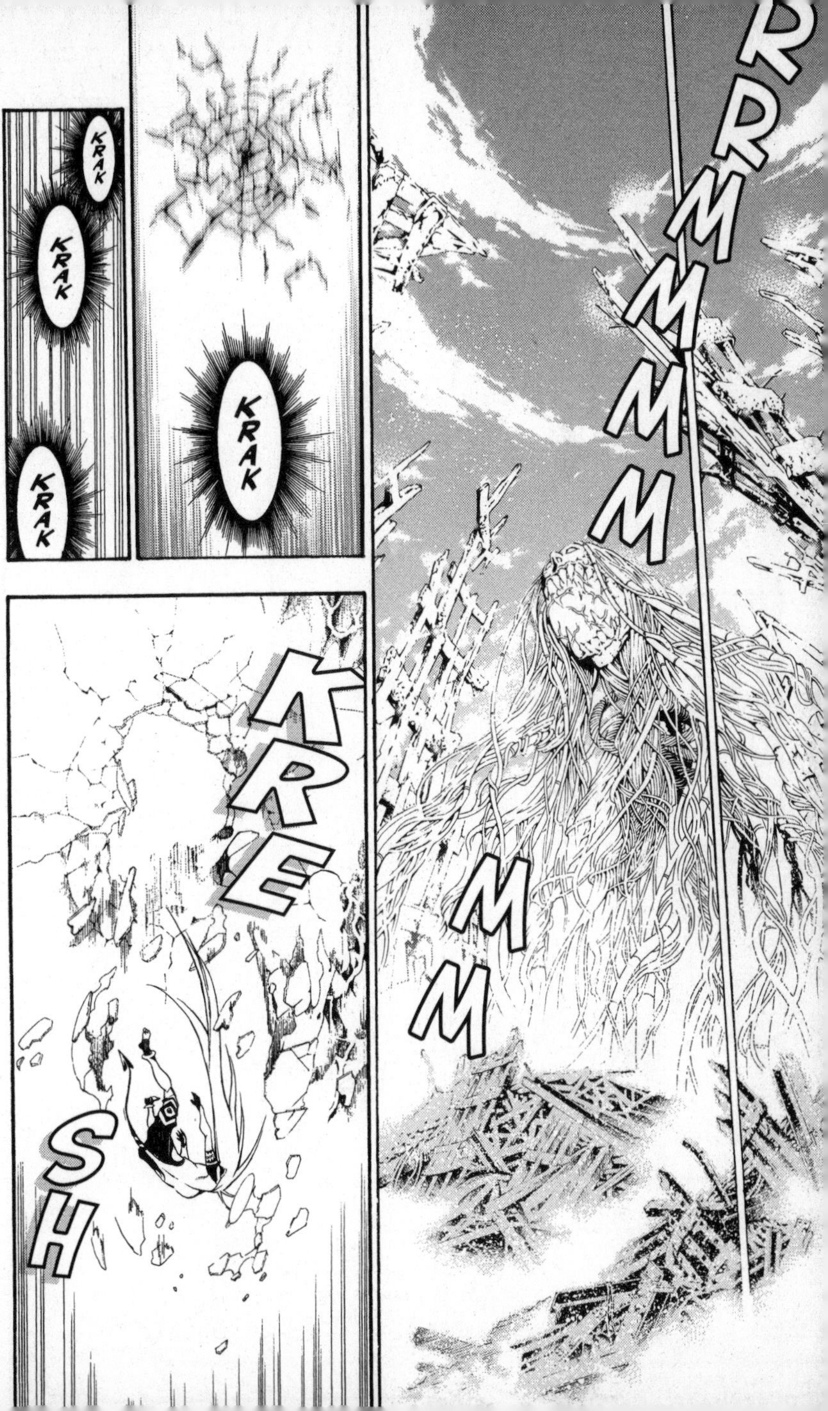
RRMMMMMM
KRAK
KRAK
KRAK
KRAK
KRESH

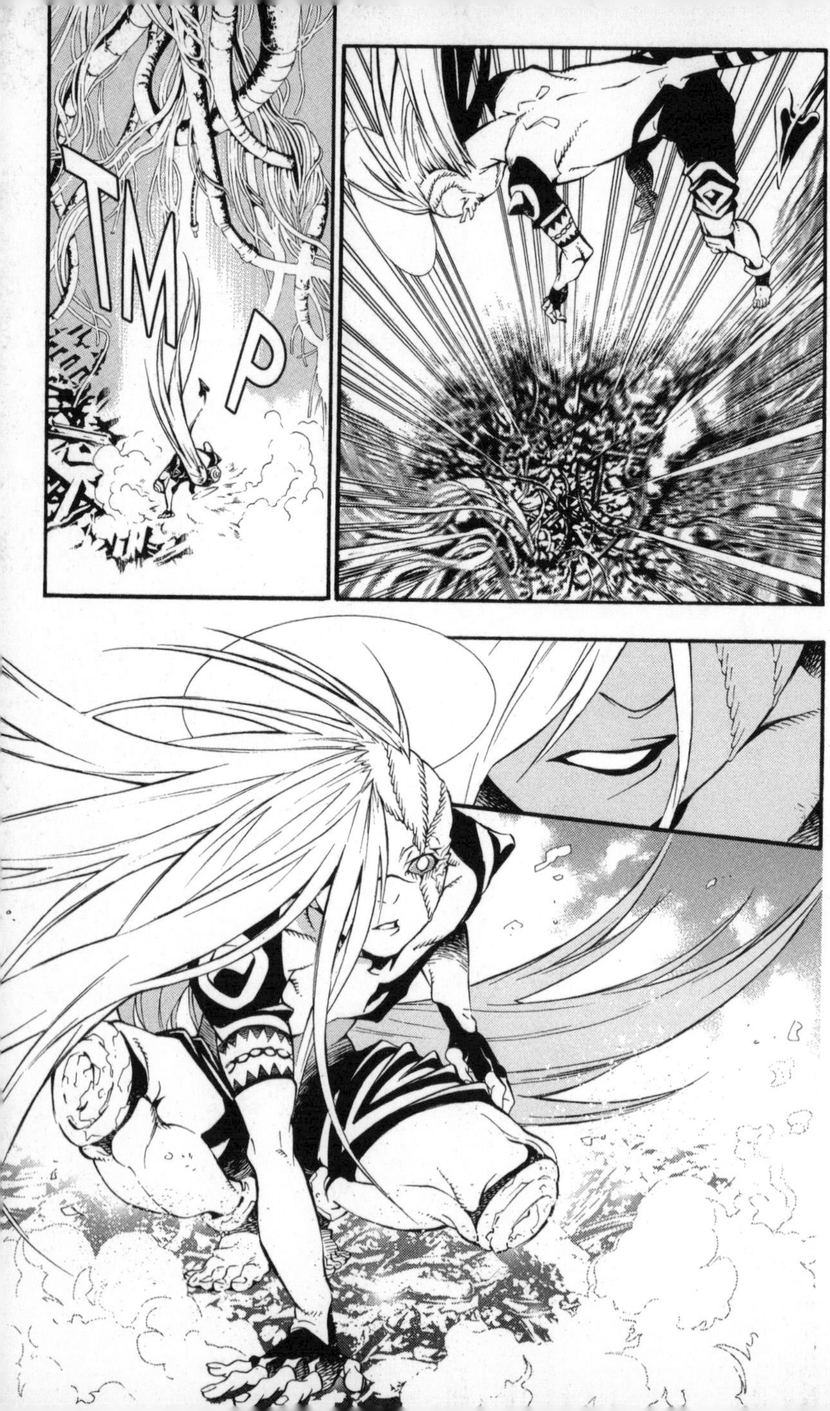
TMP

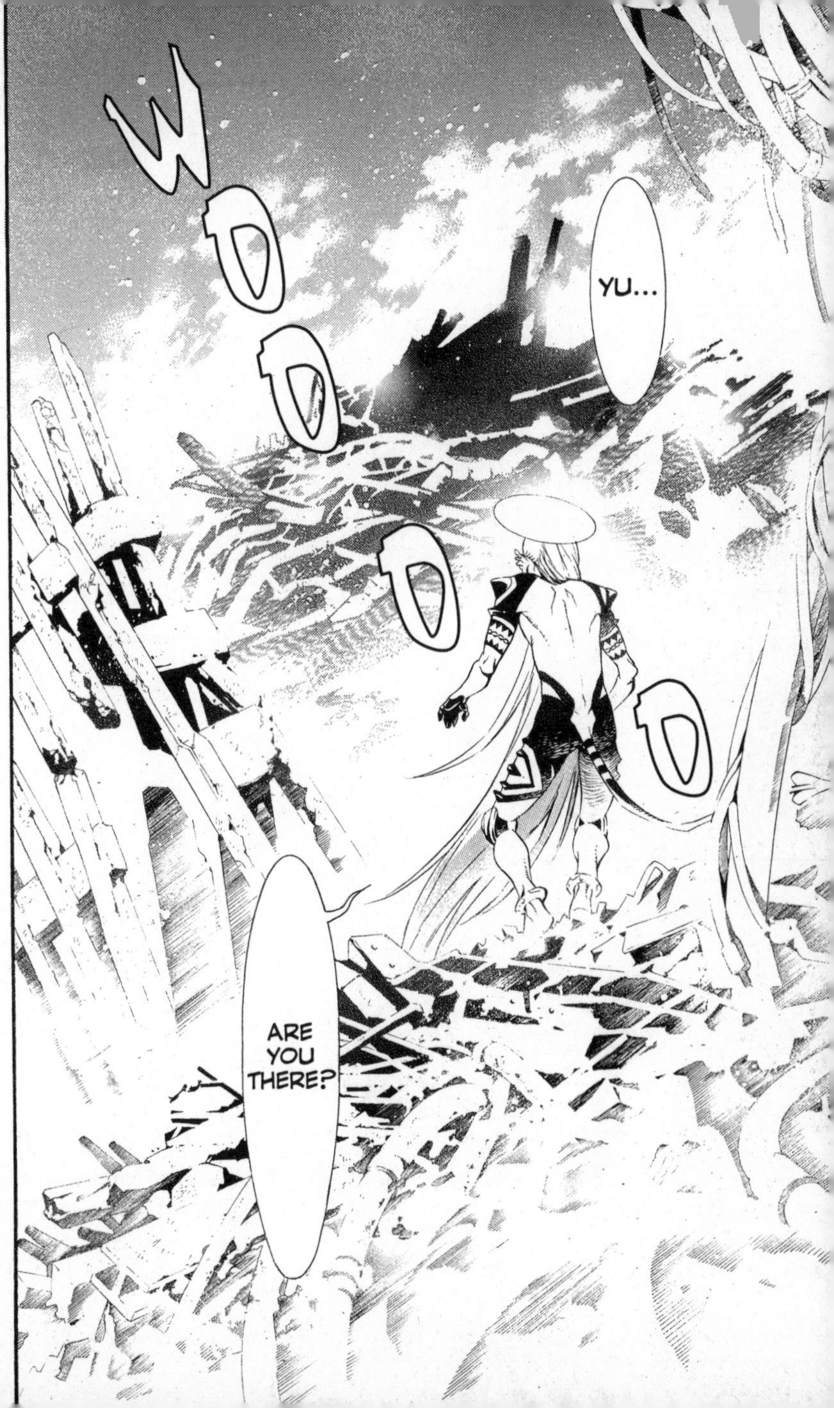
YU...
WDDDD
ARE YOU THERE?

THE 195TH NIGHT: RIPPLES

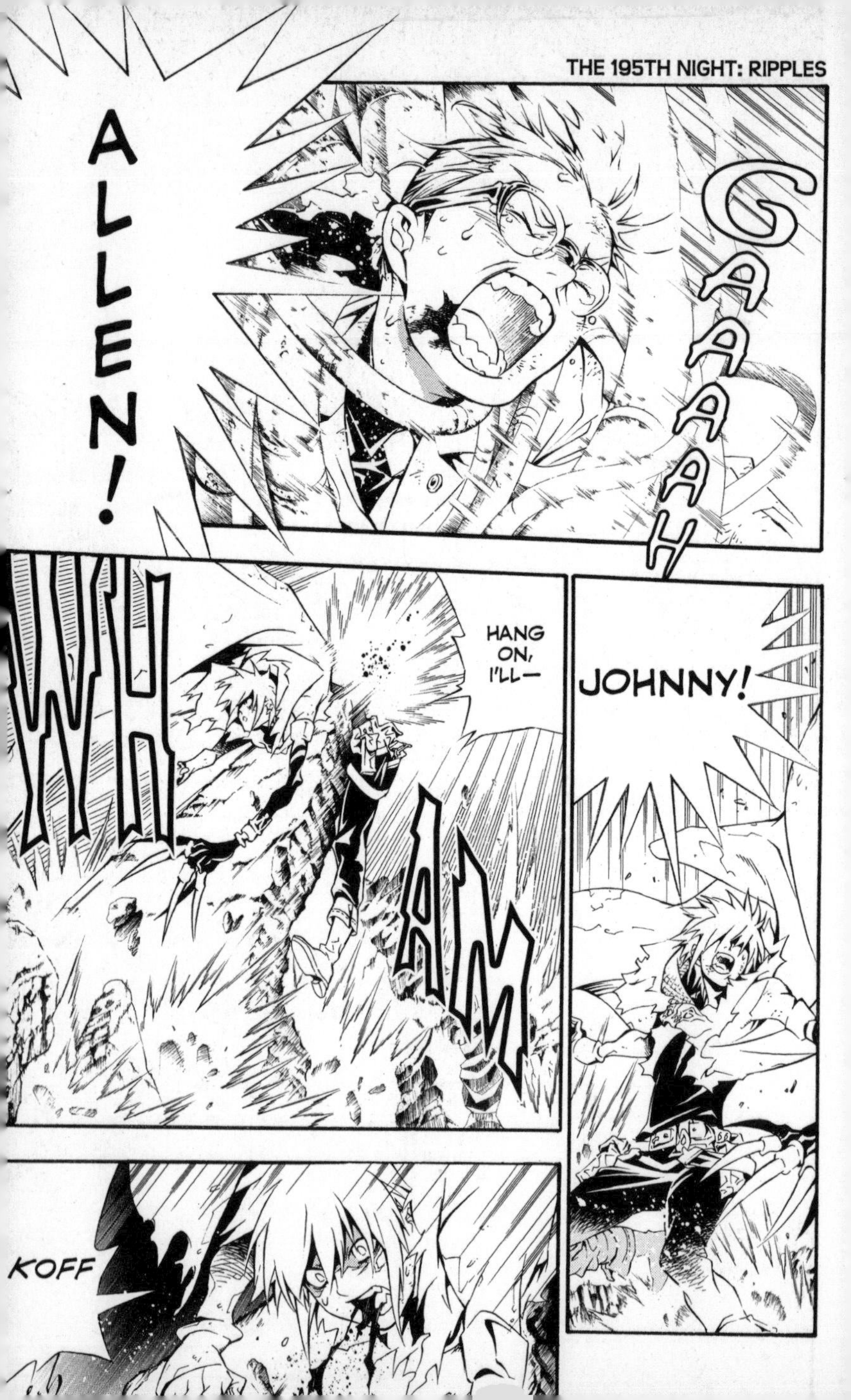
GAAAAH
ALLEN!
JOHNNY!
HANG ON, I'LL—
WHAM
KOFF

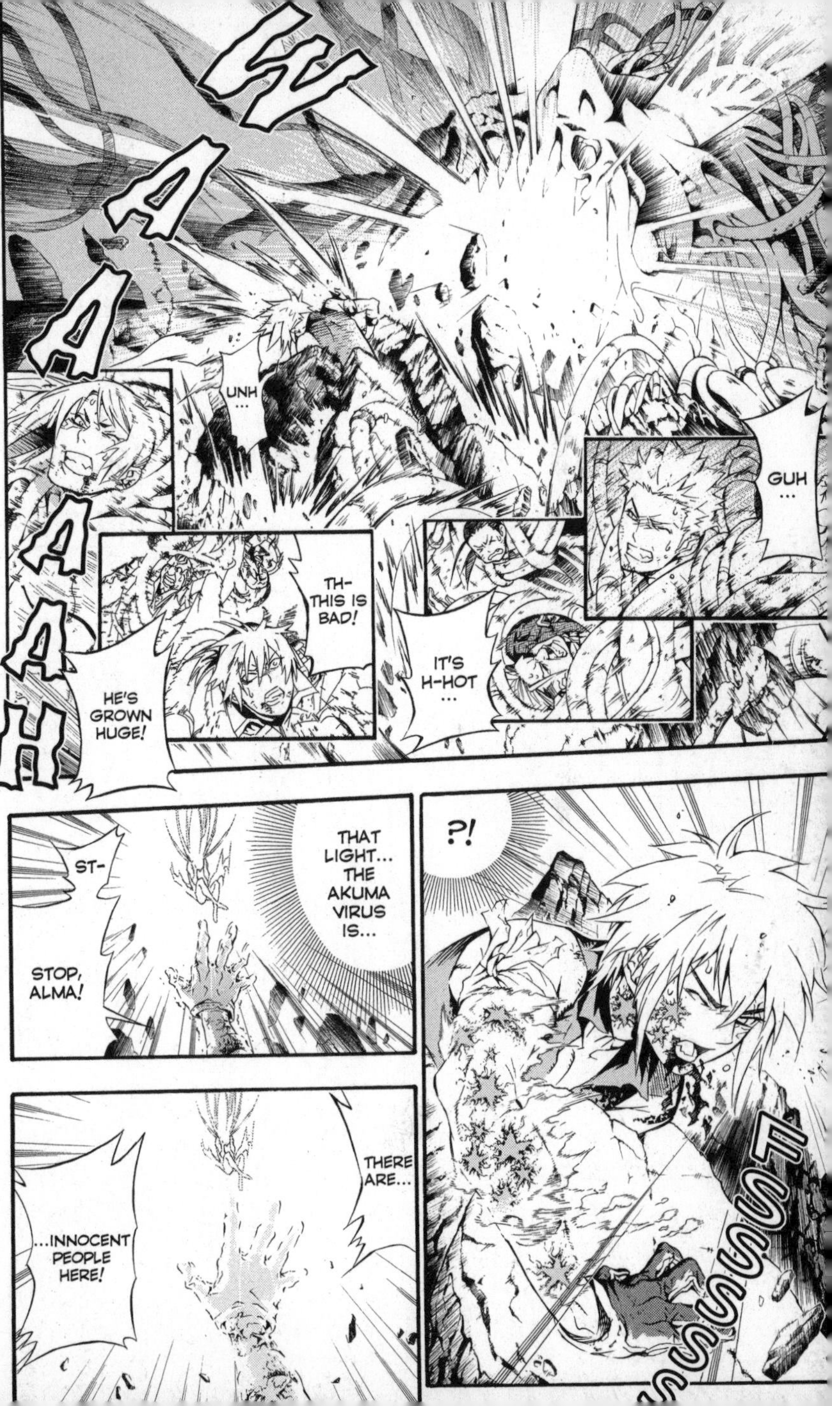
AAAAH
GUH...
IT'S H-HOT...
TH-THIS IS BAD!
UNH...
HE'S GROWN HUGE!
?!
FSSSSSSS
THAT LIGHT... THE AKUMA VIRUS IS...
ST-
STOP, ALMA!
THERE ARE...
...INNOCENT PEOPLE HERE!

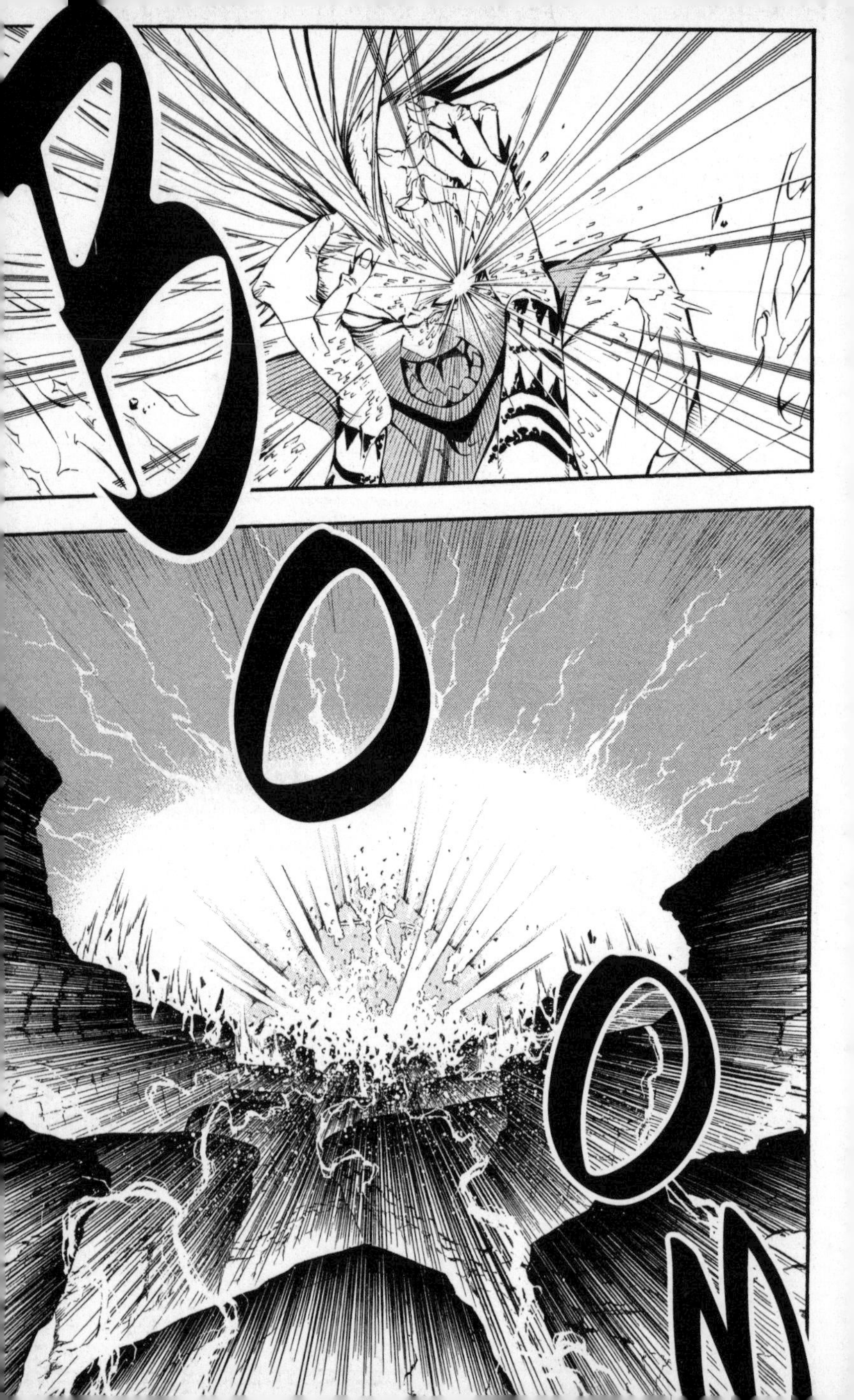
BOOM

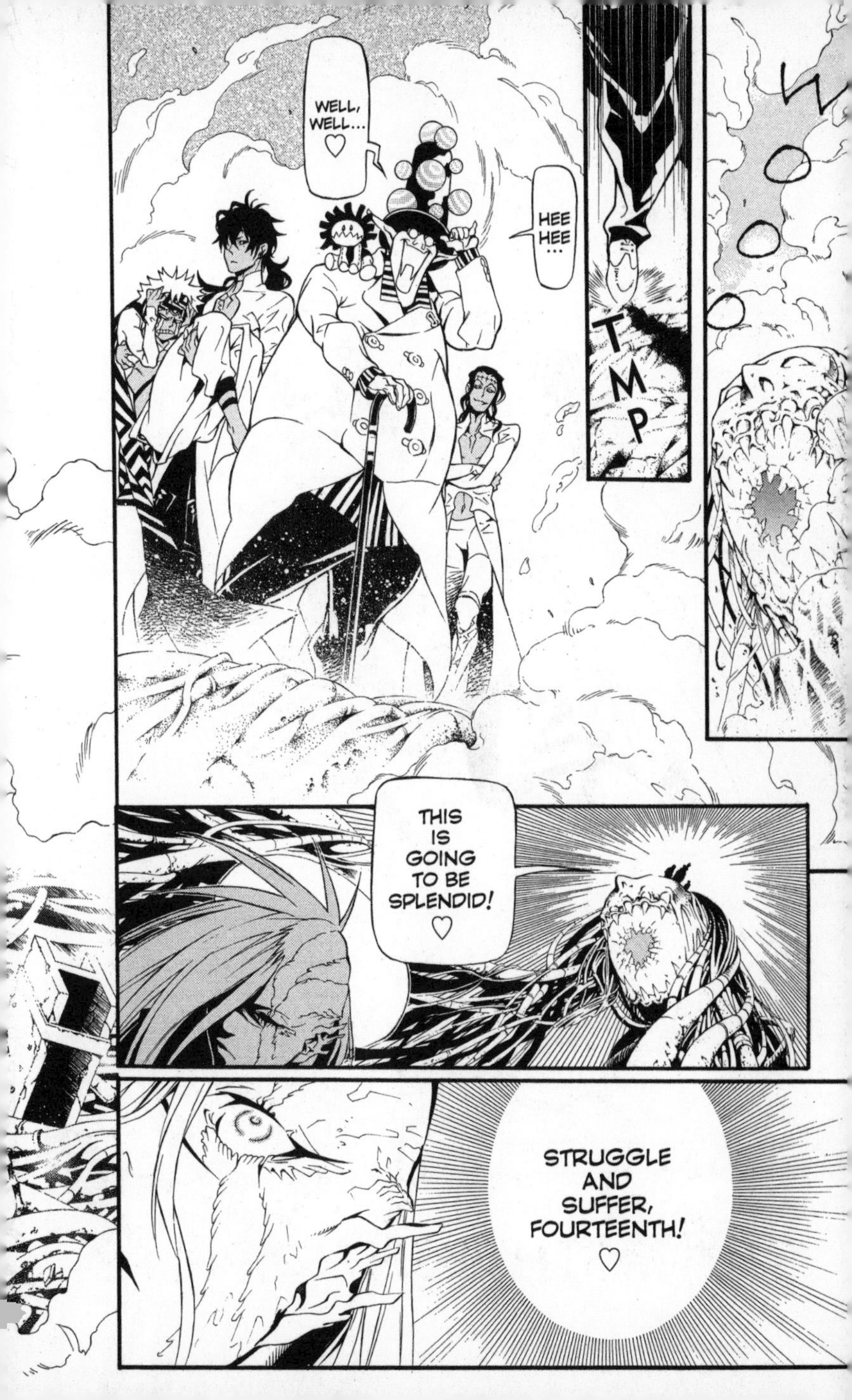
WOOO
TMP
WELL, WELL... ♡
HEE HEE...
THIS IS GOING TO BE SPLENDID! ♡
STRUGGLE AND SUFFER, FOURTEENTH! ♡

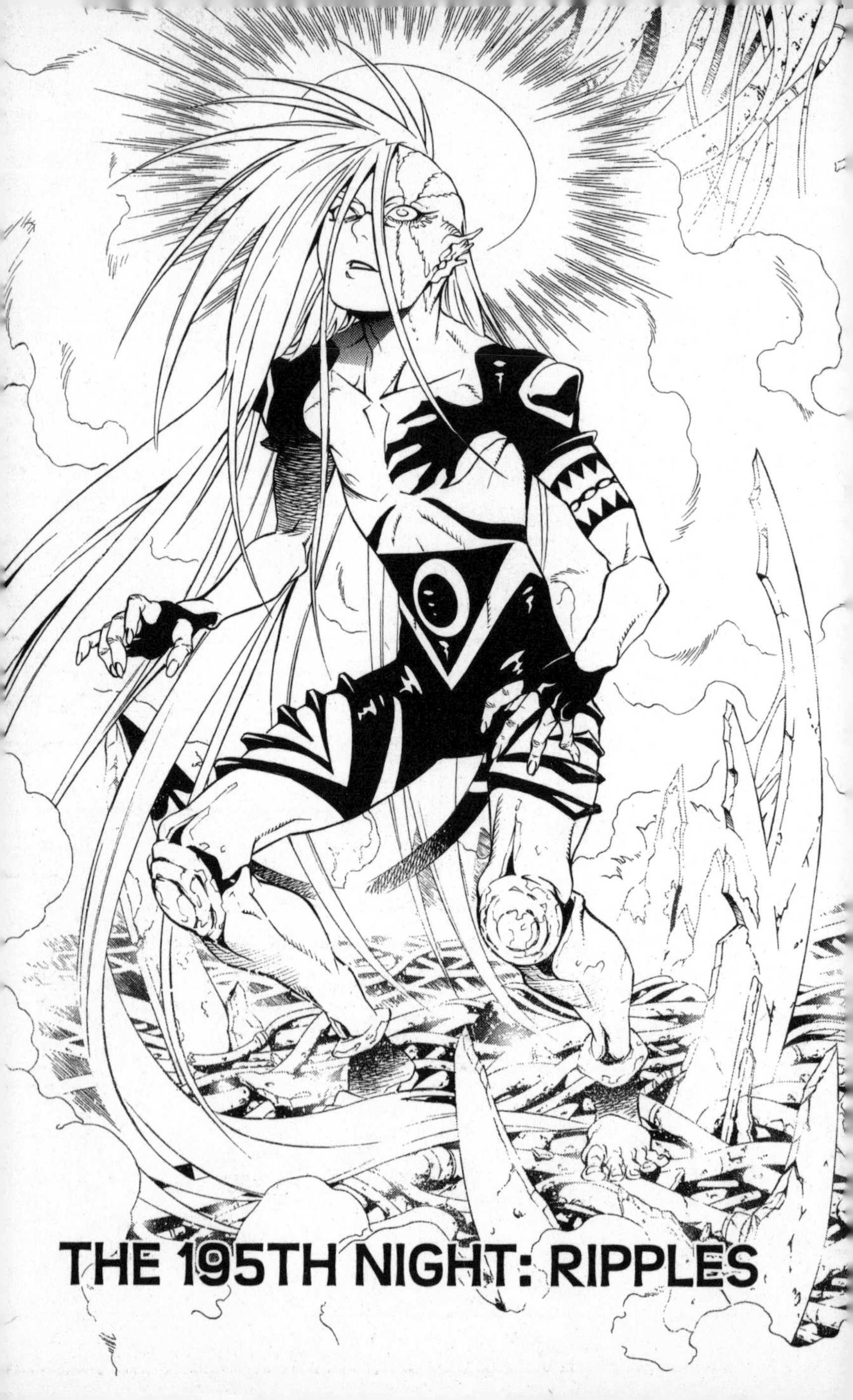

THE 195TH NIGHT: RIPPLES

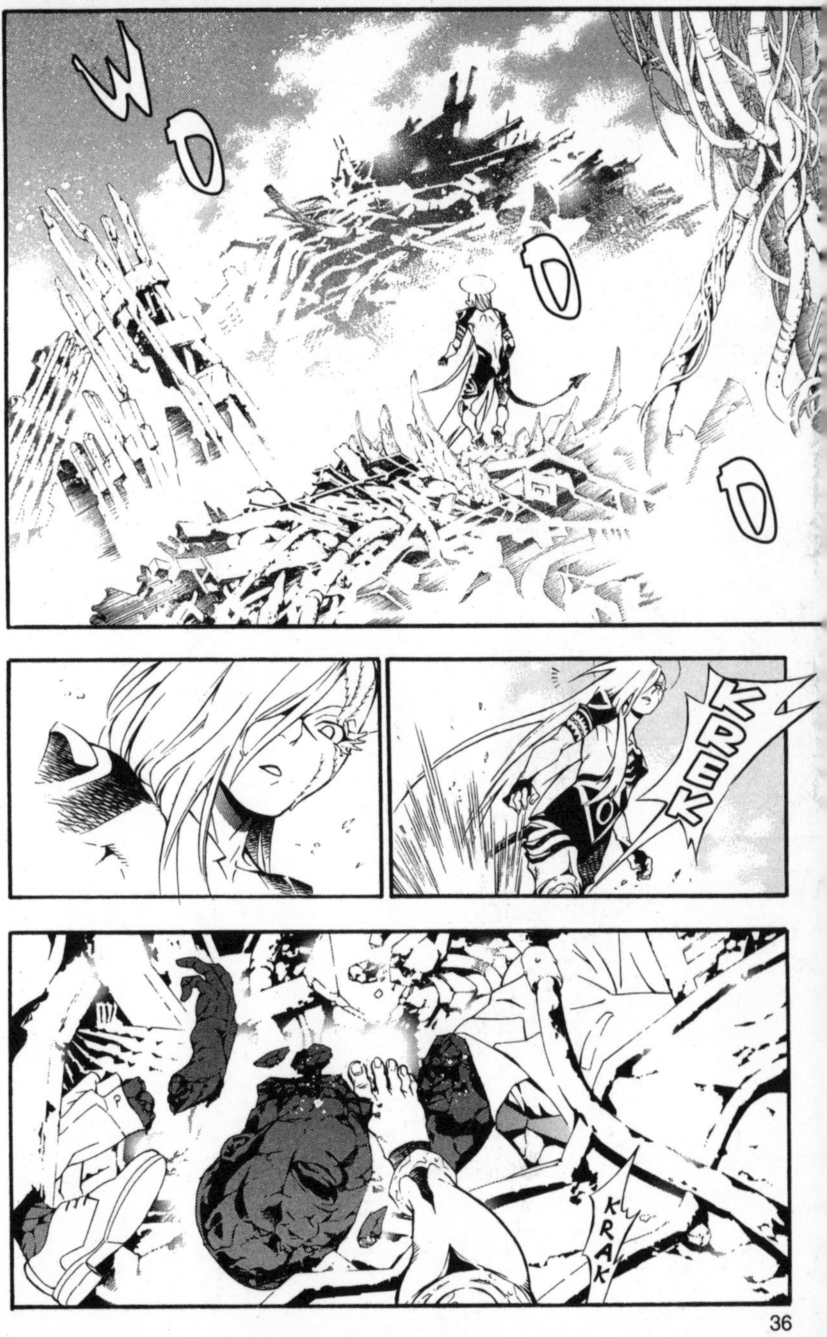
KREK
KRAK

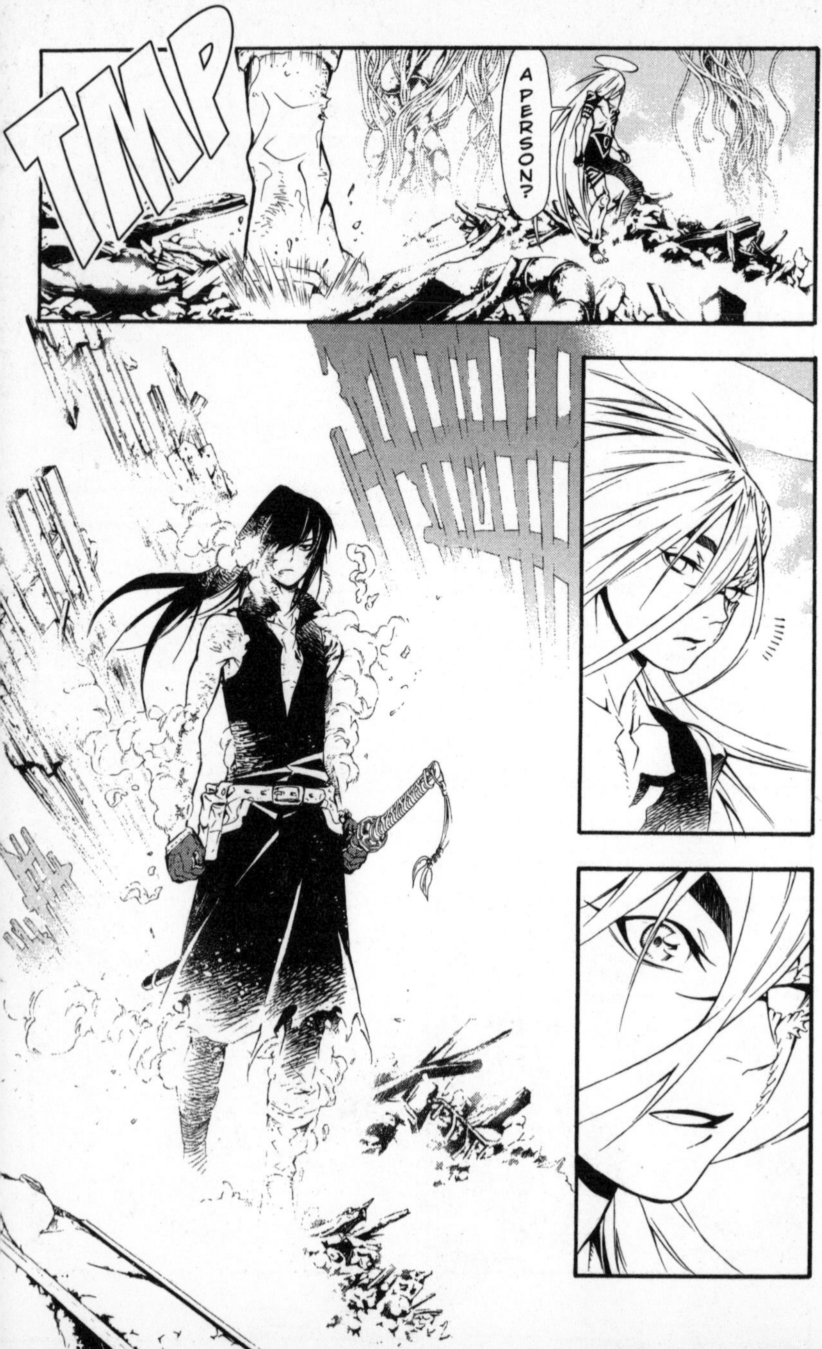
A PERSON?
TMP

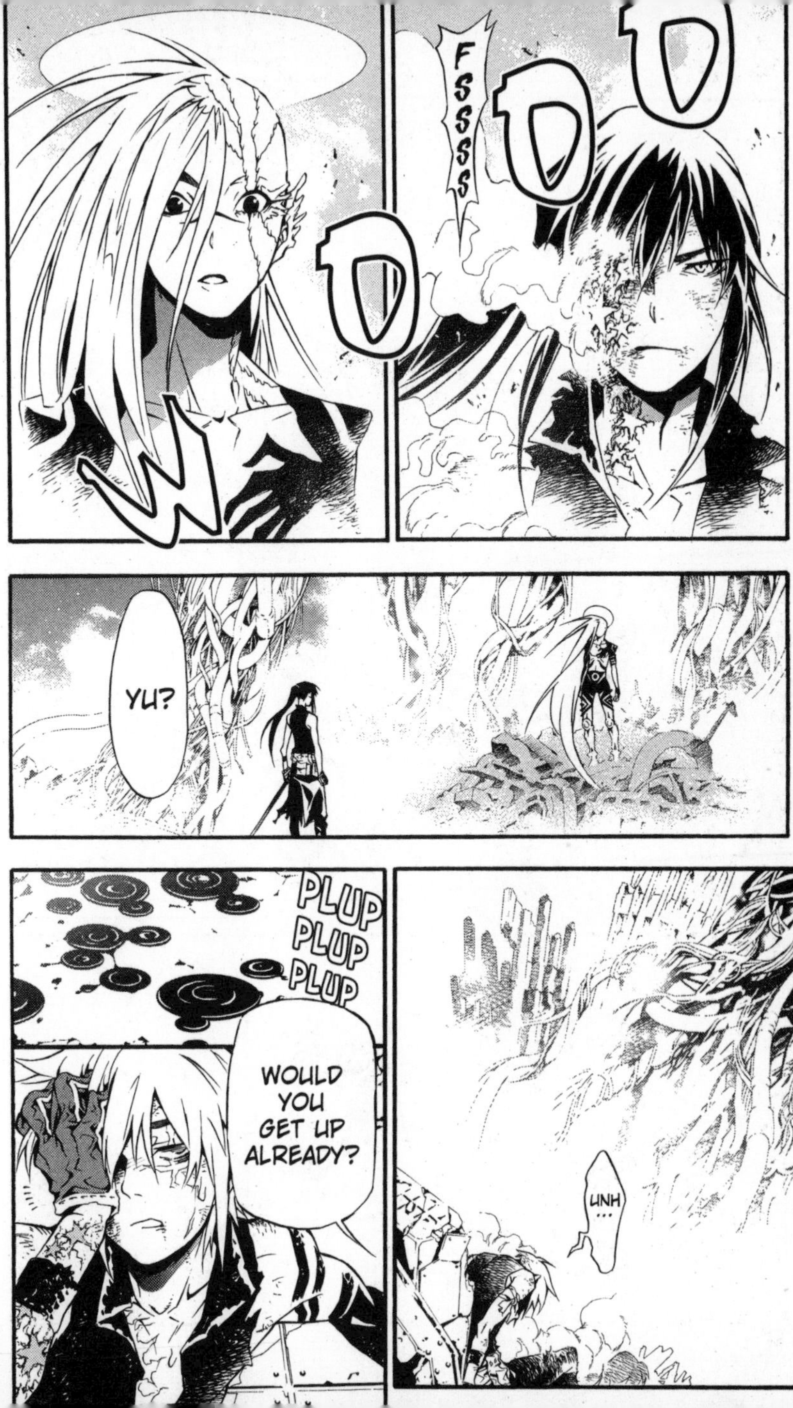
FSSSSS
DDDD
W
YU?
UNH...
PLUP
PLUP
PLUP
WOULD YOU GET UP ALREADY?

READ THIS WAY

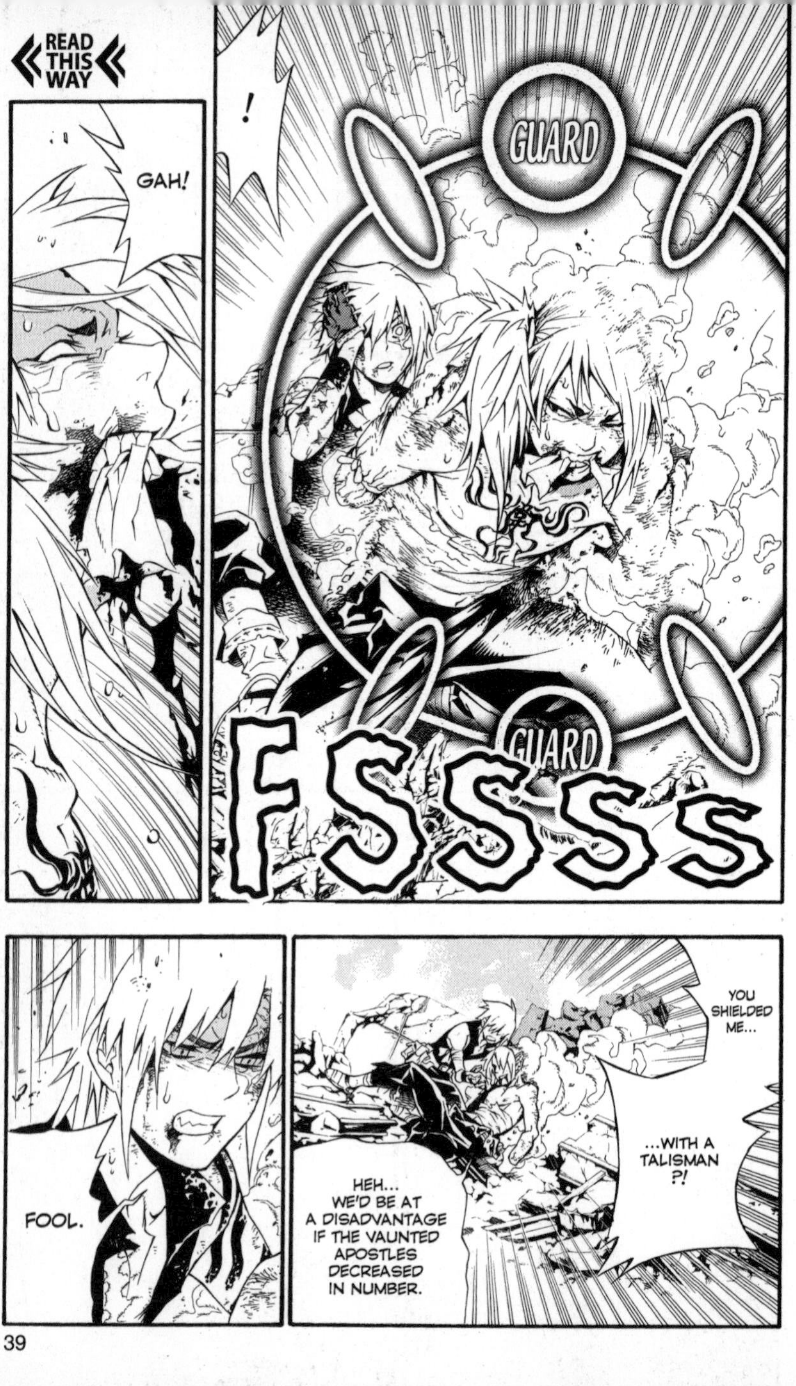

!
GUARD
GUARD
FSSSS
GAH!
YOU SHIELDED ME...
...WITH A TALISMAN?!
HEH... WE'D BE AT A DISADVANTAGE IF THE VAUNTED APOSTLES DECREASED IN NUMBER.
FOOL.

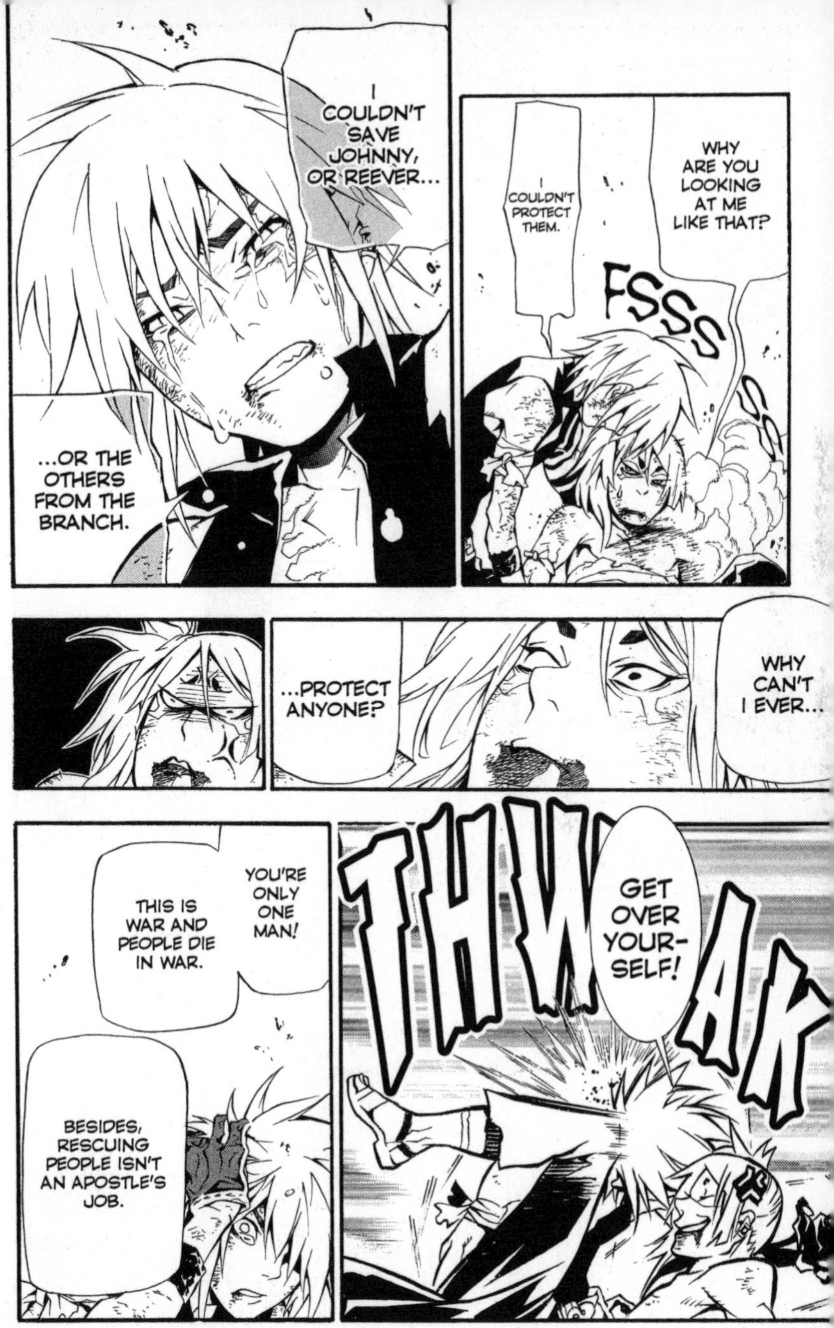
WHY ARE YOU LOOKING AT ME LIKE THAT?
I COULDN'T PROTECT THEM.
FSSSS
I COULDN'T SAVE JOHNNY, OR REEVER...
...OR THE OTHERS FROM THE BRANCH.
WHY CAN'T I EVER...
...PROTECT ANYONE?
THWAK
GET OVER YOUR-SELF!
YOU'RE ONLY ONE MAN!
THIS IS WAR AND PEOPLE DIE IN WAR.
BESIDES, RESCUING PEOPLE ISN'T AN APOSTLE'S JOB.

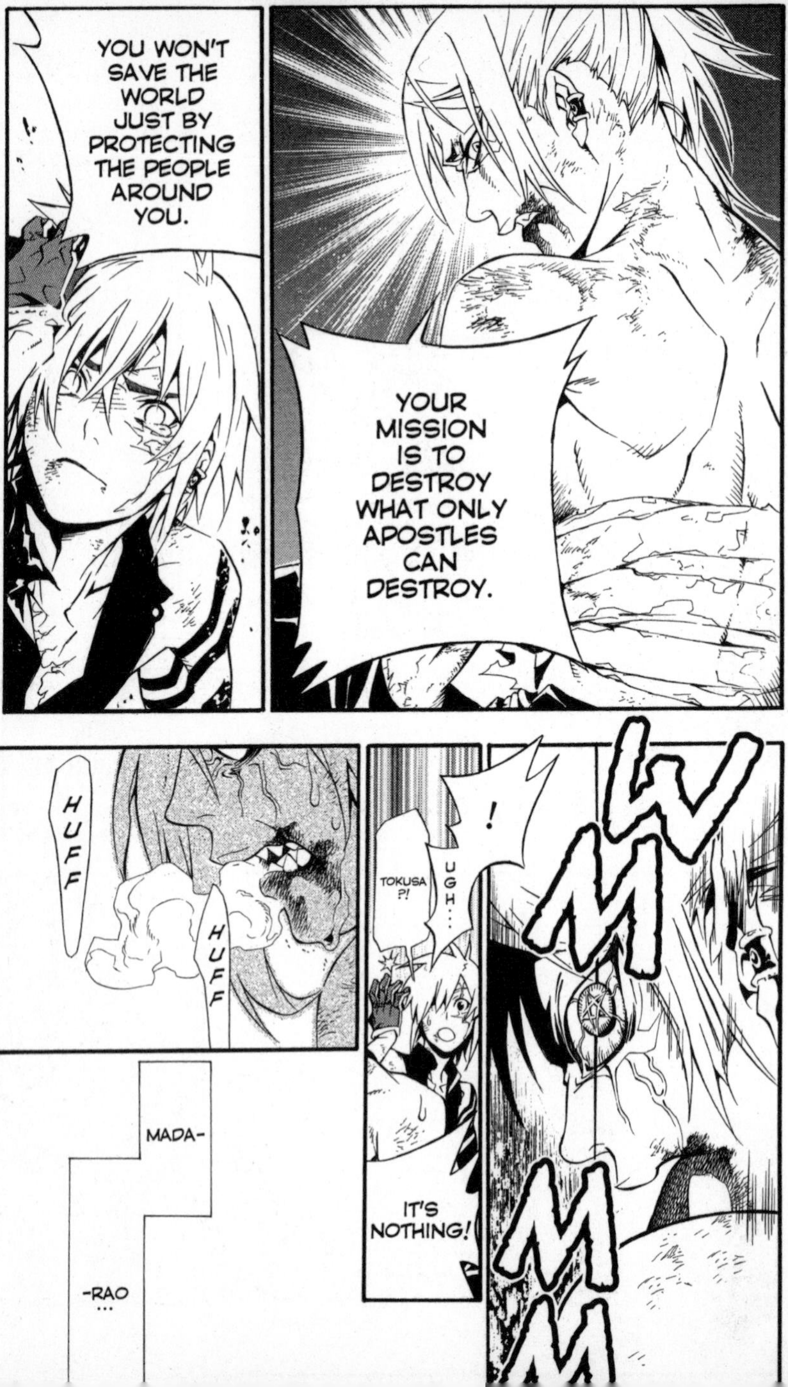
YOUR MISSION IS TO DESTROY WHAT ONLY APOSTLES CAN DESTROY.
YOU WON'T SAVE THE WORLD JUST BY PROTECTING THE PEOPLE AROUND YOU.
WMMM
!
UGH...
TOKUSA?!
IT'S NOTHING!
HUFF
HUFF
MADA-
-RAO...

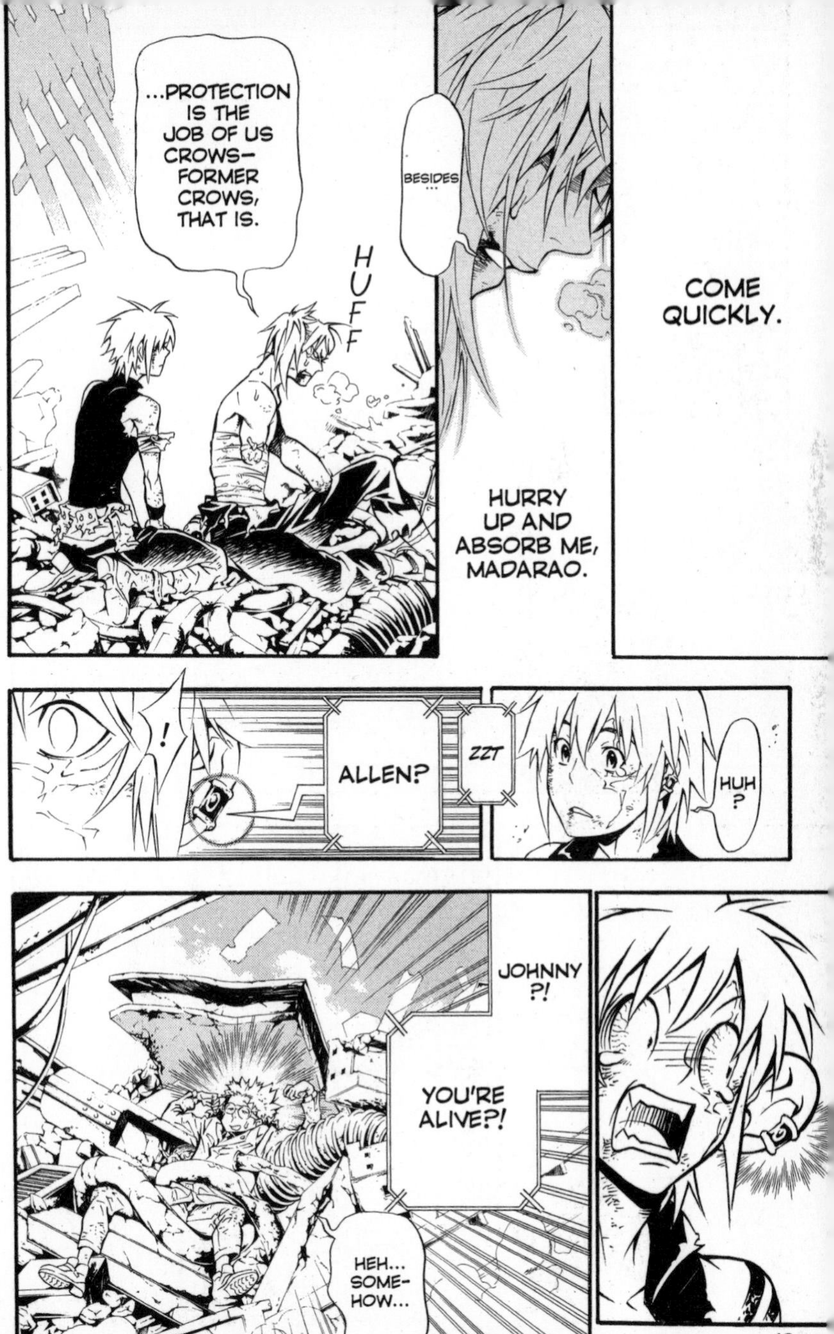
BESIDES...
COME QUICKLY.
HURRY UP AND ABSORB ME, MADARAO.
...PROTECTION IS THE JOB OF US CROWS—FORMER CROWS, THAT IS.
HUFF
HUH?
ZZT
ALLEN?
!
JOHNNY?!
YOU'RE ALIVE?!
HEH... SOME-HOW...

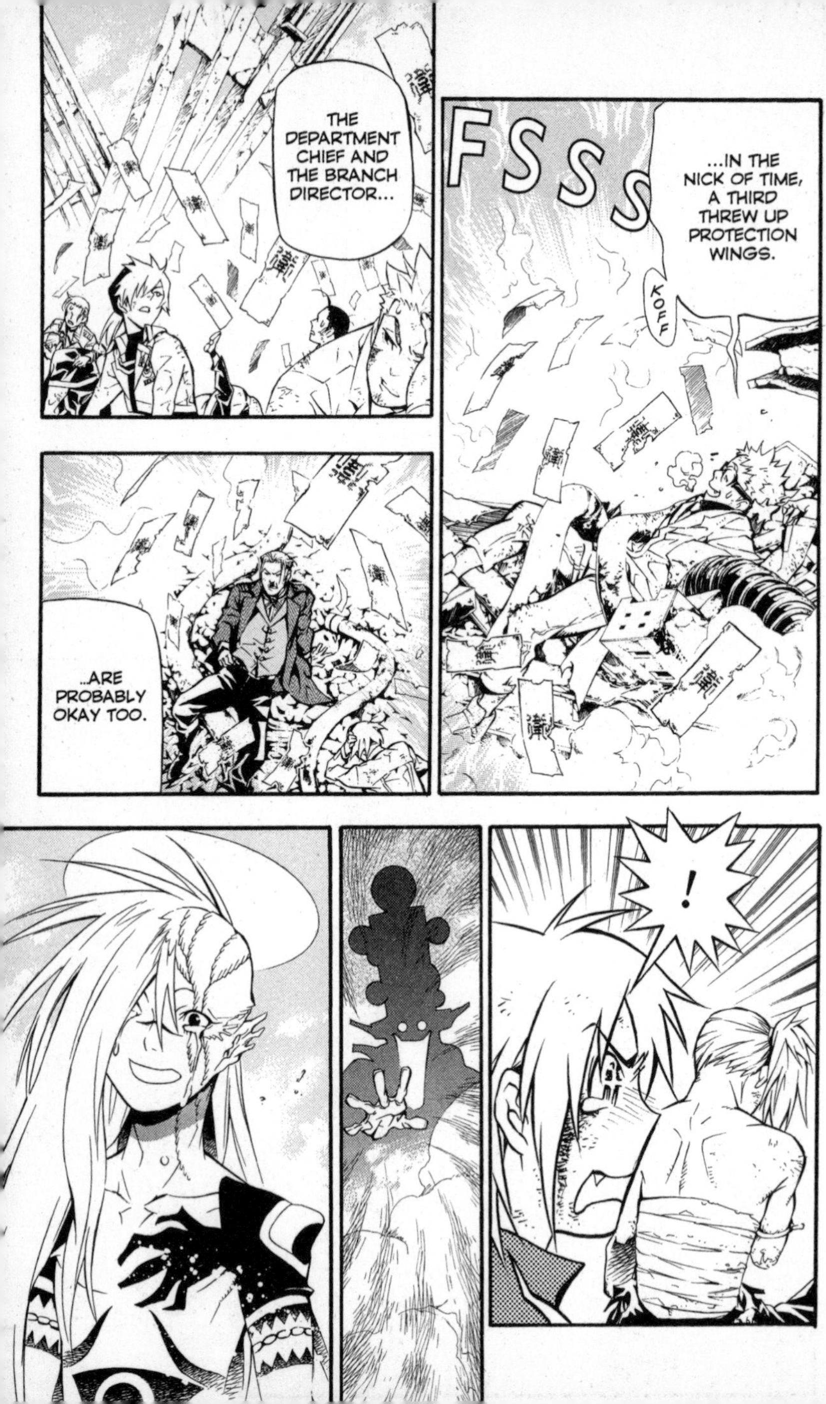
FSSS
...IN THE NICK OF TIME, A THIRD THREW UP PROTECTION WINGS.
KOFF
THE DEPARTMENT CHIEF AND THE BRANCH DIRECTOR...
..ARE PROBABLY OKAY TOO.
!

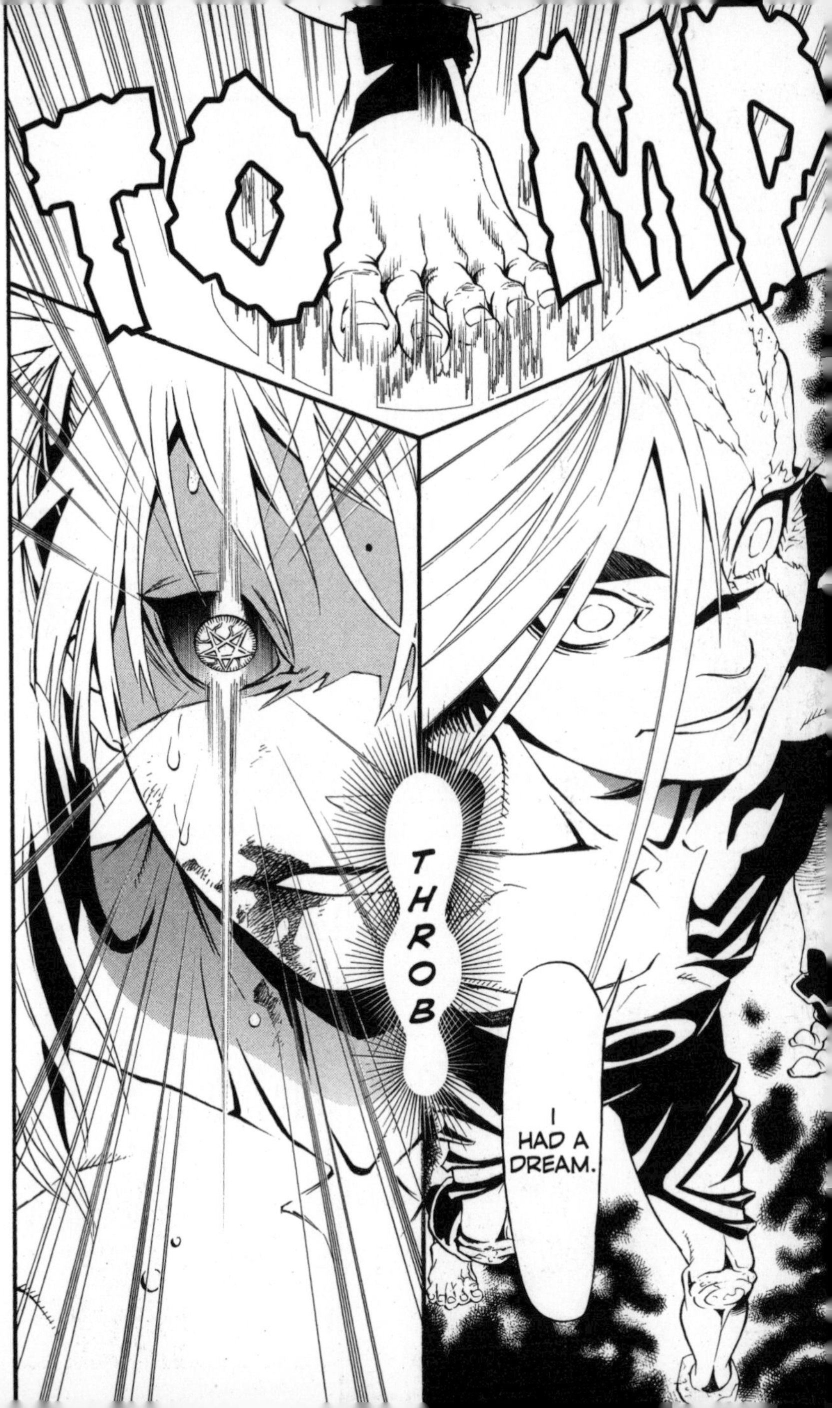
TOMP
THROB
I HAD A DREAM.

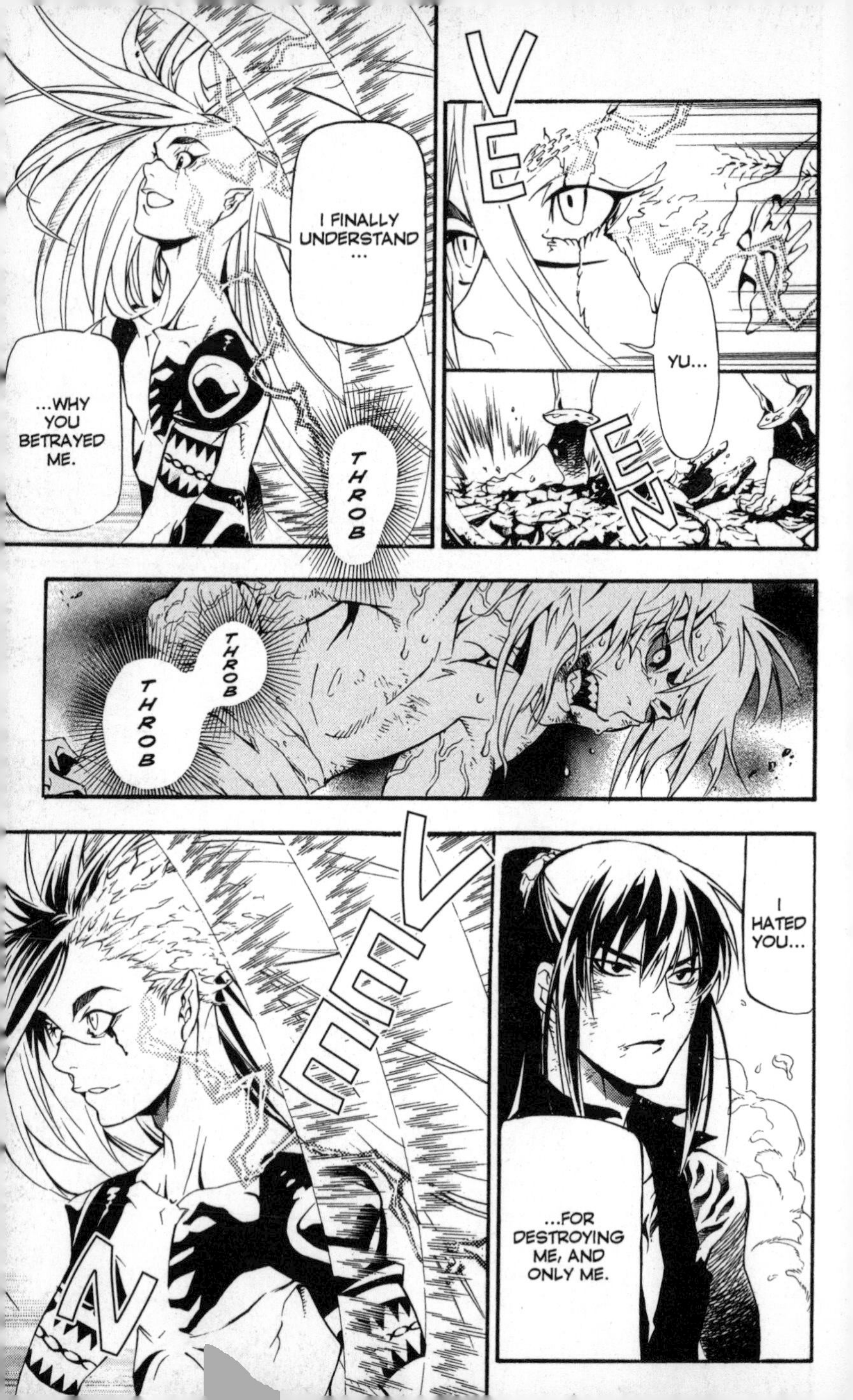
VE
YU...
EN
I FINALLY UNDERSTAND ...
...WHY YOU BETRAYED ME.
THROB
THROB THROB
I HATED YOU...
...FOR DESTROYING ME, AND ONLY ME.
VEEEN

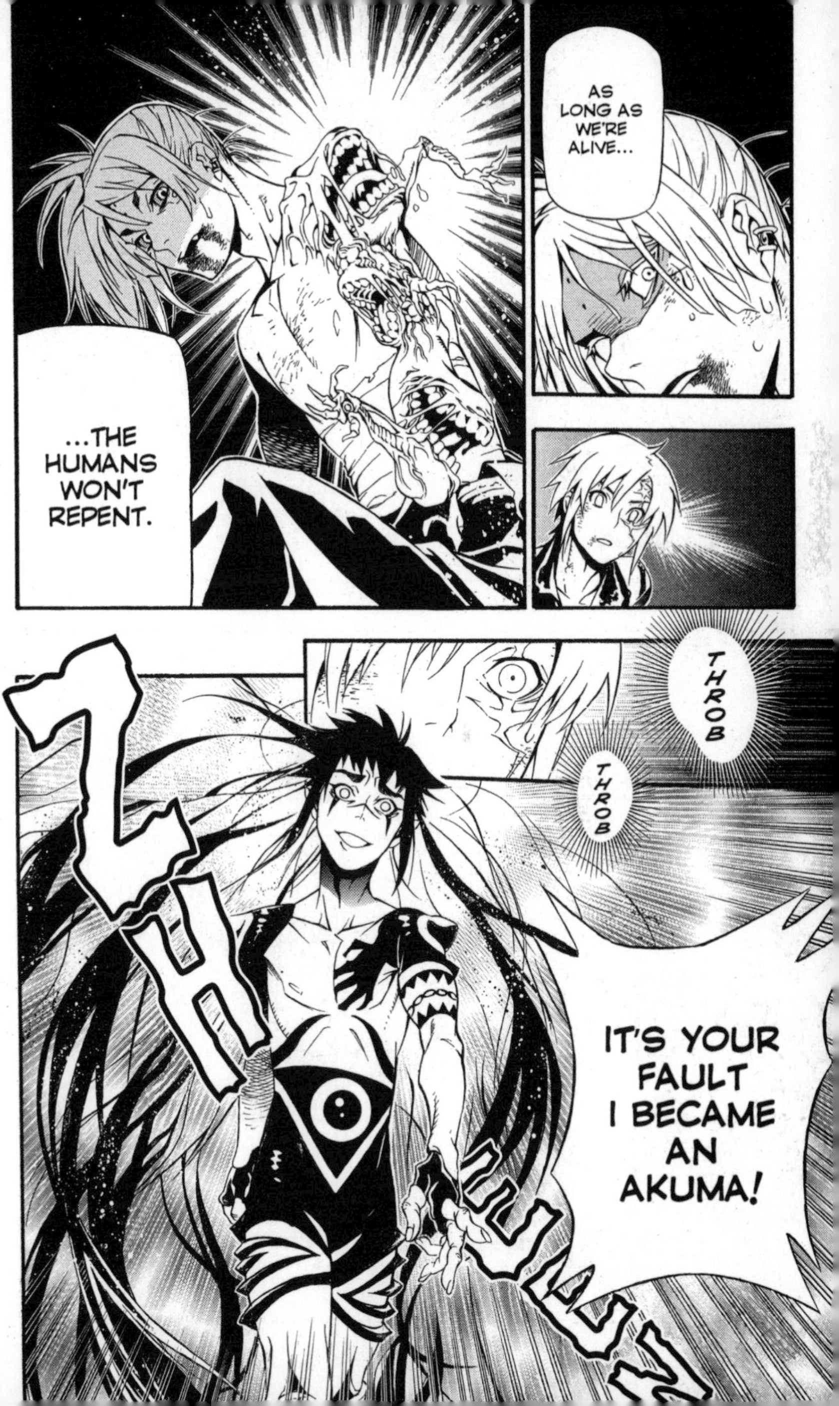
AS LONG AS WE'RE ALIVE...
...THE HUMANS WON'T REPENT.
THROB
THROB
IT'S YOUR FAULT I BECAME AN AKUMA!

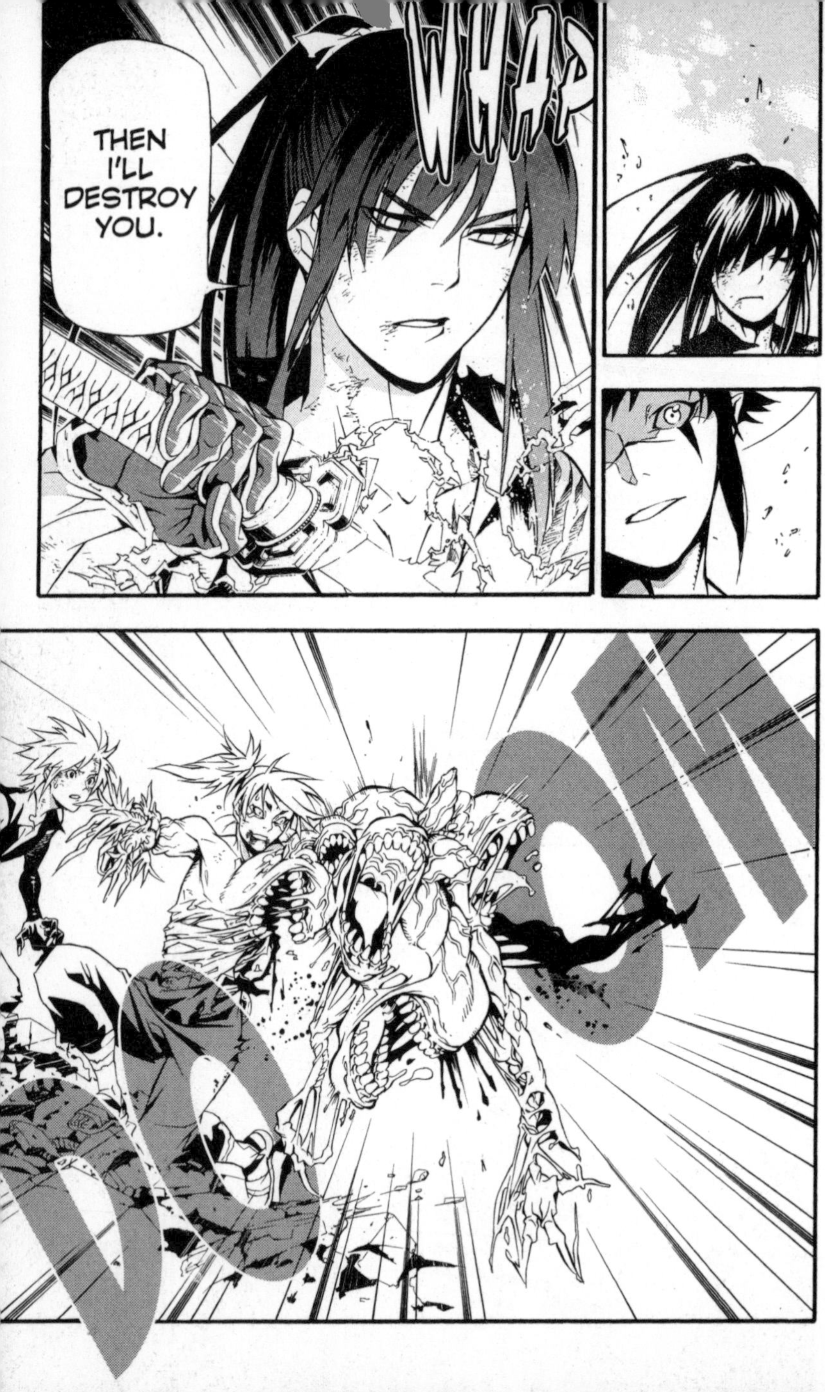
WHAP
THEN I'LL DESTROY YOU.
DOOM

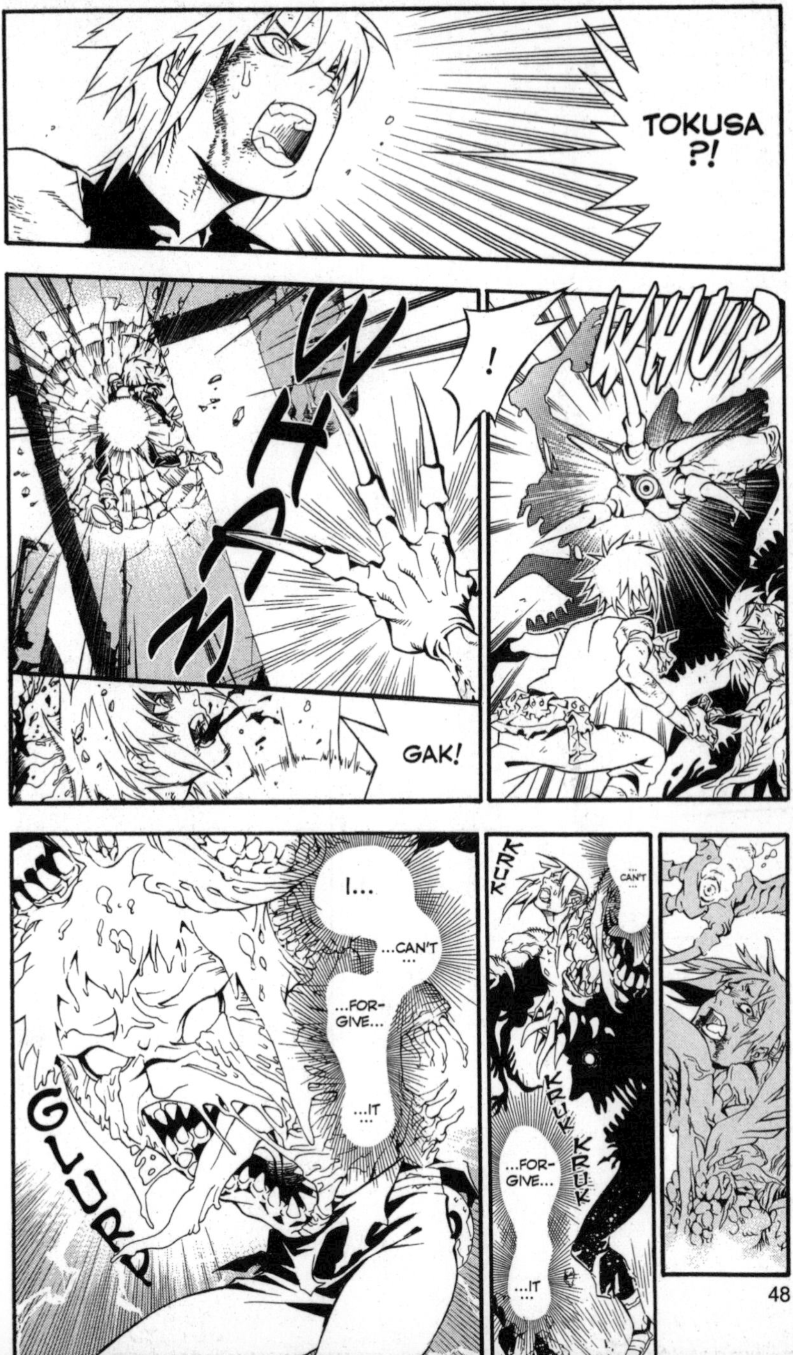

TOKUSA ?!
!
WHUP
SHAM
GAK!
KRUK
...CAN'T...
KRUK
KRUK
...FOR-GIVE...
...IT...
I...
...CAN'T...
...FOR-GIVE...
...IT...
GLURP

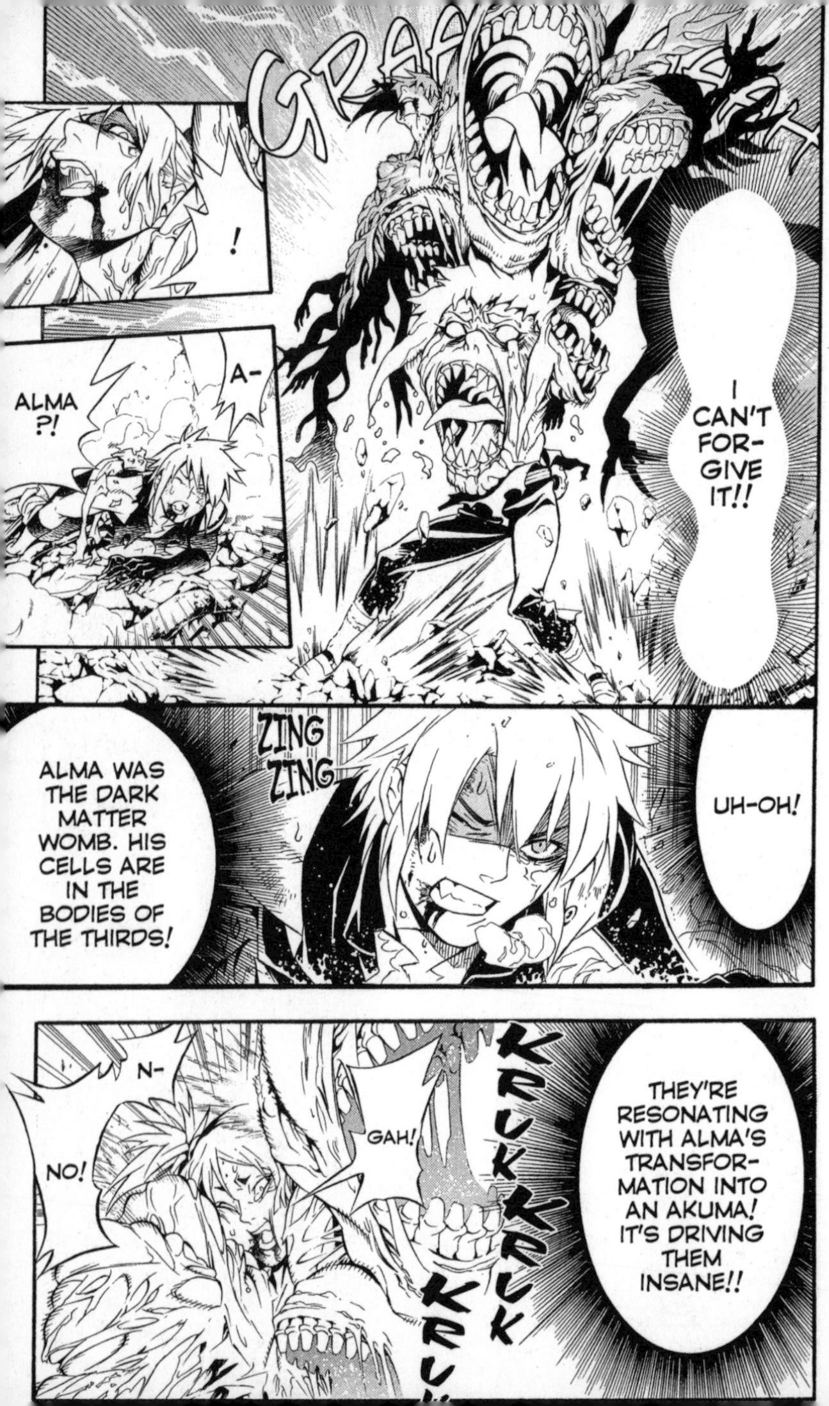
GRAA
I CAN'T FORGIVE IT!!
!
A-
ALMA ?!
UH-OH!
ZING ZING
ALMA WAS THE DARK MATTER WOMB. HIS CELLS ARE IN THE BODIES OF THE THIRDS!
THEY'RE RESONATING WITH ALMA'S TRANSFORMATION INTO AN AKUMA! IT'S DRIVING THEM INSANE!!
KRUK KRUK KRUK
GAH!
N-
NO!

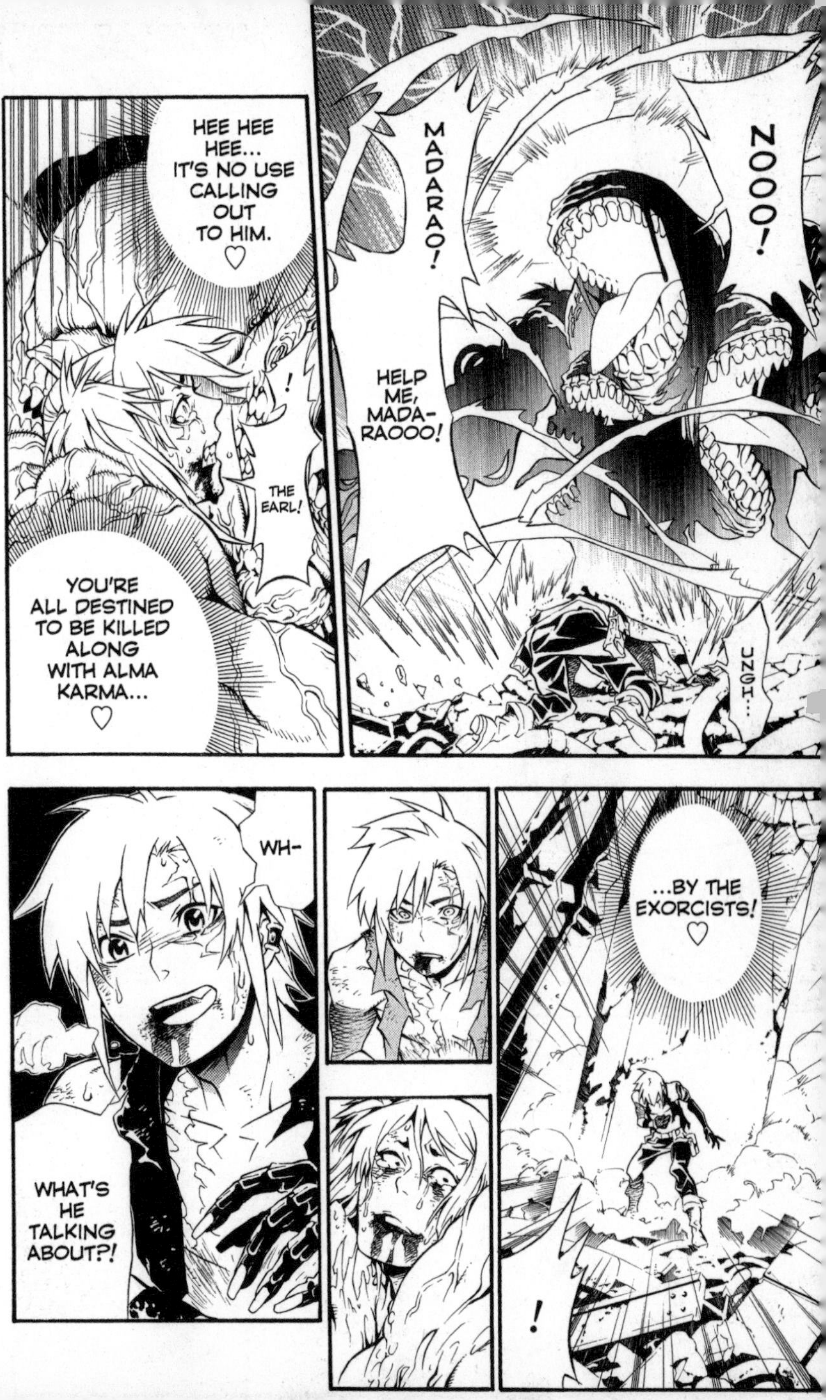
NOOOO!
MADARAO!
HELP ME, MADARAOOO!
UNGH...
HEE HEE HEE... IT'S NO USE CALLING OUT TO HIM. ♡
!
THE EARL!
YOU'RE ALL DESTINED TO BE KILLED ALONG WITH ALMA KARMA... ♡
...BY THE EXORCISTS! ♡
!
WH-
WHAT'S HE TALKING ABOUT?!

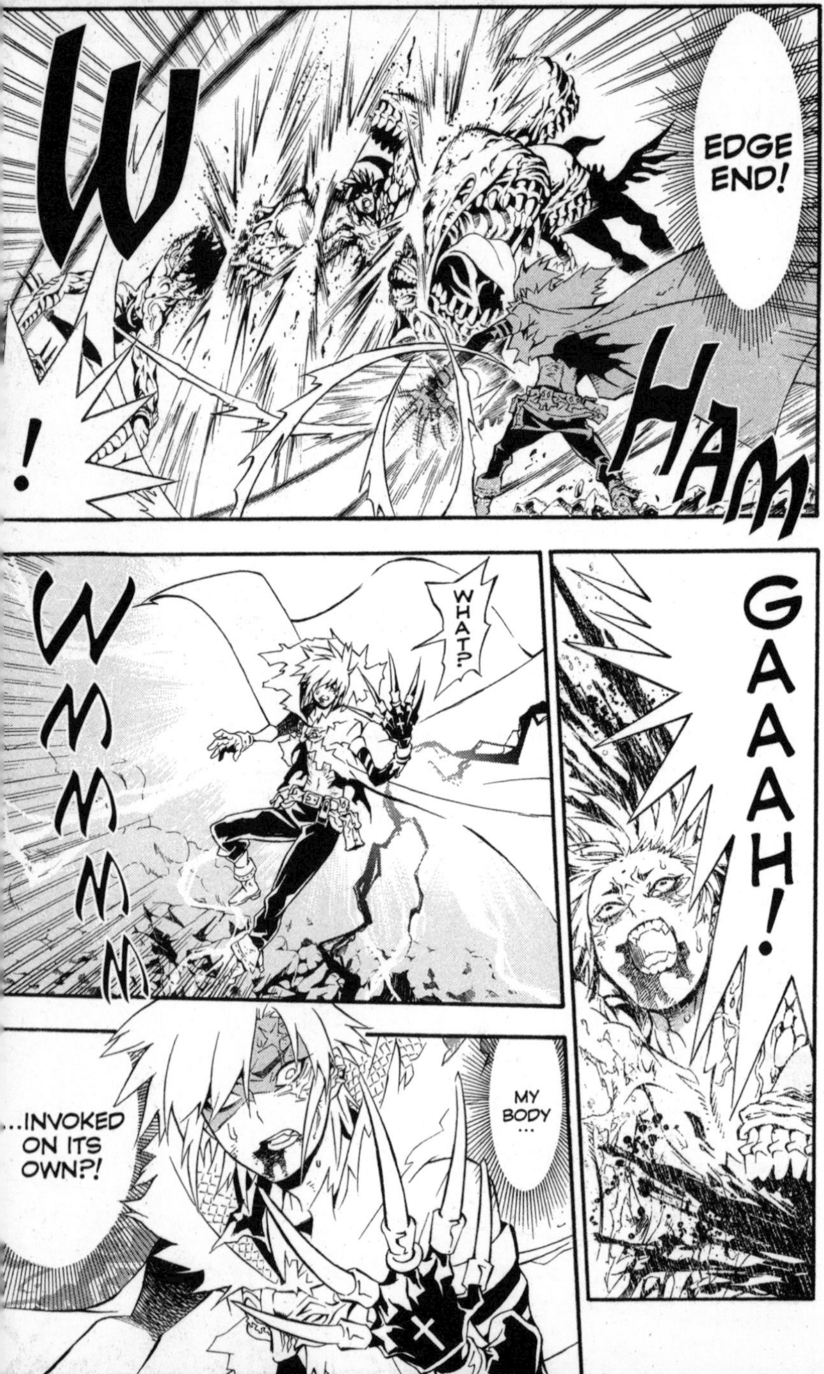
EDGE END!
WHAM!
GAAAH!
WHAT?
WMMMMN
MY BODY...
...INVOKED ON ITS OWN?!

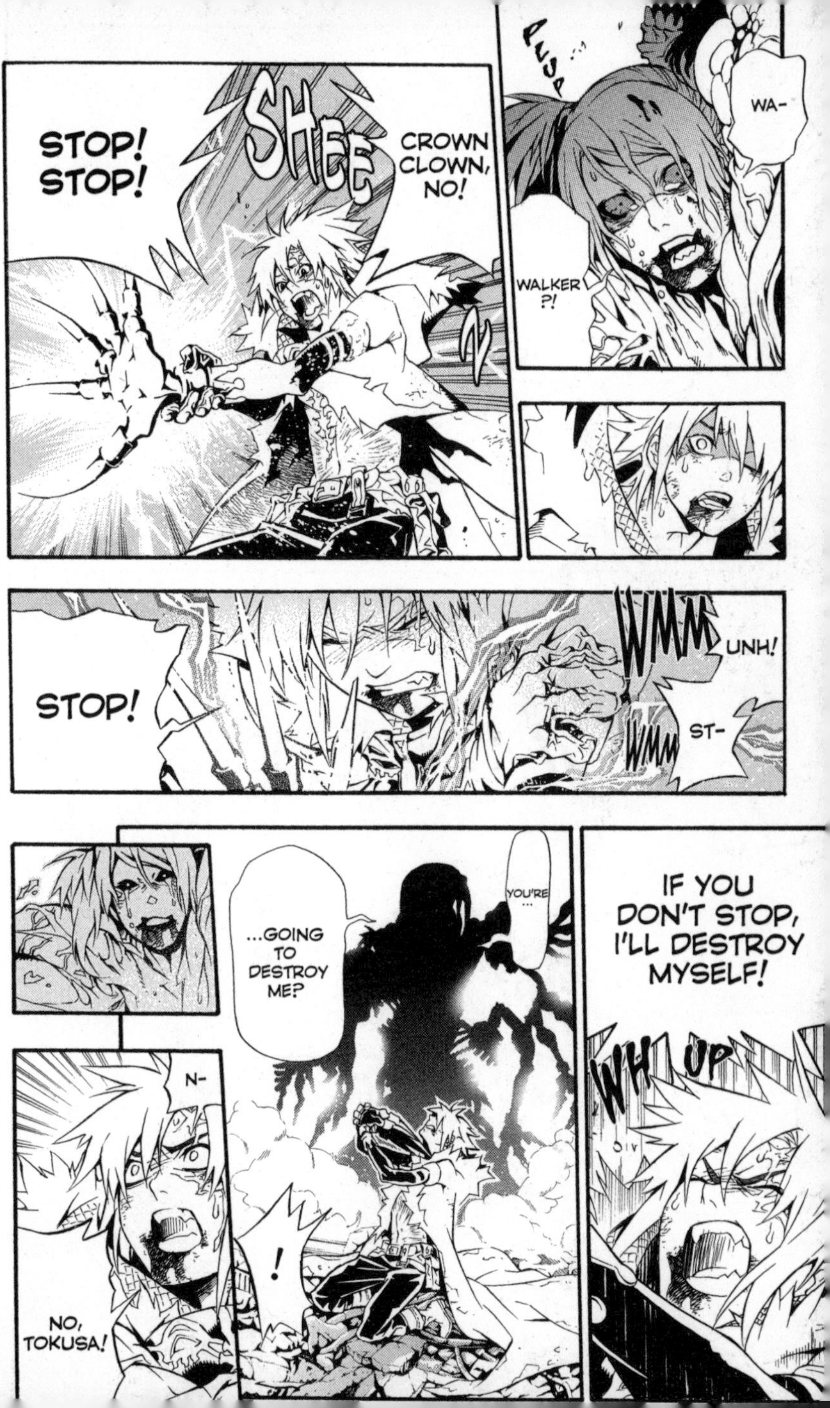
WA-
WALKER ?!
CROWN CLOWN, NO!
SHEE
STOP! STOP!
UNH!
WMM
ST-
WMM
STOP!
IF YOU DON'T STOP, I'LL DESTROY MYSELF!
WH UP
YOU'RE ...
...GOING TO DESTROY ME?
!
N-
NO, TOKUSA!

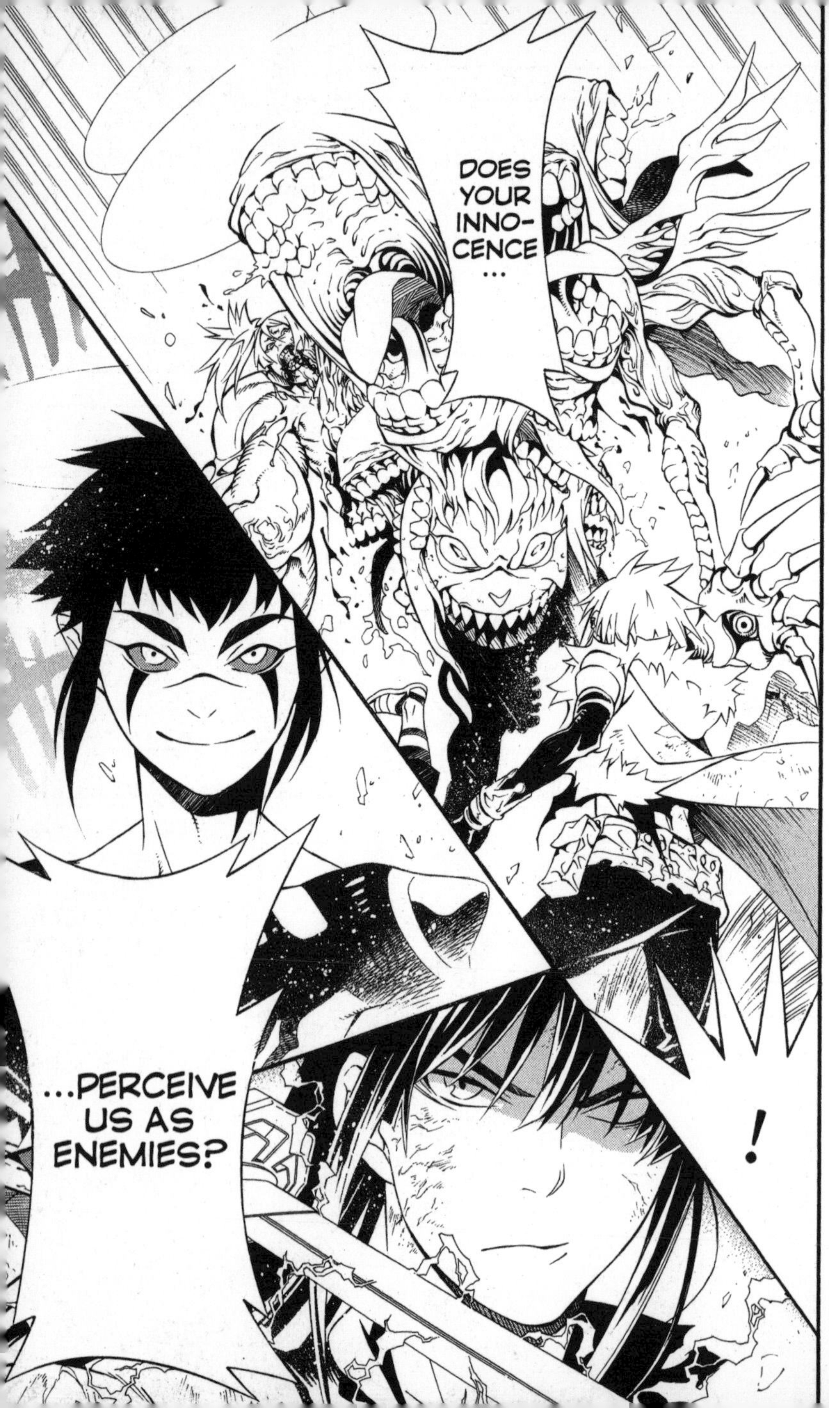
DOES YOUR INNOCENCE...
...PERCEIVE US AS ENEMIES?
!

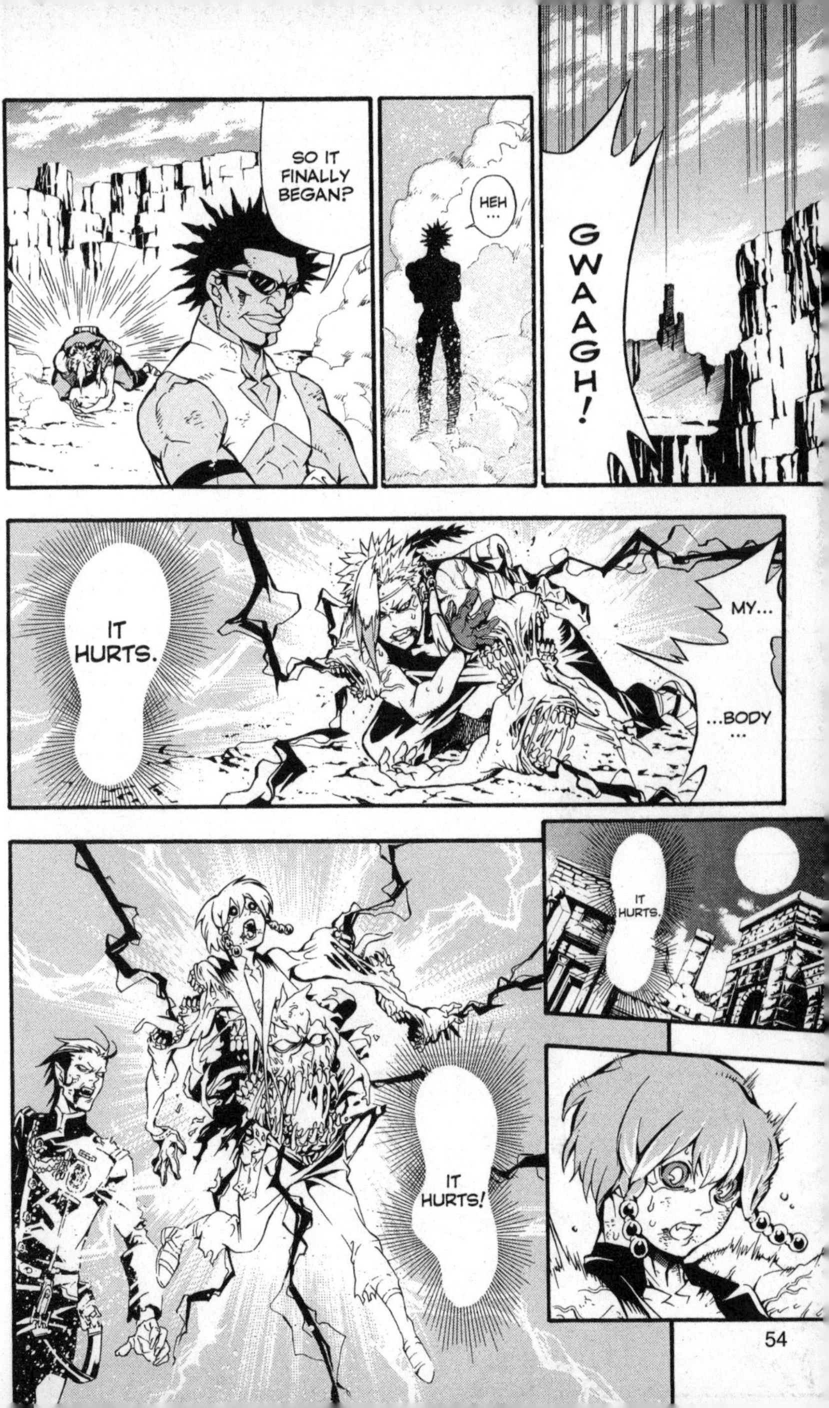
GWAAGH!
HEH ...
SO IT FINALLY BEGAN?
MY...
...BODY ...
IT HURTS.
IT HURTS.
IT HURTS!

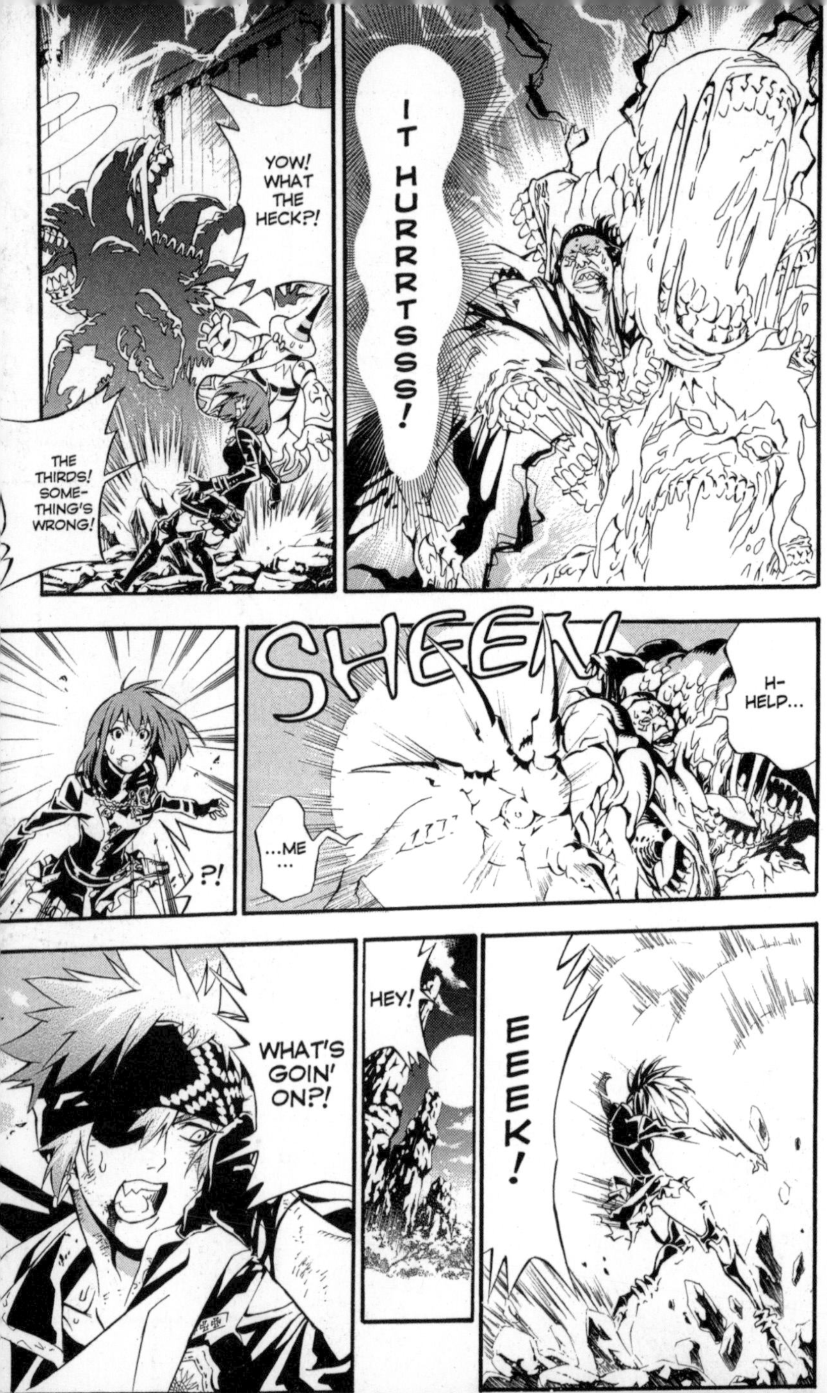
IT HURRRTSSS!
YOW! WHAT THE HECK?!
THE THIRDS! SOME-THING'S WRONG!
SHEEN
H-HELP...
...ME ...
?!
EEEK!
HEY!
WHAT'S GOIN' ON?!

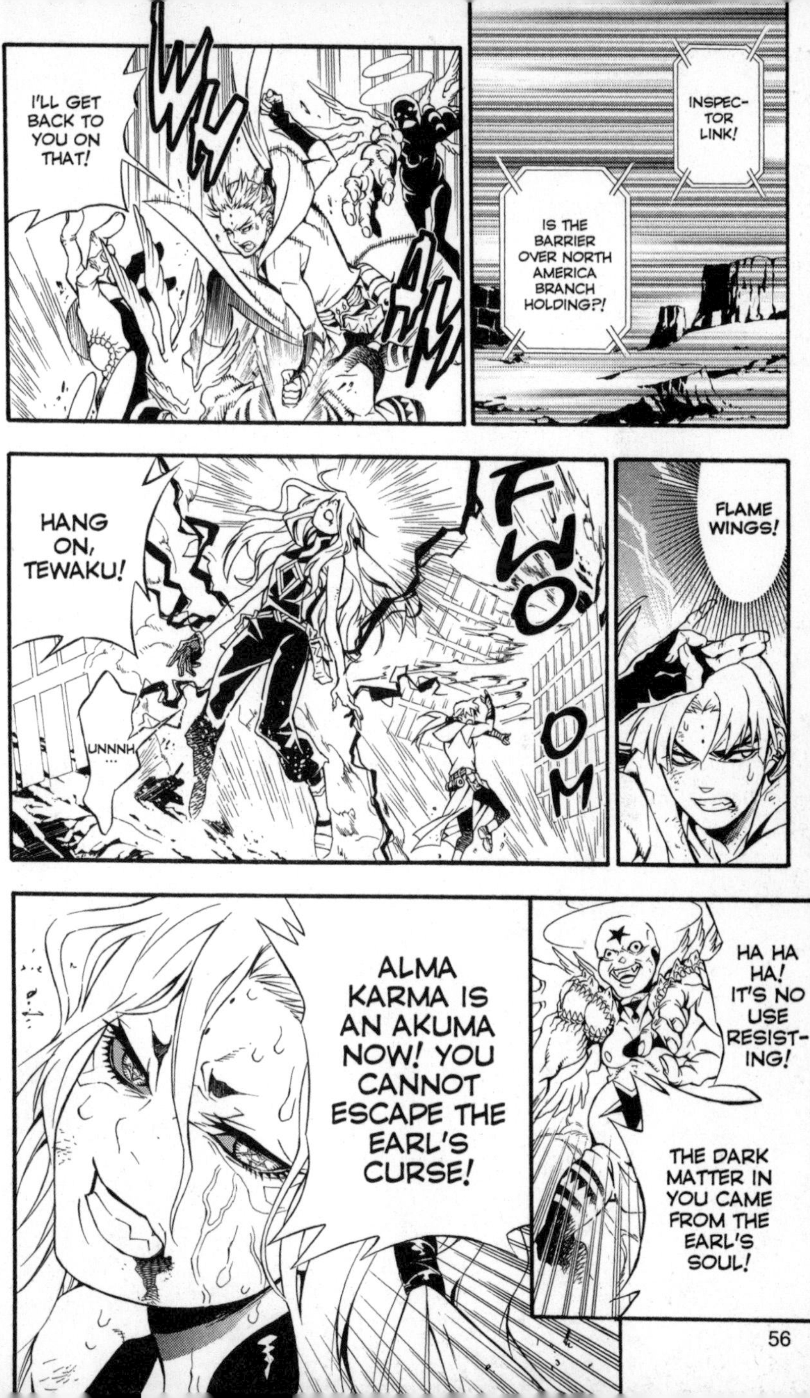
INSPECTOR LINK!
IS THE BARRIER OVER NORTH AMERICA BRANCH HOLDING?!
WHAM
I'LL GET BACK TO YOU ON THAT!
FLAME WINGS!
FWOOM
HANG ON, TEWAKU!
UNNNH...
HA HA HA! IT'S NO USE RESISTING!
THE DARK MATTER IN YOU CAME FROM THE EARL'S SOUL!
ALMA KARMA IS AN AKUMA NOW! YOU CANNOT ESCAPE THE EARL'S CURSE!

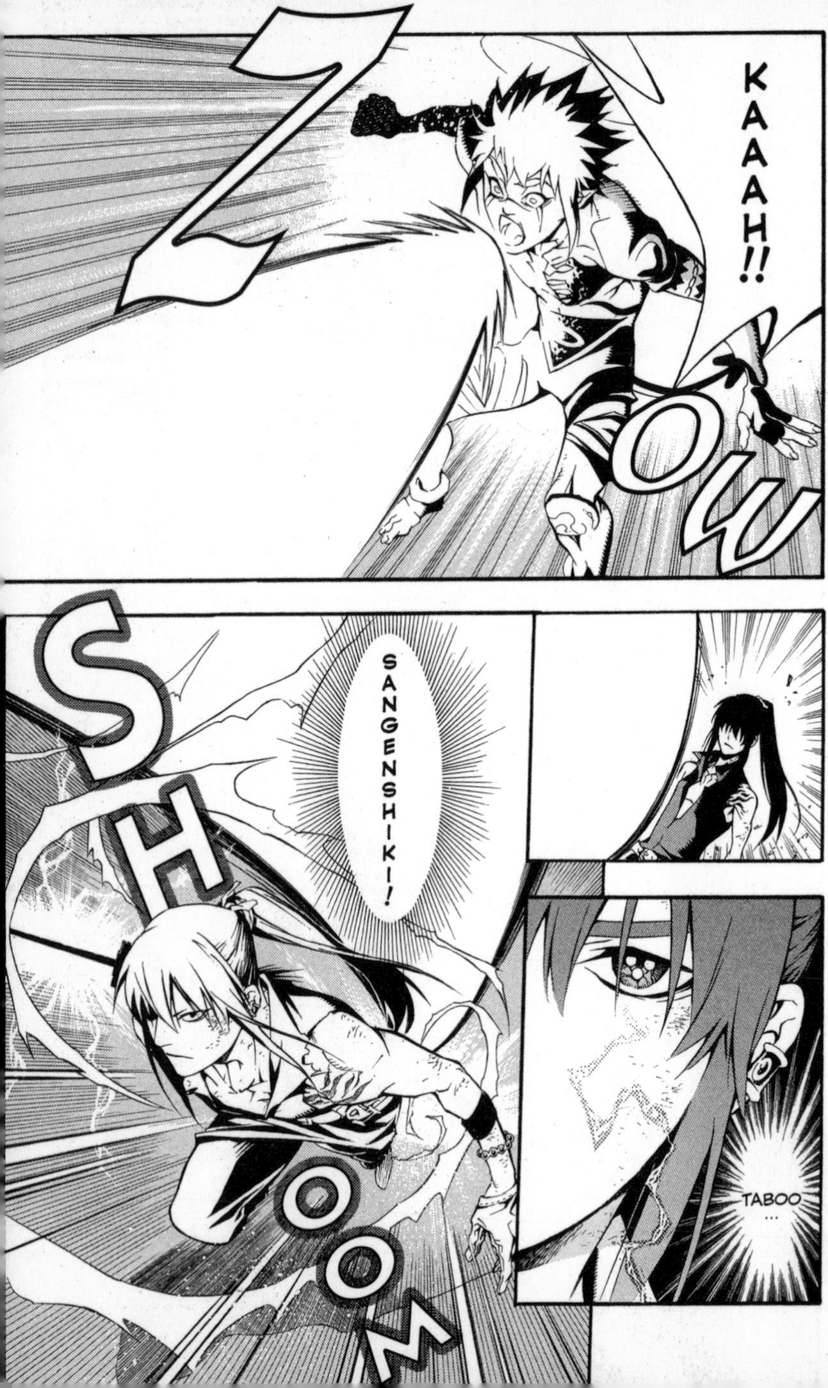
KAAAAH!!
ZOW
!
TABOO ...
SANGENSHIKI!
SHOOM

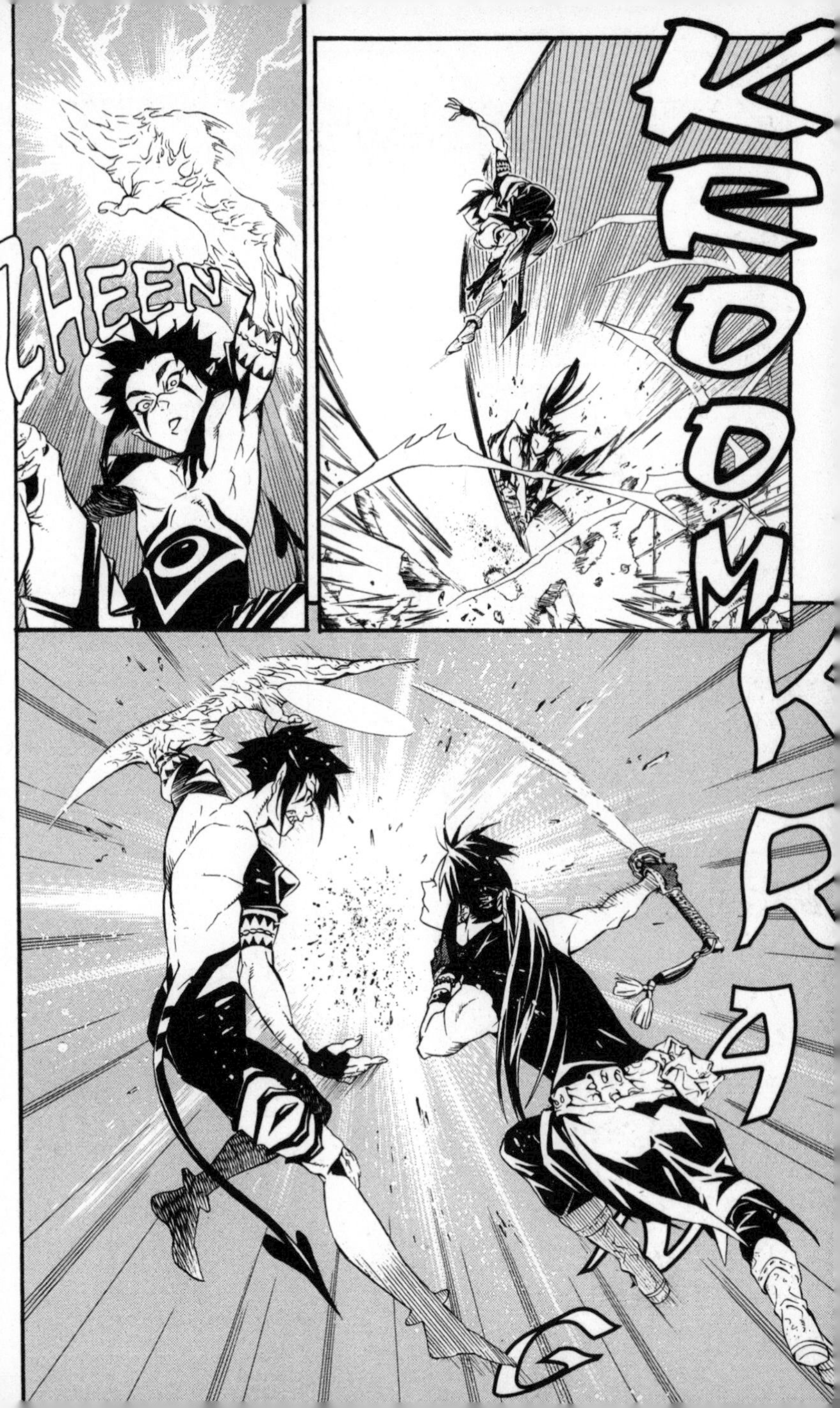
KRDOM
ZHEEN
KRAG

READ THIS WAY

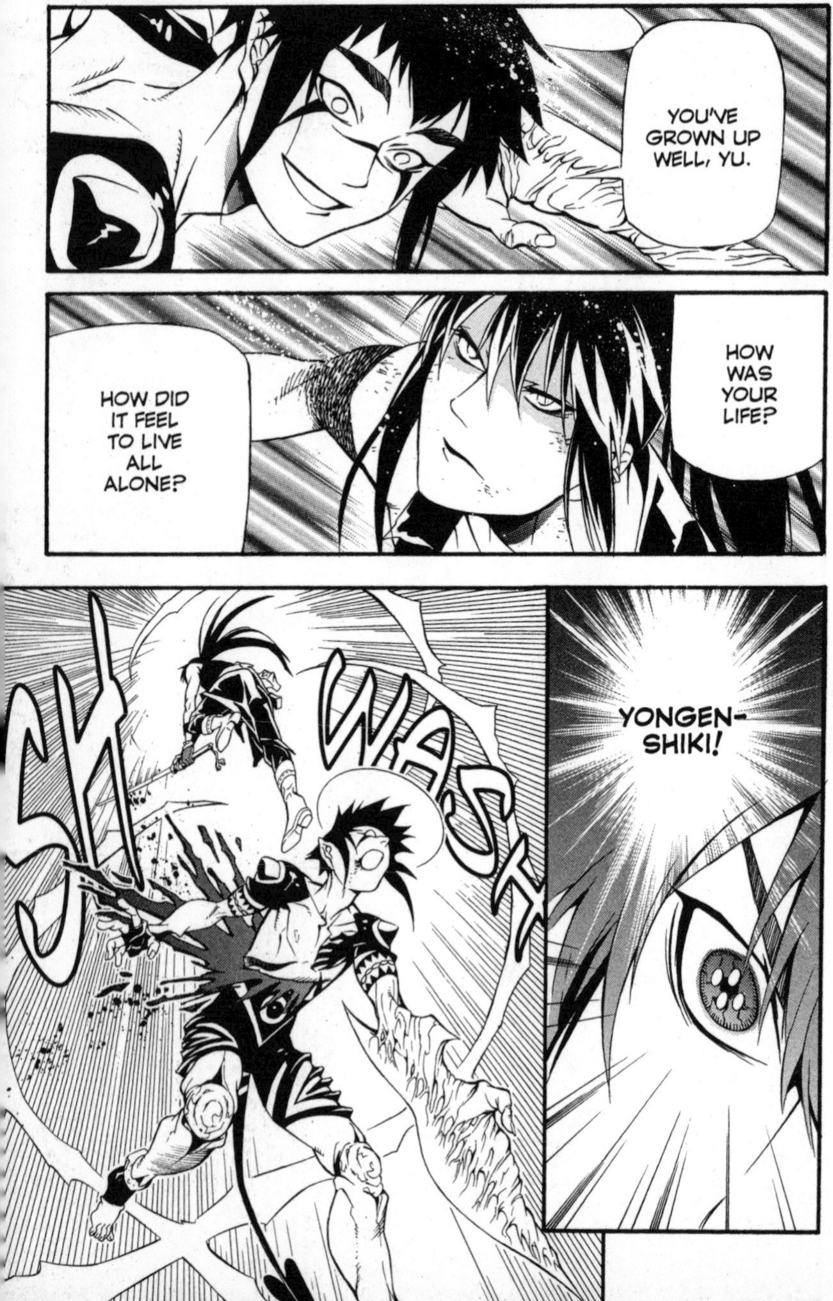
YOU'VE GROWN UP WELL, YU.
HOW WAS YOUR LIFE?
HOW DID IT FEEL TO LIVE ALL ALONE?
YONGEN-SHIKI!
WASH
SH

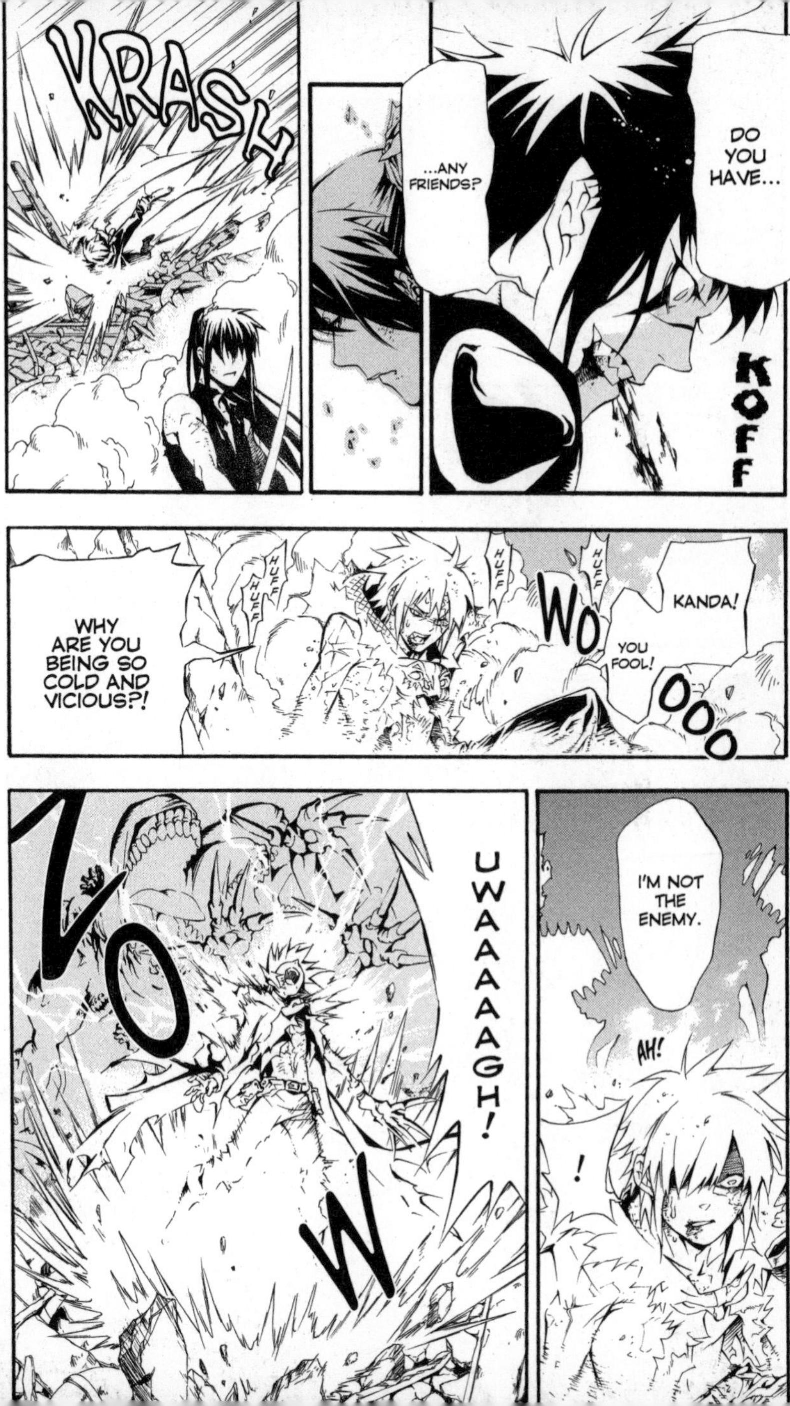
DO YOU HAVE...
...ANY FRIENDS?
KOFF
KRASH
KANDA!
YOU FOOL!
WOOOO
HUFF HUFF
HUFF HUFF
WHY ARE YOU BEING SO COLD AND VICIOUS?!
I'M NOT THE ENEMY.
AH!
!
UWAAAAAGH!

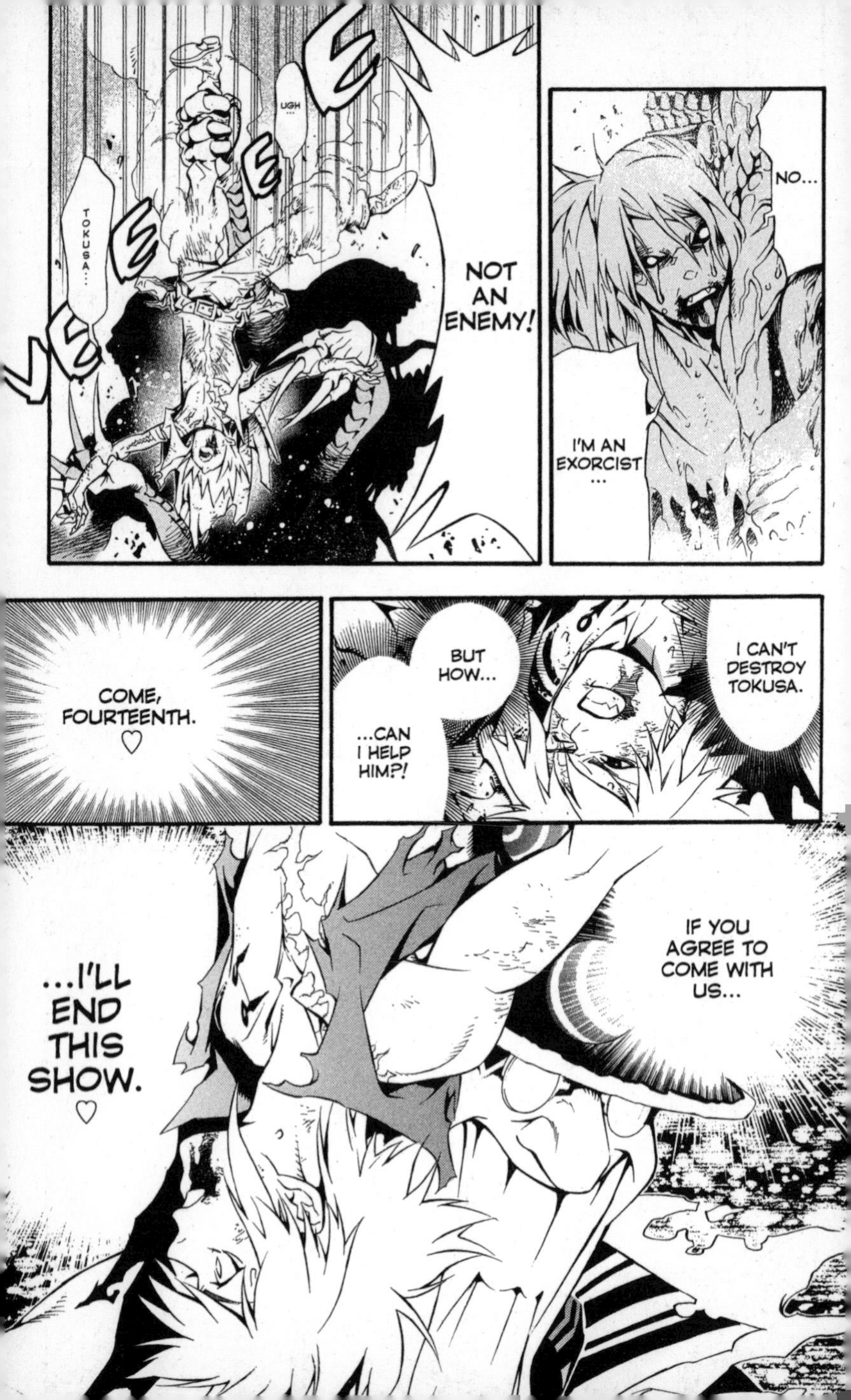
NO...
I'M AN EXORCIST ...
UGH ...
TOKUSA...
NOT AN ENEMY!
I CAN'T DESTROY TOKUSA.
BUT HOW...
...CAN I HELP HIM?!
COME, FOURTEENTH. ♡
IF YOU AGREE TO COME WITH US...
...I'LL END THIS SHOW. ♡

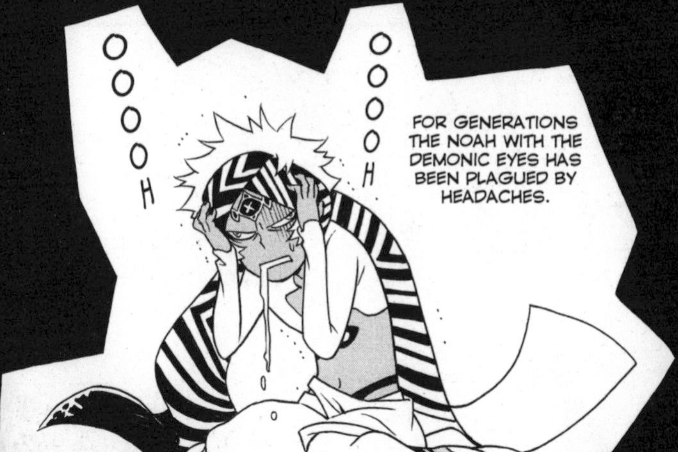
FOR GENERATIONS THE NOAH WITH THE DEMONIC EYES HAS BEEN PLAGUED BY HEADACHES.
OOOOH
OOOOH

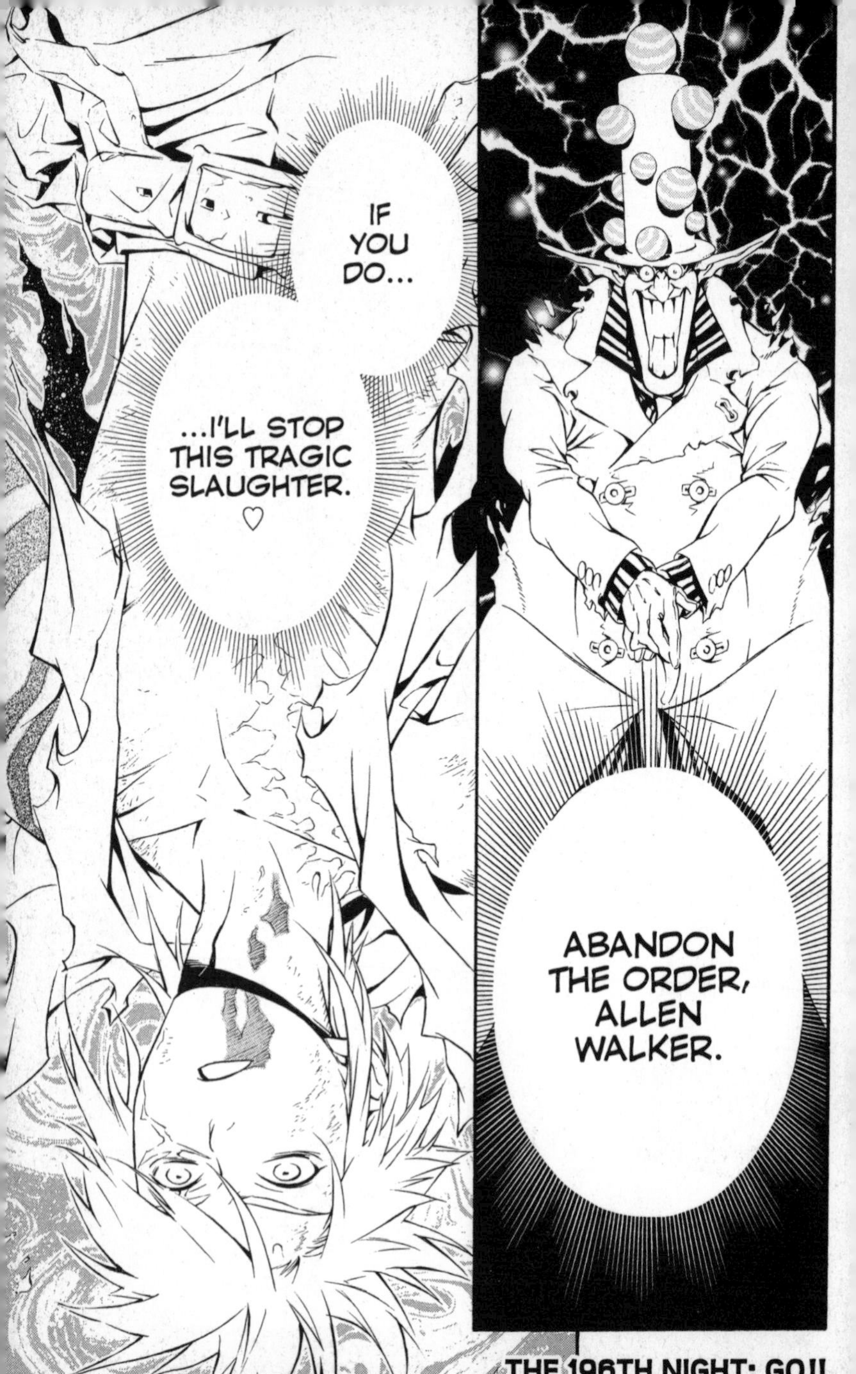
ABANDON THE ORDER, ALLEN WALKER.
IF YOU DO...
...I'LL STOP THIS TRAGIC SLAUGHTER. ♡

THE 196TH NIGHT: GO!!

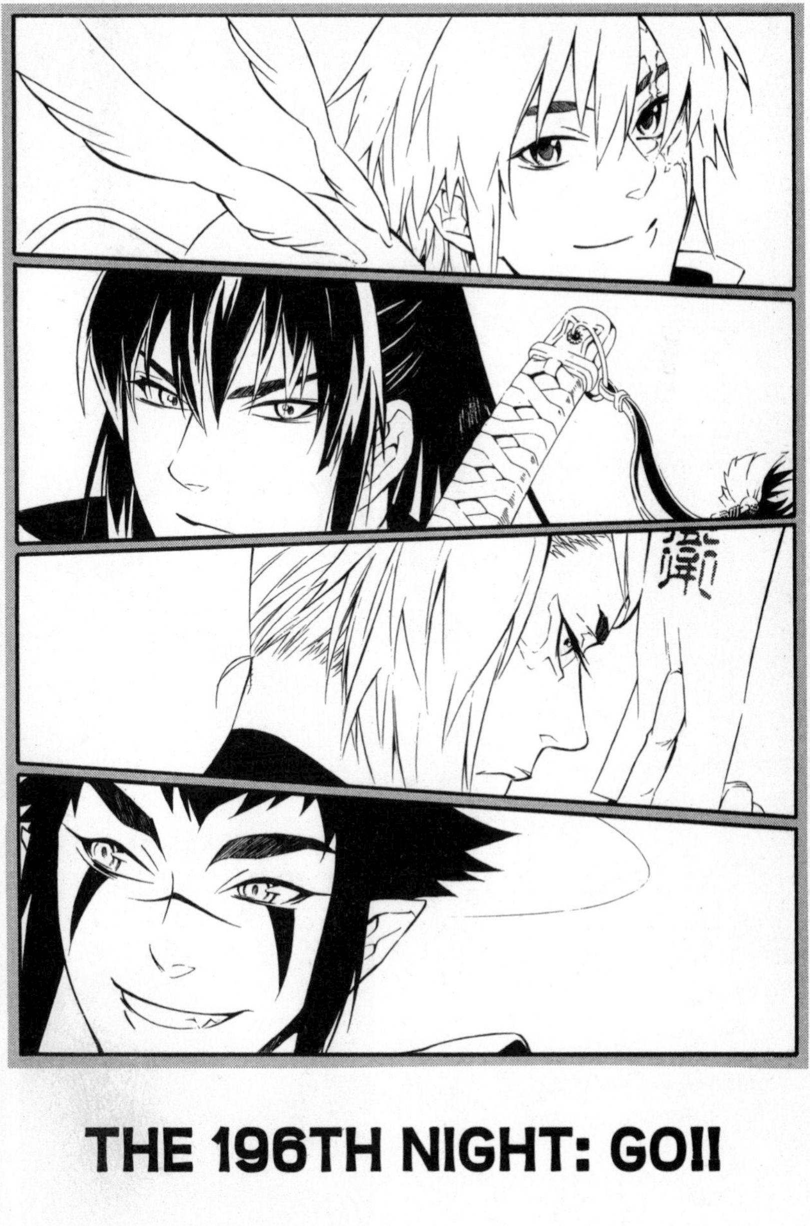

THE 196TH NIGHT: GO!!

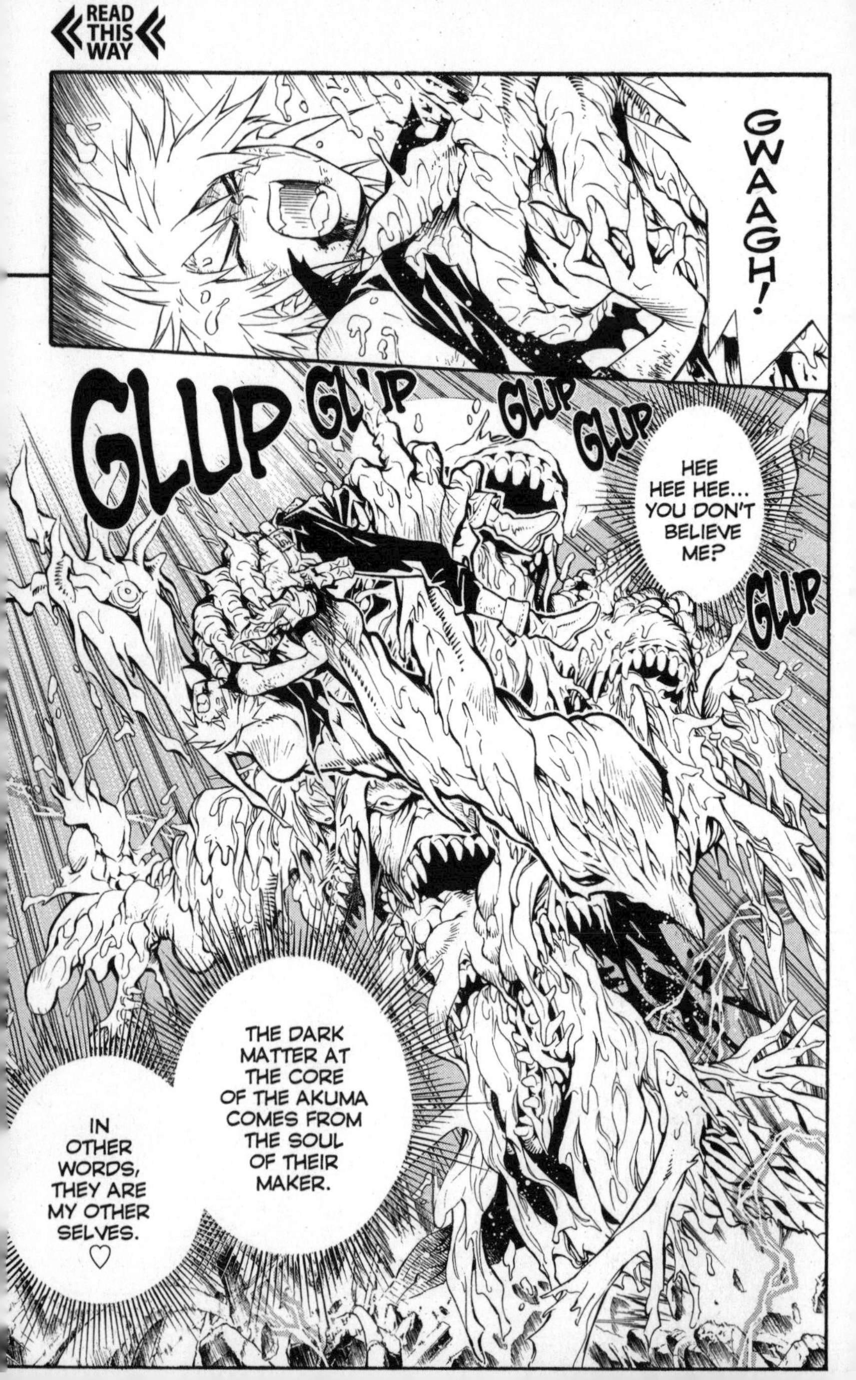
READ THIS WAY
GWAAGH!
GLUP
GLUP
GLUP
GLUP
HEE HEE HEE... YOU DON'T BELIEVE ME?
GLUP
THE DARK MATTER AT THE CORE OF THE AKUMA COMES FROM THE SOUL OF THEIR MAKER.
IN OTHER WORDS, THEY ARE MY OTHER SELVES. ♡

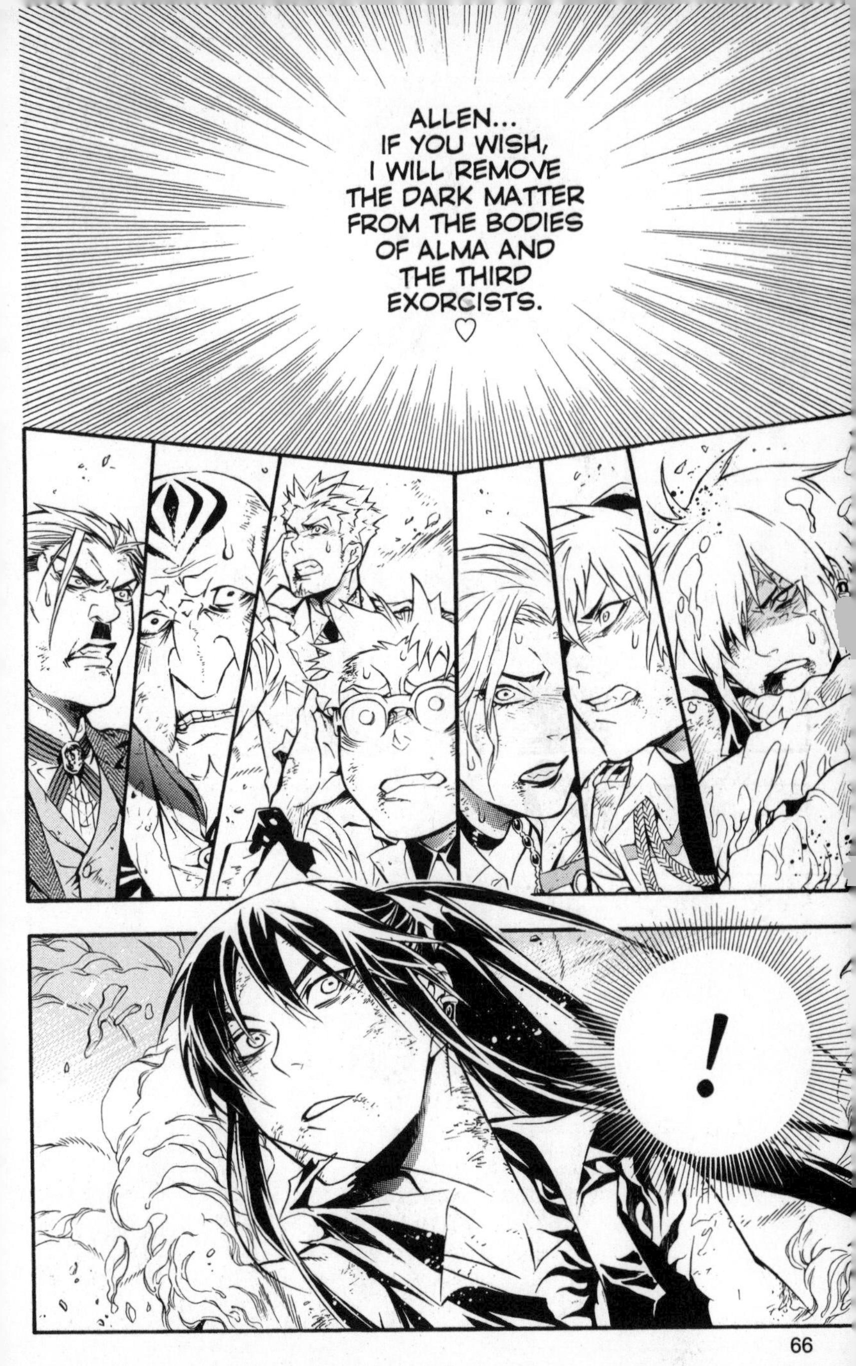
ALLEN... IF YOU WISH, I WILL REMOVE THE DARK MATTER FROM THE BODIES OF ALMA AND THE THIRD EXORCISTS. ♡
!

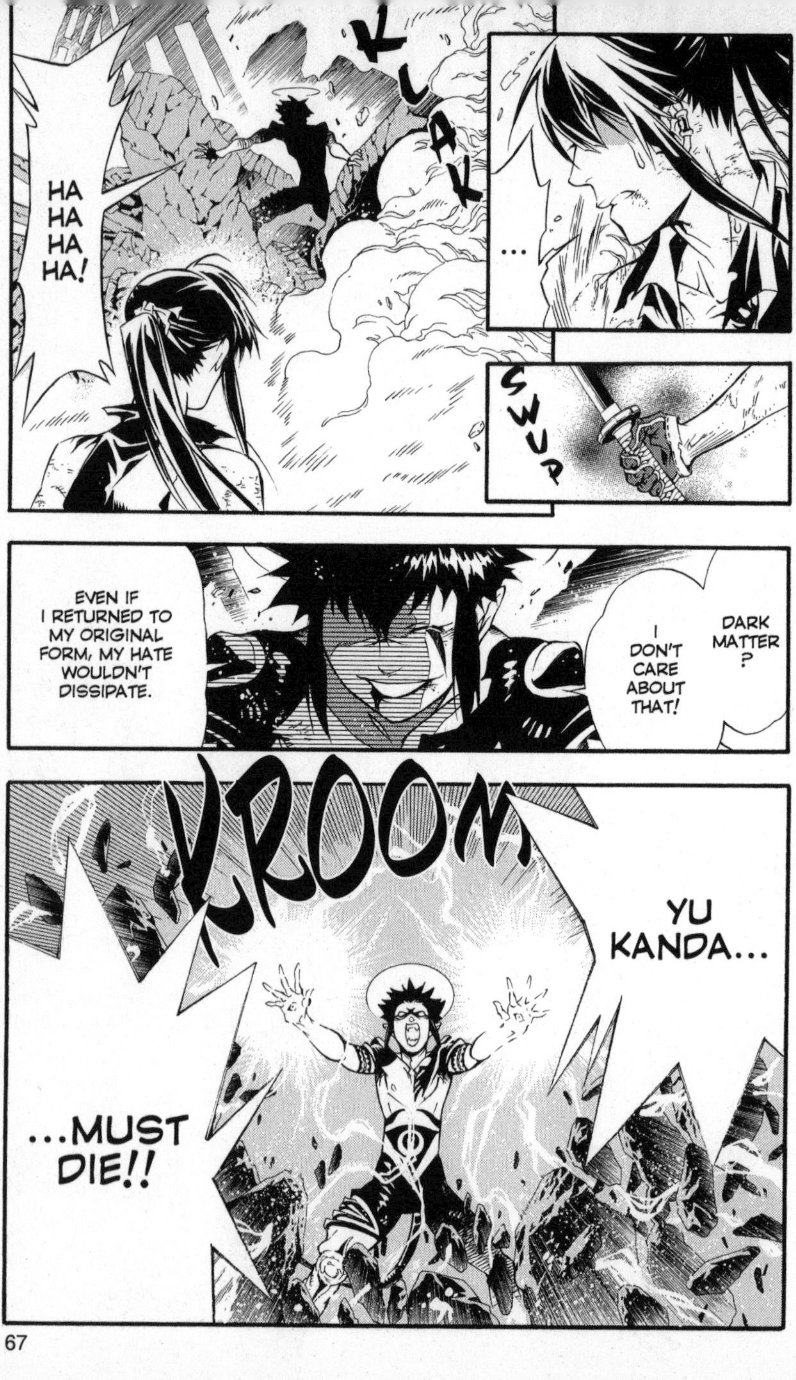
...
SWUP
KLAK
HA HA HA HA!
DARK MATTER?
I DON'T CARE ABOUT THAT!
EVEN IF I RETURNED TO MY ORIGINAL FORM, MY HATE WOULDN'T DISSIPATE.
KROOM
YU KANDA...
...MUST DIE!!

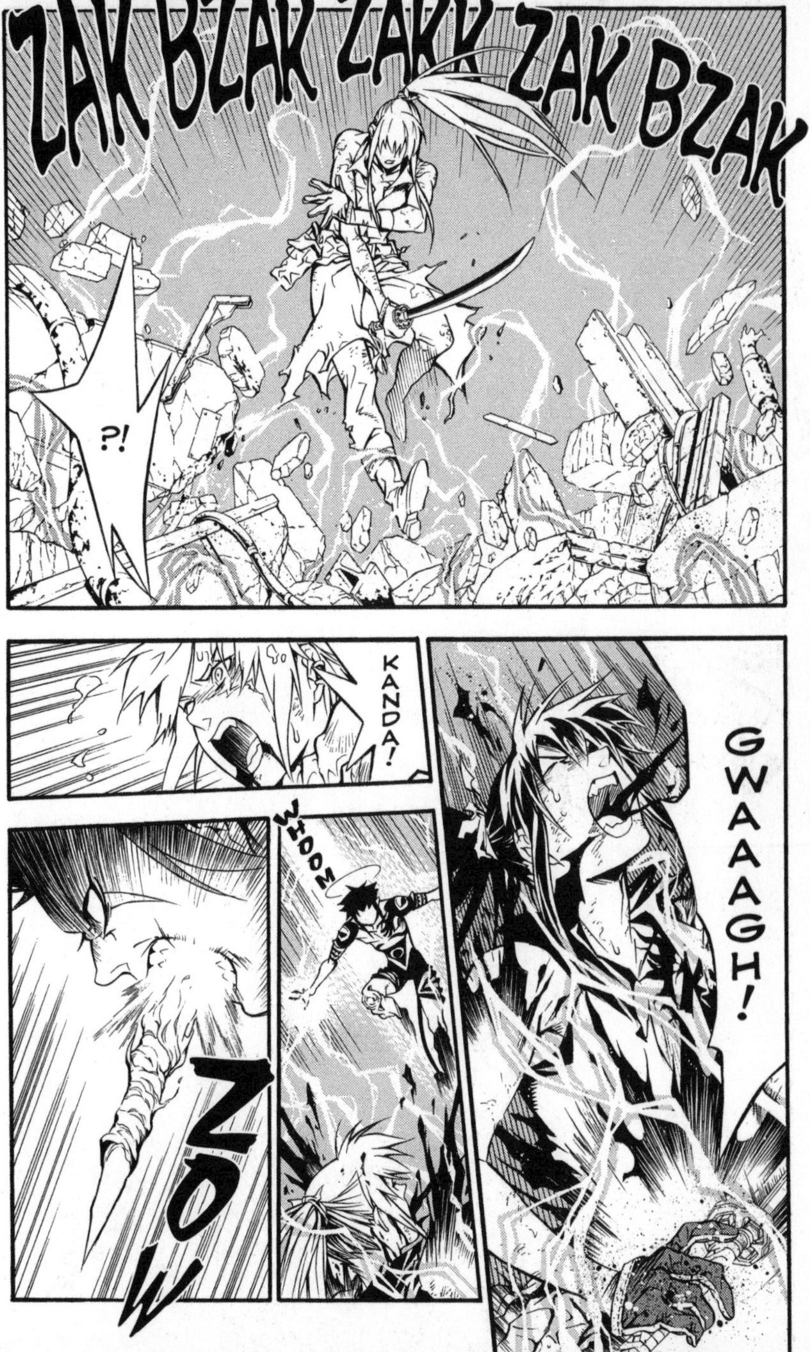
ZAK BZAK ZAKK ZAK BZAK
?!
GWAAAAGH!
KANDA!
WHOOM
ZOOM

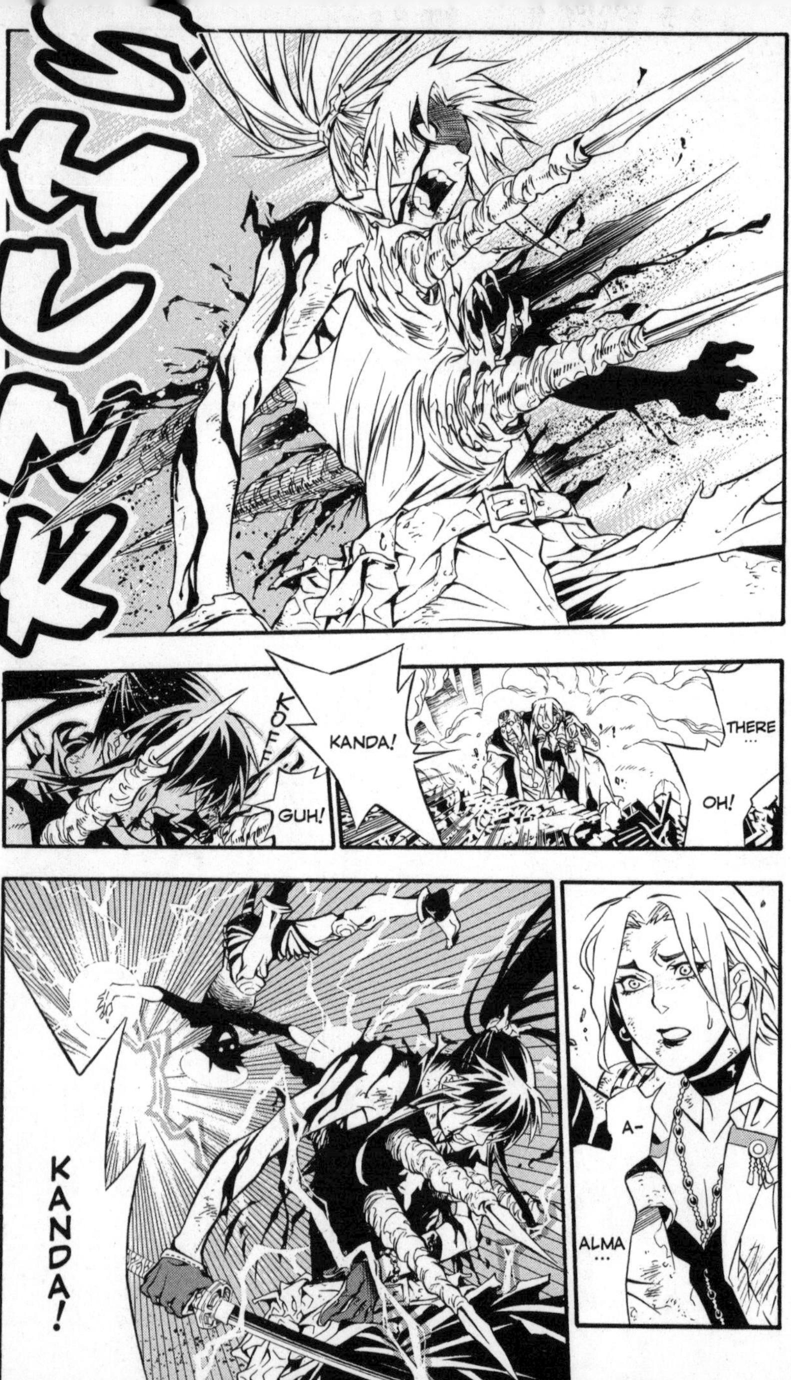
THERE...
OH!
KANDA!
KOFF
GUH!
A-
ALMA...
KANDA!

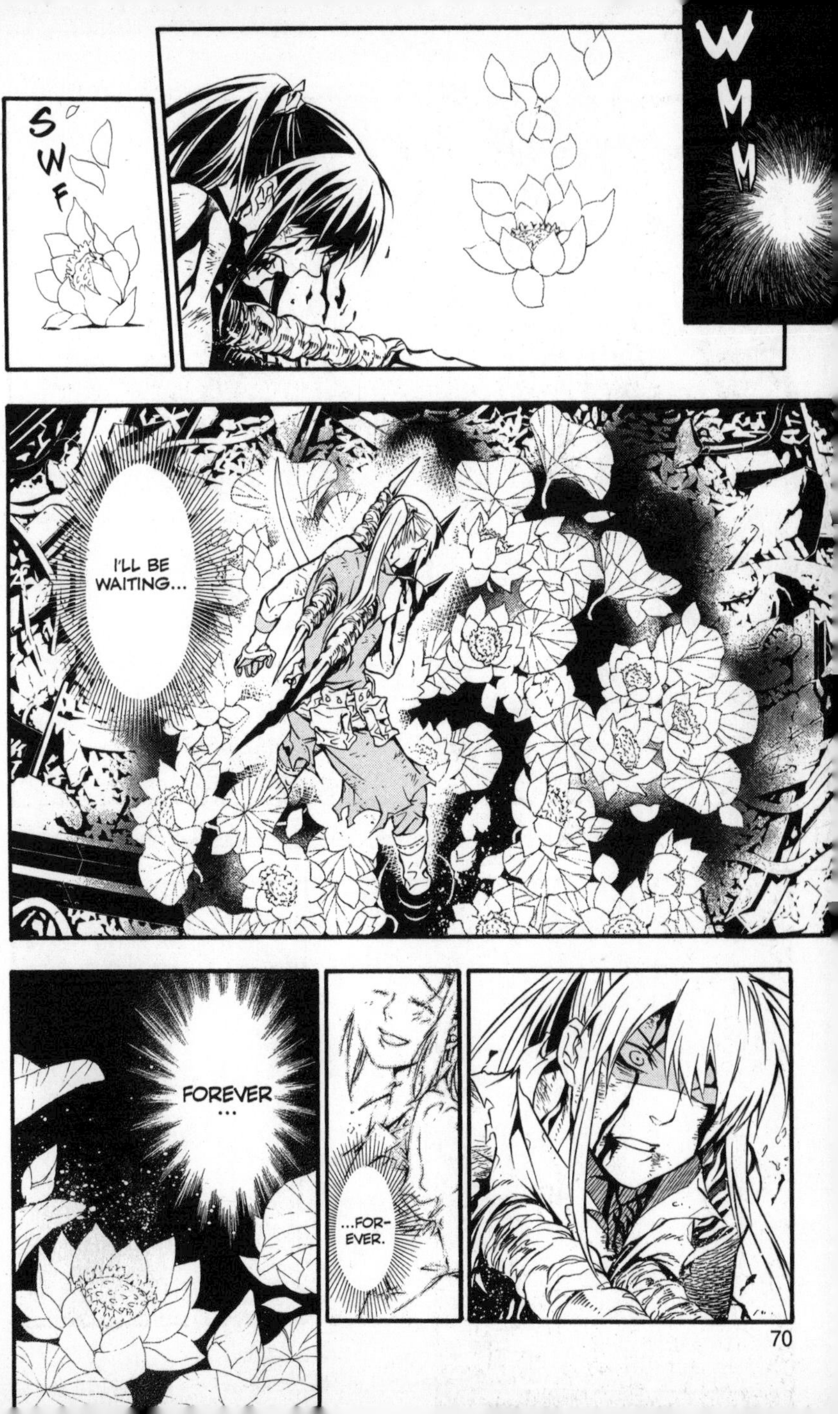
WMM
SWF
I'LL BE WAITING...
...FOR-EVER.
FOREVER ...

READ THIS WAY

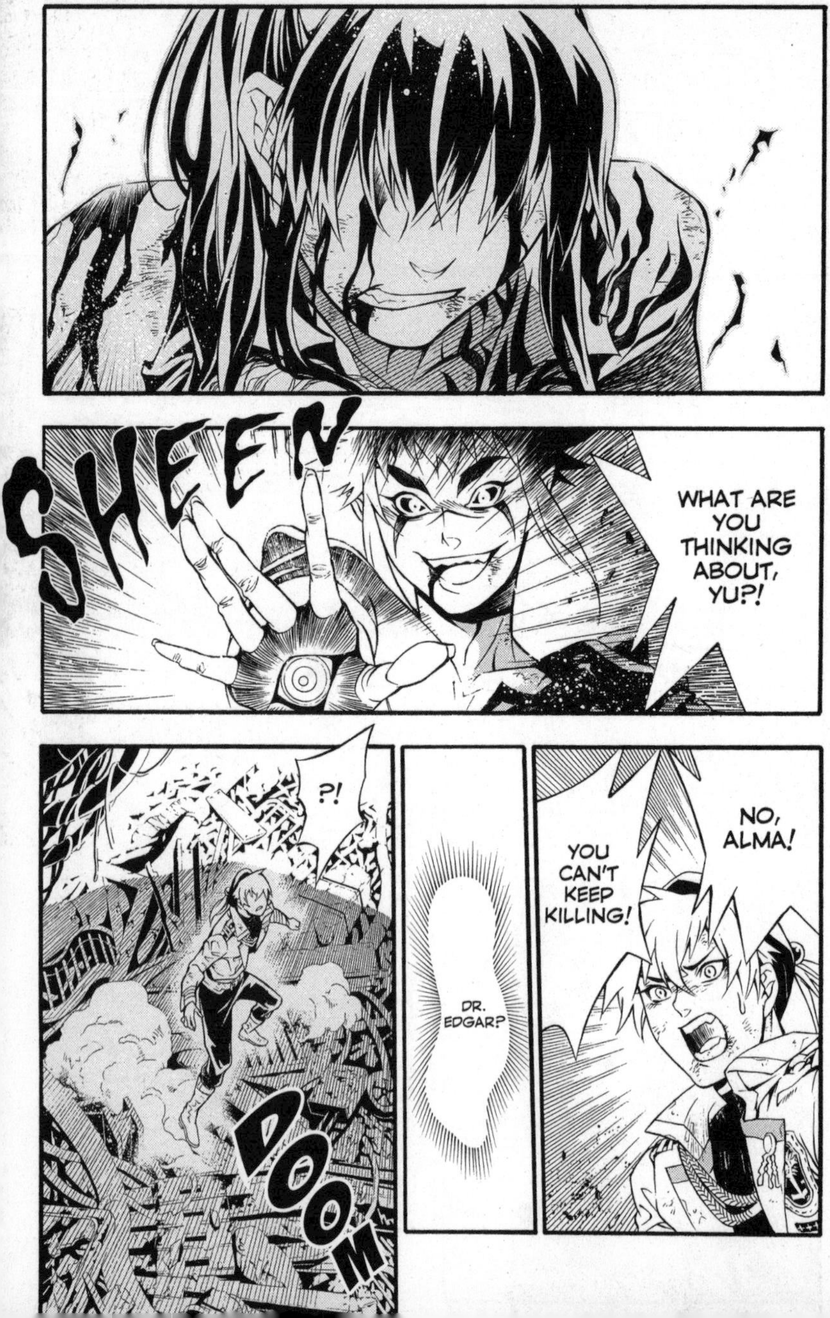

WHAT ARE YOU THINKING ABOUT, YU?!
SHEEN
NO, ALMA!
YOU CAN'T KEEP KILLING!
DR. EDGAR?
?!
DOOM

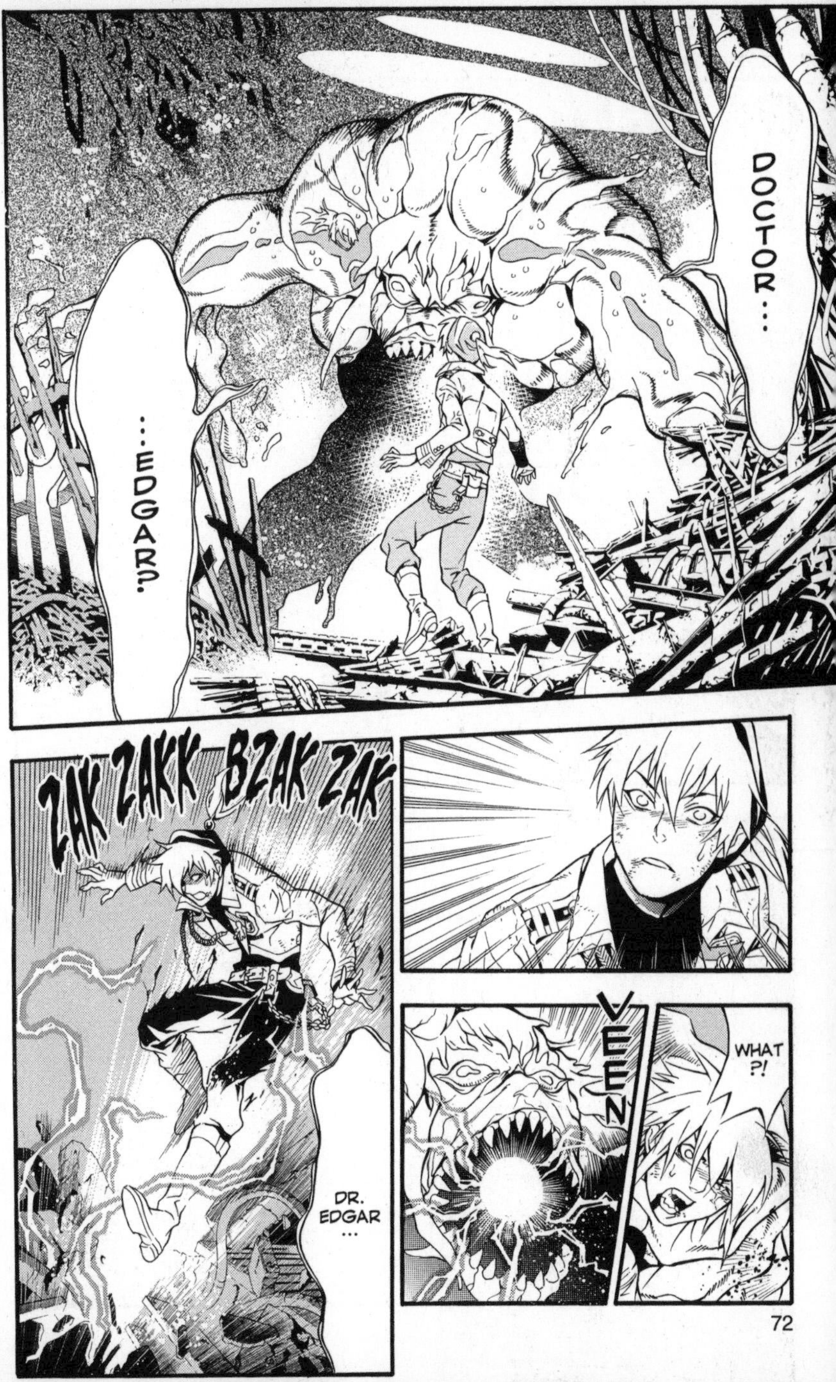
DOCTOR...
...EDGAR?
WHAT ?!
VEEN
ZAK ZAKK BZAK ZAK
DR. EDGAR ...

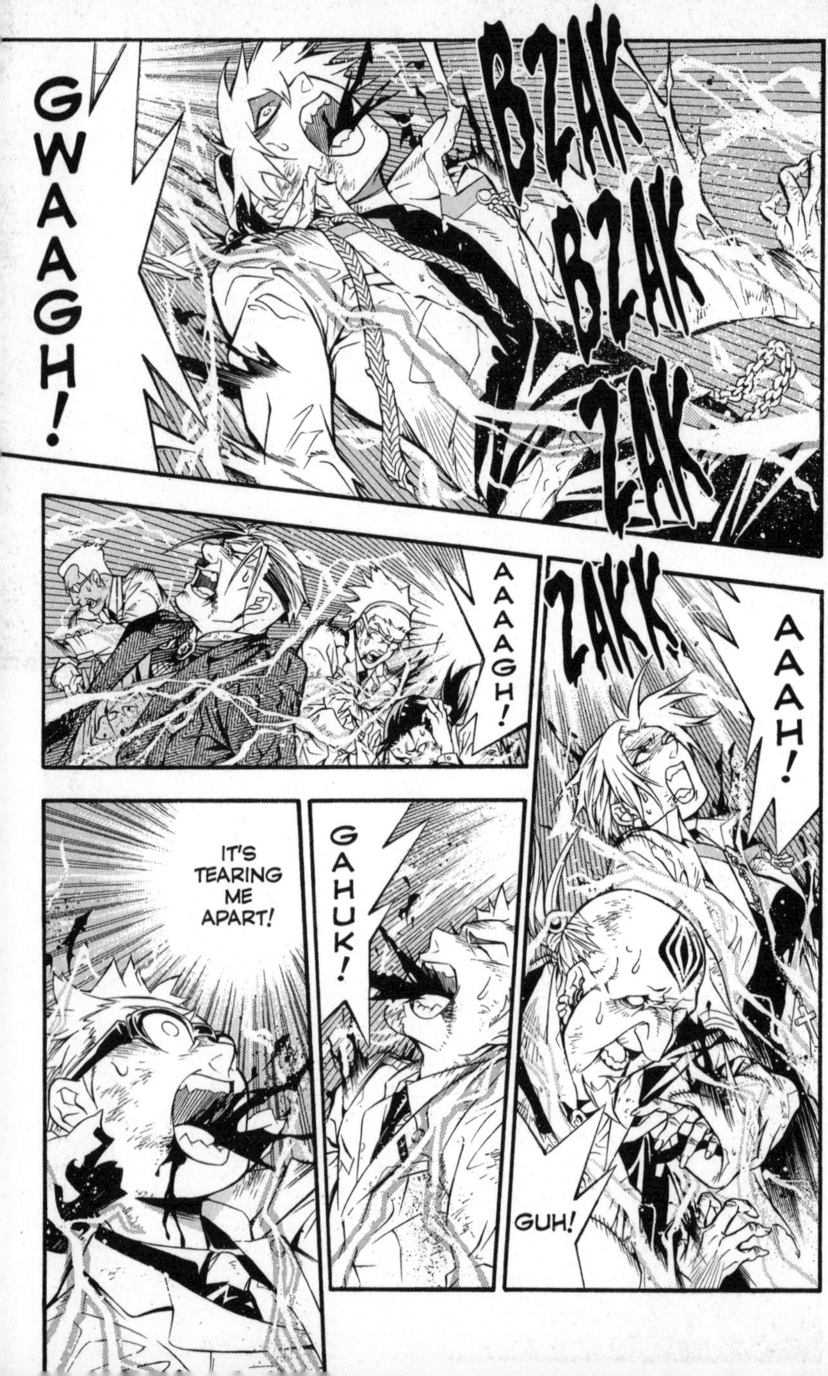
BZAK
BZAK
ZAK
GWAAGH!
ZAKK
AAAAH!
GUH!
AAAAAGH!
GAHUK!
IT'S TEARING ME APART!

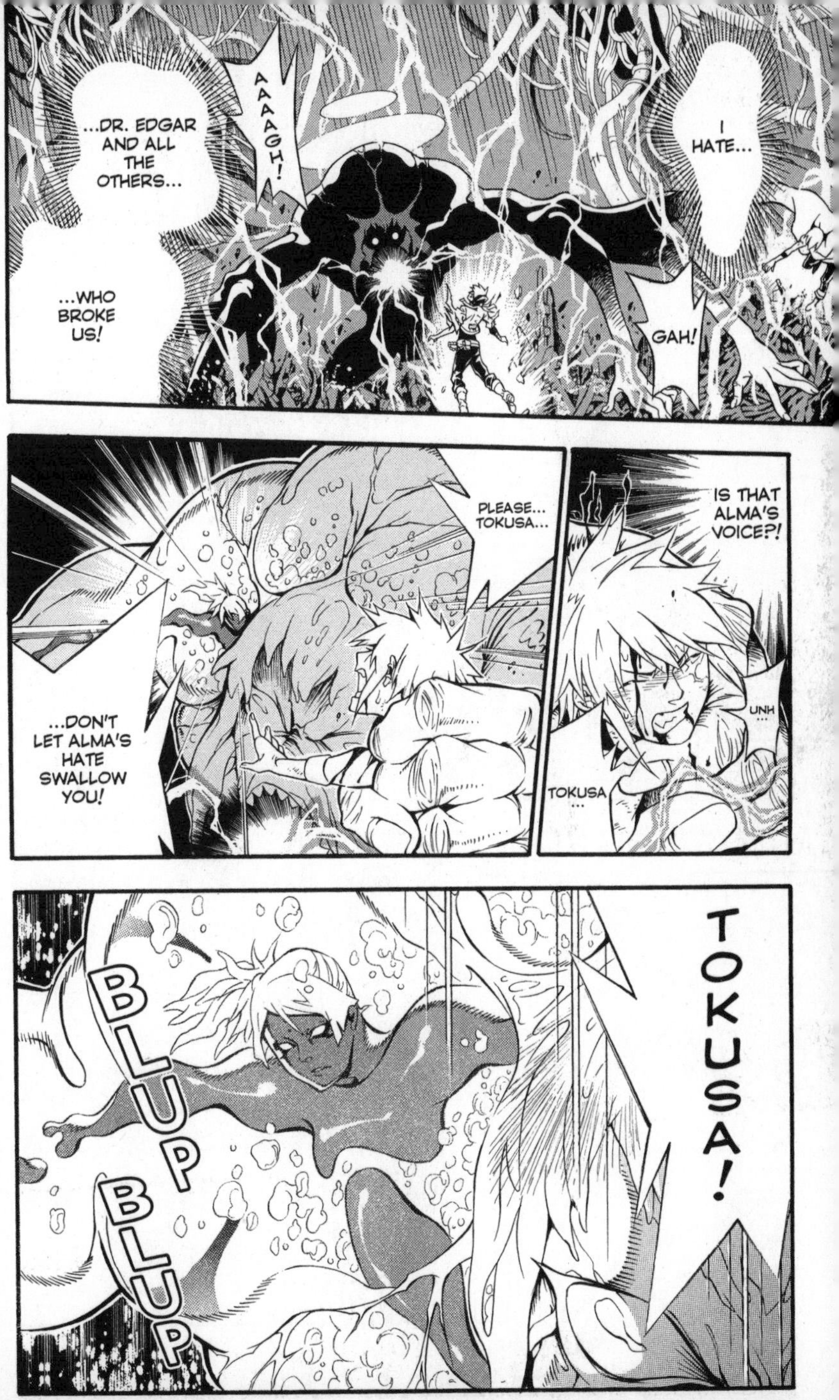
I HATE...
AAAAGH!
...DR. EDGAR AND ALL THE OTHERS...
GAH!
...WHO BROKE US!
IS THAT ALMA'S VOICE?!
UNH...
TOKUSA...
PLEASE... TOKUSA...
...DON'T LET ALMA'S HATE SWALLOW YOU!
TOKUSA!
BLUP BLUP

READ THIS WAY

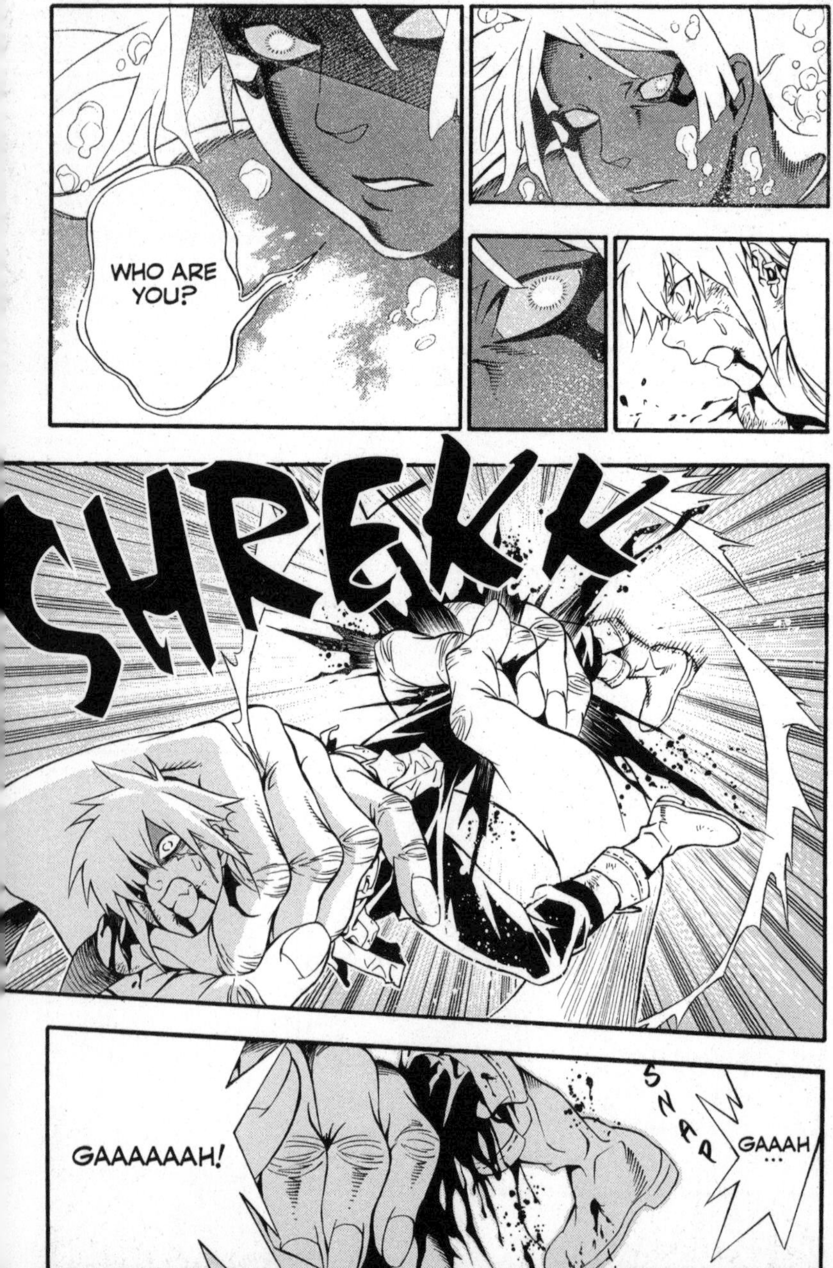
WHO ARE YOU?
SHREKK
SNAP
GAAAH ...
GAAAAAAH!

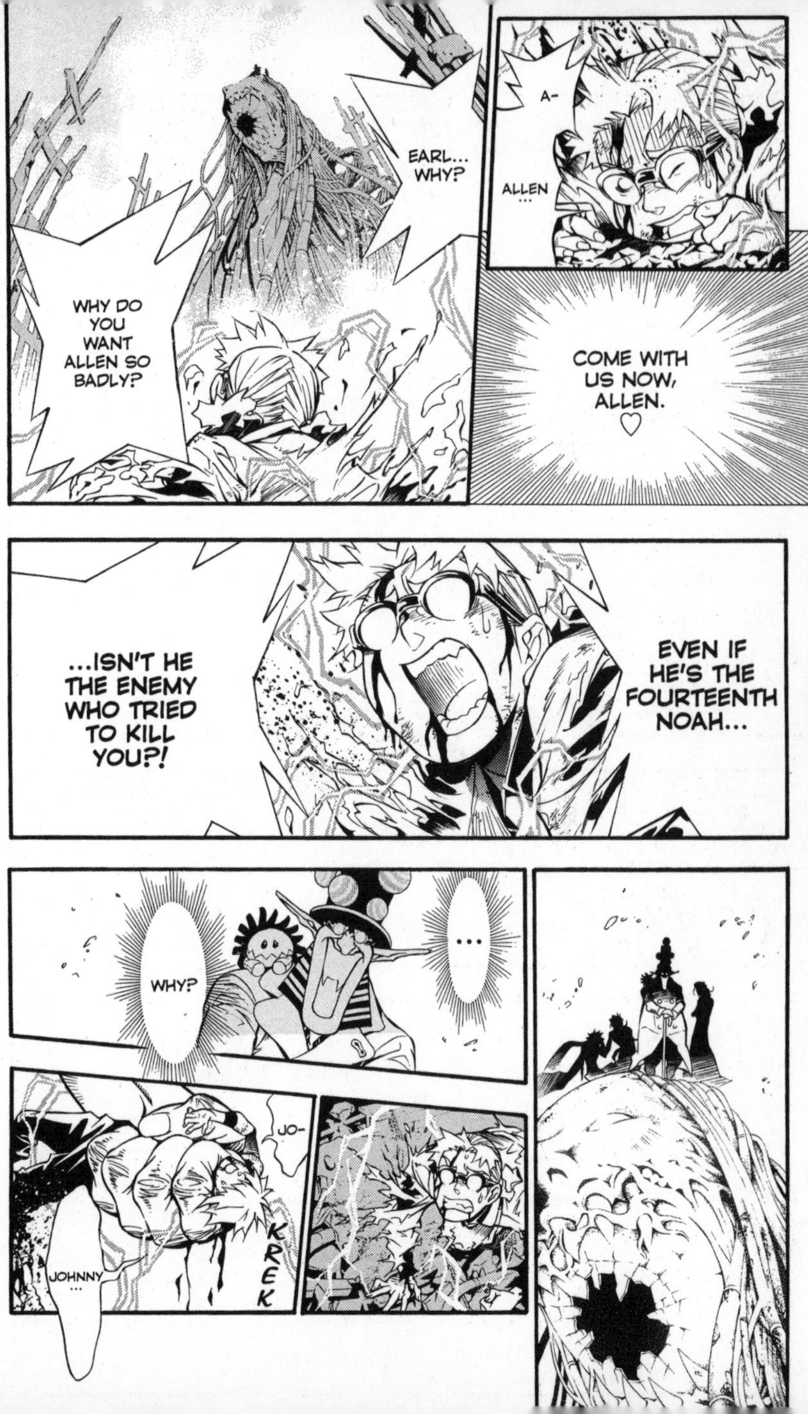
A-
ALLEN ...
COME WITH US NOW, ALLEN. ♡
EARL... WHY?
WHY DO YOU WANT ALLEN SO BADLY?
EVEN IF HE'S THE FOURTEENTH NOAH...
...ISN'T HE THE ENEMY WHO TRIED TO KILL YOU?!
...
WHY?
JO-
KREK
JOHNNY ...

READ THIS WAY

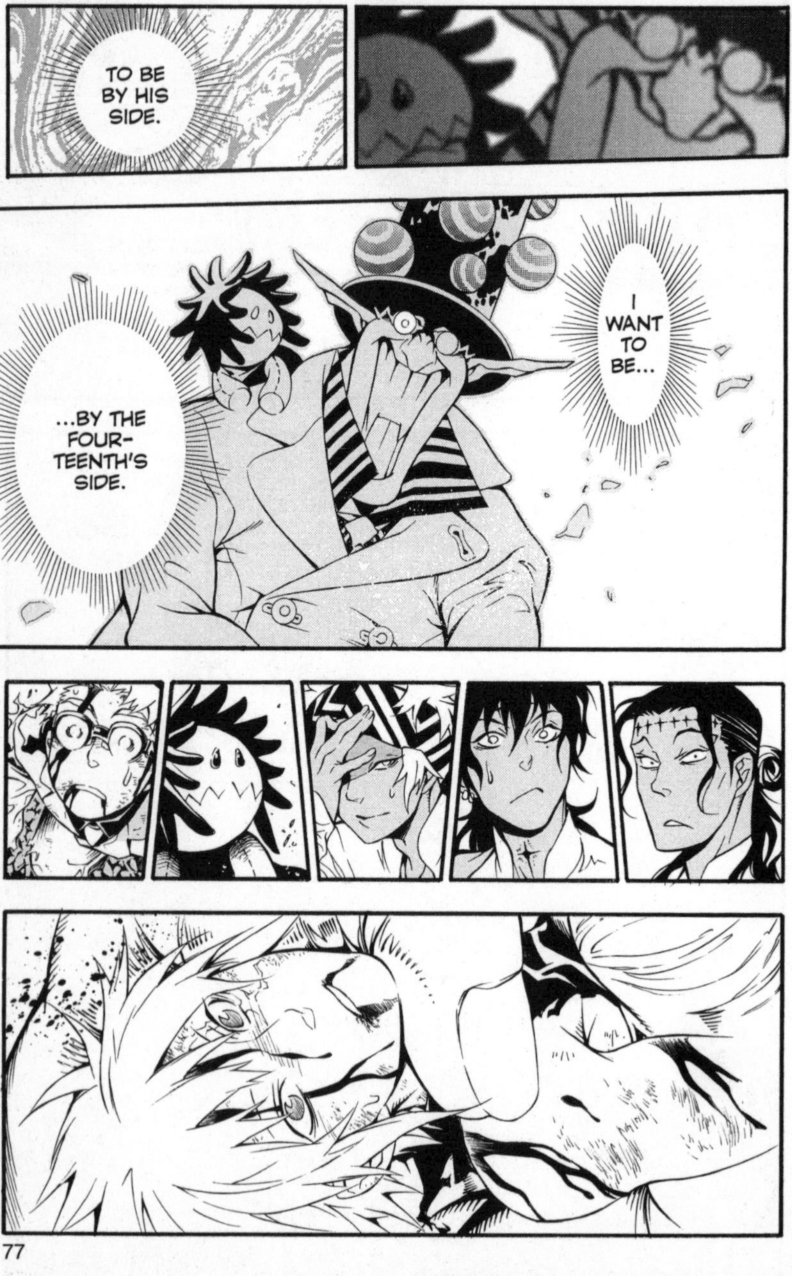
TO BE BY HIS SIDE.
I WANT TO BE...
...BY THE FOURTEENTH'S SIDE.

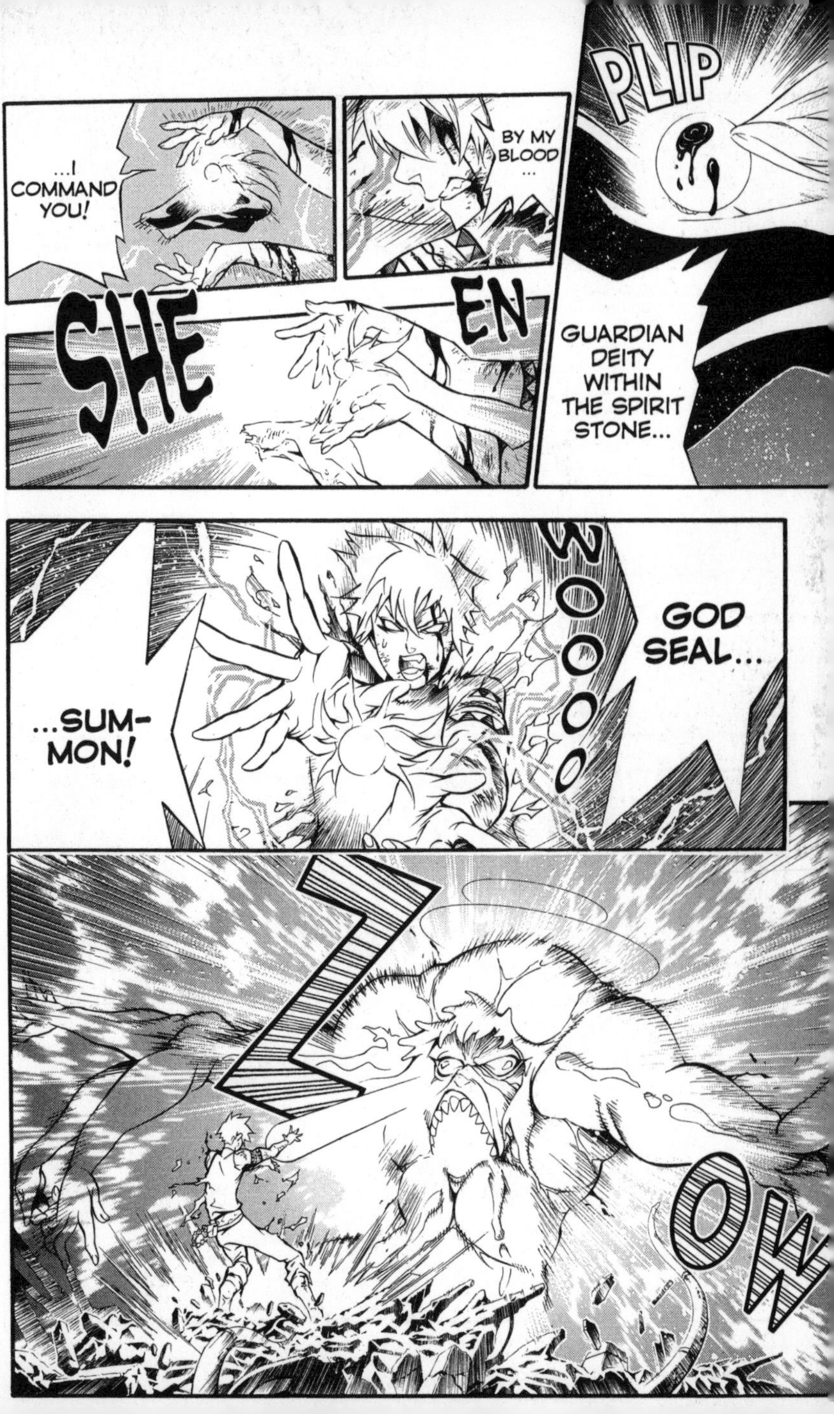
PLIP
GUARDIAN DEITY WITHIN THE SPIRIT STONE...
BY MY BLOOD ...
...I COMMAND YOU!
SHE
EN
BOOOOO
GOD SEAL...
...SUM-MON!
Z
OW

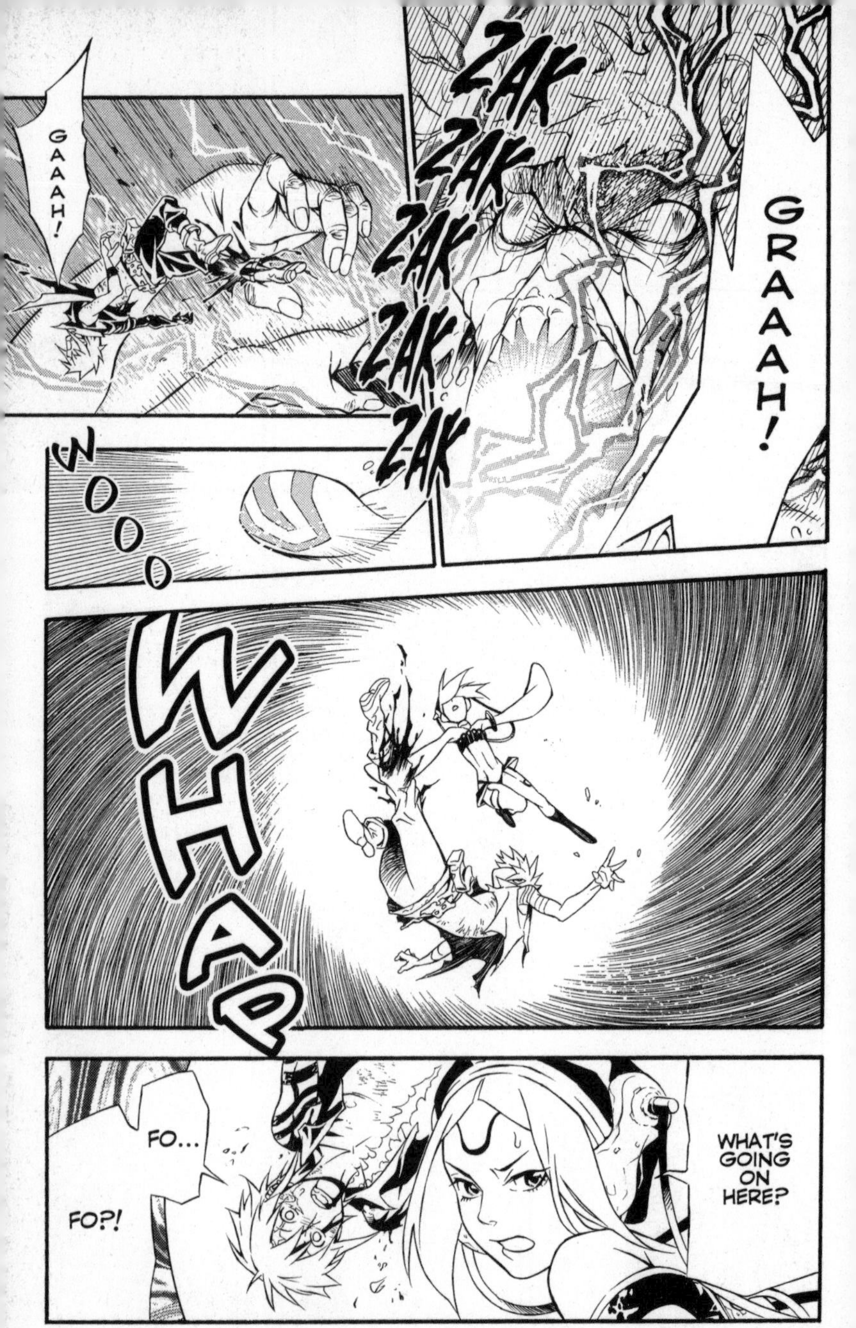
GRAAAH!
ZAK ZAK ZAK ZAK ZAK ZAK
GAAAH!
WOOOO
WHAP
WHAT'S GOING ON HERE?
FO...
FO?!

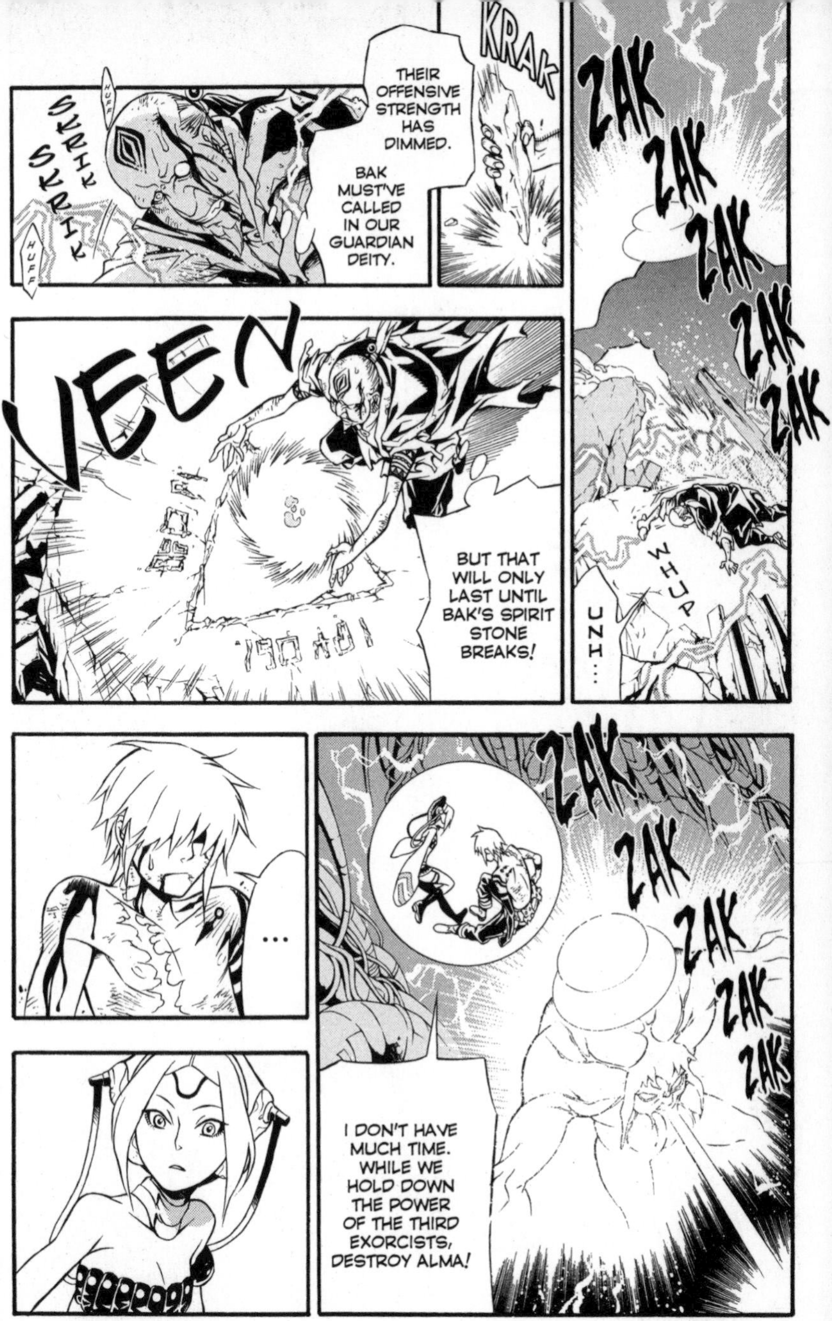
ZAK
ZAK
ZAK
ZAK
ZAK
ZAK
WHUP
UNH...
KRAK
THEIR OFFENSIVE STRENGTH HAS DIMMED.
BAK MUST'VE CALLED IN OUR GUARDIAN DEITY.
HUFF
SKRIK SKRIK
HUFF HUFF
VEEN
BUT THAT WILL ONLY LAST UNTIL BAK'S SPIRIT STONE BREAKS!
ZAK
ZAK
ZAK
ZAK
ZAK
I DON'T HAVE MUCH TIME. WHILE WE HOLD DOWN THE POWER OF THE THIRD EXORCISTS, DESTROY ALMA!
...

READ THIS WAY

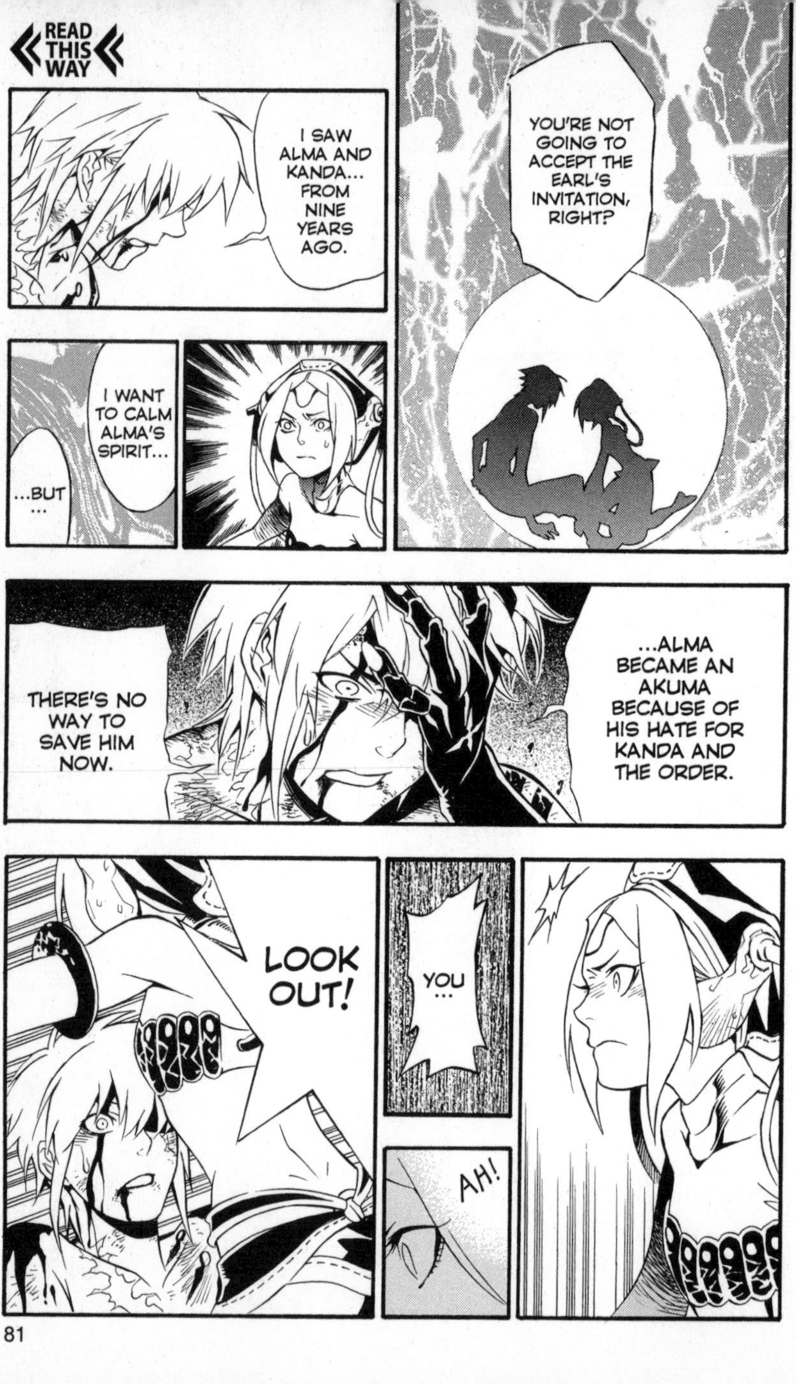
YOU'RE NOT GOING TO ACCEPT THE EARL'S INVITATION, RIGHT?
I SAW ALMA AND KANDA... FROM NINE YEARS AGO.
I WANT TO CALM ALMA'S SPIRIT...
...BUT ...
...ALMA BECAME AN AKUMA BECAUSE OF HIS HATE FOR KANDA AND THE ORDER.
THERE'S NO WAY TO SAVE HIM NOW.
YOU ...
AH!
LOOK OUT!

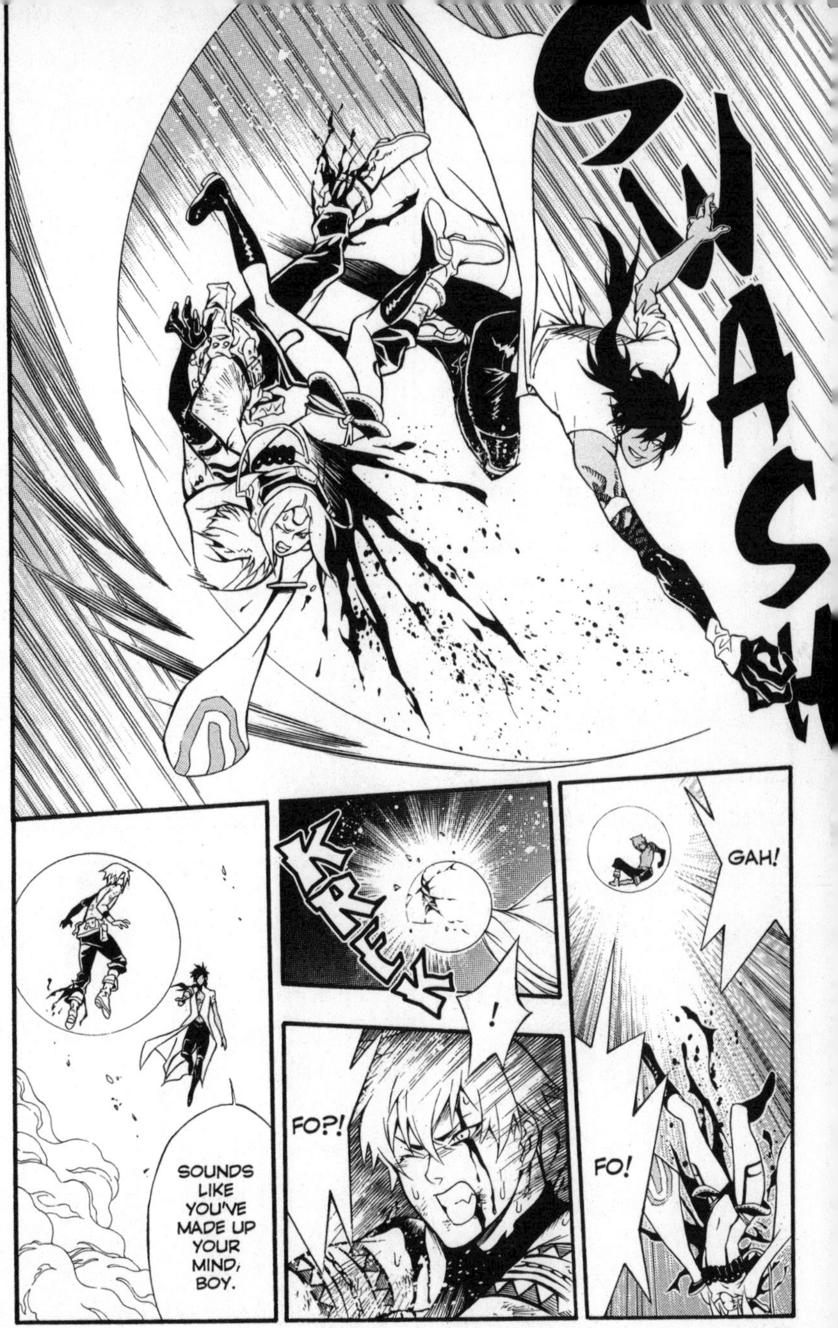
SWASH
GAH!
FO!
KREK
!
FO?!
SOUNDS LIKE YOU'VE MADE UP YOUR MIND, BOY.

READ THIS WAY

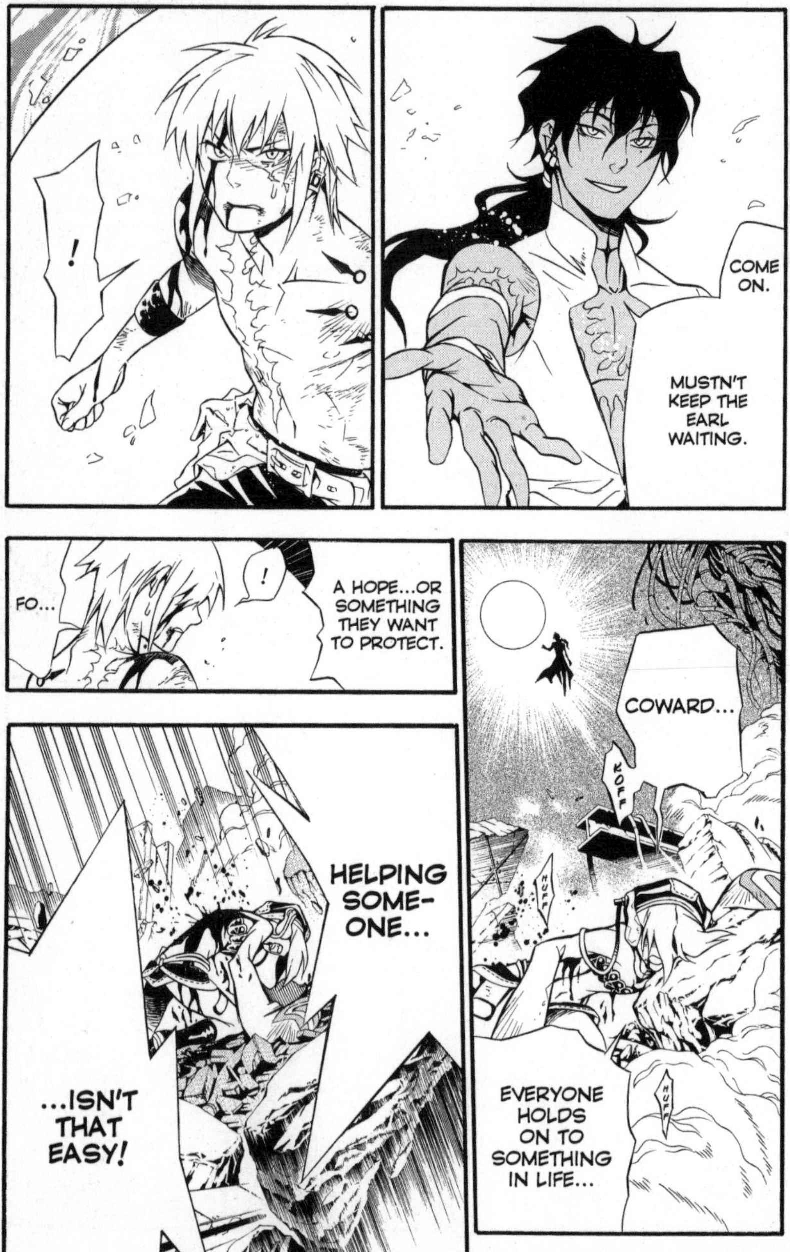
COME ON.
MUSTN'T KEEP THE EARL WAITING.
!
COWARD...
KOFF
HUFF
HUFF
EVERYONE HOLDS ON TO SOMETHING IN LIFE...
A HOPE...OR SOMETHING THEY WANT TO PROTECT.
!
FO...
HELPING SOME-ONE...
...ISN'T THAT EASY!

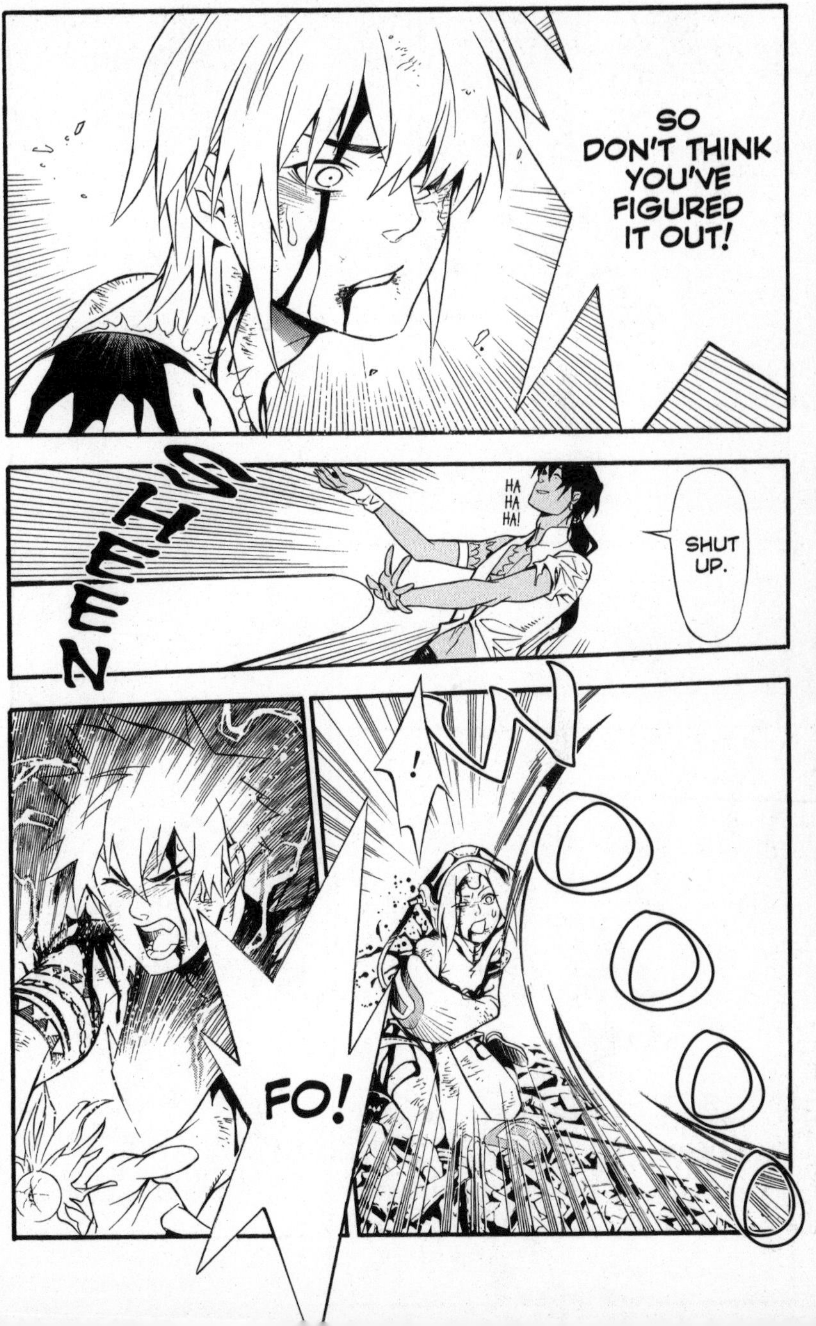
SO DON'T THINK YOU'VE FIGURED IT OUT!
SHUT UP.
HA HA HA!
SHEEN
W
!
OOOO
FO!

READ THIS WAY

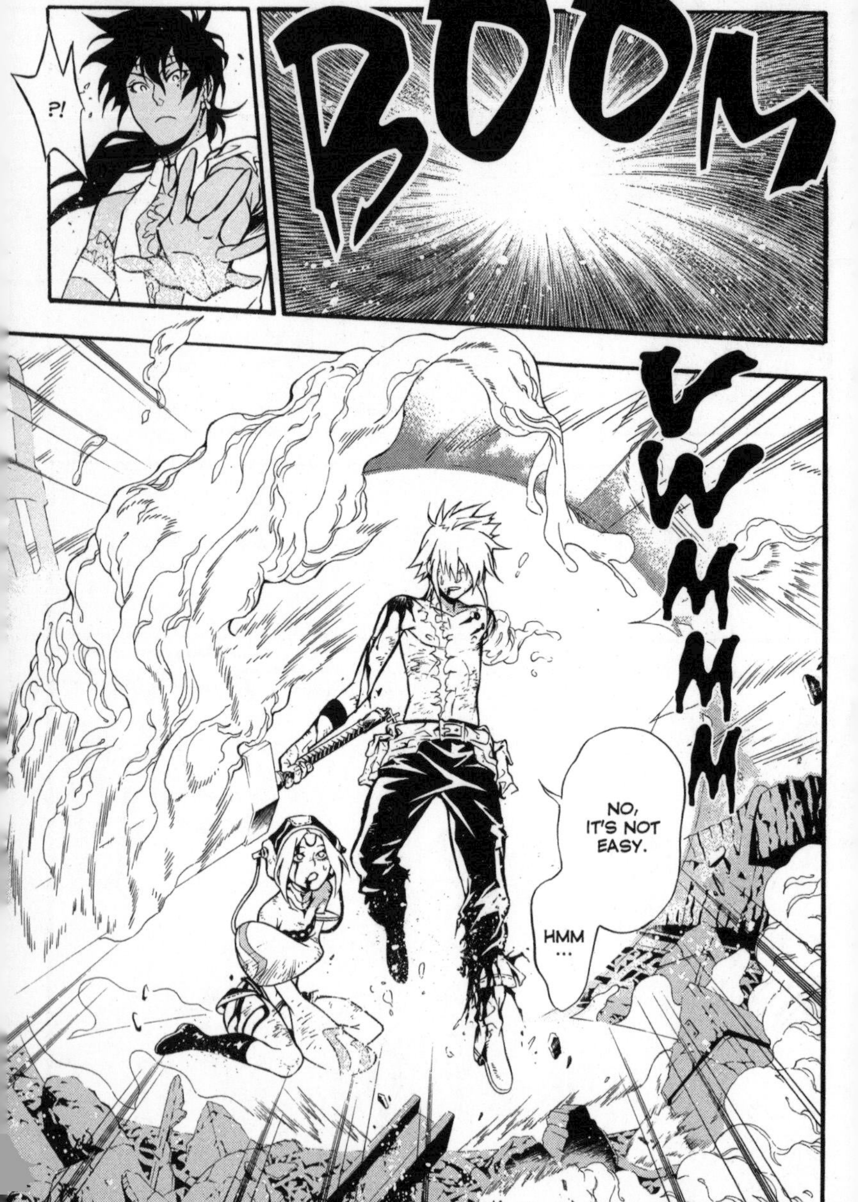
BOOM
?!
VWMMMM
NO, IT'S NOT EASY.
HMM ...

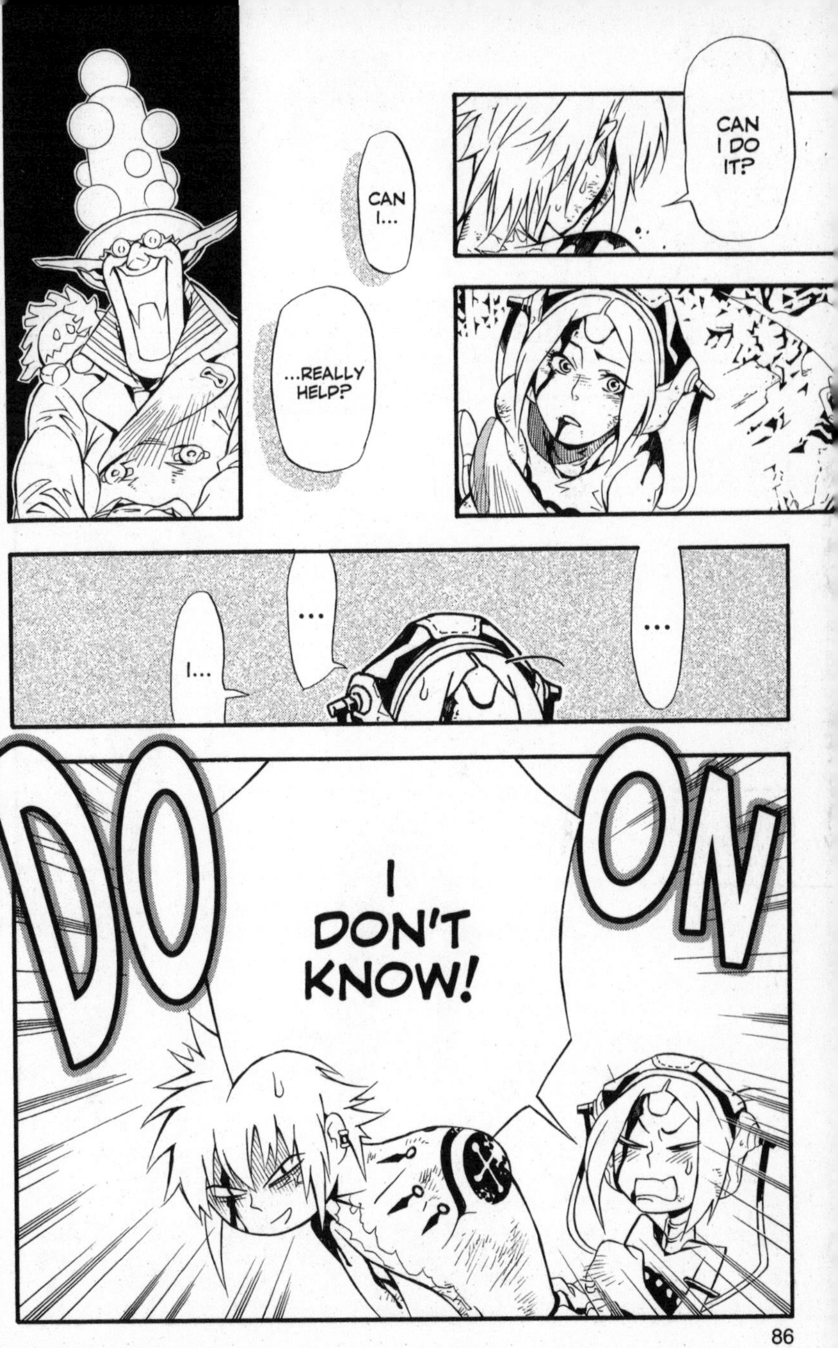
CAN I DO IT?
CAN I...
...REALLY HELP?
...
...
I...
DO ON
I DON'T KNOW!

READ THIS WAY

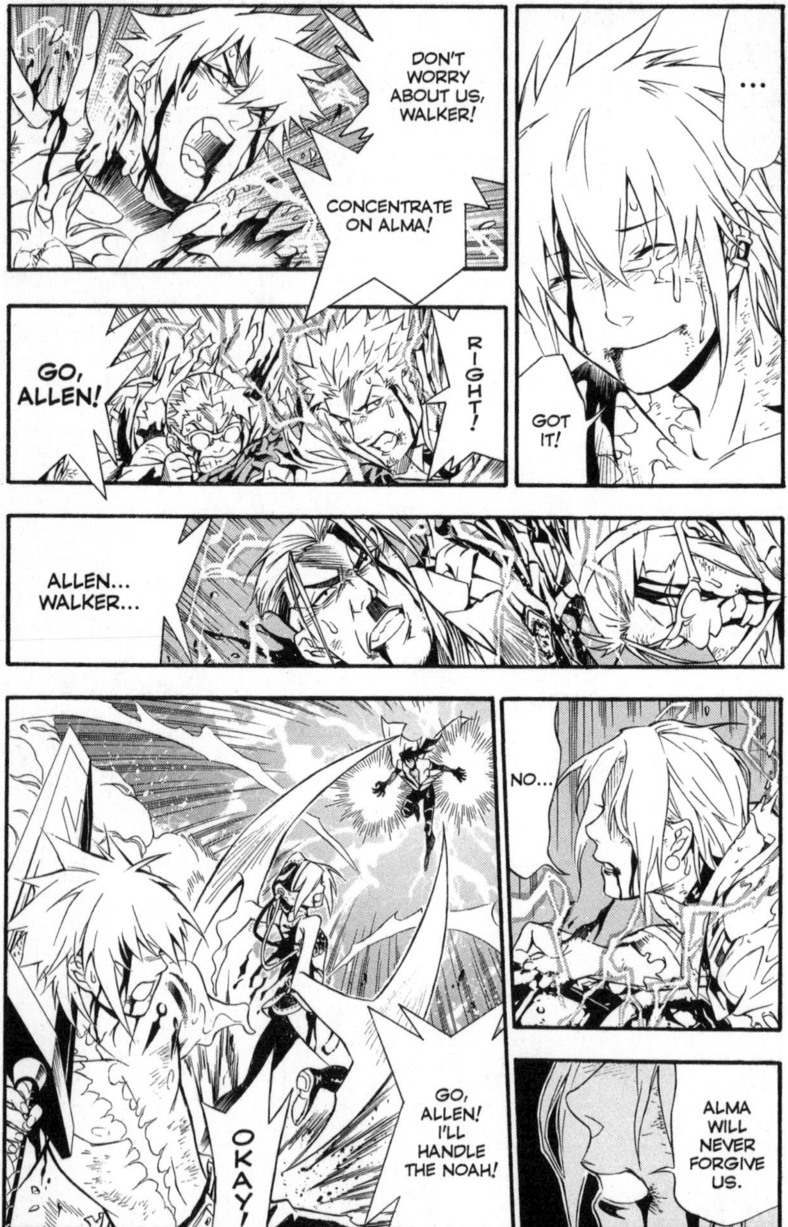
...
GOT IT!
DON'T WORRY ABOUT US, WALKER!
CONCENTRATE ON ALMA!
RIGHT!
GO, ALLEN!
ALLEN... WALKER...
NO...
ALMA WILL NEVER FORGIVE US.
GO, ALLEN! I'LL HANDLE THE NOAH!
OKAY!

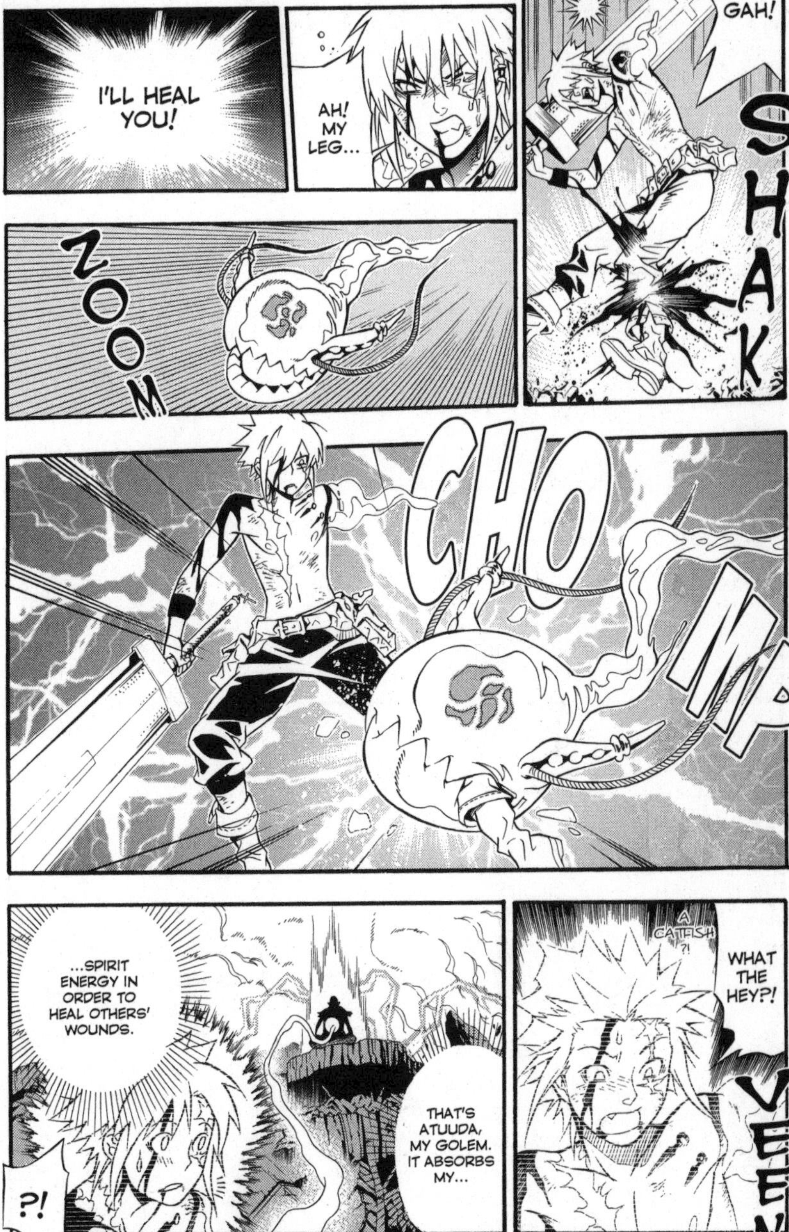
GAH!
SHAK
AH! MY LEG...
I'LL HEAL YOU!
ZOOM
CHOMP
A CATFISH?!
WHAT THE HEY?!
VEEN
THAT'S ATUUDA, MY GOLEM. IT ABSORBS MY...
...SPIRIT ENERGY IN ORDER TO HEAL OTHERS' WOUNDS.
?!

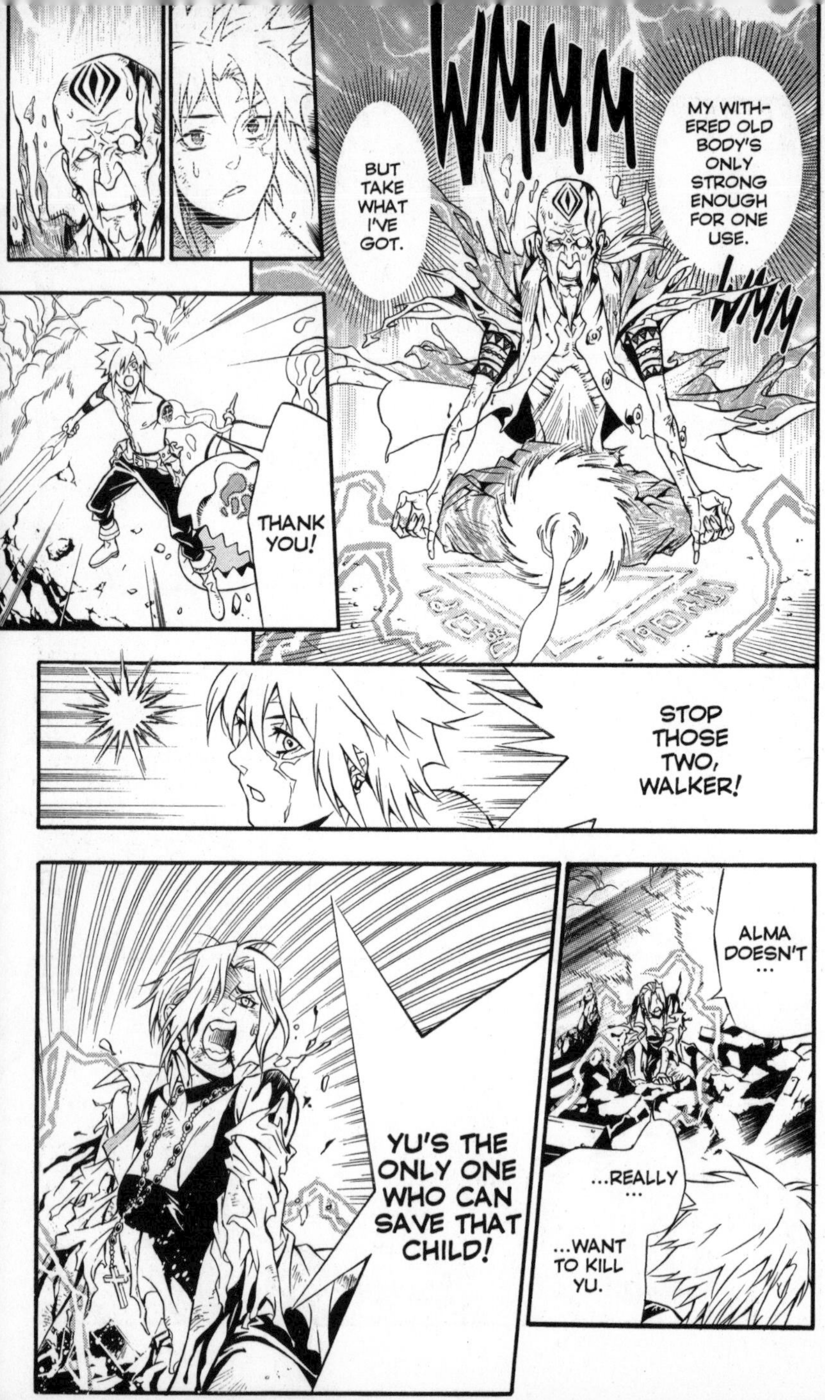
WMMM
MY WITH-ERED OLD BODY'S ONLY STRONG ENOUGH FOR ONE USE.
BUT TAKE WHAT I'VE GOT.
WMM
THANK YOU!
STOP THOSE TWO, WALKER!
ALMA DOESN'T ...
...REALLY ...
...WANT TO KILL YU.
YU'S THE ONLY ONE WHO CAN SAVE THAT CHILD!

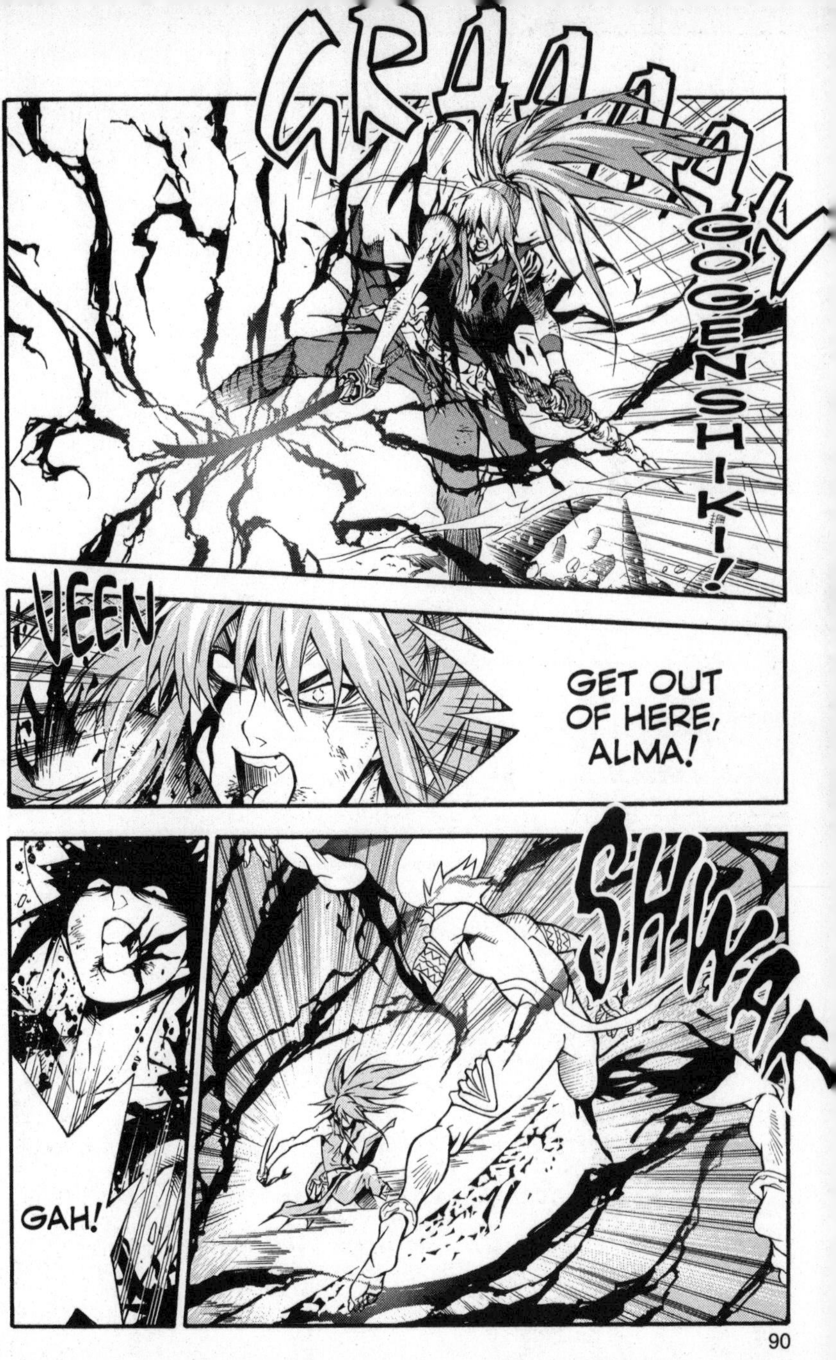
GRAAAAY
GOGENSHIKI!
VEEN
GET OUT OF HERE, ALMA!
SHWAK
GAH!

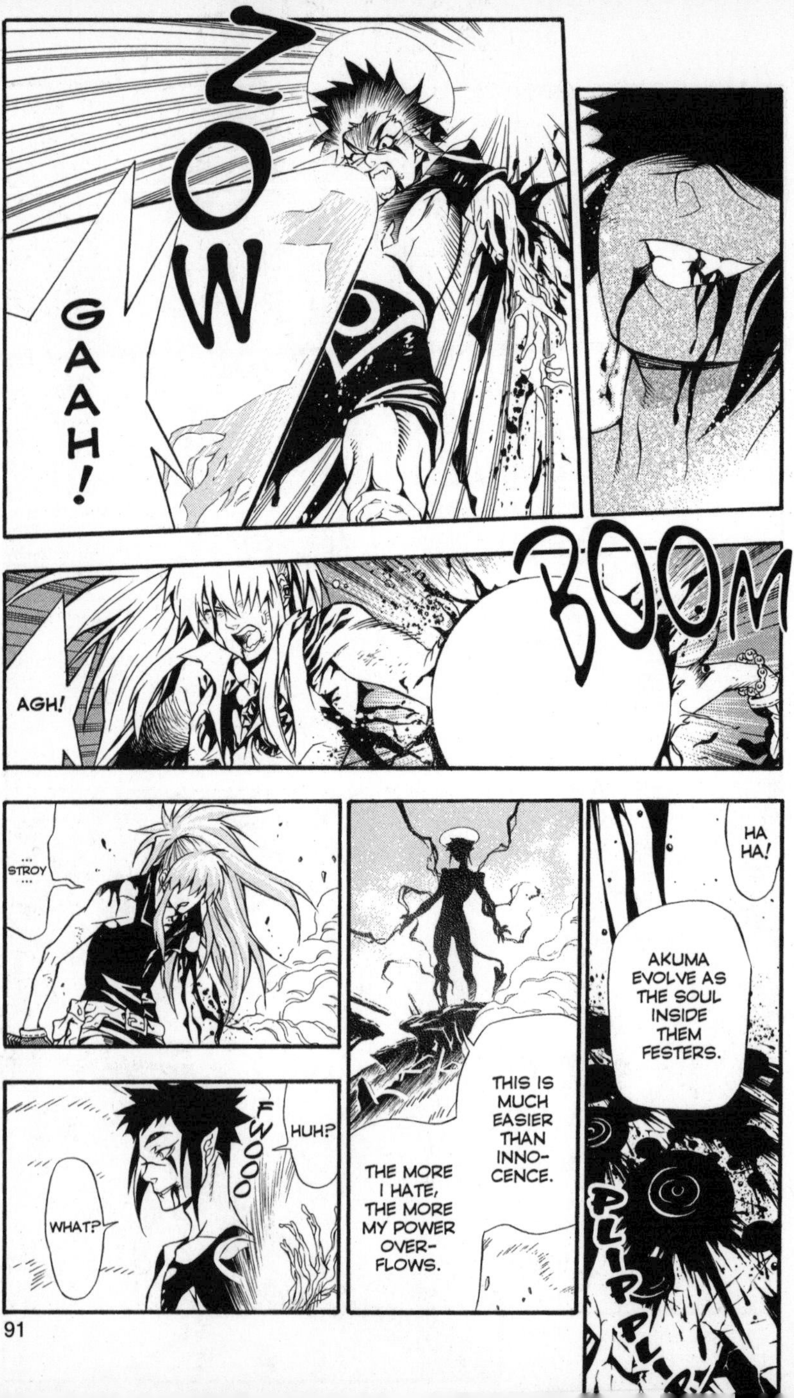
ZOW
GAAH!
BOOM
AGH!
HA HA!
AKUMA EVOLVE AS THE SOUL INSIDE THEM FESTERS.
PLIP PLIP
THIS IS MUCH EASIER THAN INNO-CENCE.
THE MORE I HATE, THE MORE MY POWER OVER-FLOWS.
...STROY...
FWOOO
HUH?
WHAT?

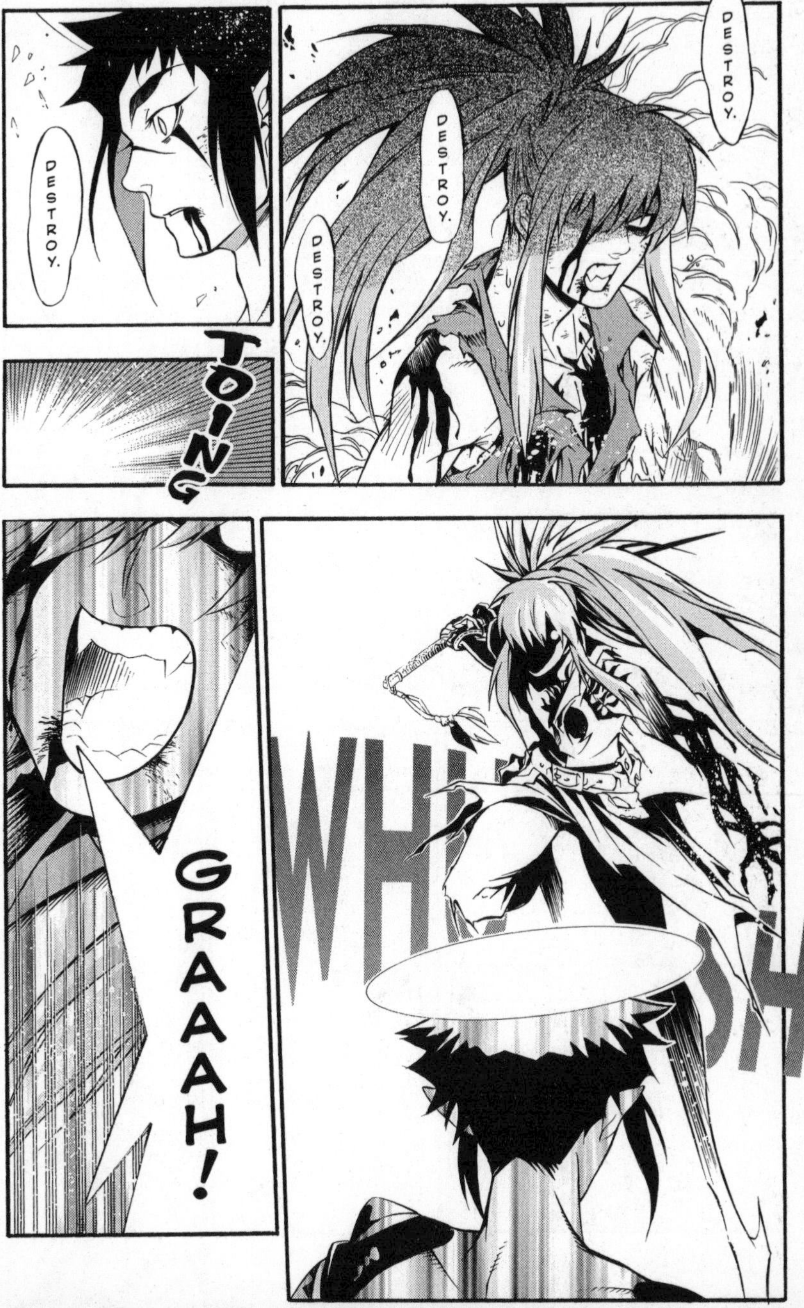
DESTROY.
DESTROY.
DESTROY.
DESTROY.
TOING
GRAAAH!

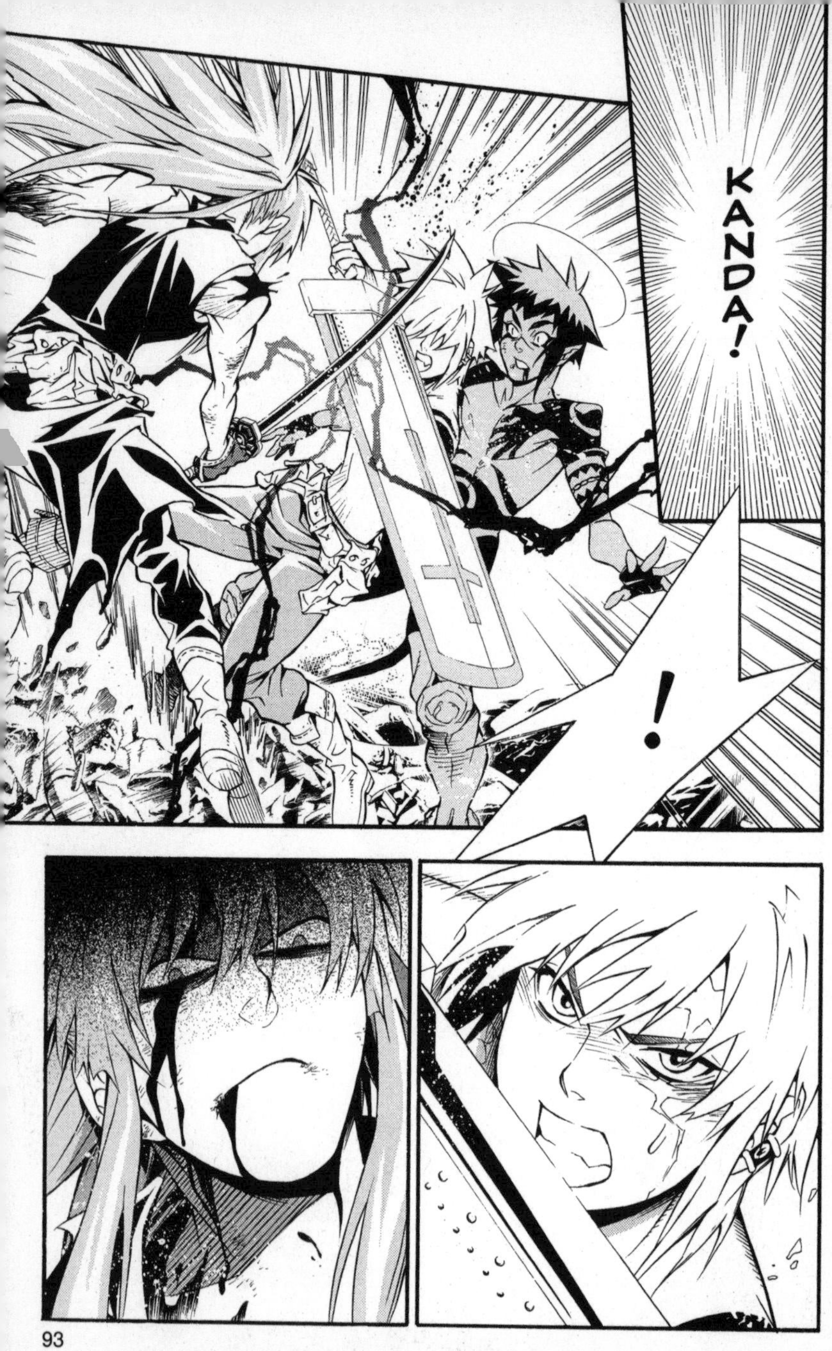
KANDA!
!

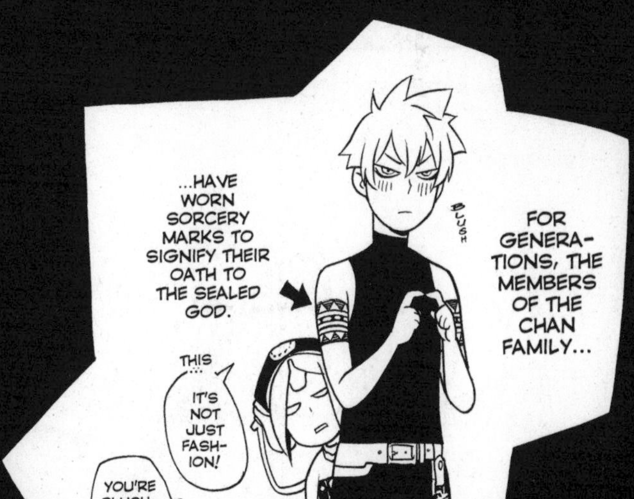
FOR GENERATIONS, THE MEMBERS OF THE CHAN FAMILY...
BLUSH
...HAVE WORN SORCERY MARKS TO SIGNIFY THEIR OATH TO THE SEALED GOD.
THIS...
IT'S NOT JUST FASHION!
YOU'RE BLUSHING?

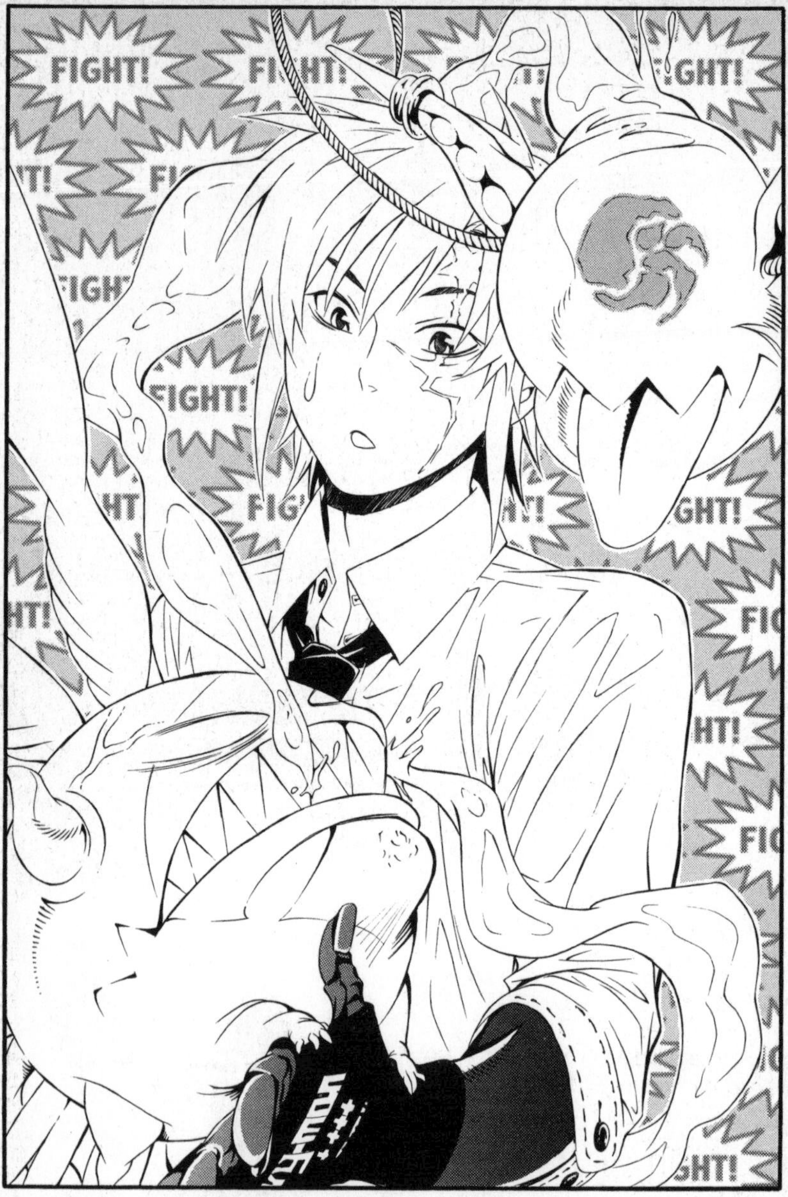
FIGHT!
FIGHT!

THE 197TH NIGHT: PASSING EACH OTHER BY

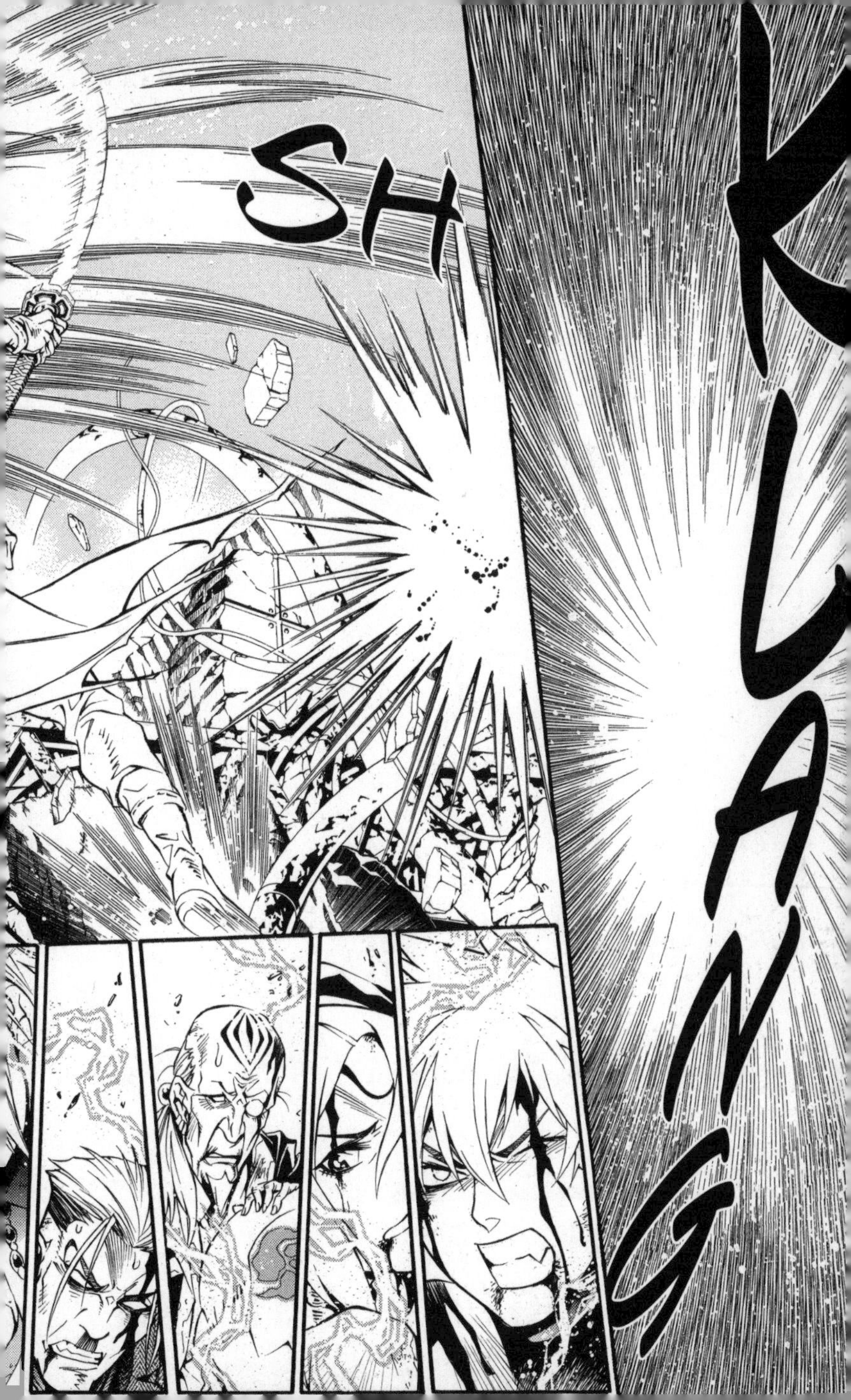
KLANG
SH

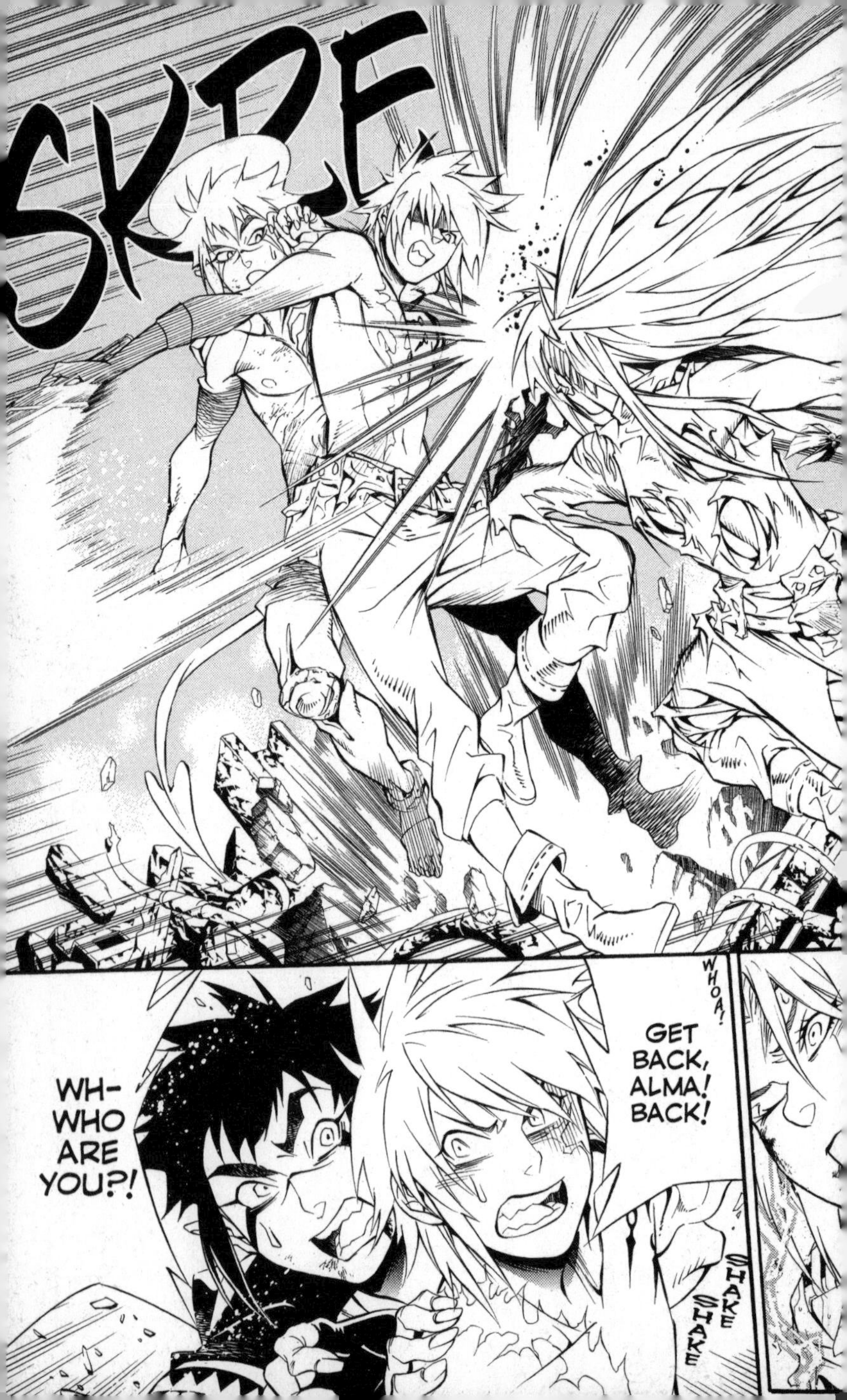
WHOA!
GET BACK, ALMA! BACK!
WH-WHO ARE YOU?!
SHAKE SHAKE

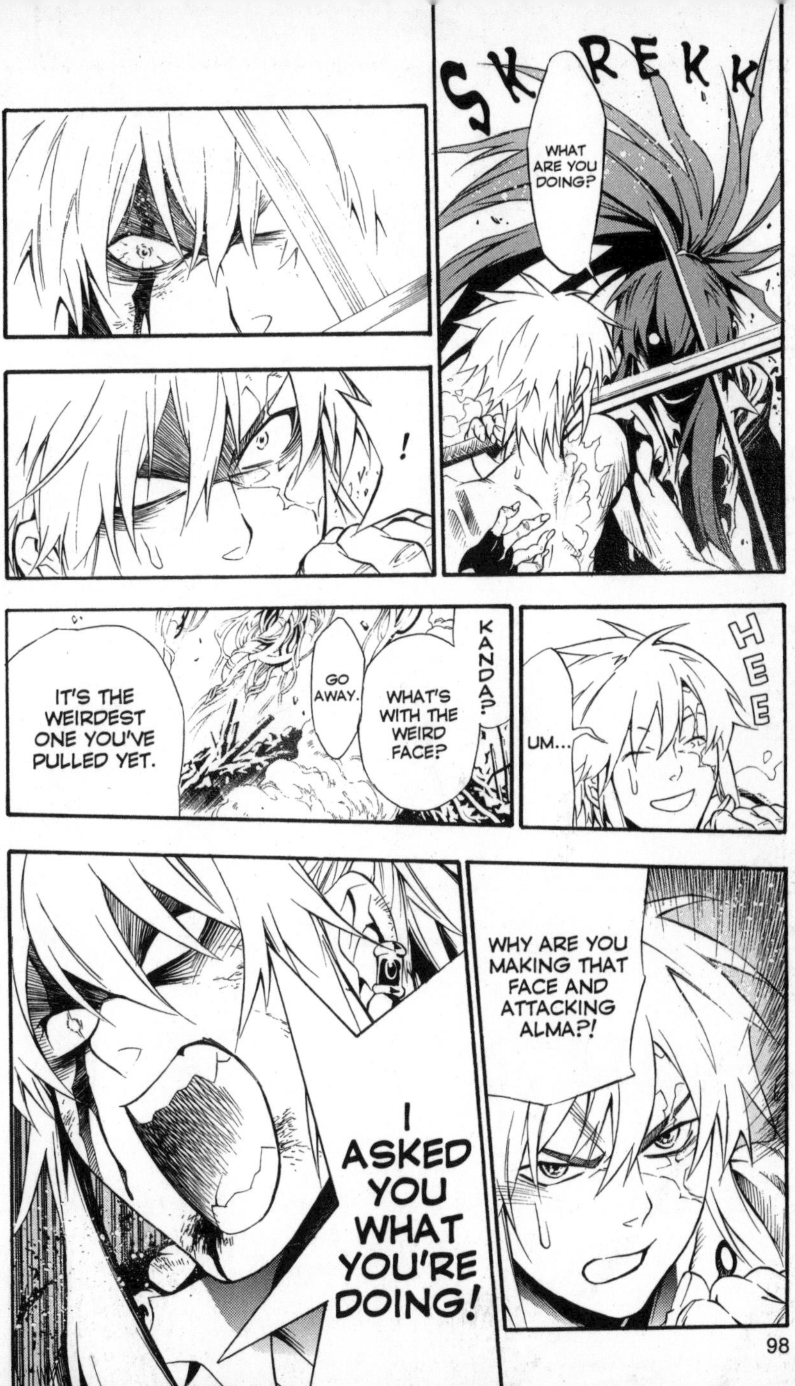
SKREKK
WHAT ARE YOU DOING?
!
HEE
UM...
KANDA?
WHAT'S WITH THE WEIRD FACE?
GO AWAY.
IT'S THE WEIRDEST ONE YOU'VE PULLED YET.
WHY ARE YOU MAKING THAT FACE AND ATTACKING ALMA?!
I ASKED YOU WHAT YOU'RE DOING!

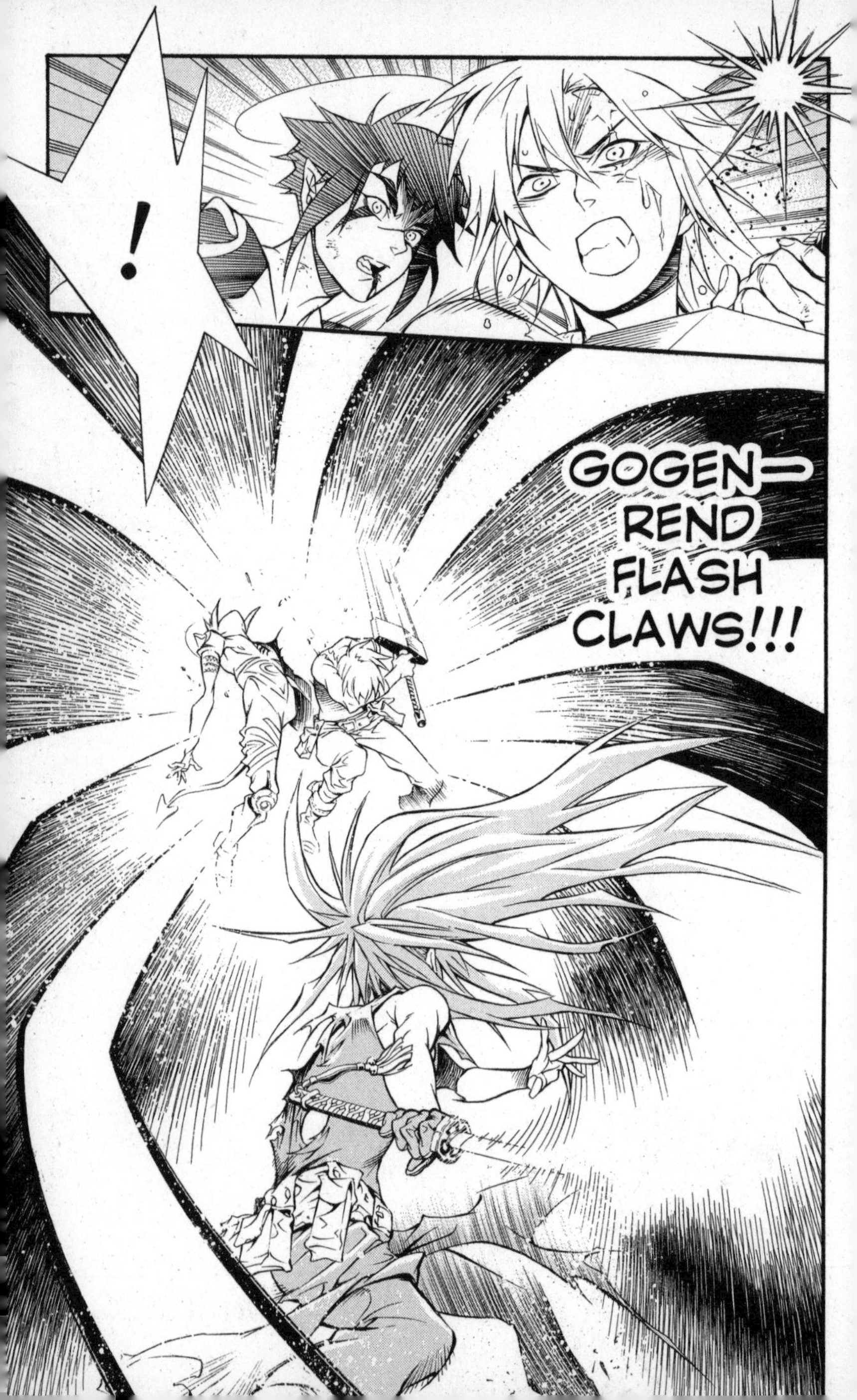
!
GOGEN—
REND
FLASH
CLAWS!!!

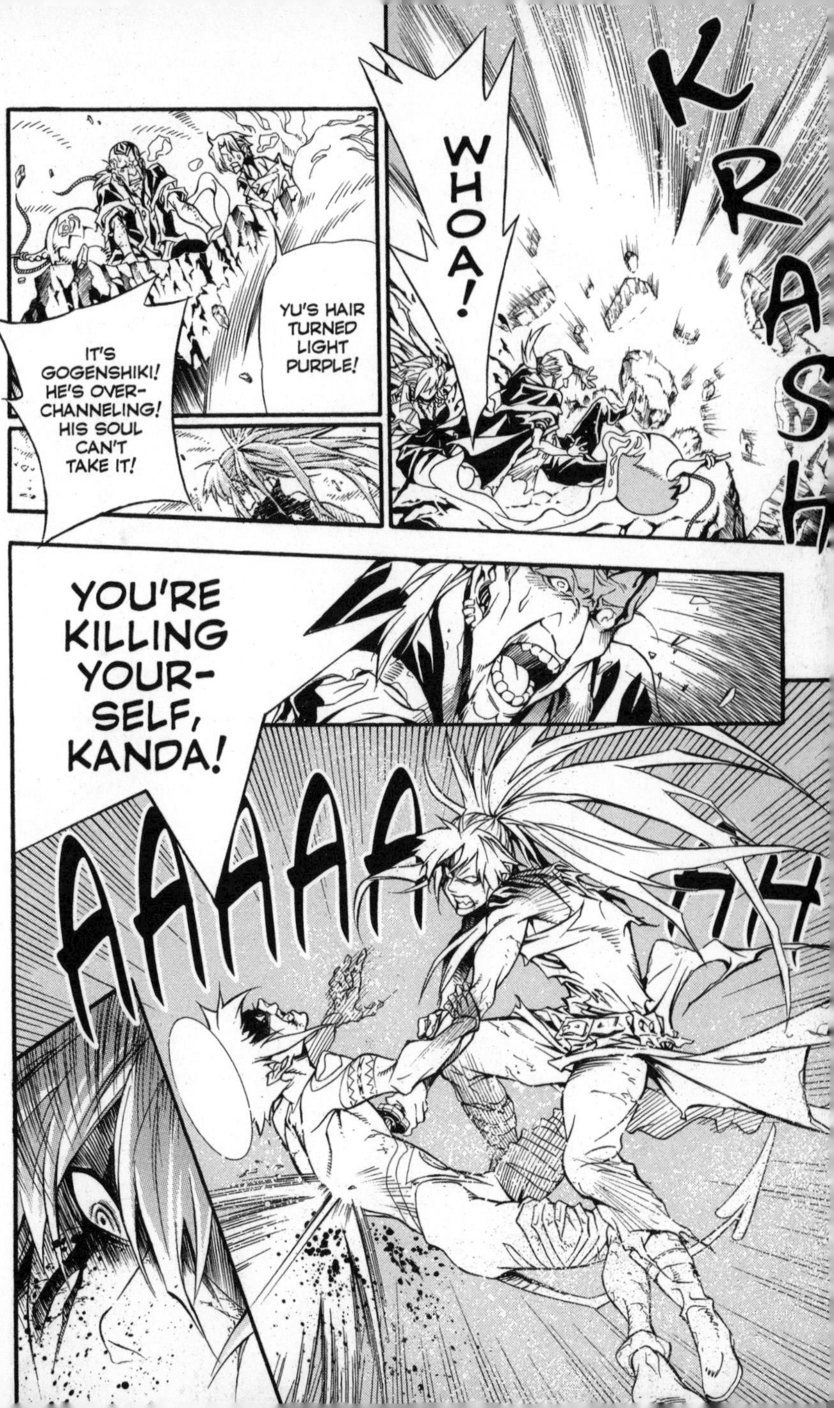
KRASH
WHOA!
YU'S HAIR TURNED LIGHT PURPLE!
IT'S GOGENSHIKI! HE'S OVER-CHANNELING! HIS SOUL CAN'T TAKE IT!
YOU'RE KILLING YOUR-SELF, KANDA!
AAAAA

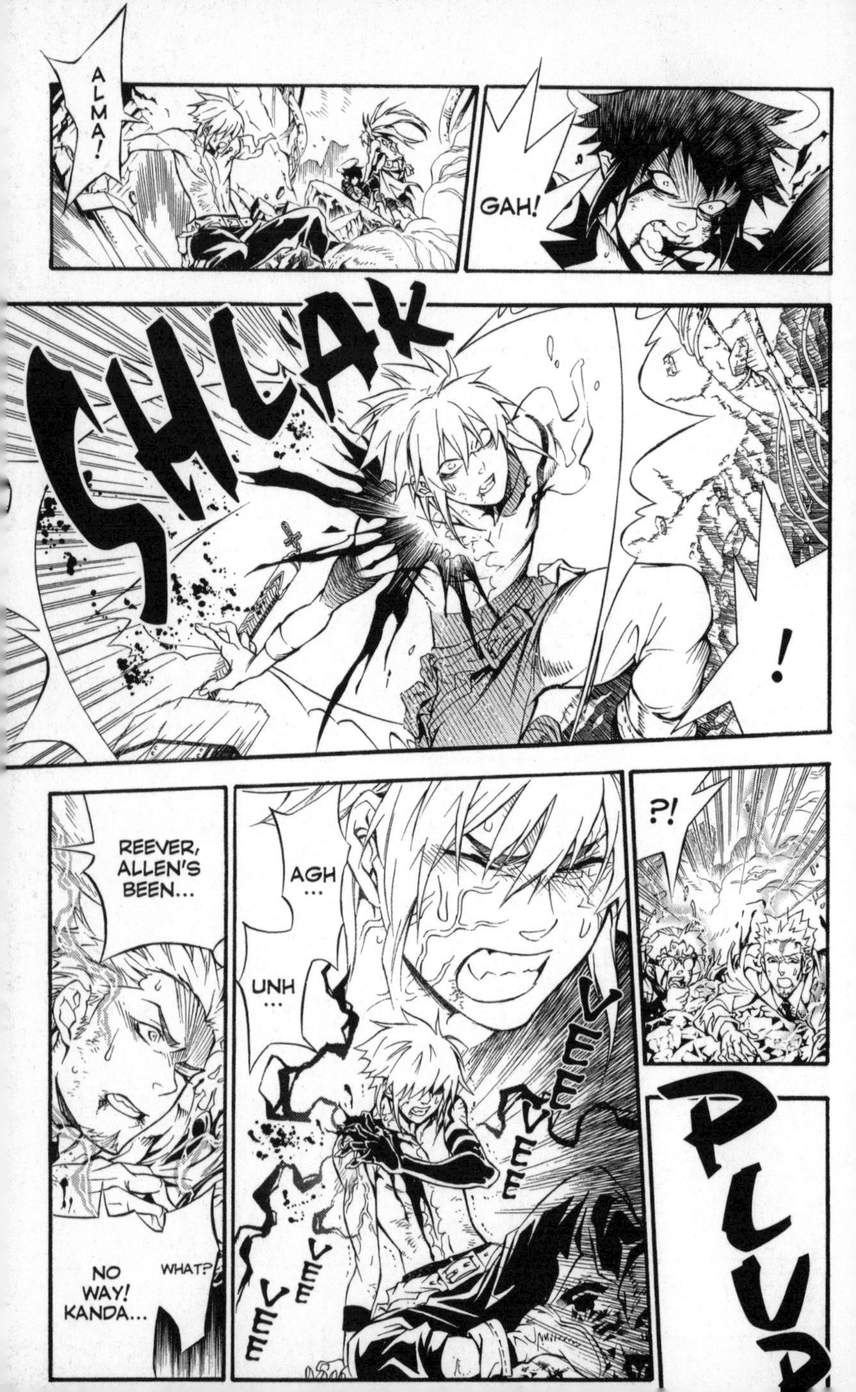
GAH!
ALMA!
SHLAK
!
?!
PLUD
AGH...
UNH...
VEE VEE VEE
VEE VEE
REEVER, ALLEN'S BEEN...
WHAT?
NO WAY! KANDA...

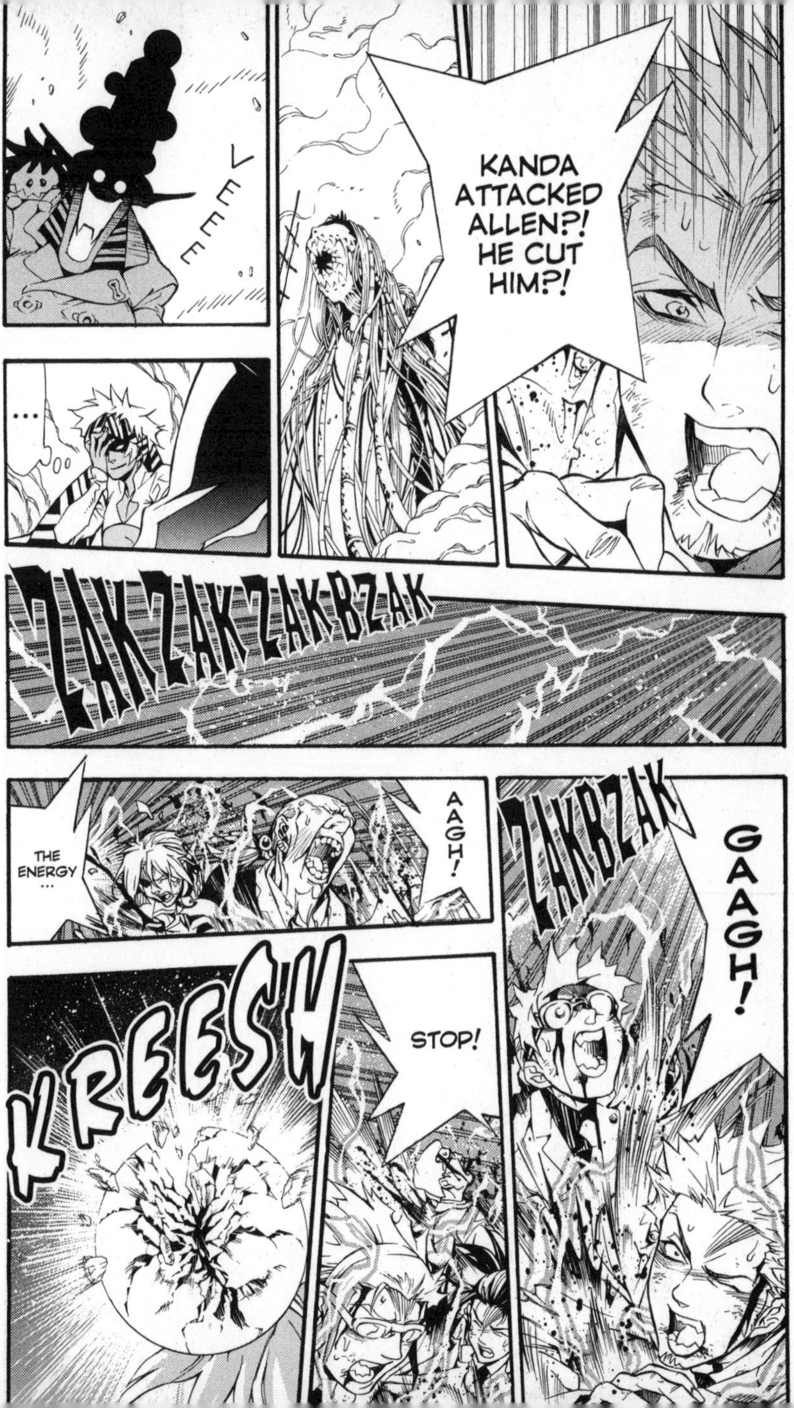
KANDA ATTACKED ALLEN?! HE CUT HIM?!
VEEEE
...
ZAKZAKZAKBZAK
ZAKBZAK
GAAGH!
AAGH!
THE ENERGY ...
STOP!
KREESH

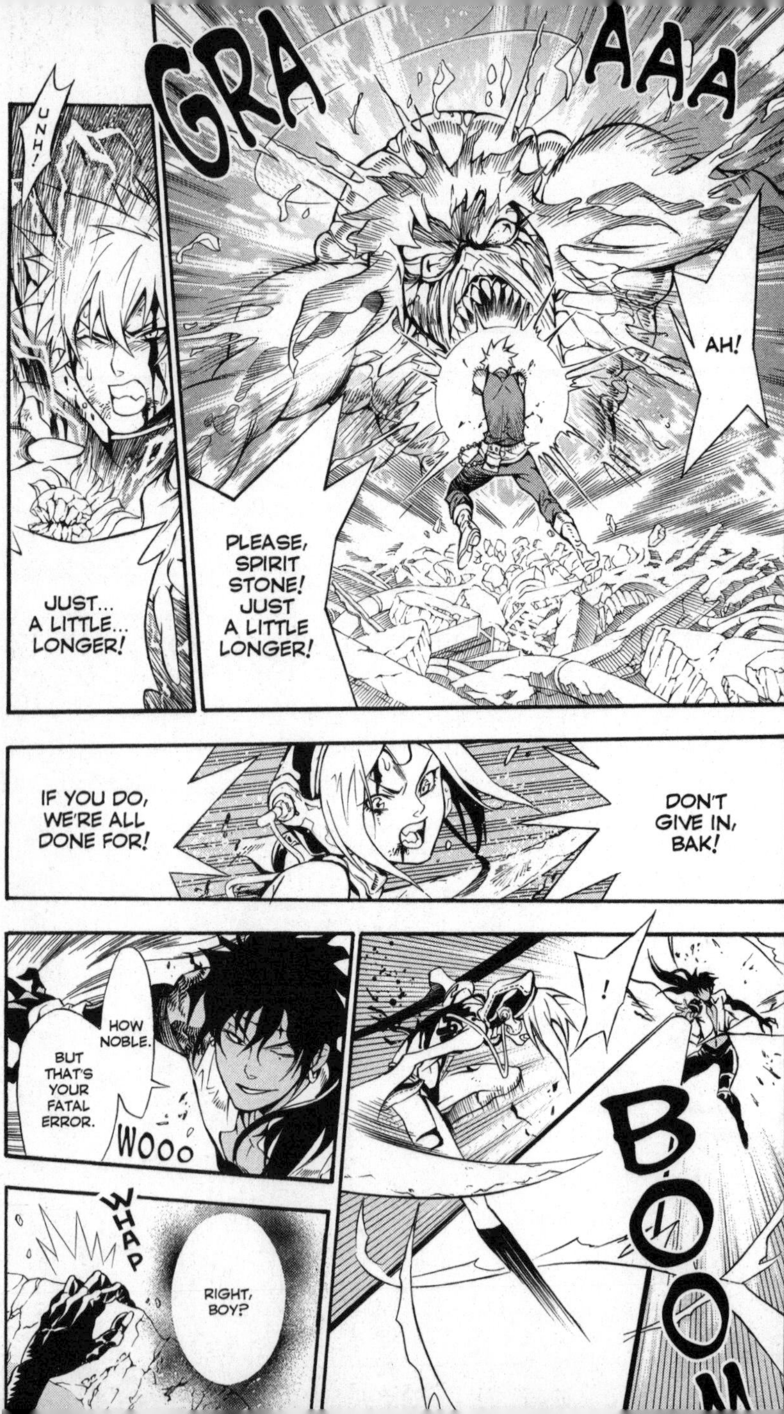
GRA AAA
AH!
PLEASE, SPIRIT STONE! JUST A LITTLE LONGER!
UNH!
JUST... A LITTLE... LONGER!
DON'T GIVE IN, BAK!
IF YOU DO, WE'RE ALL DONE FOR!
!
BOOM
HOW NOBLE.
BUT THAT'S YOUR FATAL ERROR.
WOOO
WHAP
RIGHT, BOY?

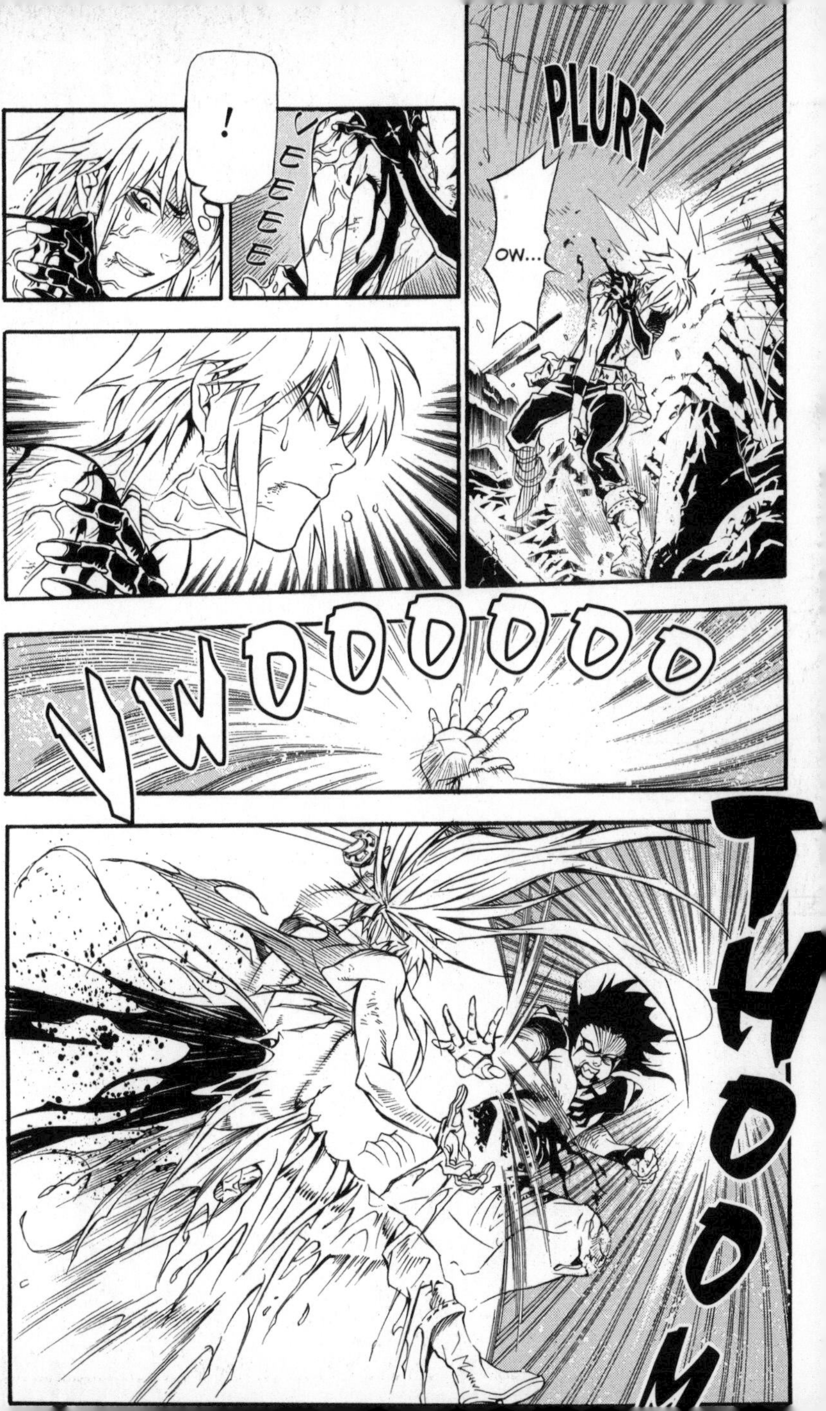
PLURT
OW...
EEEEEE
!
VWOOOOOOO
THOOOM

READ THIS WAY

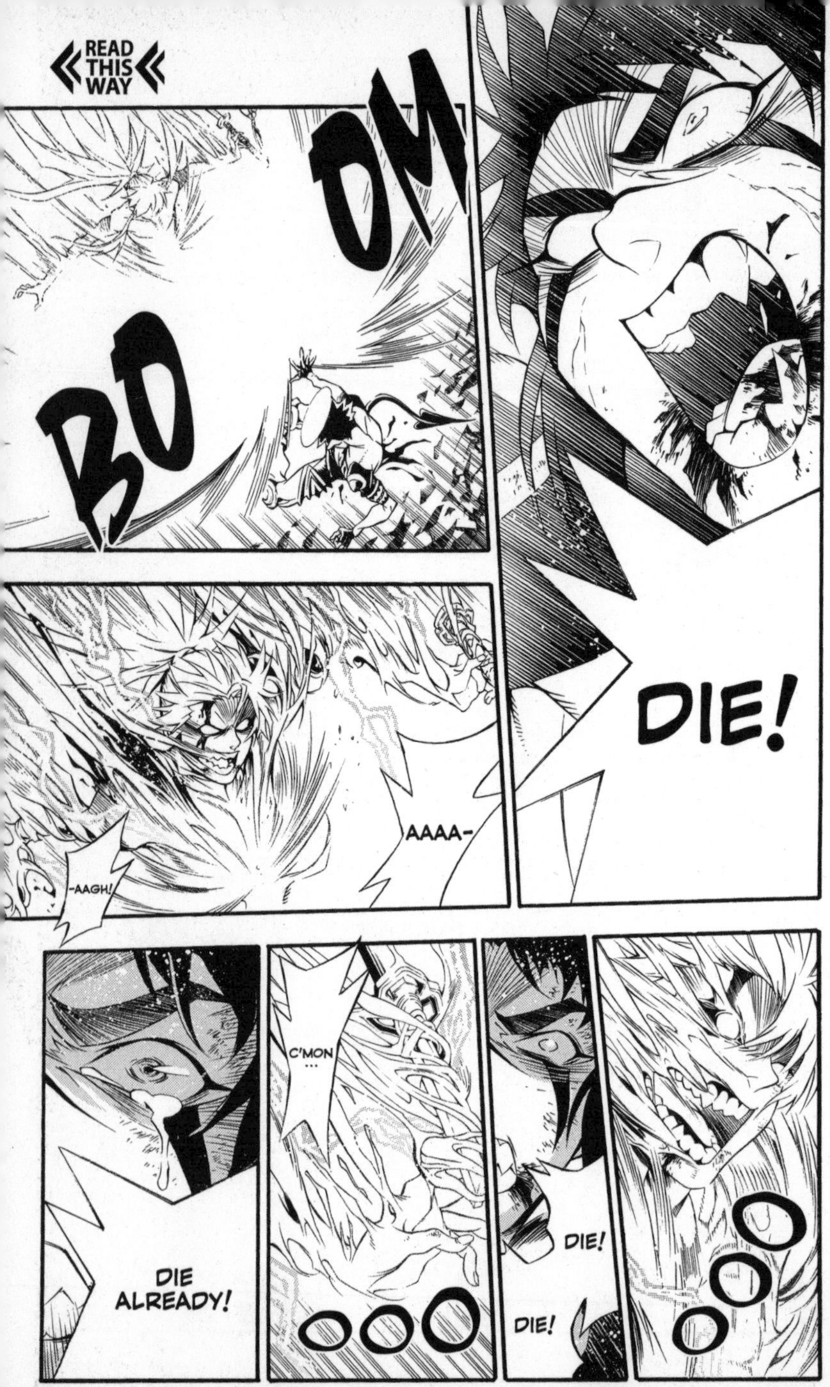
DIE!
BOOM
AAAA-
-AAGH!
OOO
DIE!
DIE!
C'MON...
OOO
DIE ALREADY!

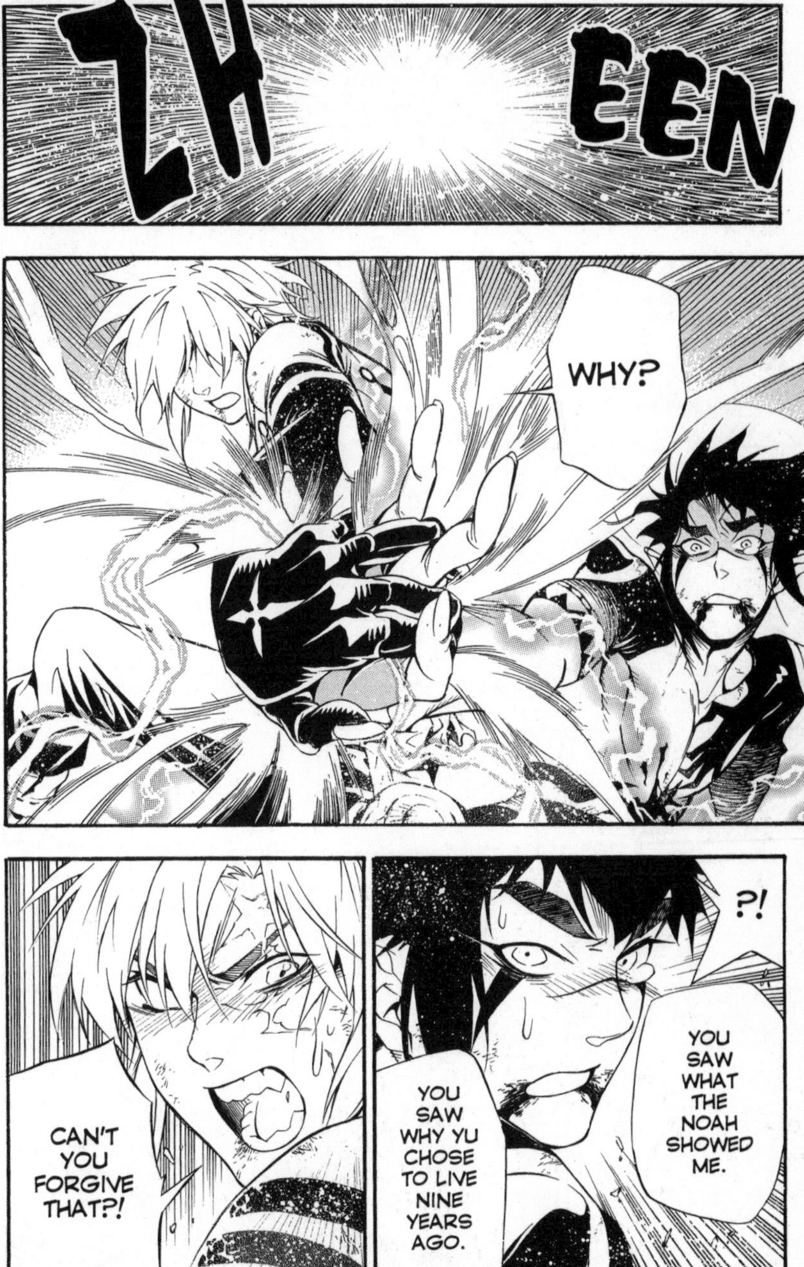
ZH EEN
WHY?
?!
YOU SAW WHAT THE NOAH SHOWED ME.
YOU SAW WHY YU CHOSE TO LIVE NINE YEARS AGO.
CAN'T YOU FORGIVE THAT?!

READ THIS WAY

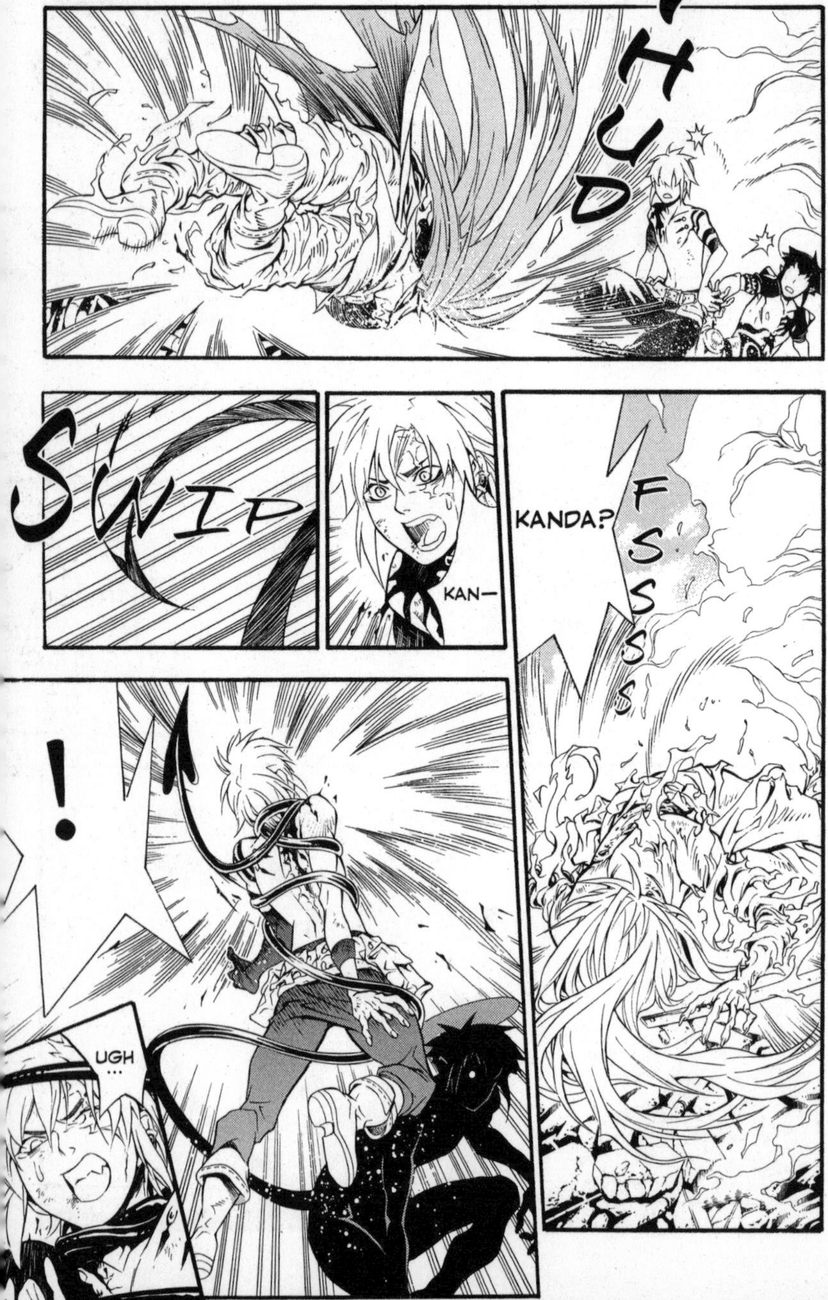
THUD
KANDA?
FSSSS
KAN—
SWIP
!
UGH ...

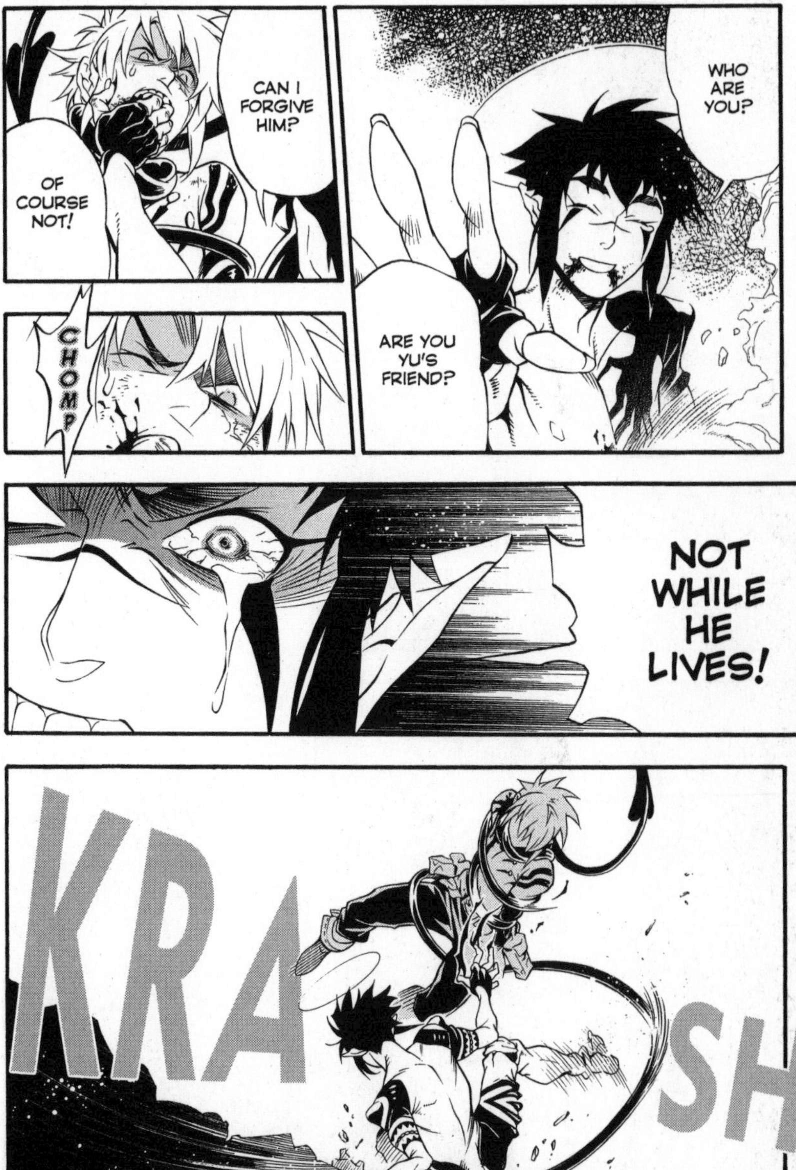
WHO ARE YOU?
ARE YOU YU'S FRIEND?
CAN I FORGIVE HIM?
OF COURSE NOT!
CHOMP
NOT WHILE HE LIVES!
KRASH

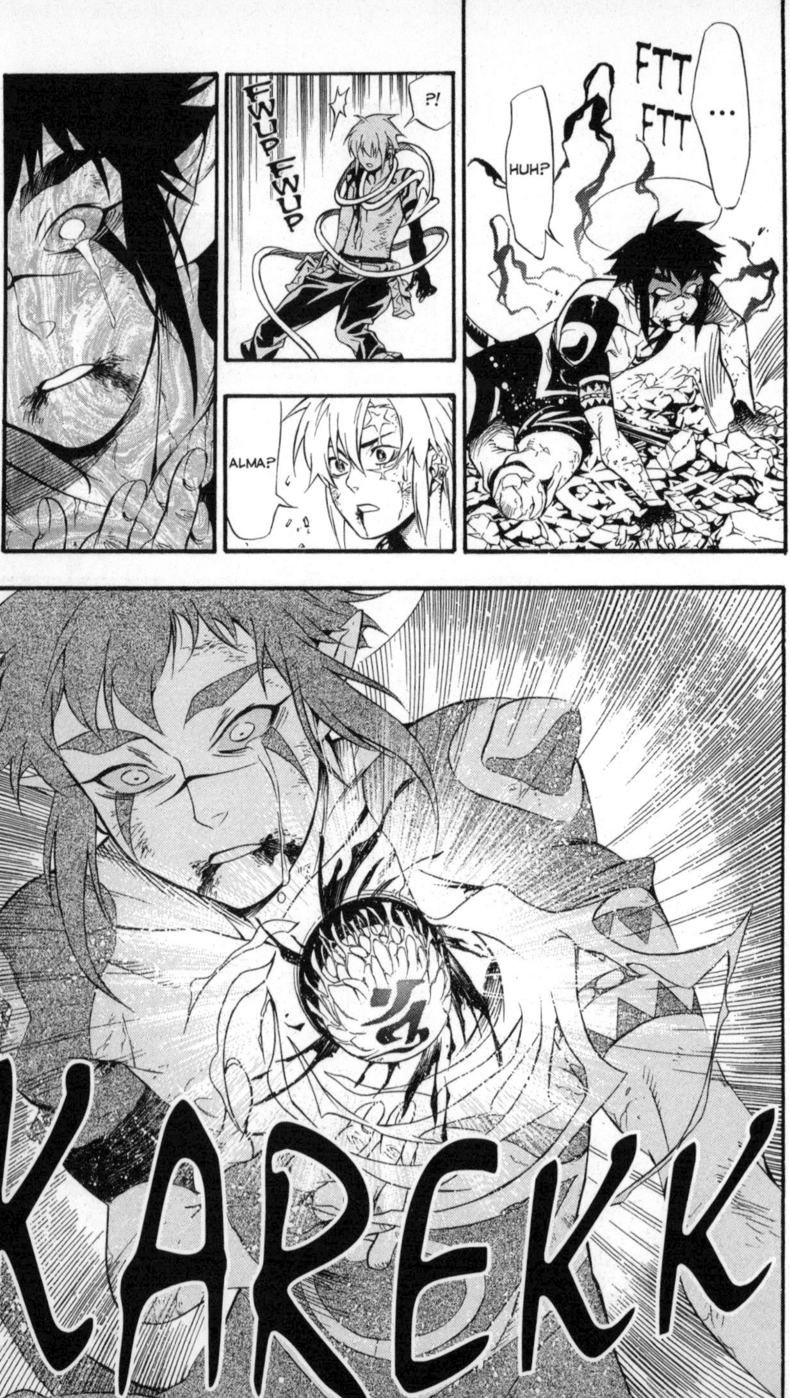
...
FTT FTT
HUH?
?!
FWUP FWUP
ALMA?
KAREKK

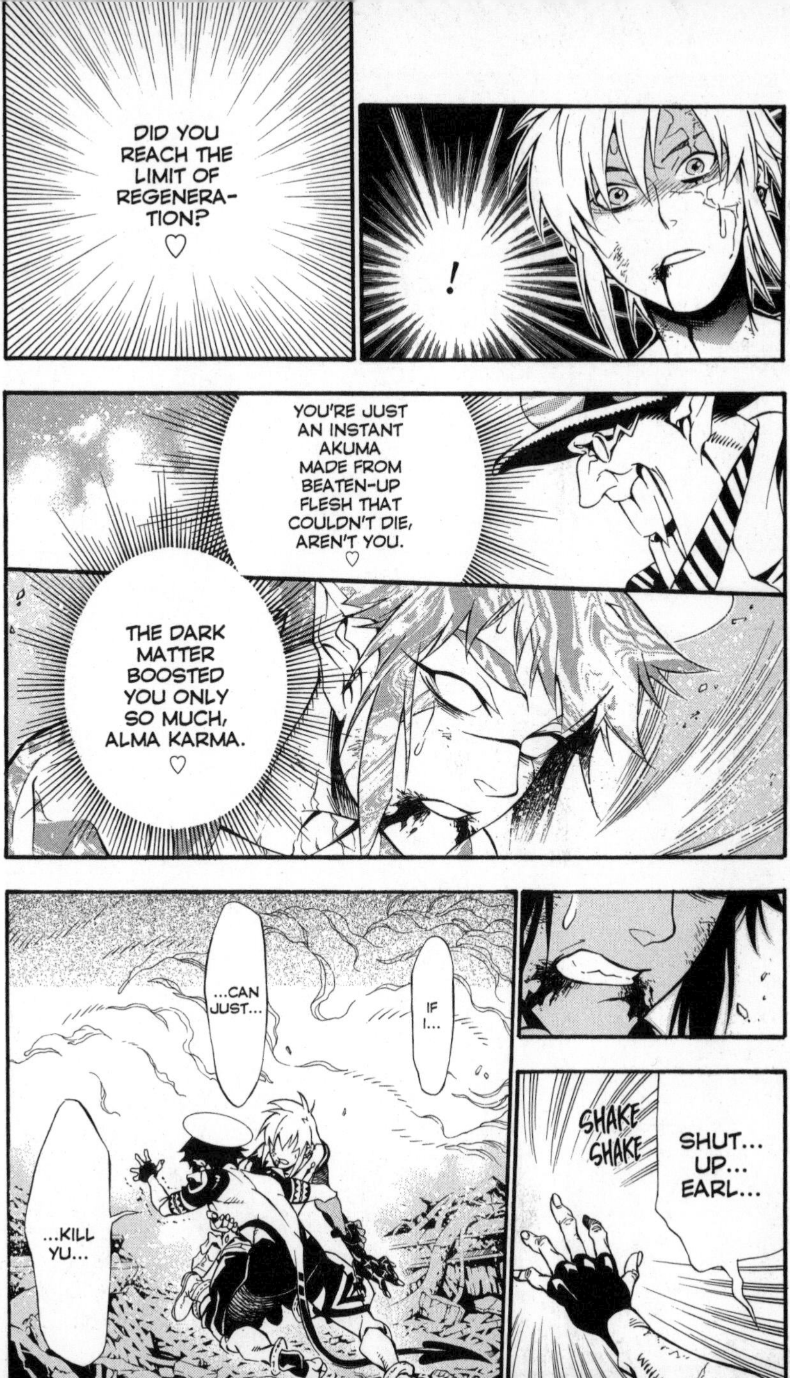
!
DID YOU REACH THE LIMIT OF REGENERA-TION? ♡
YOU'RE JUST AN INSTANT AKUMA MADE FROM BEATEN-UP FLESH THAT COULDN'T DIE, AREN'T YOU. ♡
THE DARK MATTER BOOSTED YOU ONLY SO MUCH, ALMA KARMA. ♡
SHAKE SHAKE
SHUT... UP... EARL...
IF I...
...CAN JUST...
...KILL YU...

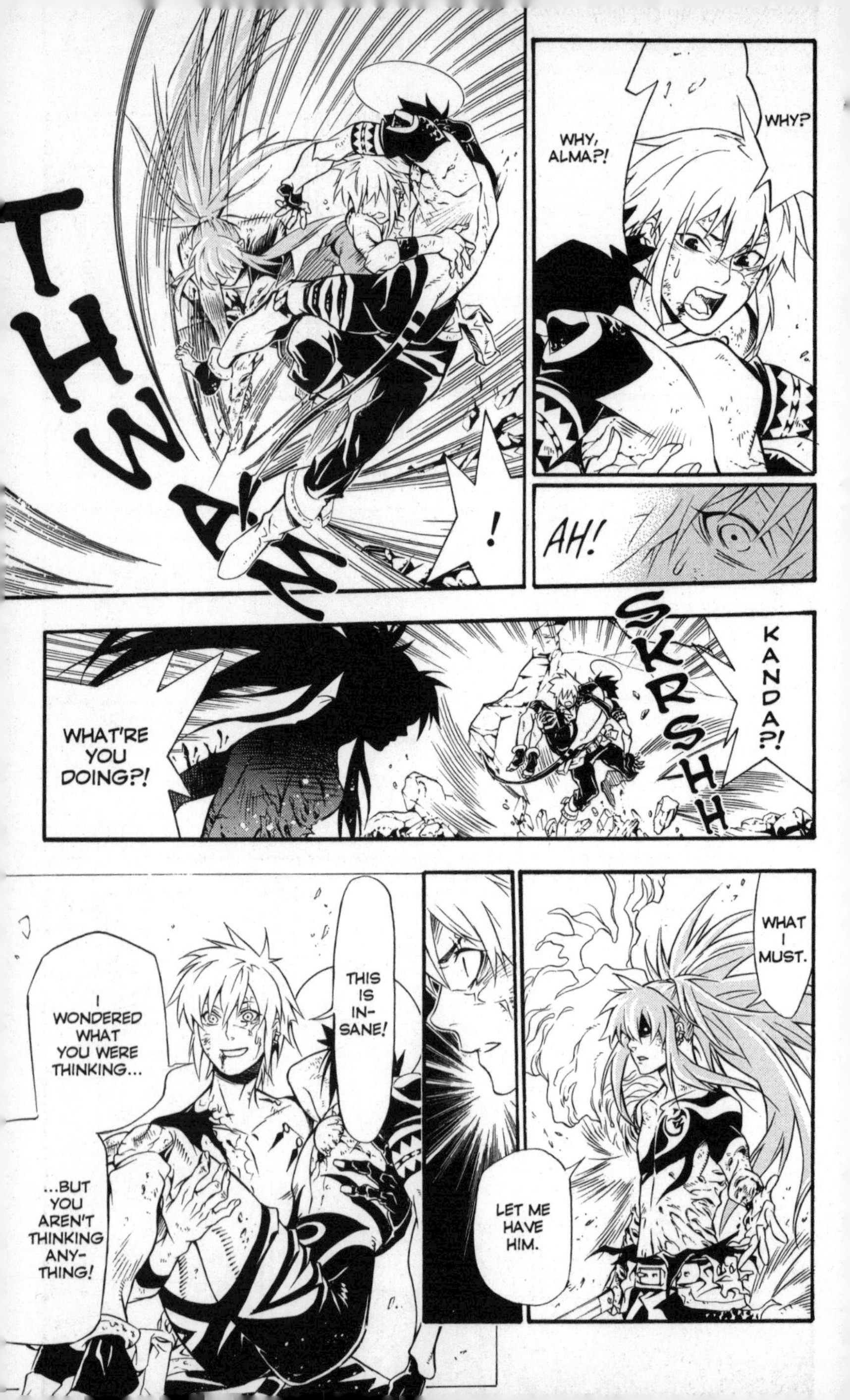
WHY?
WHY, ALMA?!
AH!
!
THWAM
KANDA?!
SKRSHH
WHAT'RE YOU DOING?!
WHAT I MUST.
THIS IS IN-SANE!
LET ME HAVE HIM.
I WONDERED WHAT YOU WERE THINKING...
...BUT YOU AREN'T THINKING ANY-THING!

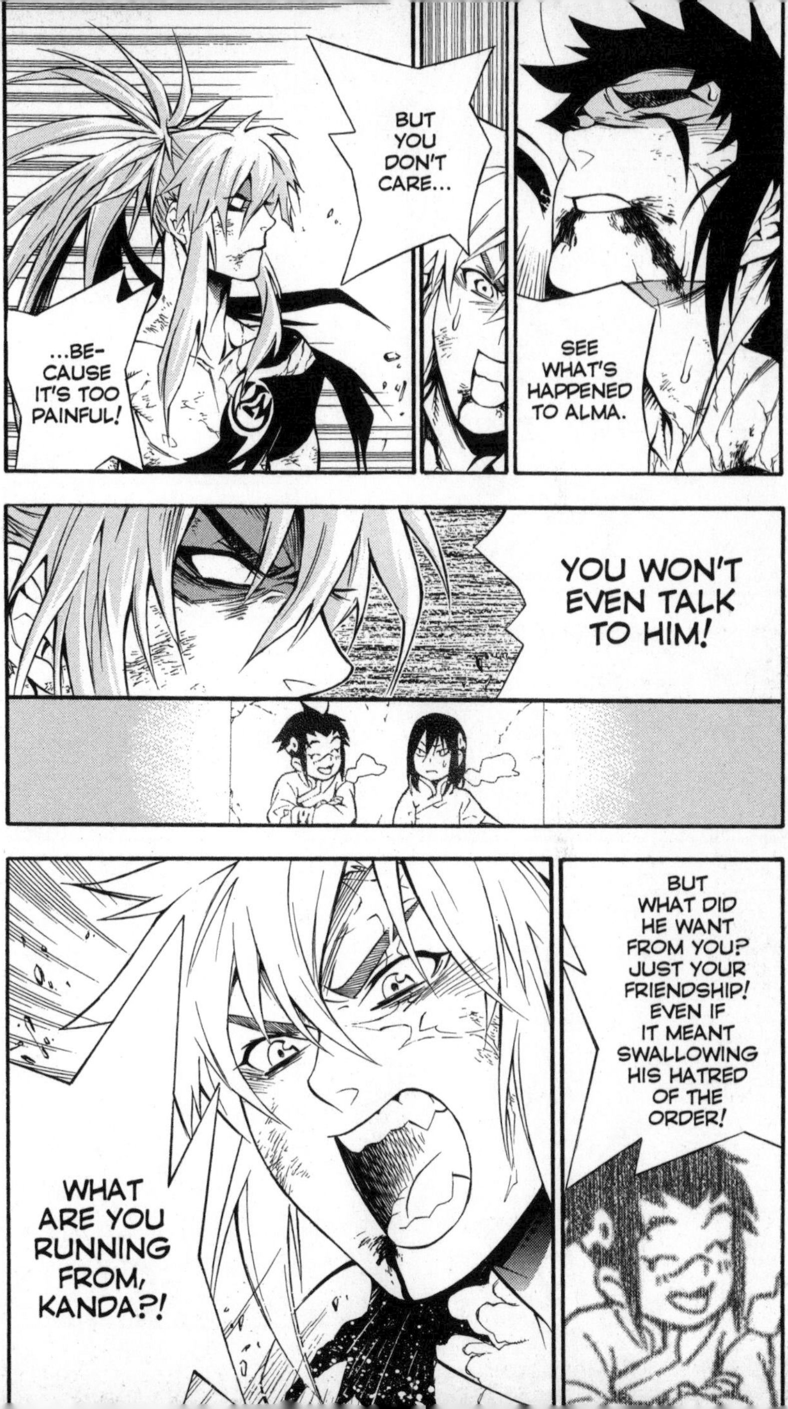
SEE WHAT'S HAPPENED TO ALMA.
BUT YOU DON'T CARE...
...BE-CAUSE IT'S TOO PAINFUL!
YOU WON'T EVEN TALK TO HIM!
BUT WHAT DID HE WANT FROM YOU? JUST YOUR FRIENDSHIP! EVEN IF IT MEANT SWALLOWING HIS HATRED OF THE ORDER!
WHAT ARE YOU RUNNING FROM, KANDA?!

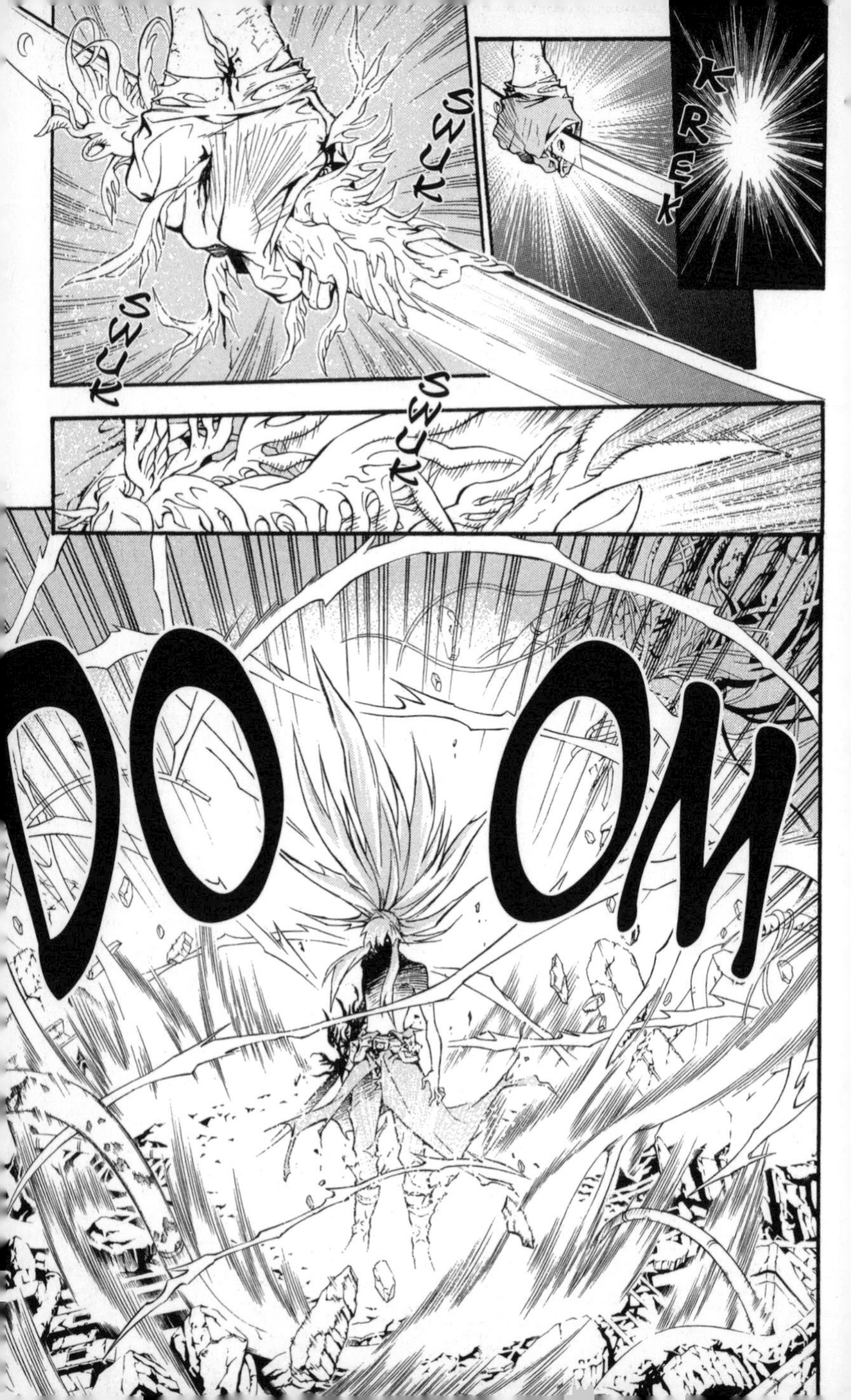
KREK
SWUK
SWUK
SWUK
DOOM

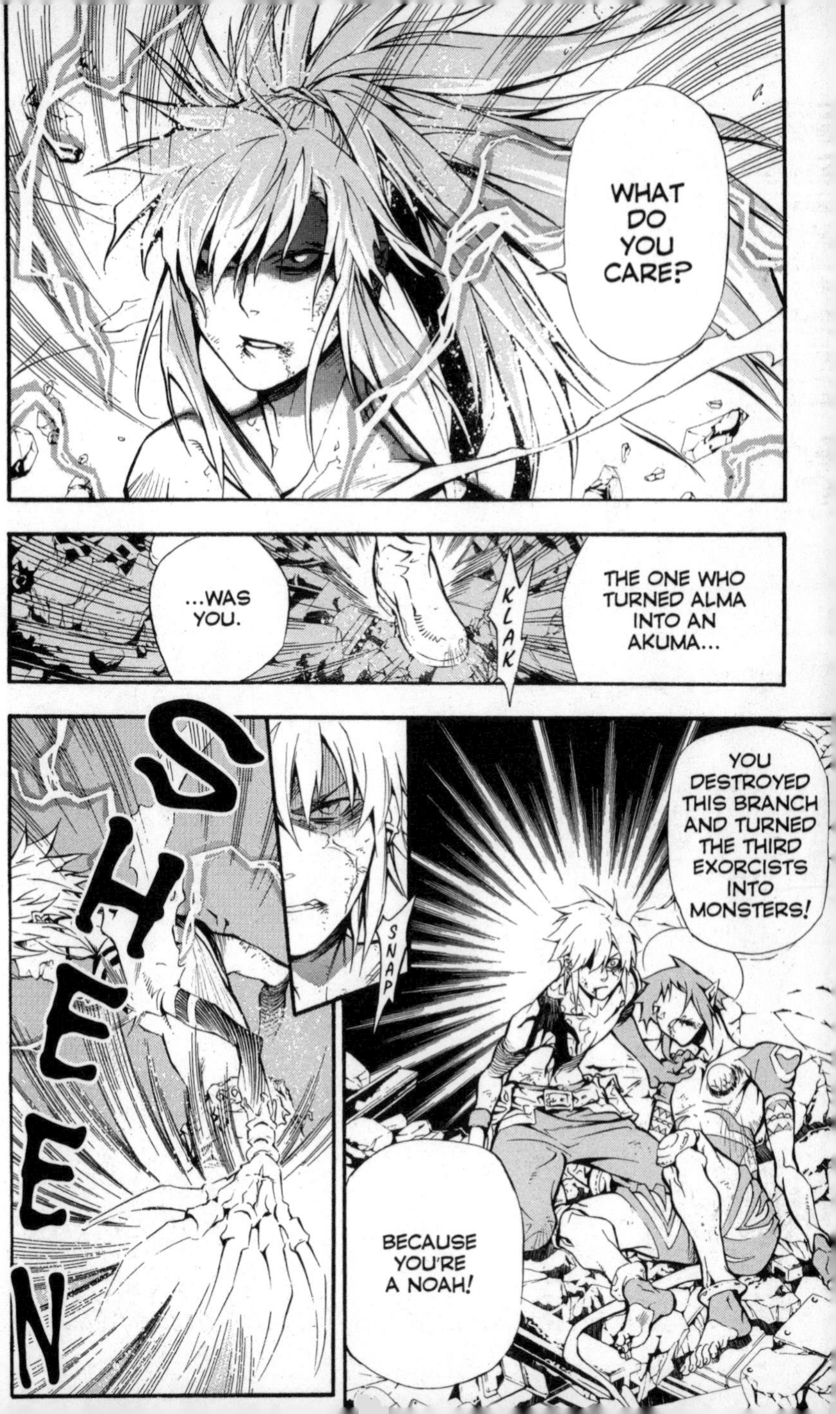
WHAT DO YOU CARE?
THE ONE WHO TURNED ALMA INTO AN AKUMA...
KLAK
...WAS YOU.
YOU DESTROYED THIS BRANCH AND TURNED THE THIRD EXORCISTS INTO MONSTERS!
BECAUSE YOU'RE A NOAH!
SNAP
SHEEN

READ THIS WAY

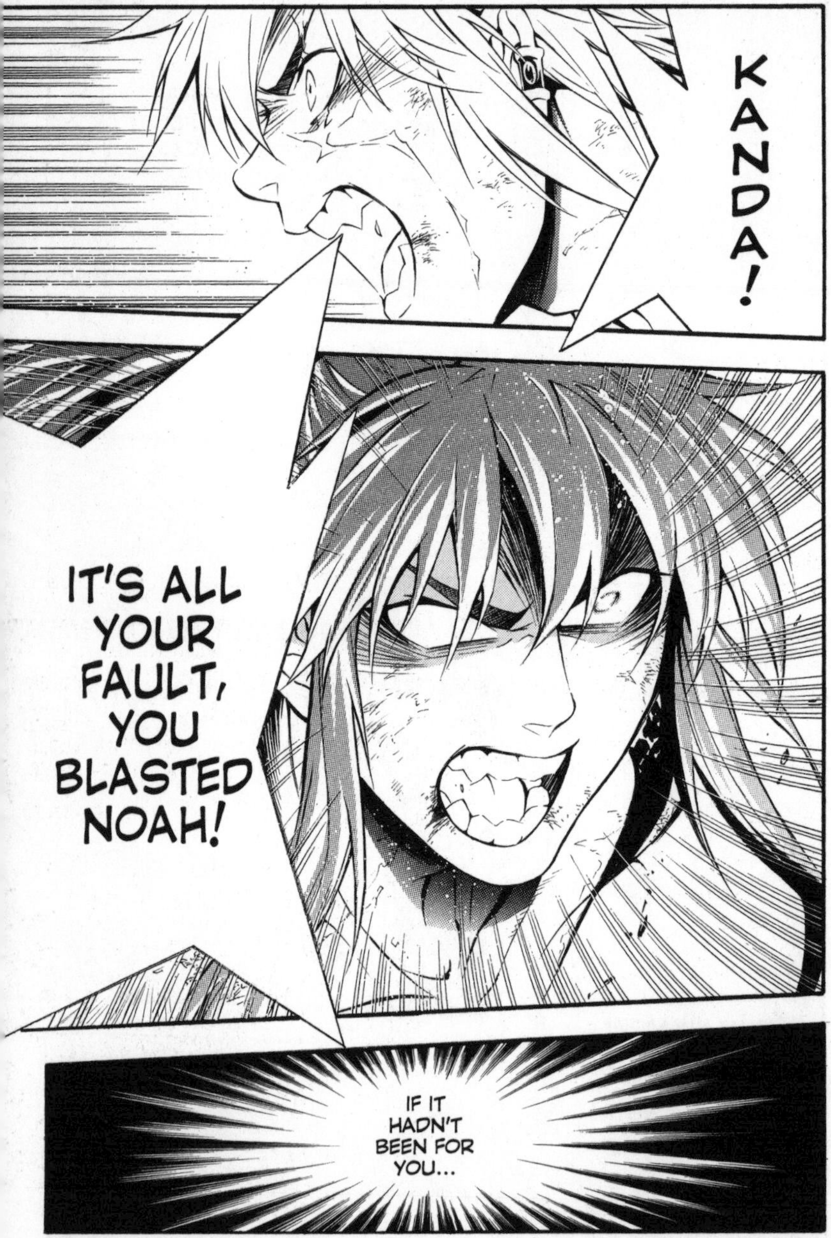
KANDA!
IT'S ALL YOUR FAULT, YOU BLASTED NOAH!
IF IT HADN'T BEEN FOR YOU...

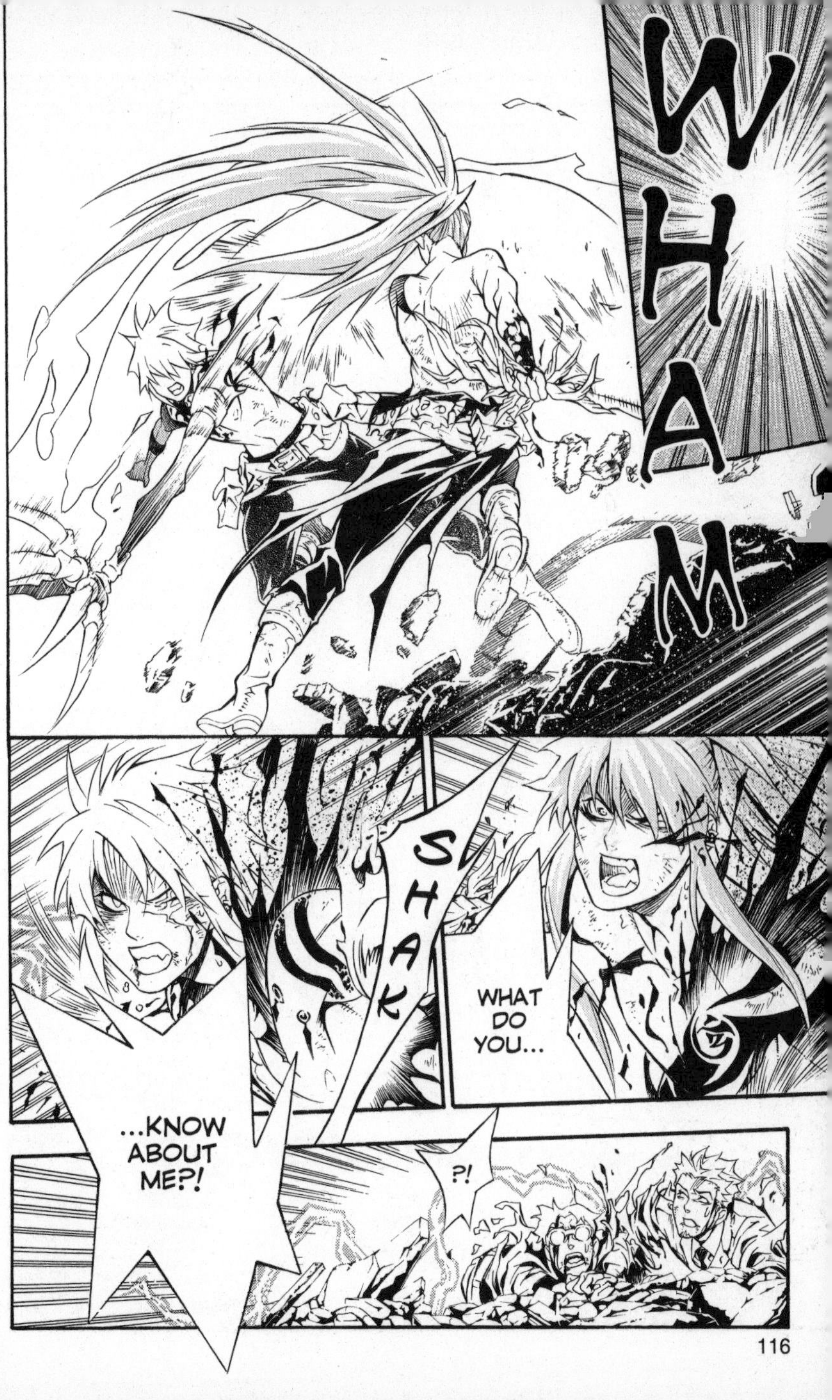
WHAM
WHAT DO YOU...
SHAK
...KNOW ABOUT ME?!
?!

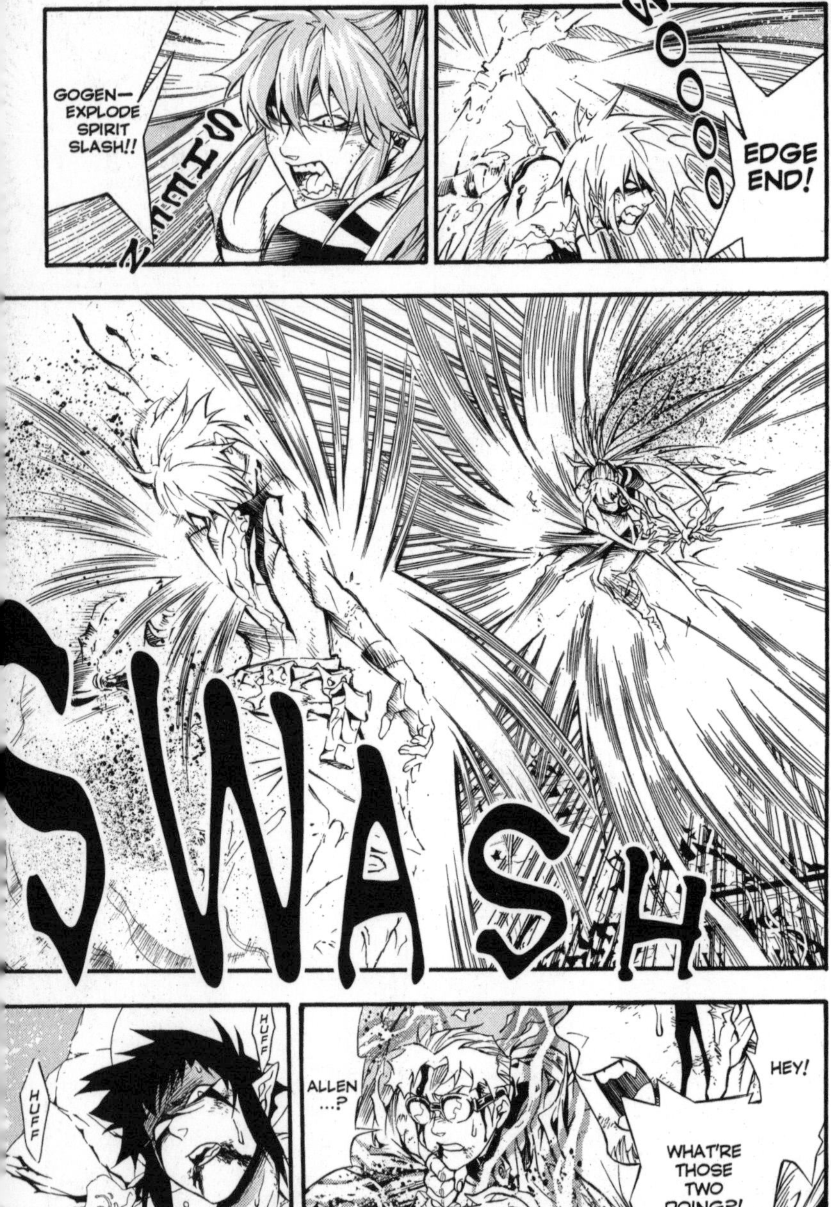
WOOOOOO
EDGE END!
GOGEN— EXPLODE SPIRIT SLASH!!
SHWWN
SWASH
HEY!
WHAT'RE THOSE TWO DOING?!
ALLEN ...?
HUFF
HUFF

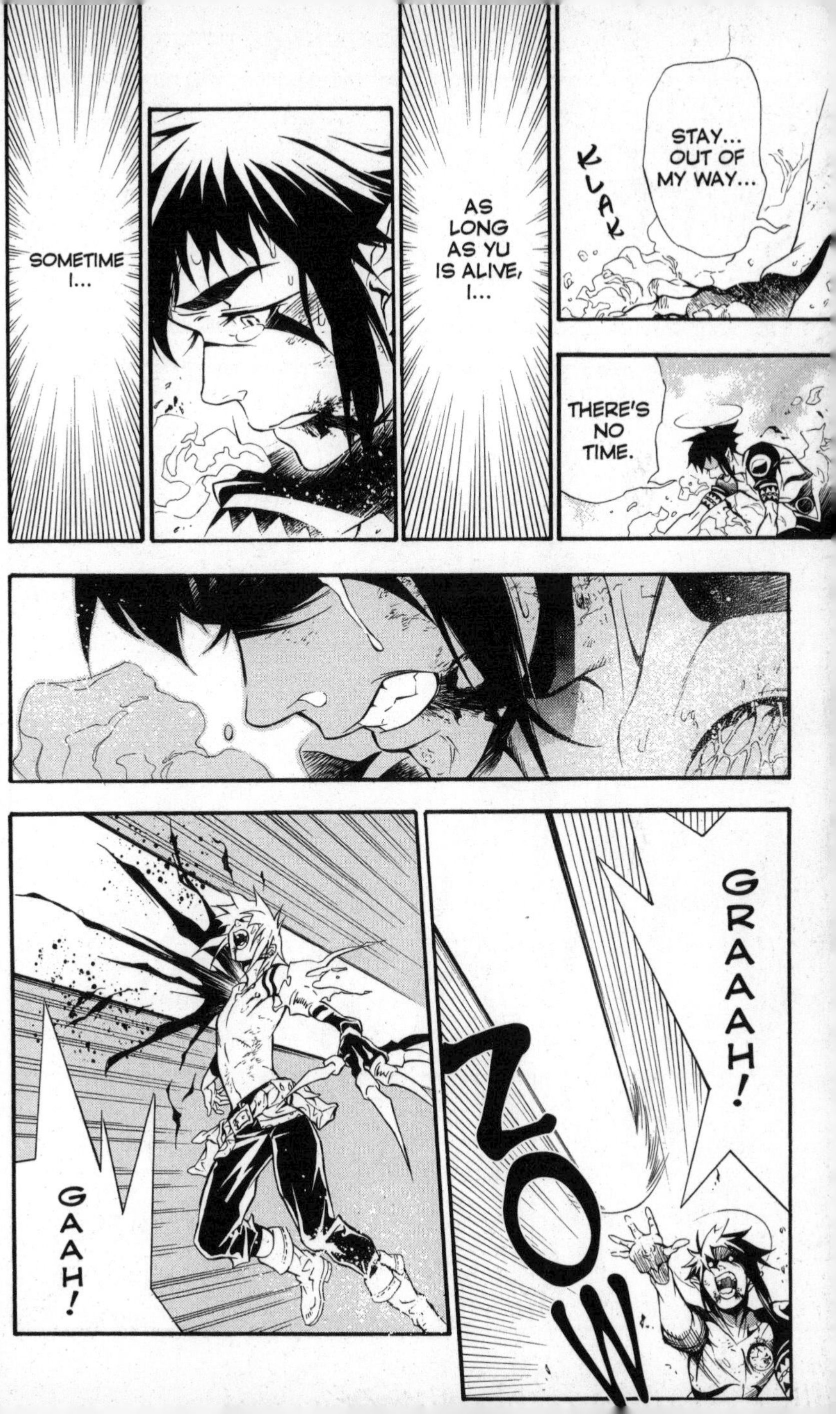
STAY... OUT OF MY WAY...
KLAK
THERE'S NO TIME.
AS LONG AS YU IS ALIVE, I...
SOMETIME I...
GRAAAH!
ZOOM
GAAH!

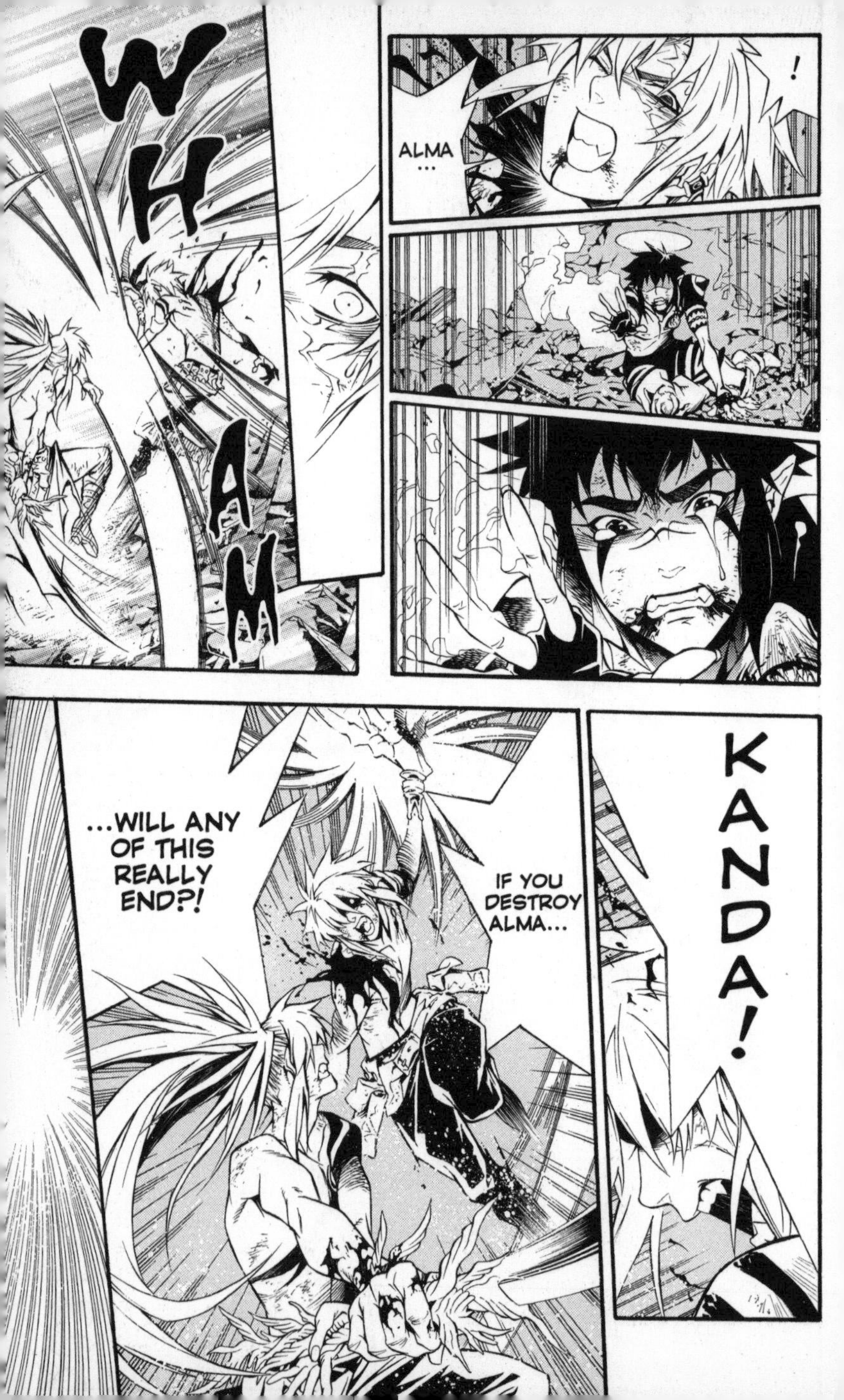
!
ALMA ...
WHAM
KANDA!
IF YOU DESTROY ALMA...
...WILL ANY OF THIS REALLY END?!

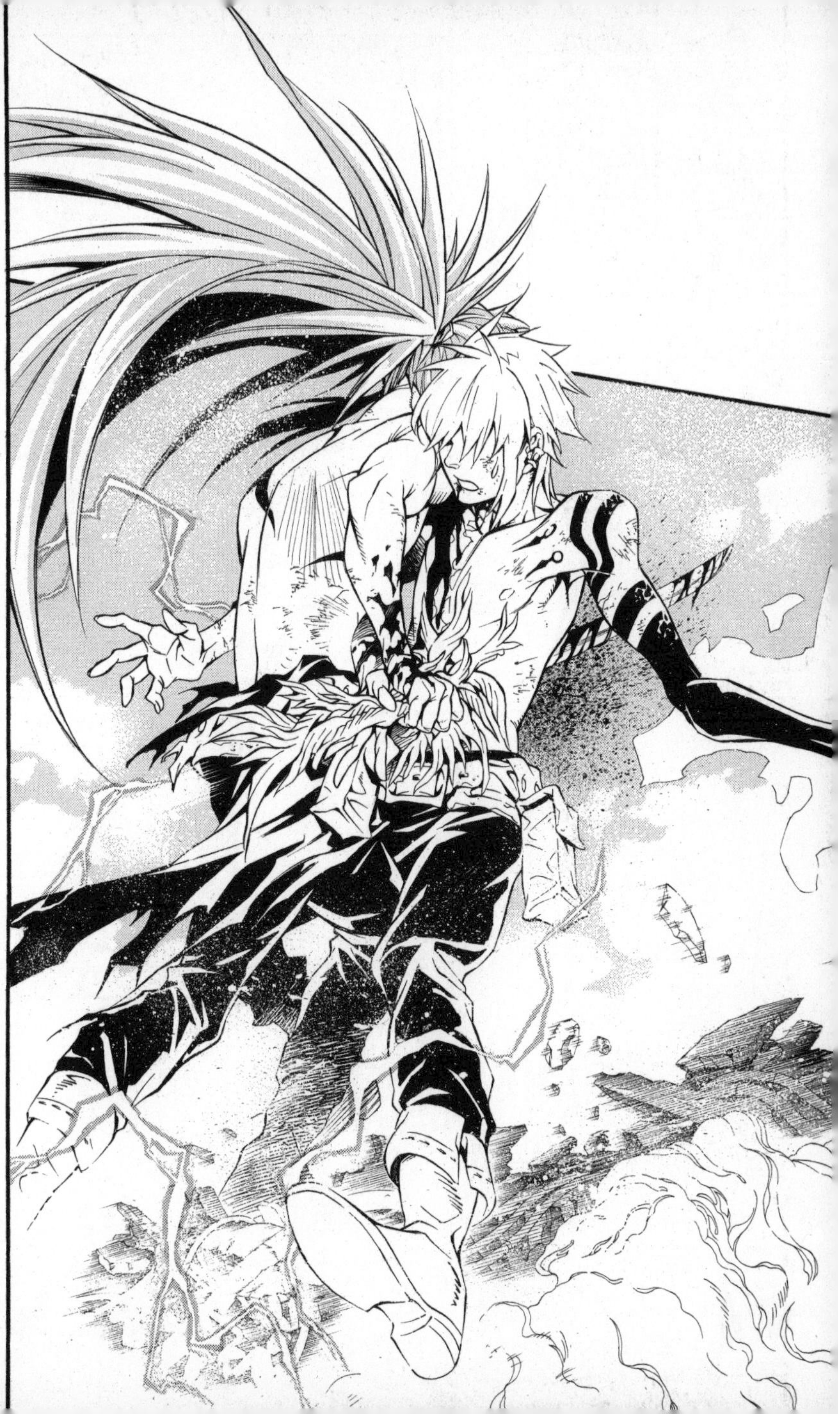

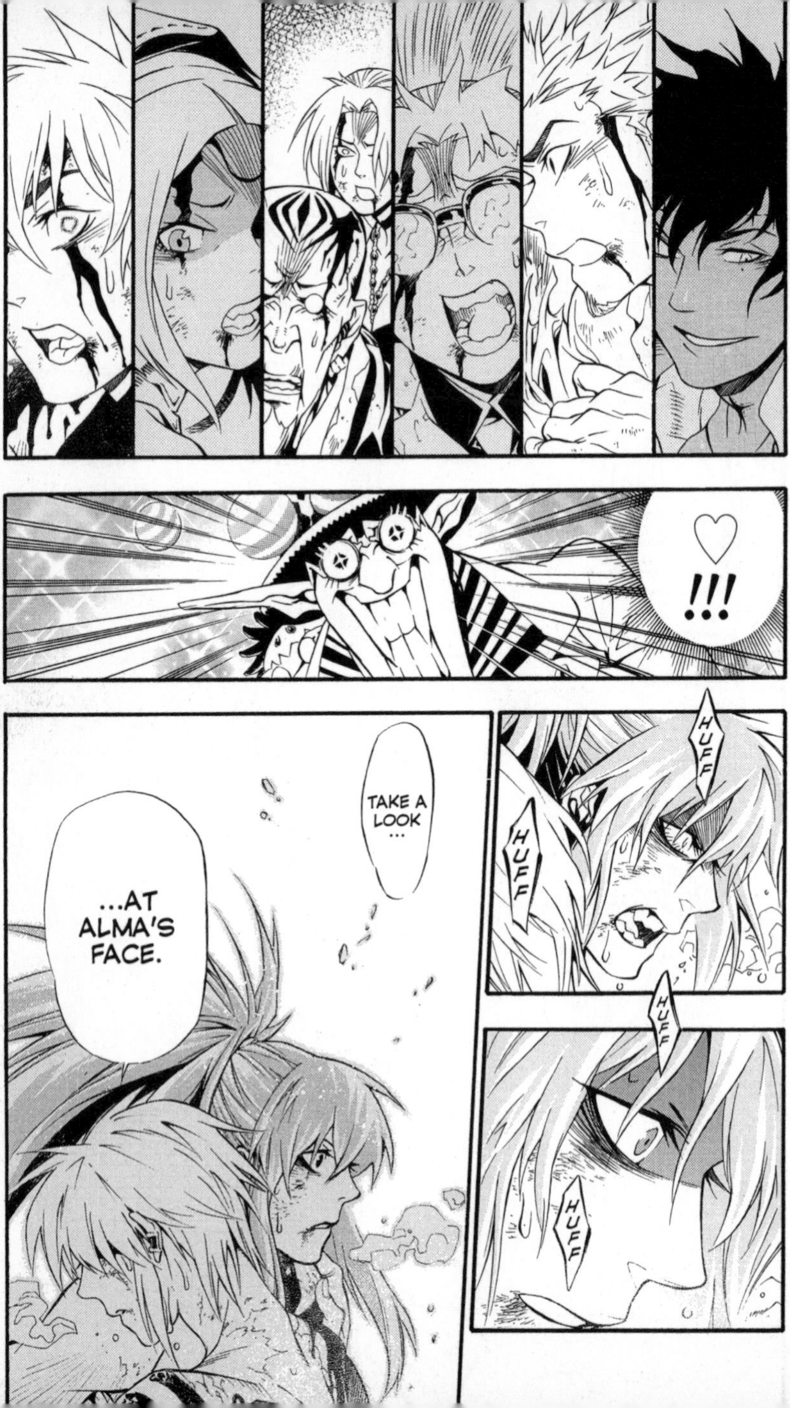
♥ !!!
HUFF
HUFF
HUFF
HUFF
TAKE A LOOK ...
...AT ALMA'S FACE.

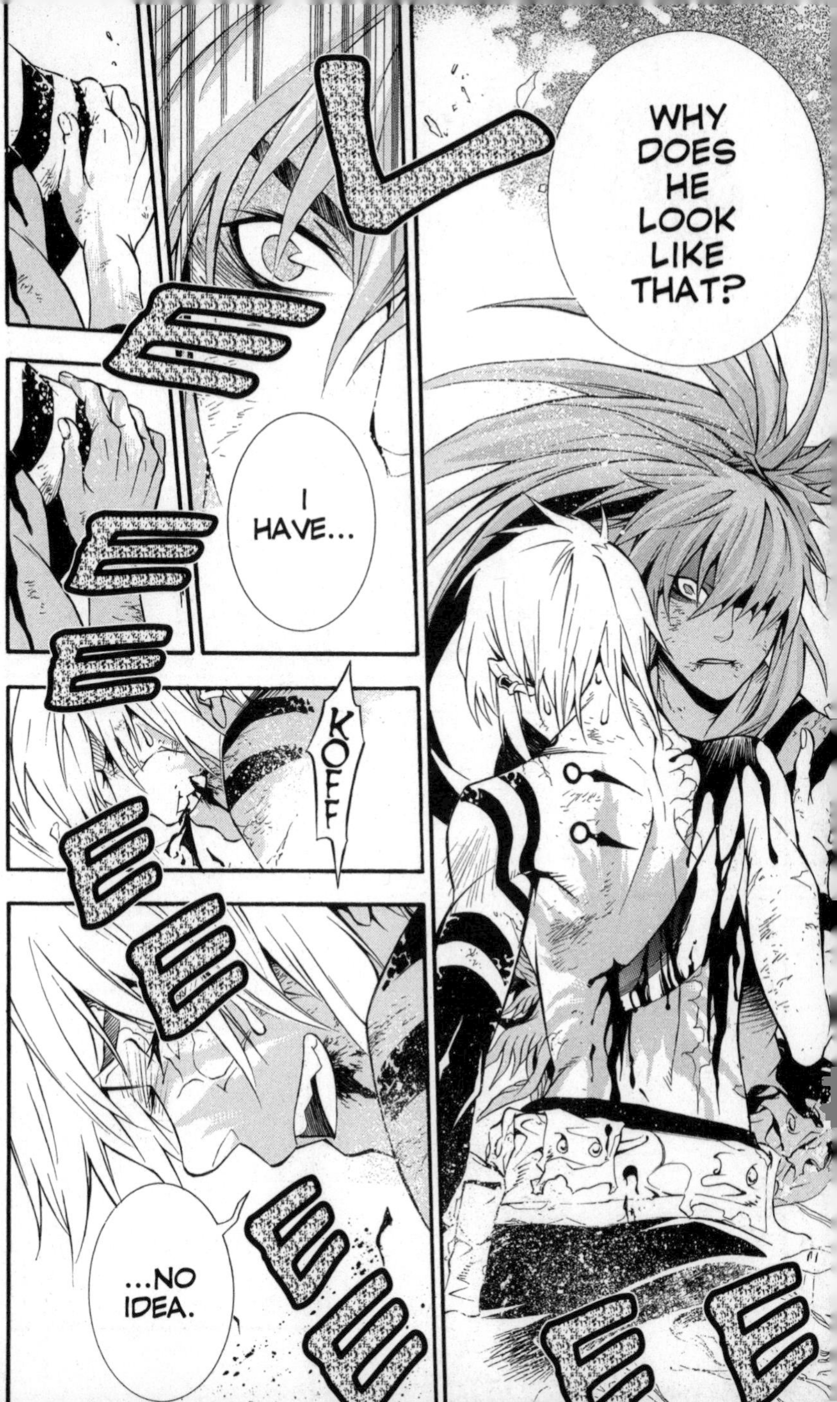
WHY DOES HE LOOK LIKE THAT?
I HAVE...
KOFF
...NO IDEA.

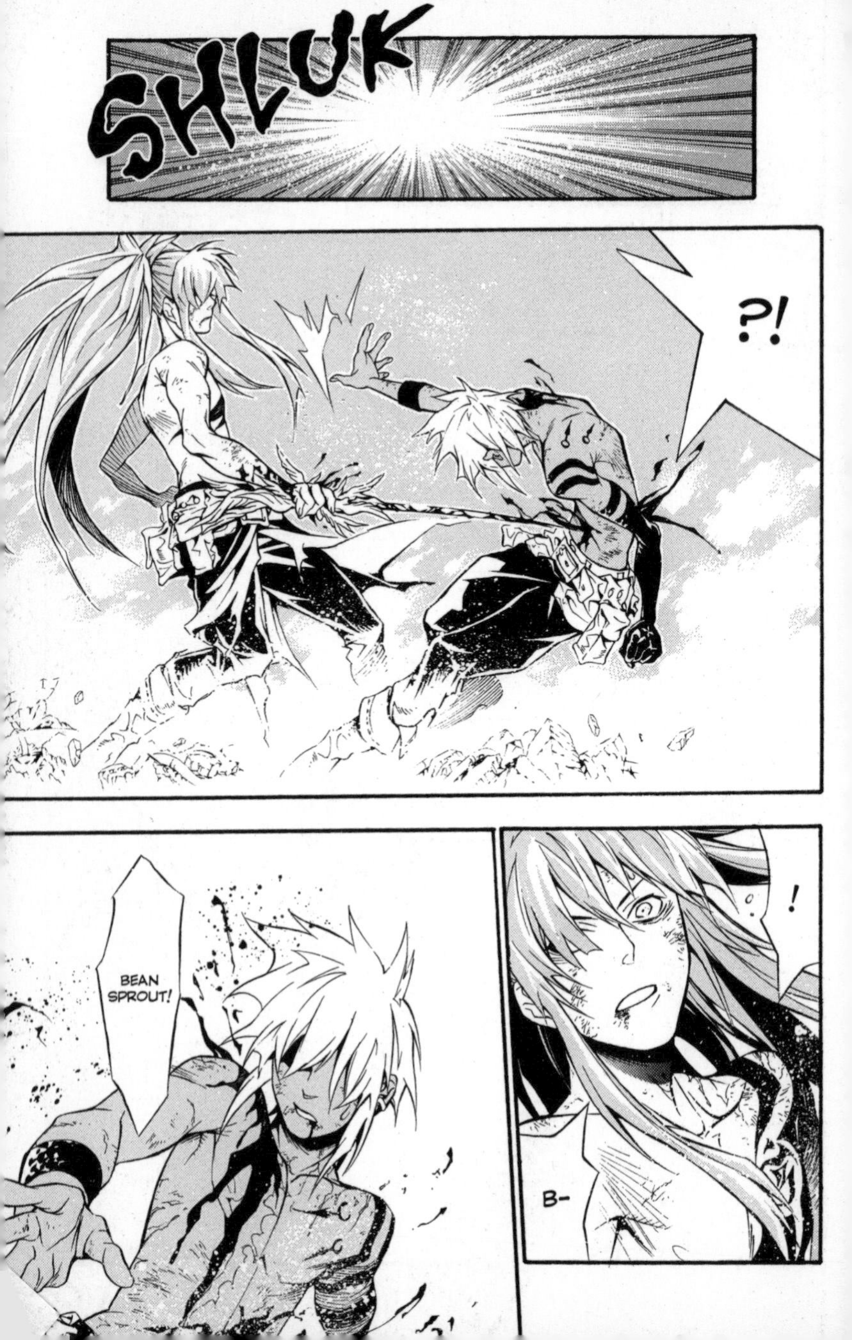
SHLUK
?!
!
B-
BEAN SPROUT!

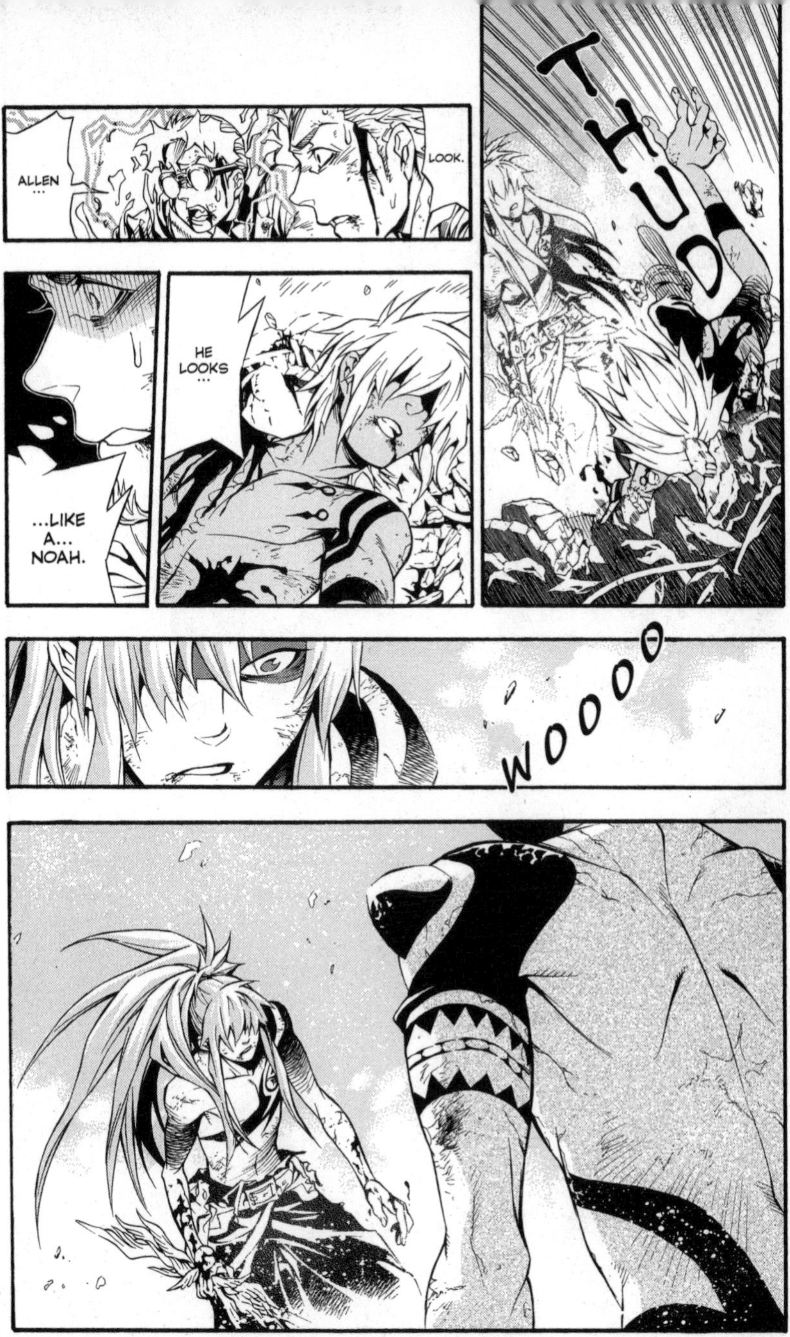
THUD
LOOK.
ALLEN ...
HE LOOKS ...
...LIKE A... NOAH.
WOOOO

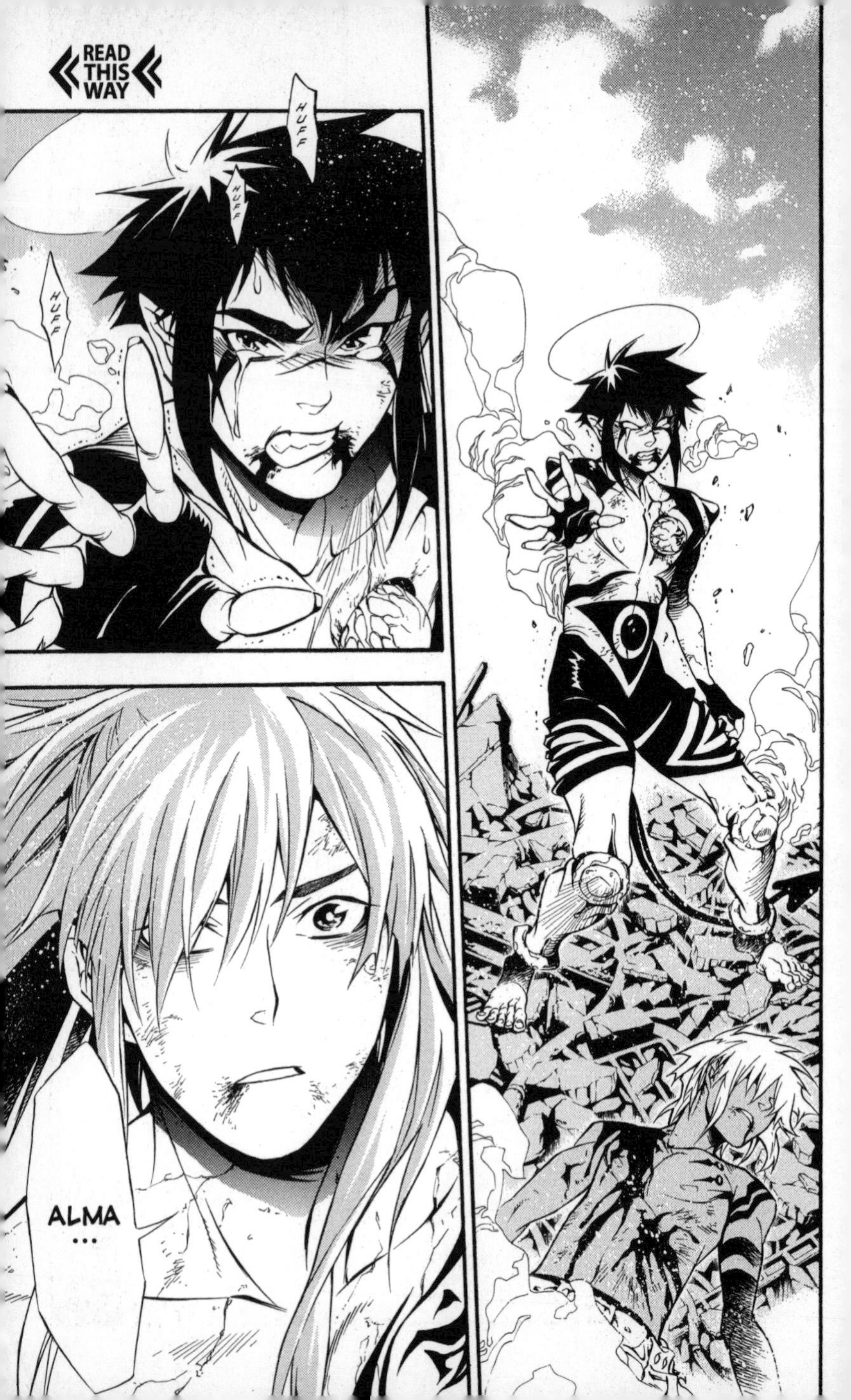
READ THIS WAY
HUFF
HUFF
HUFF
ALMA
...

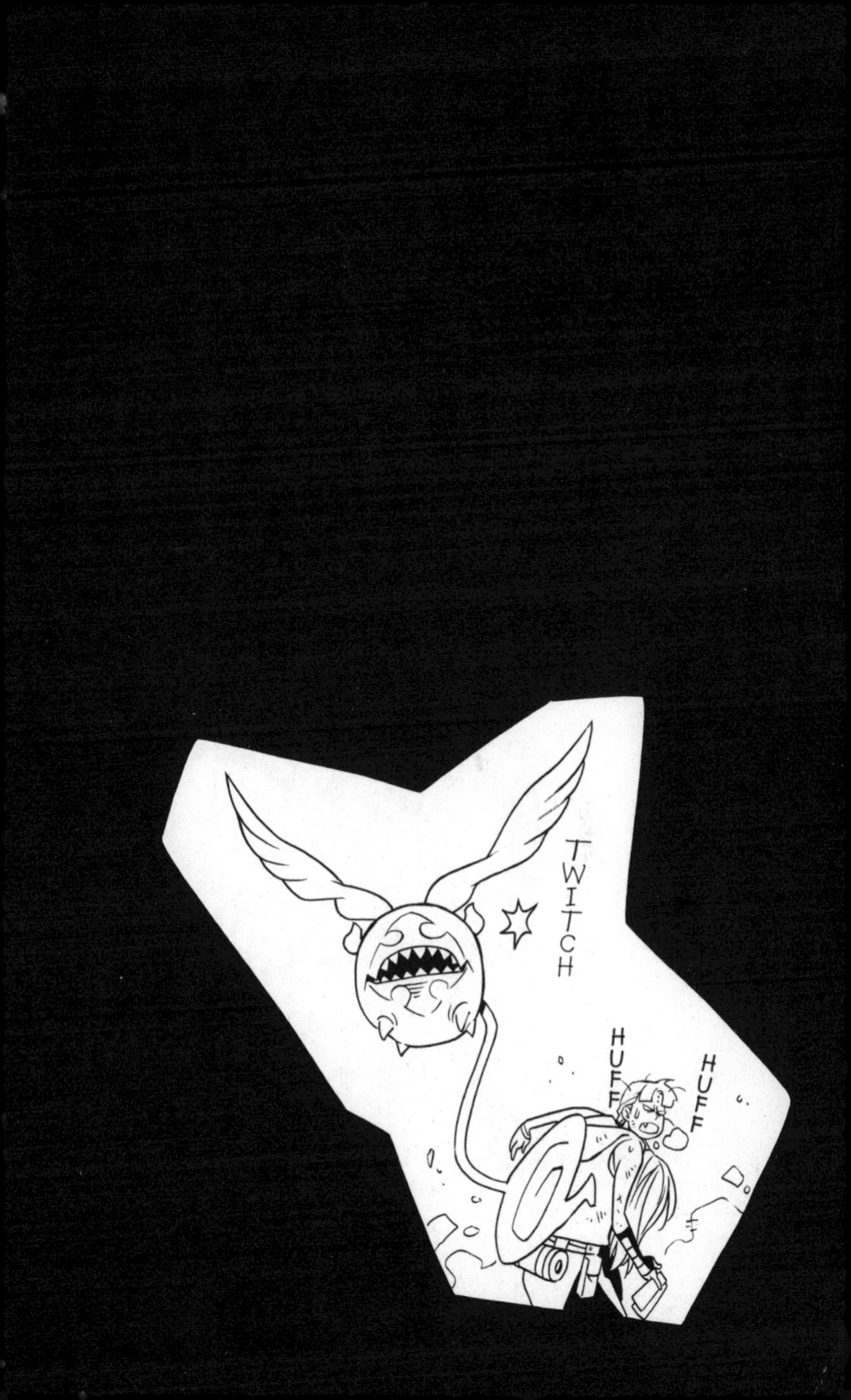
TWITCH
HUFF
HUFF

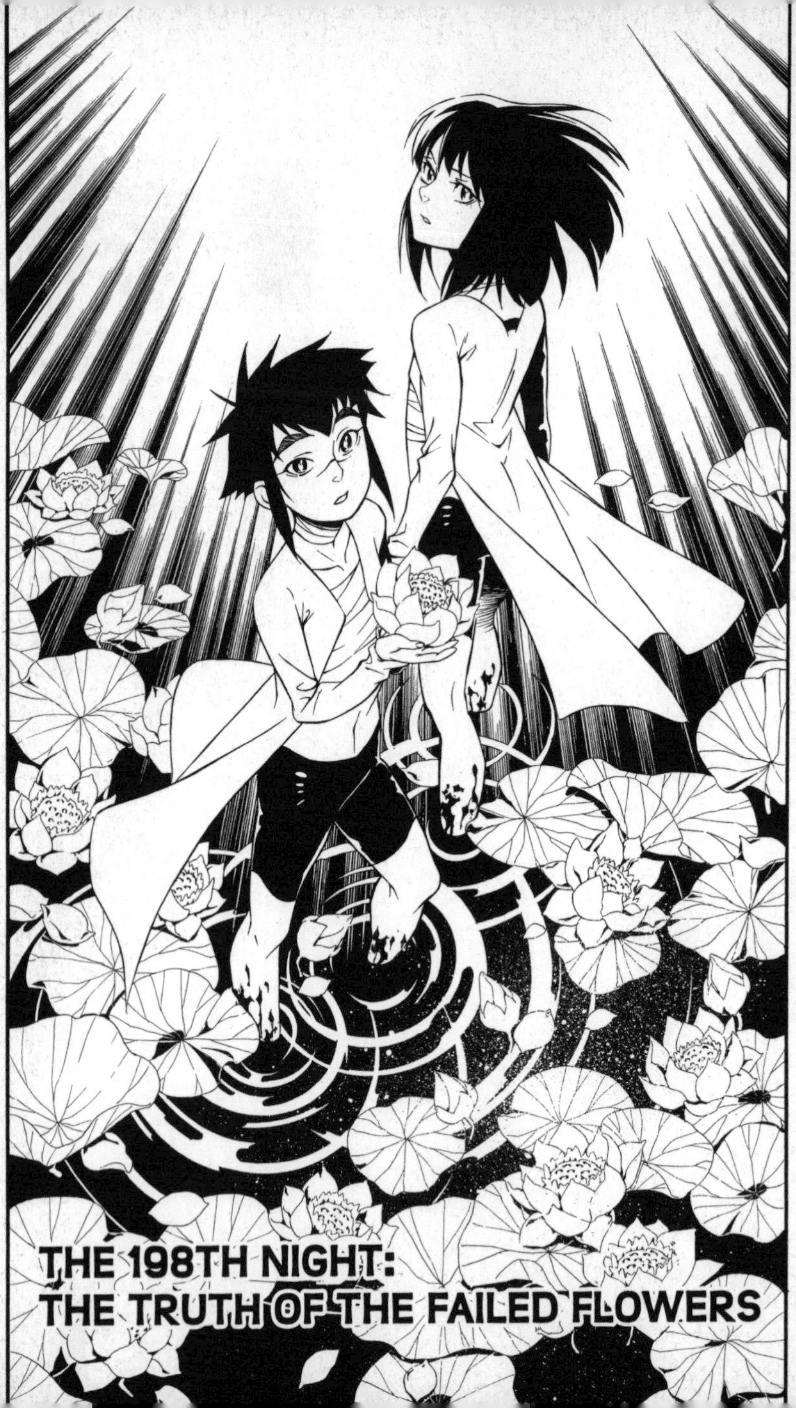
THE 198TH NIGHT:
THE TRUTH OF THE FAILED FLOWERS

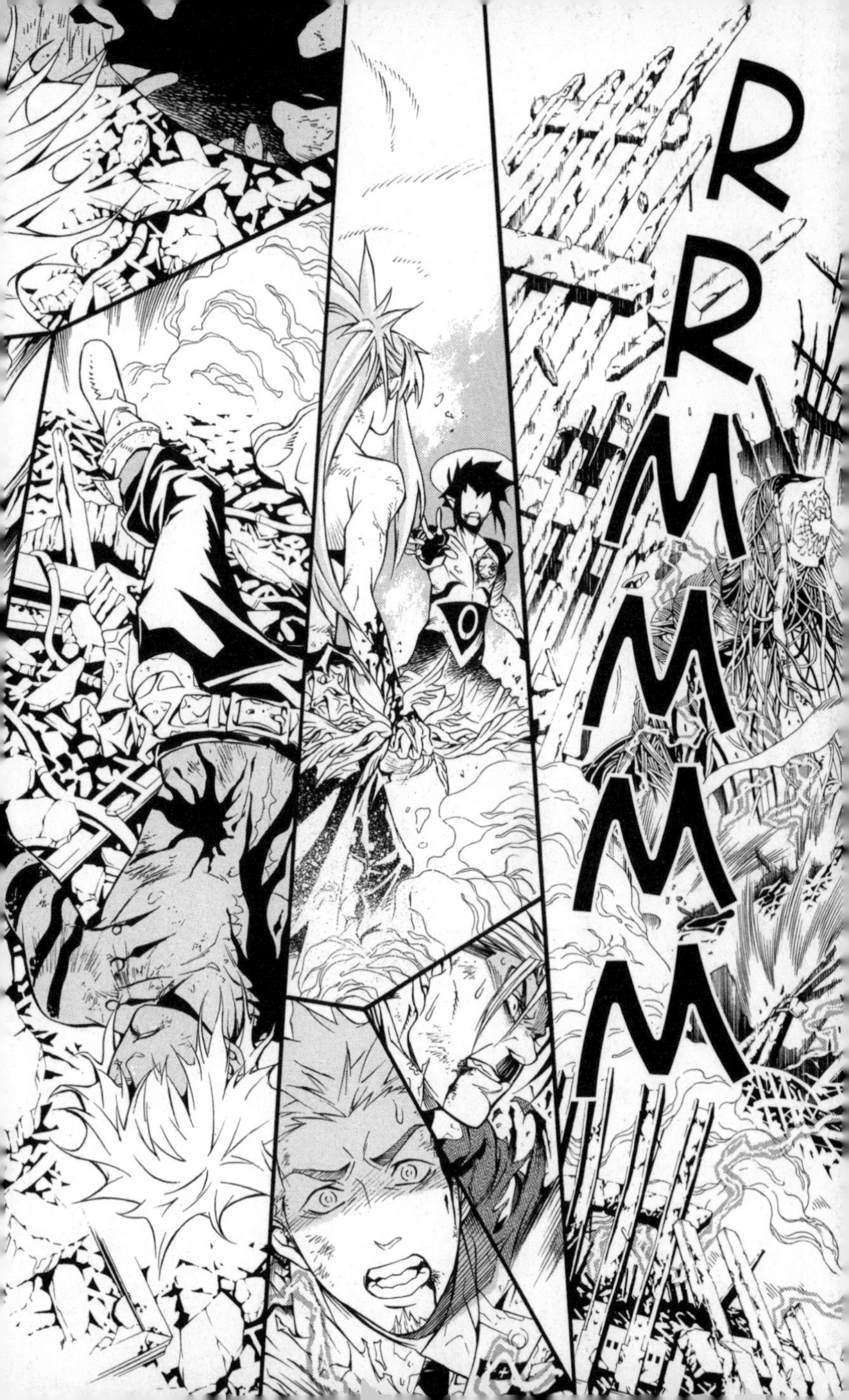
RRMMMMM

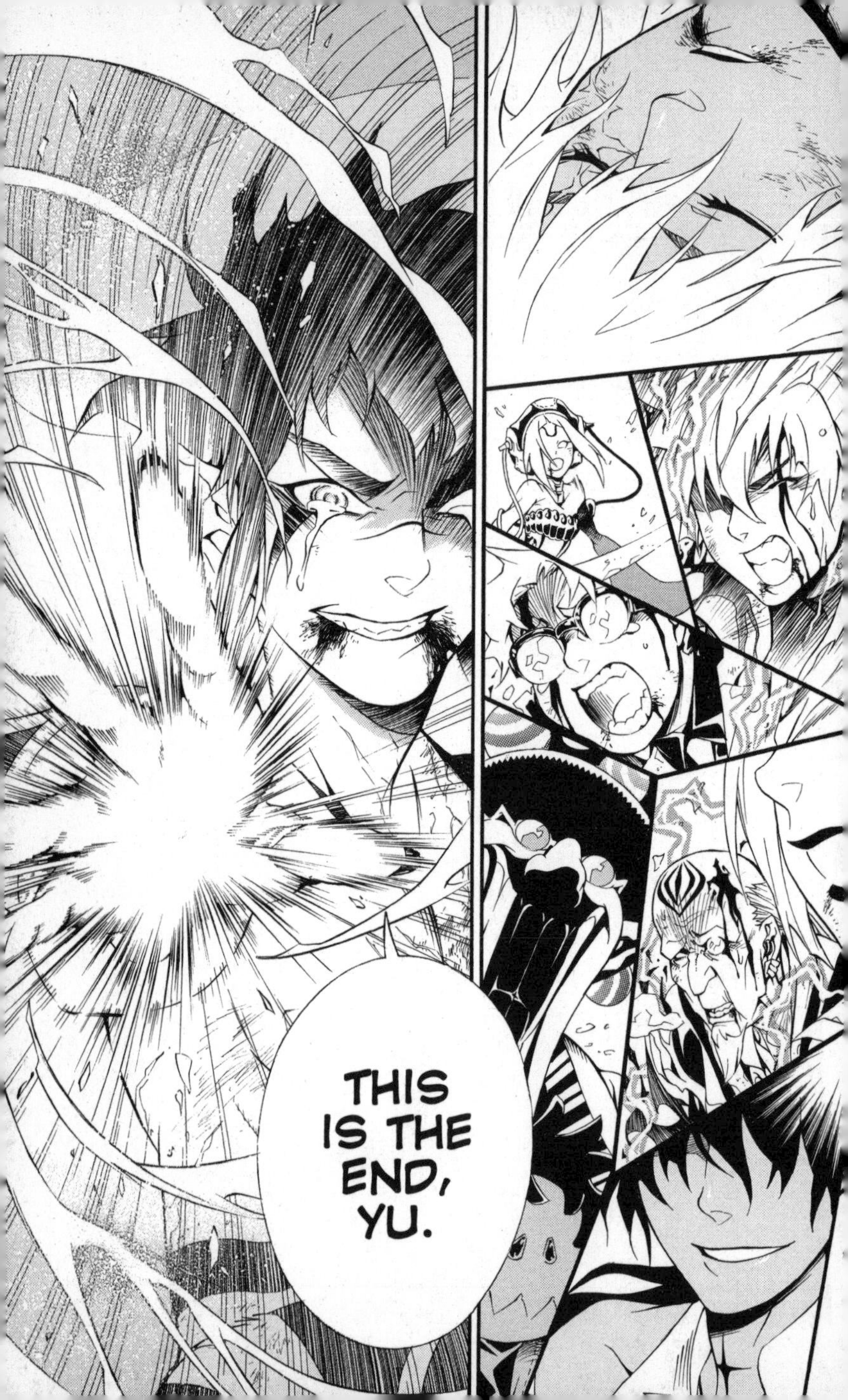
THIS IS THE END, YU.

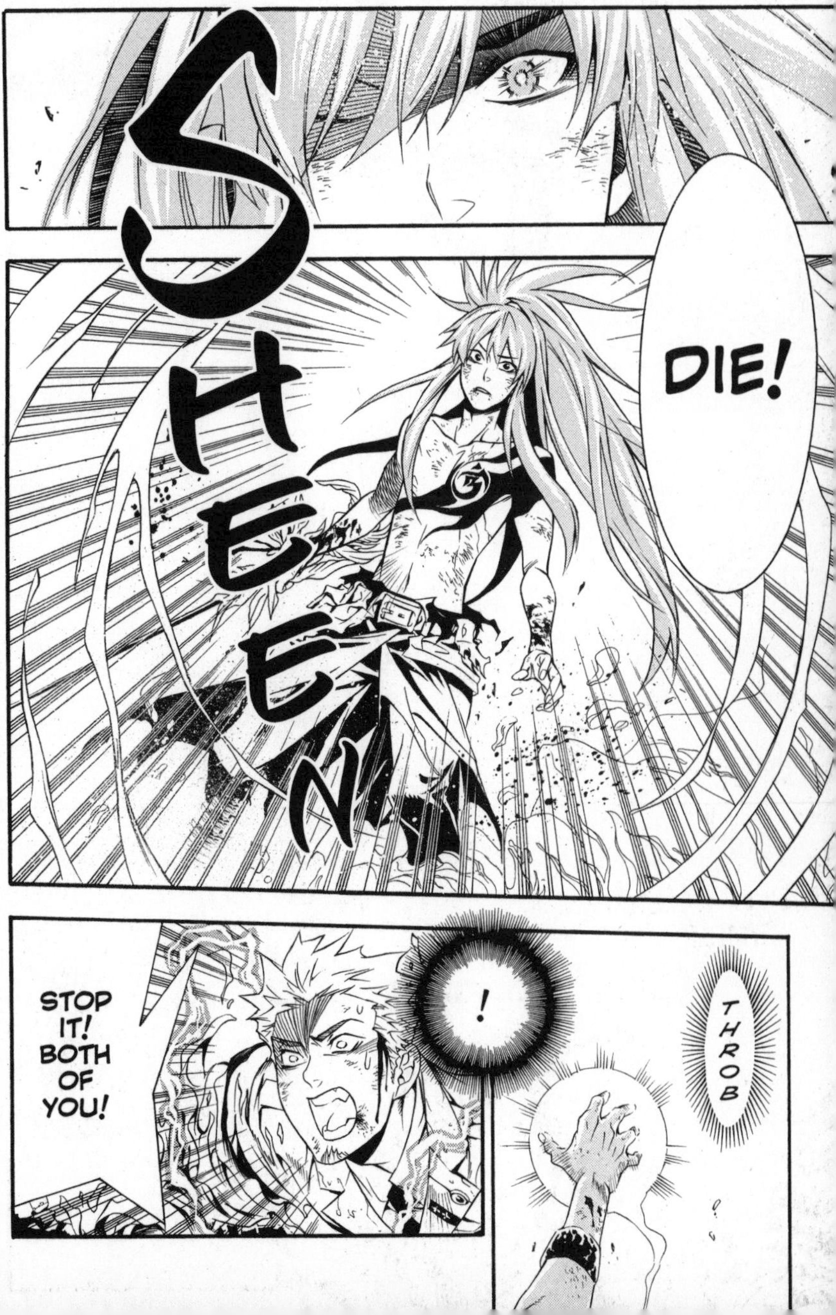
SHEEEN
DIE!
THROB
!
STOP IT! BOTH OF YOU!

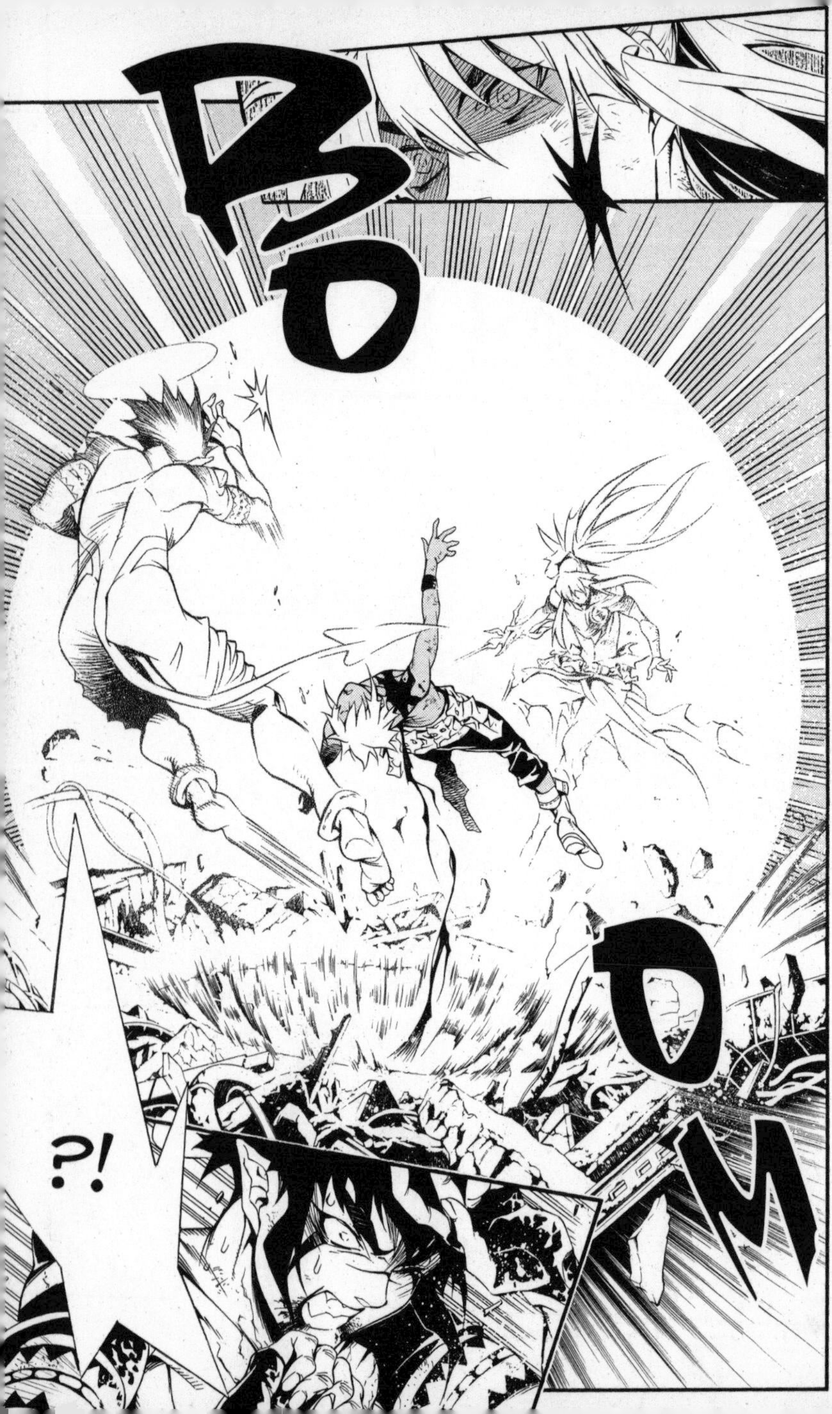
BADOOM
?!

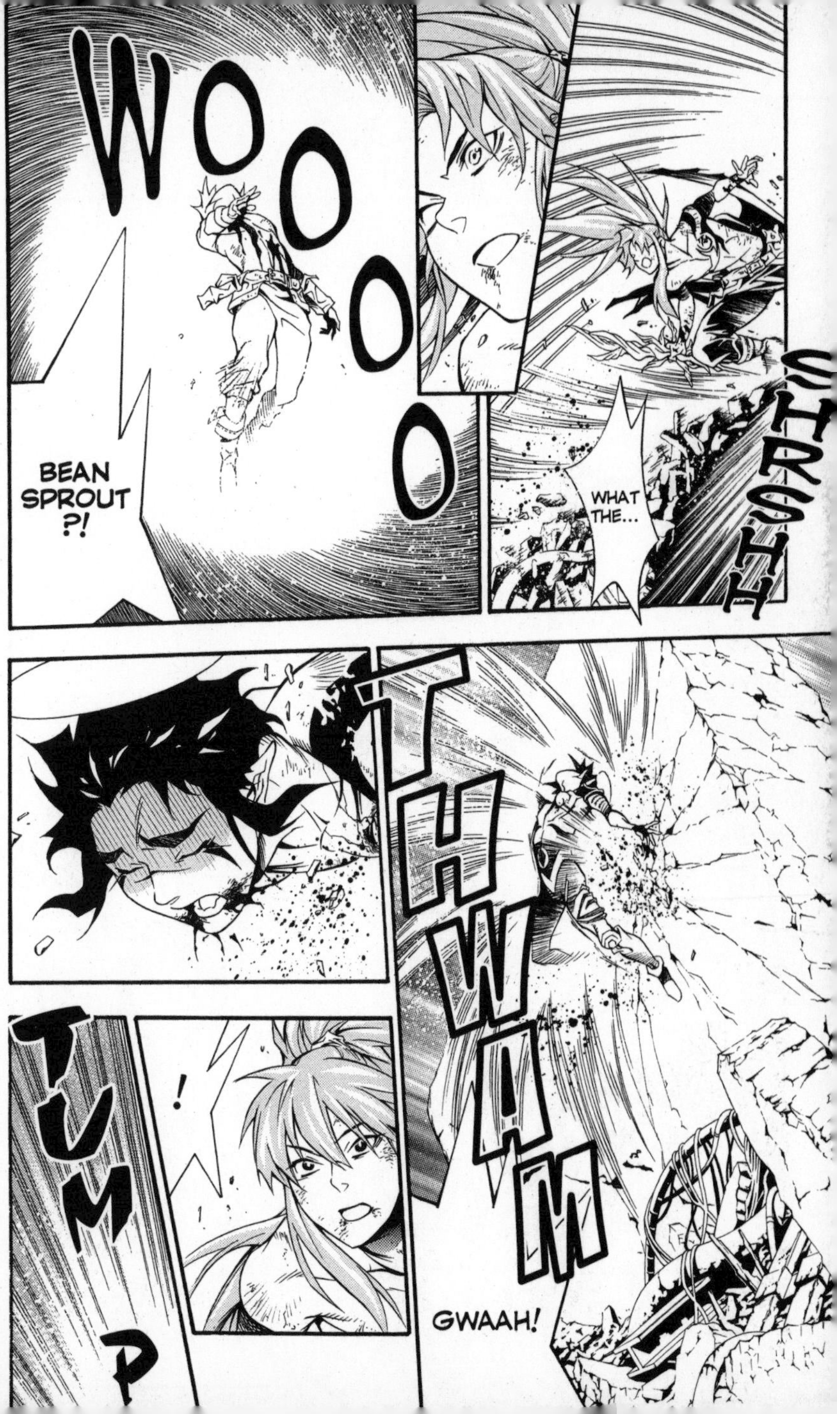
SHRSHH
WHAT THE...
WOOOO
BEAN SPROUT ?!
THWAM
GWAAH!
!
TUMP

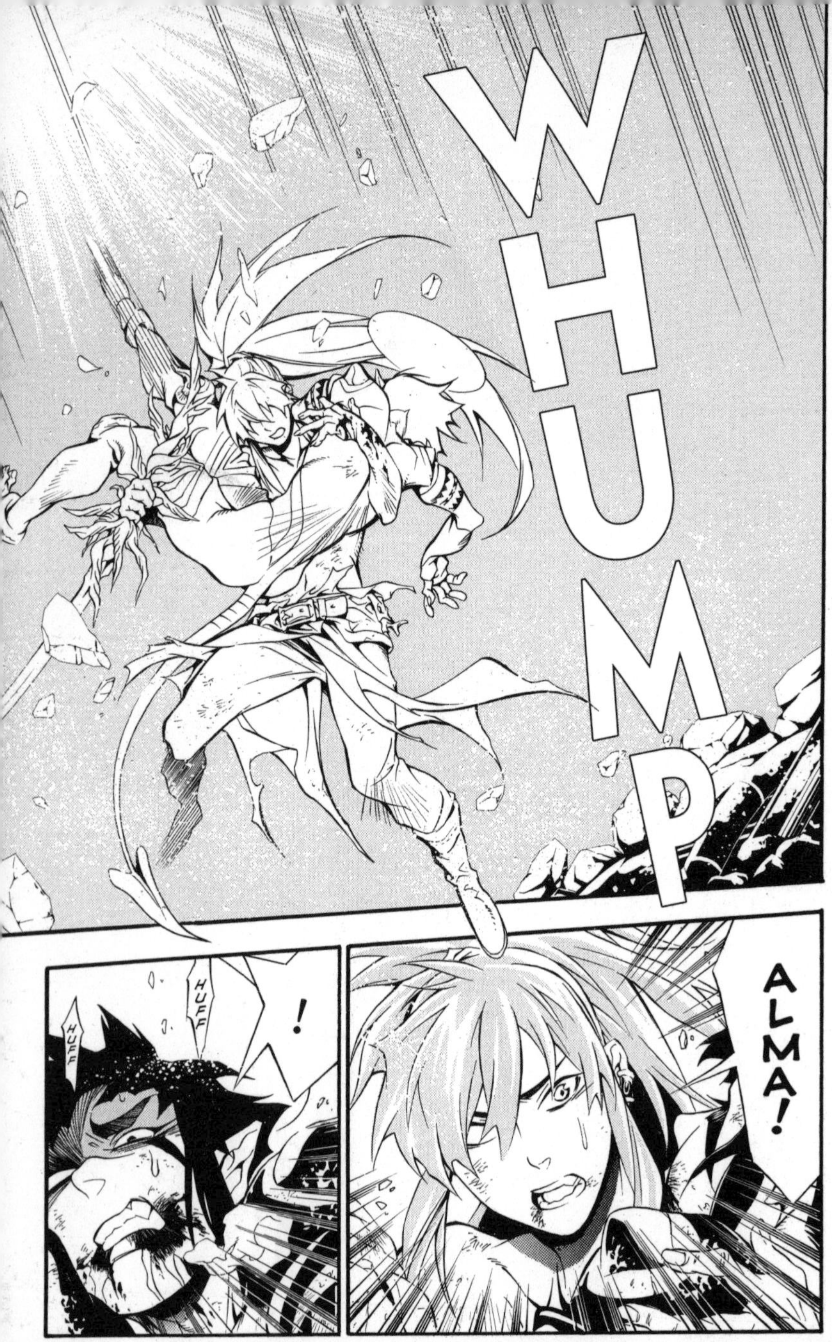
WHUMP
ALMA!
HUFF
HUFF
!

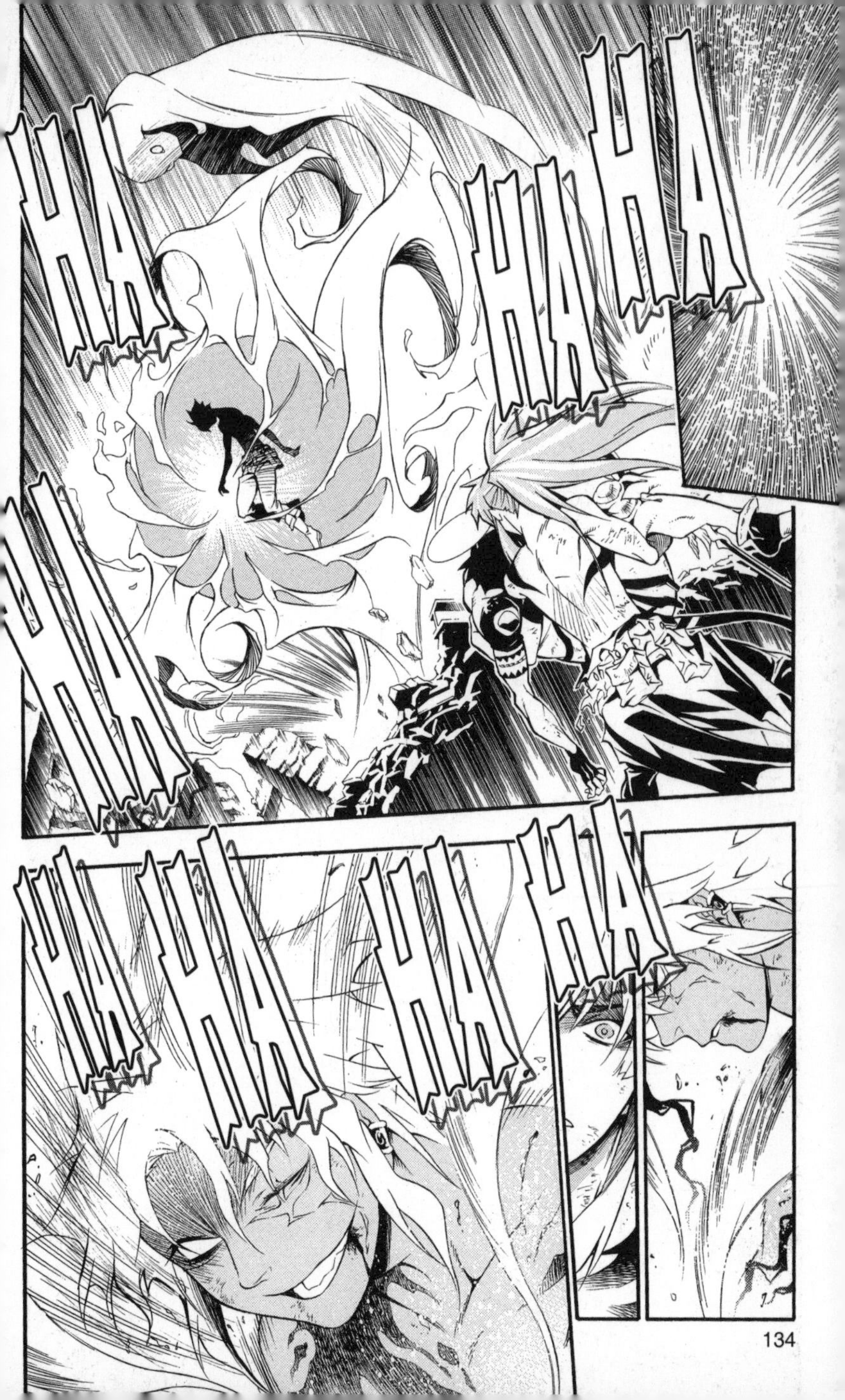
HA HA HA
HA
HA HA
HA HA HA
HA HA HA

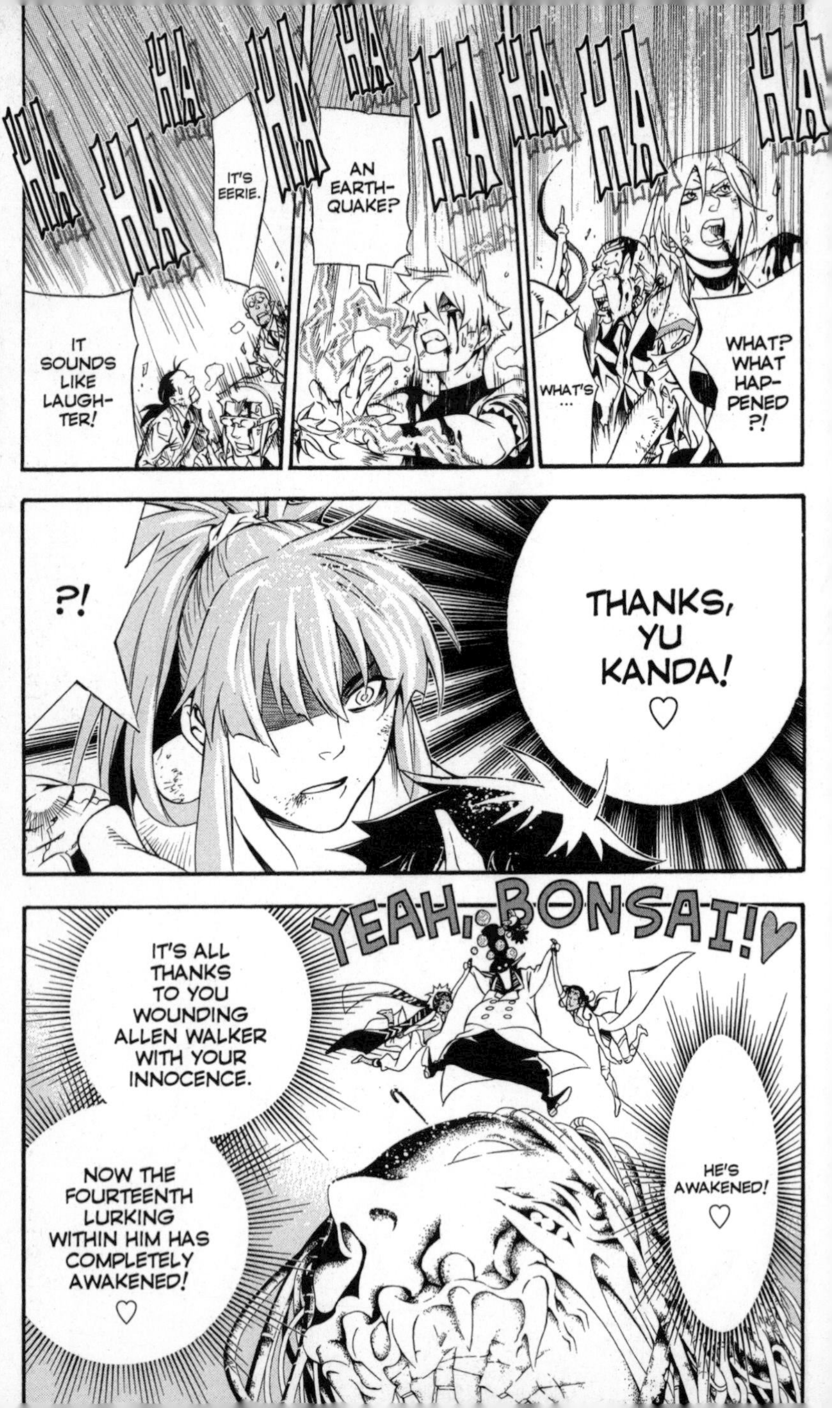
HA HA HA HA HA HA HA HA HA
WHAT? WHAT HAPPENED ?!
WHAT'S...
AN EARTH-QUAKE?
IT'S EERIE.
IT SOUNDS LIKE LAUGHTER!
THANKS, YU KANDA! ♡
?!
YEAH, BONSAI!♥
IT'S ALL THANKS TO YOU WOUNDING ALLEN WALKER WITH YOUR INNOCENCE.
NOW THE FOURTEENTH LURKING WITHIN HIM HAS COMPLETELY AWAKENED! ♡
HE'S AWAKENED! ♡

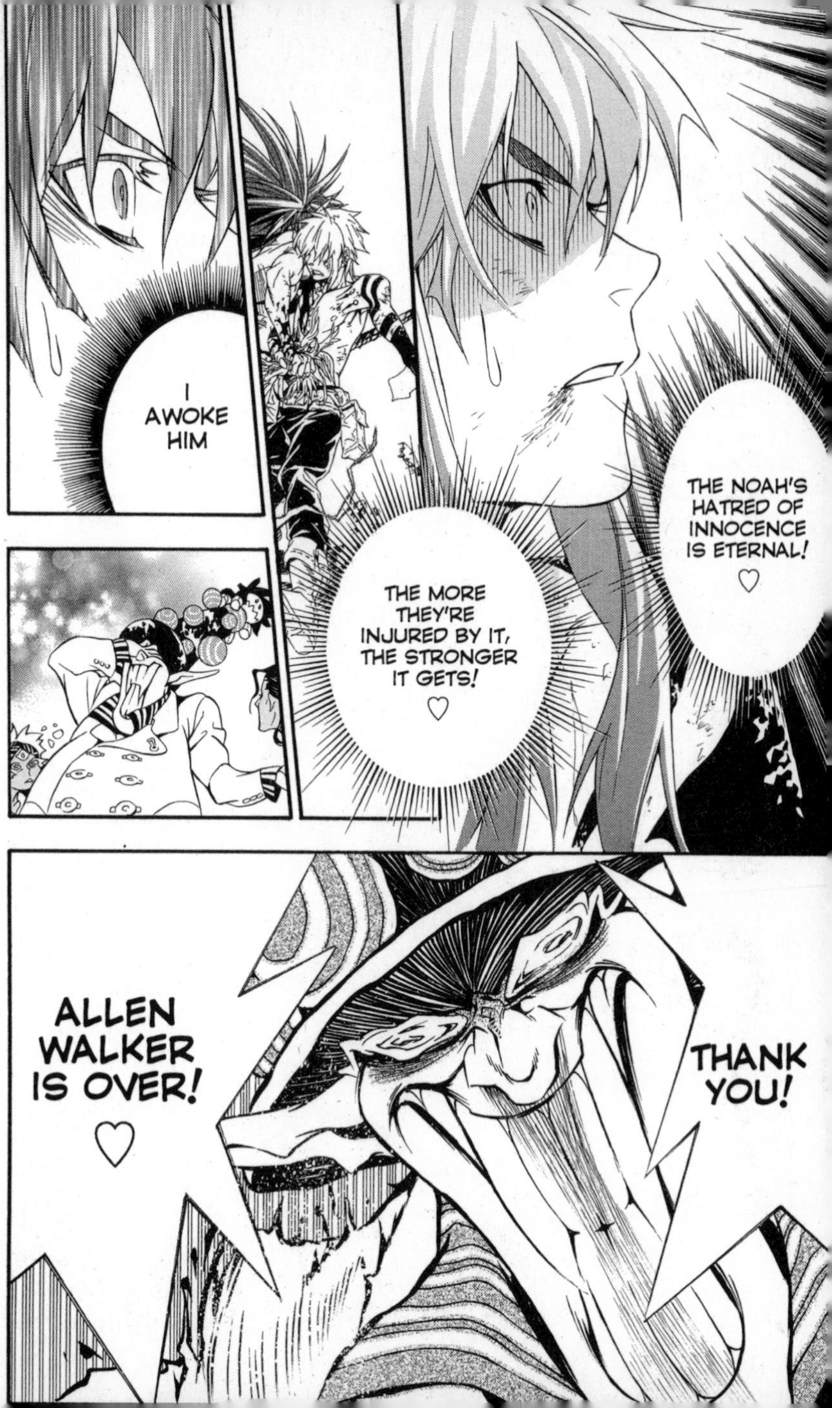
THE NOAH'S HATRED OF INNOCENCE IS ETERNAL! ♡
THE MORE THEY'RE INJURED BY IT, THE STRONGER IT GETS! ♡
I AWOKE HIM
THANK YOU!
ALLEN WALKER IS OVER! ♡

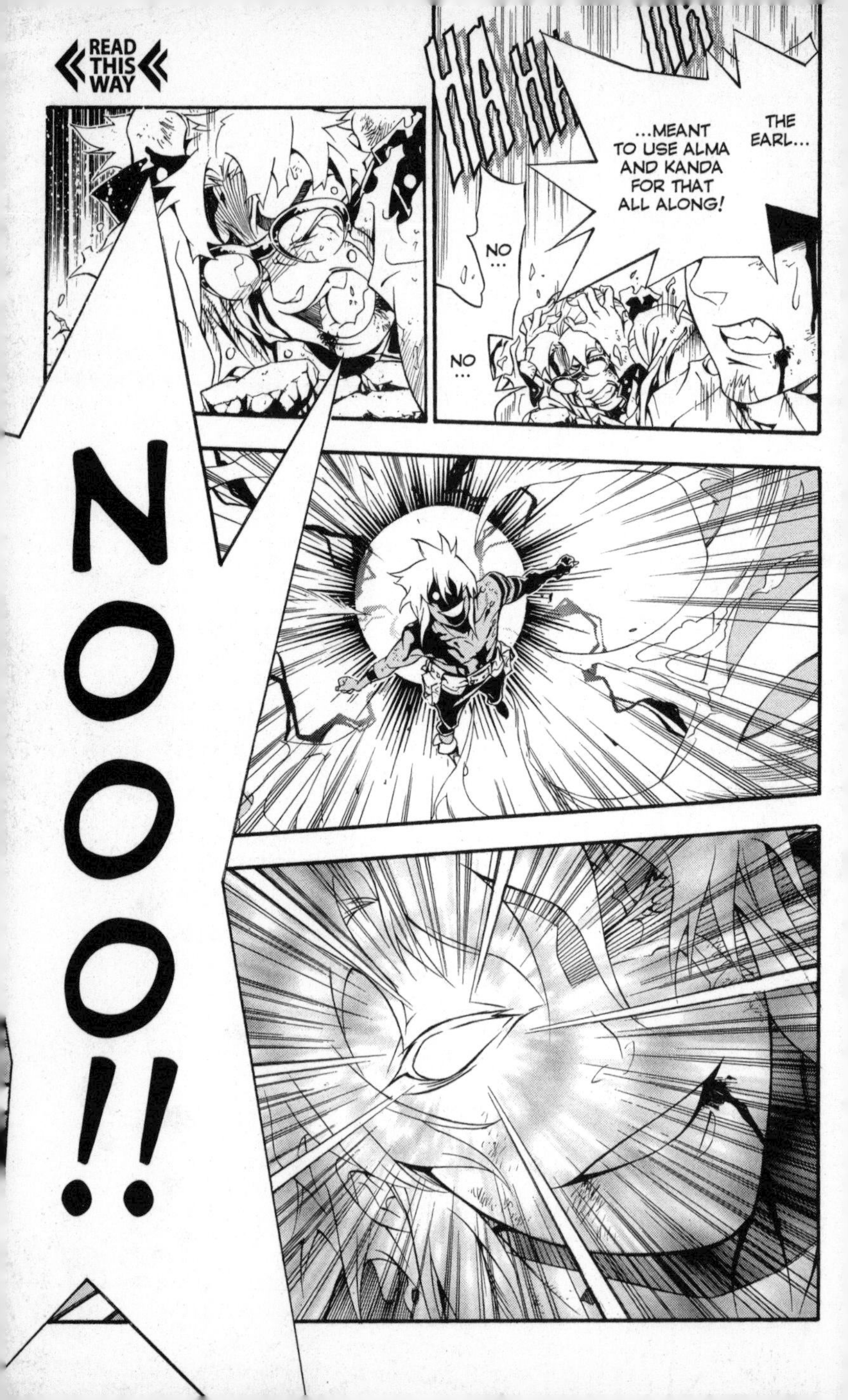
READ THIS WAY
HAHAHA
THE EARL...
...MEANT TO USE ALMA AND KANDA FOR THAT ALL ALONG!
NO...
NO...
NOOOO!!

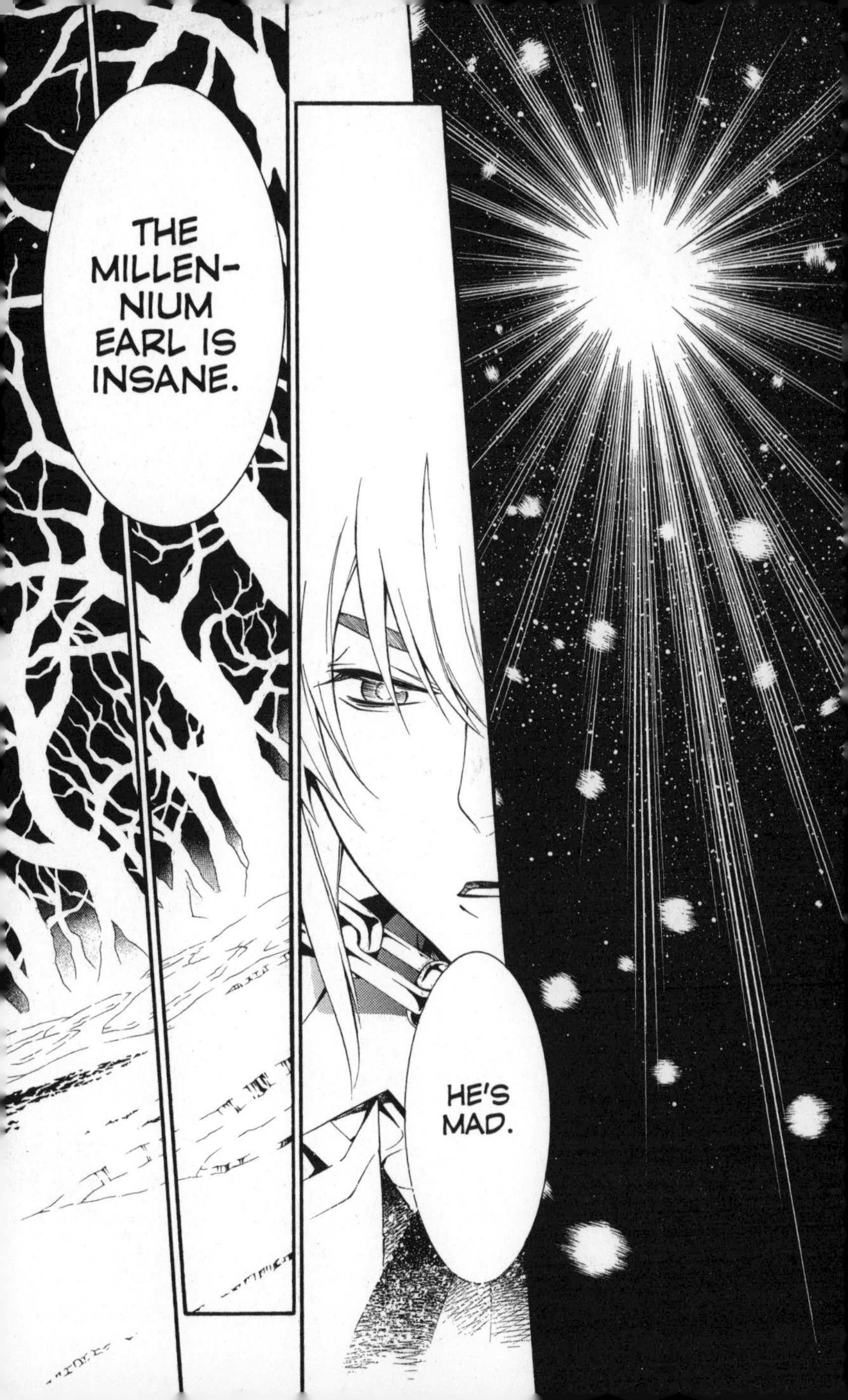
HE'S MAD.
THE MILLEN-NIUM EARL IS INSANE.

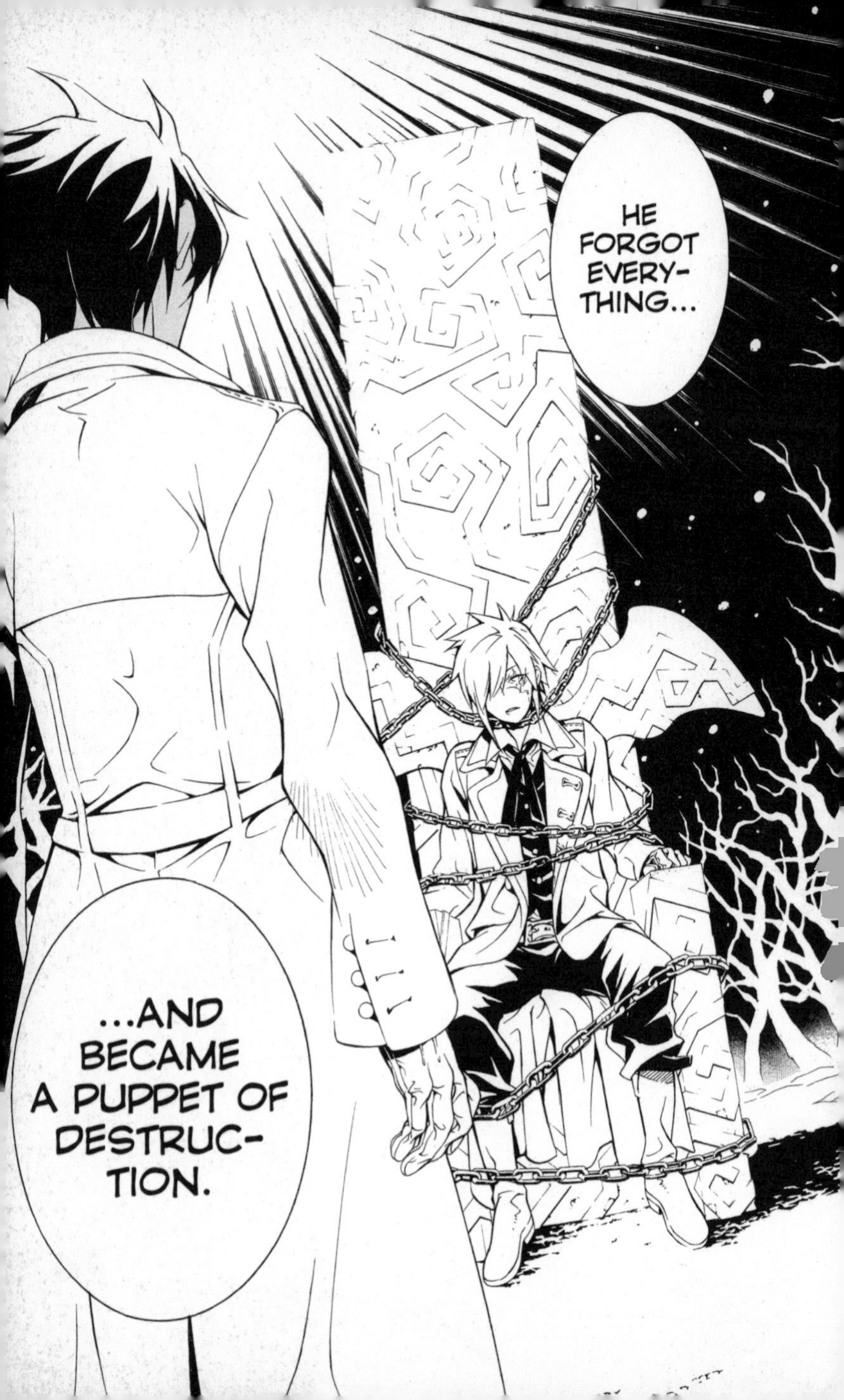
HE FORGOT EVERY-THING...
...AND BECAME A PUPPET OF DESTRUC-TION.

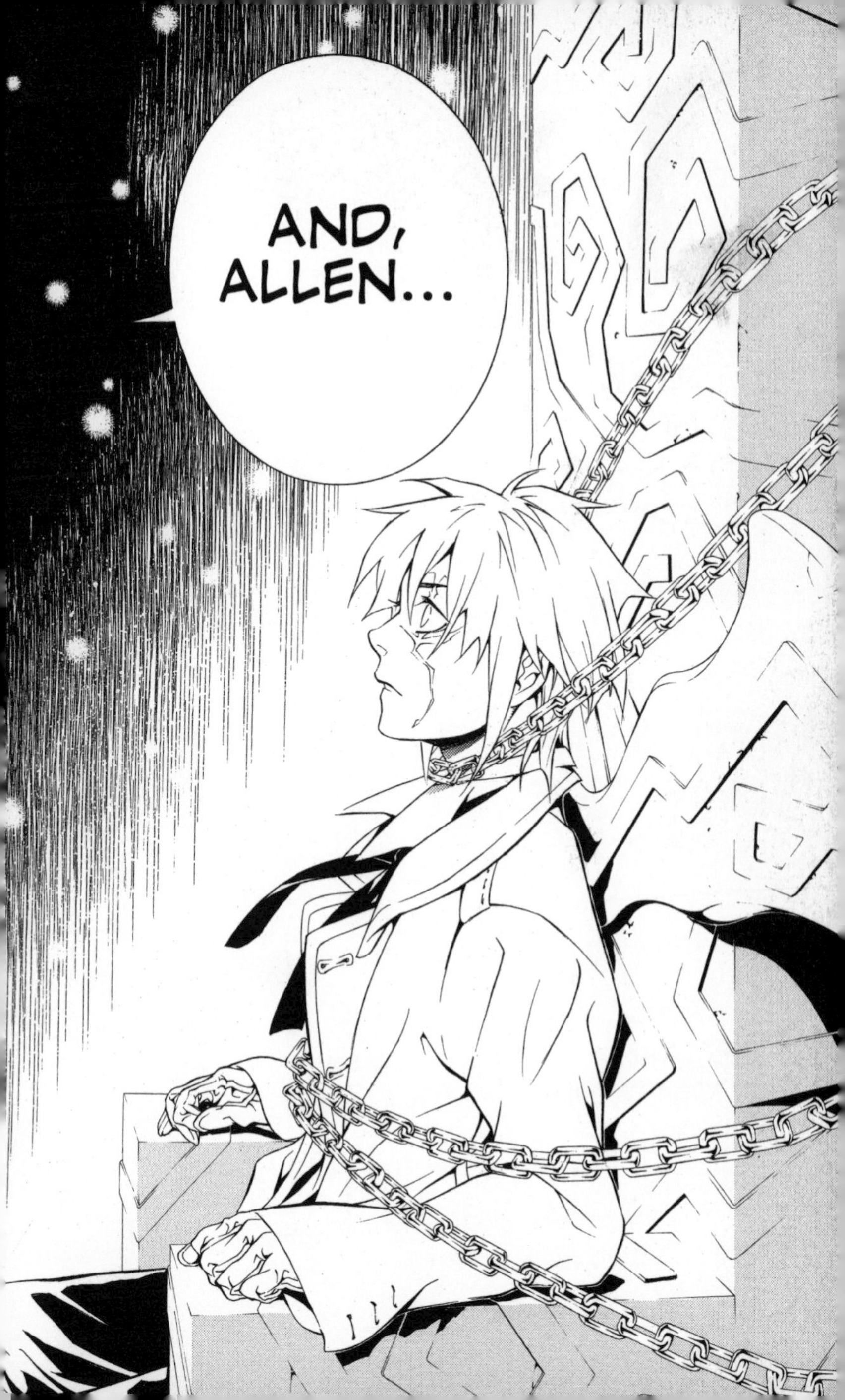
AND, ALLEN...

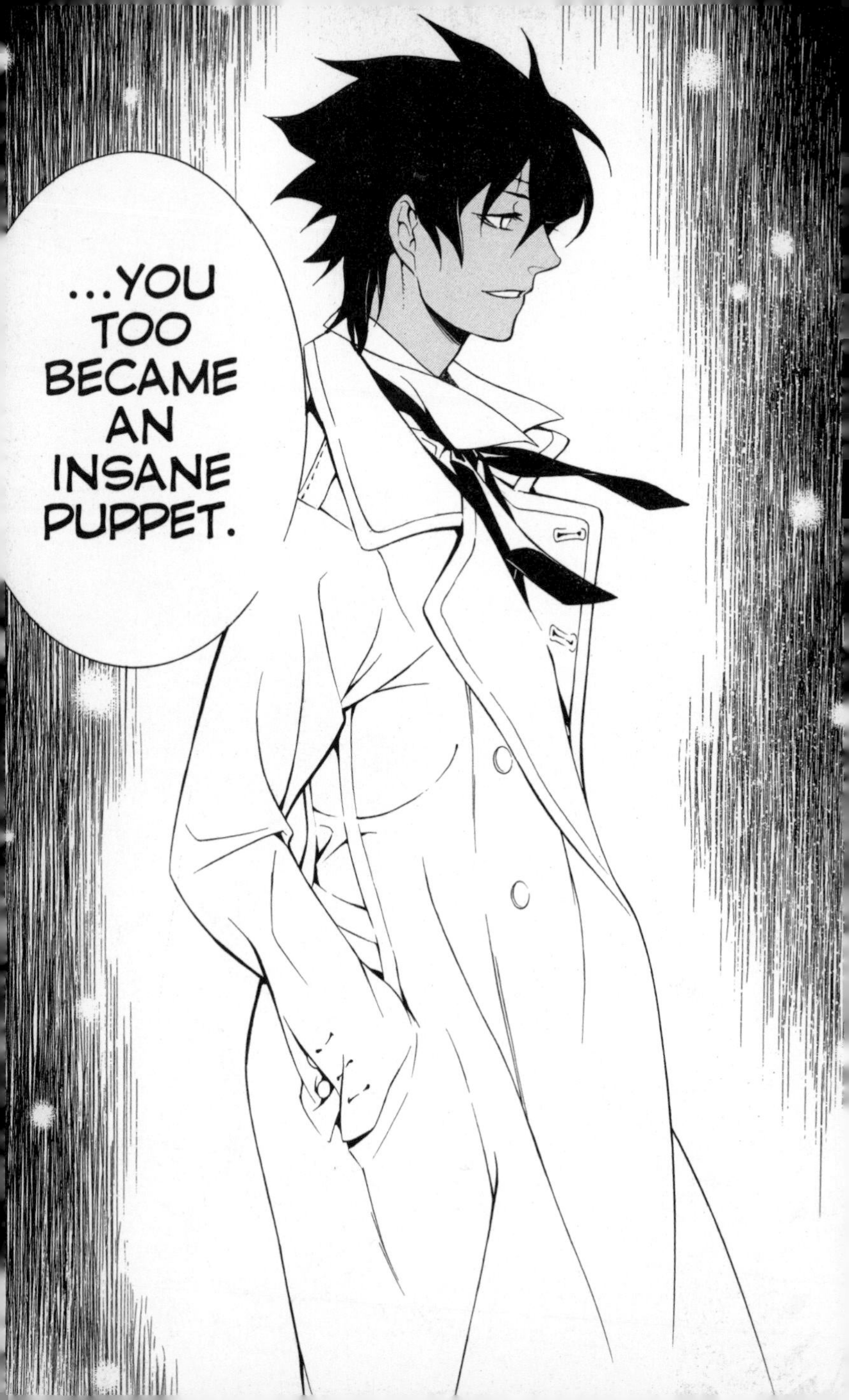
...YOU TOO BECAME AN INSANE PUPPET.

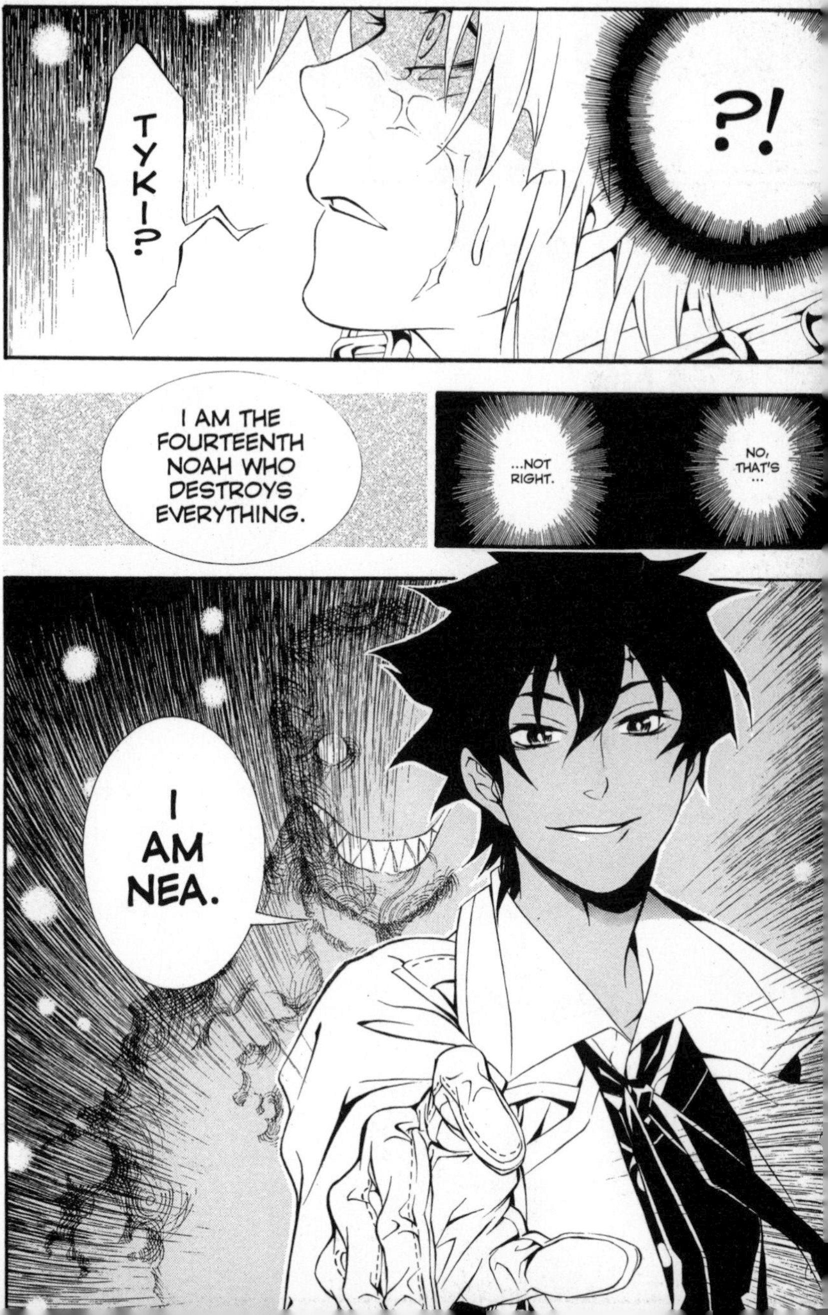
?!
TYKI?
NO, THAT'S ...
...NOT RIGHT.
I AM THE FOURTEENTH NOAH WHO DESTROYS EVERYTHING.
I AM NEA.

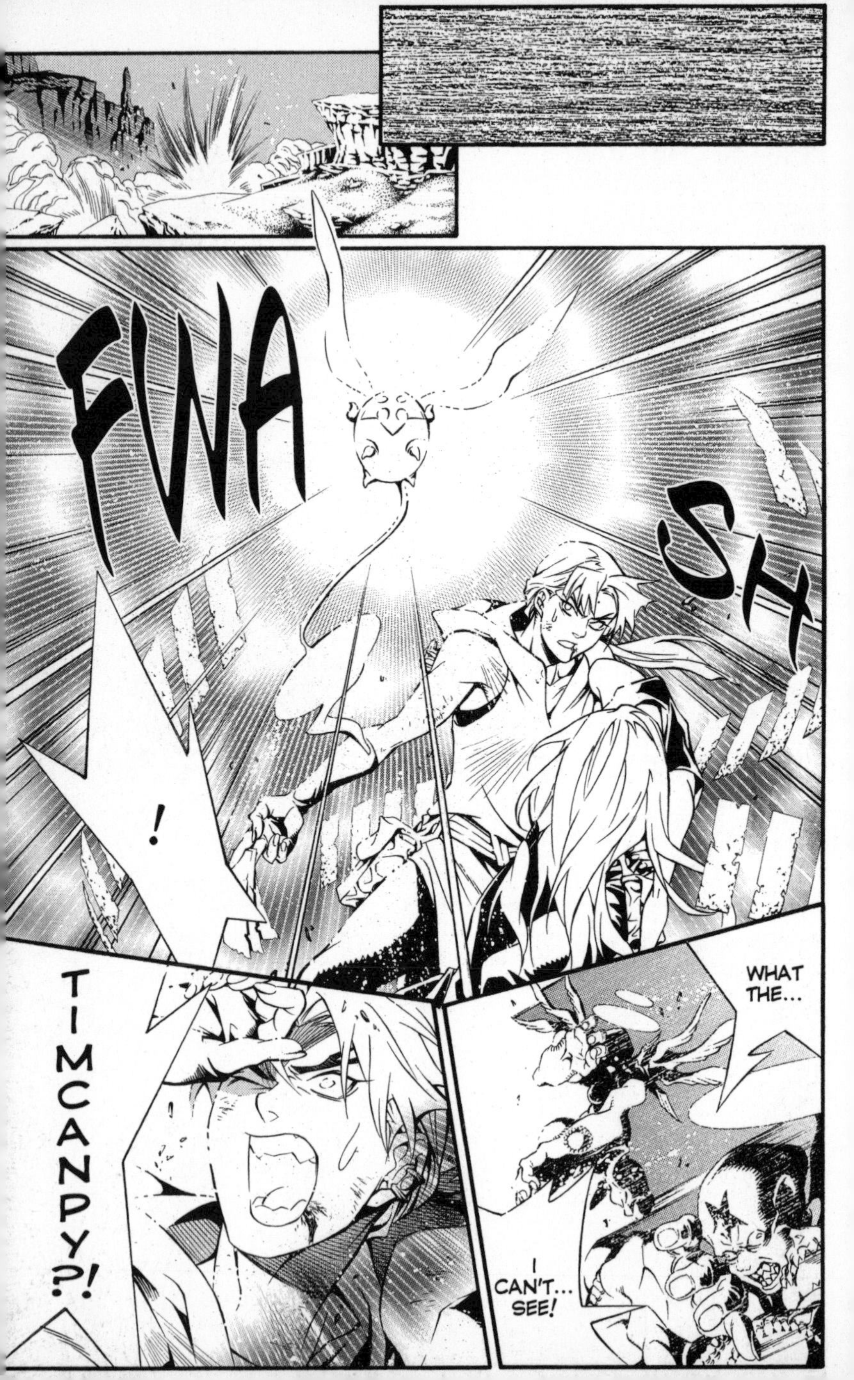
FWA
SH
!
WHAT THE...
I CAN'T... SEE!
TIMCANPY?!

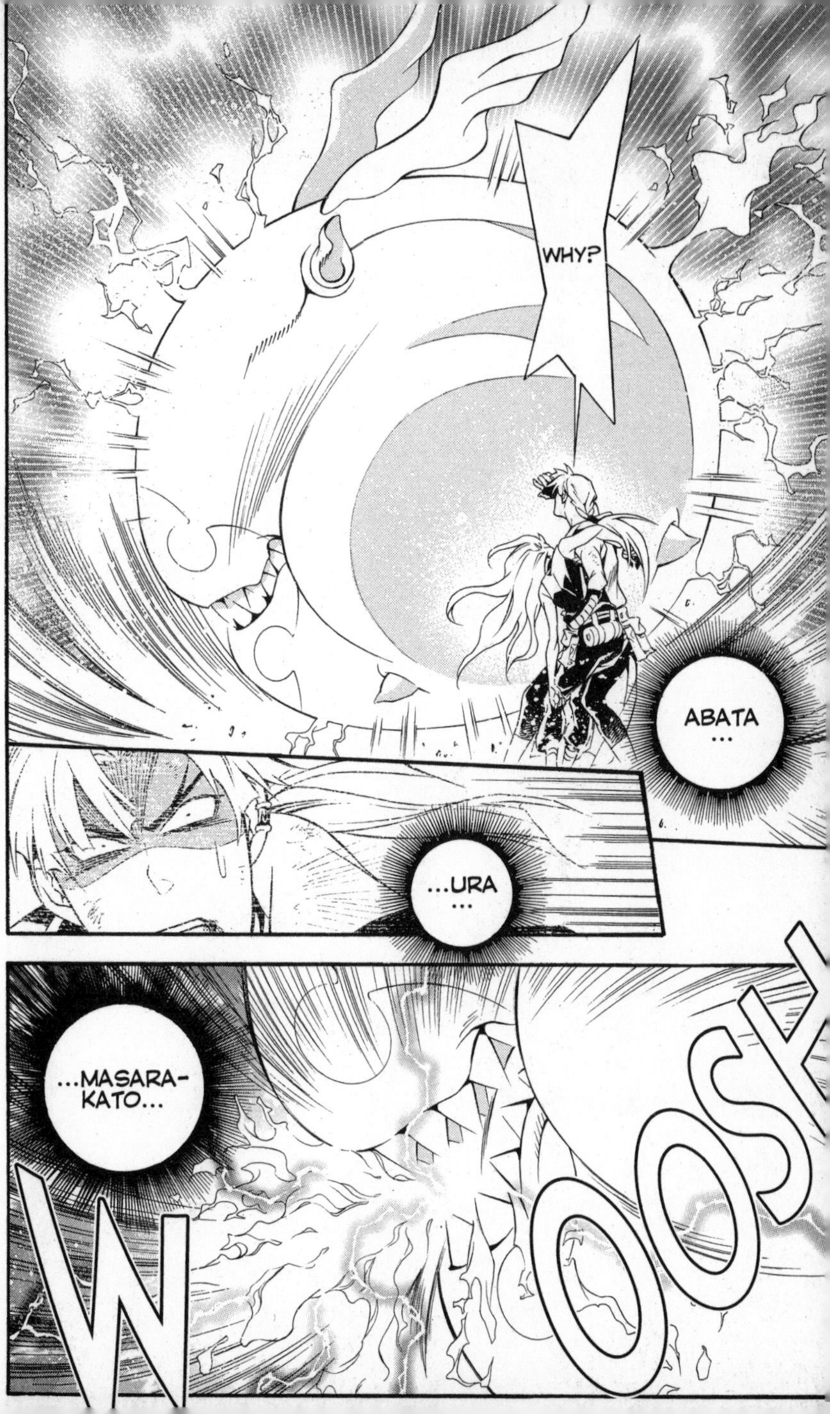
WHY?
ABATA ...
...URA ...
...MASARA-KATO...
WHOOSH

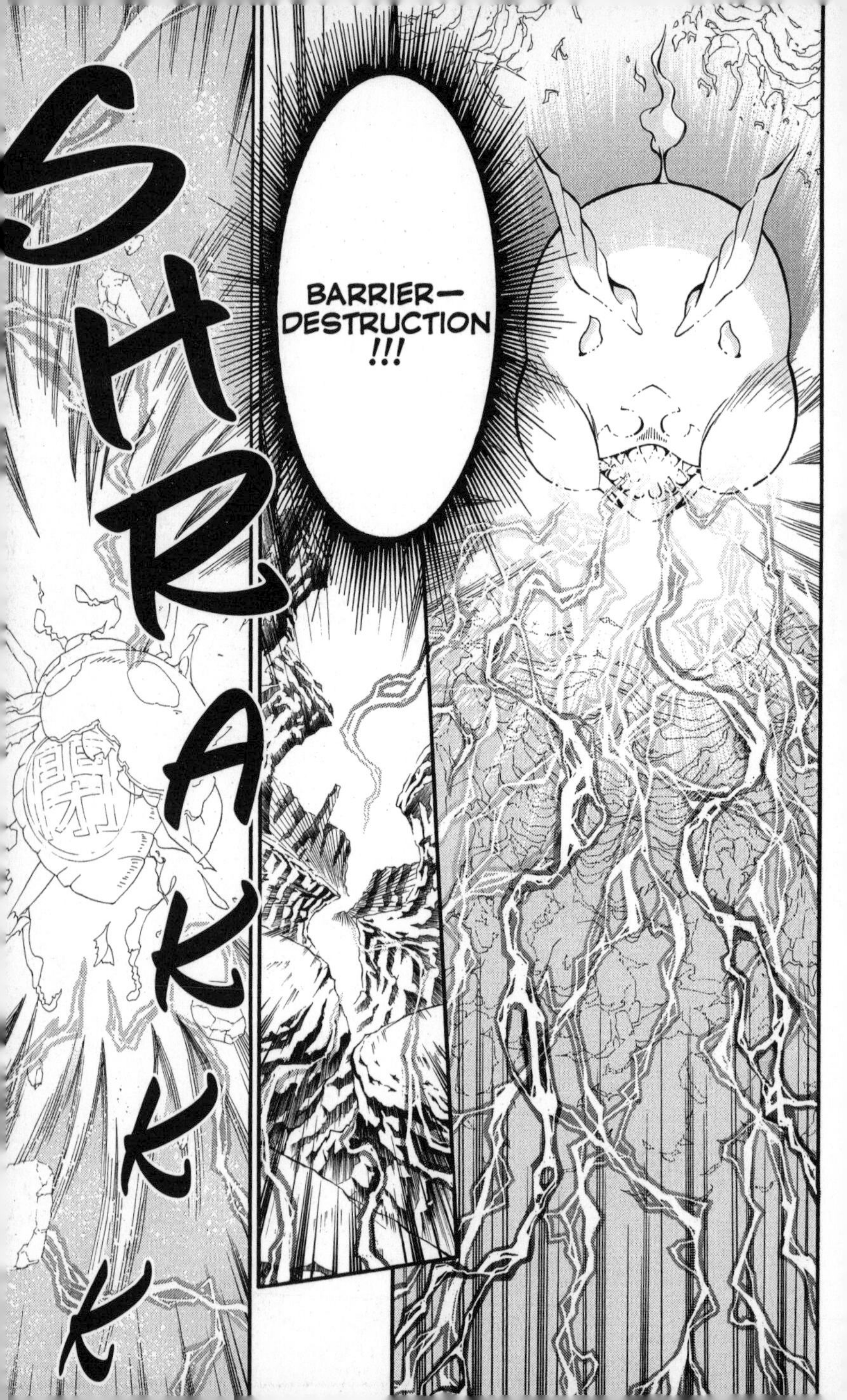
BARRIER-DESTRUCTION !!!
SHRAKKKK

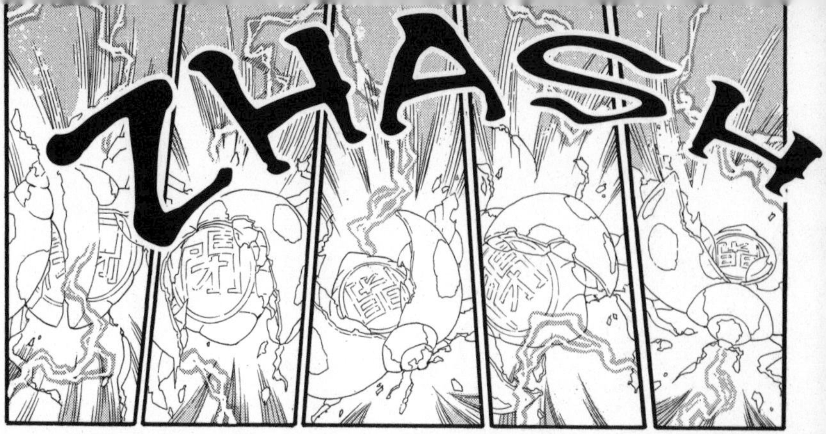
ZHASH
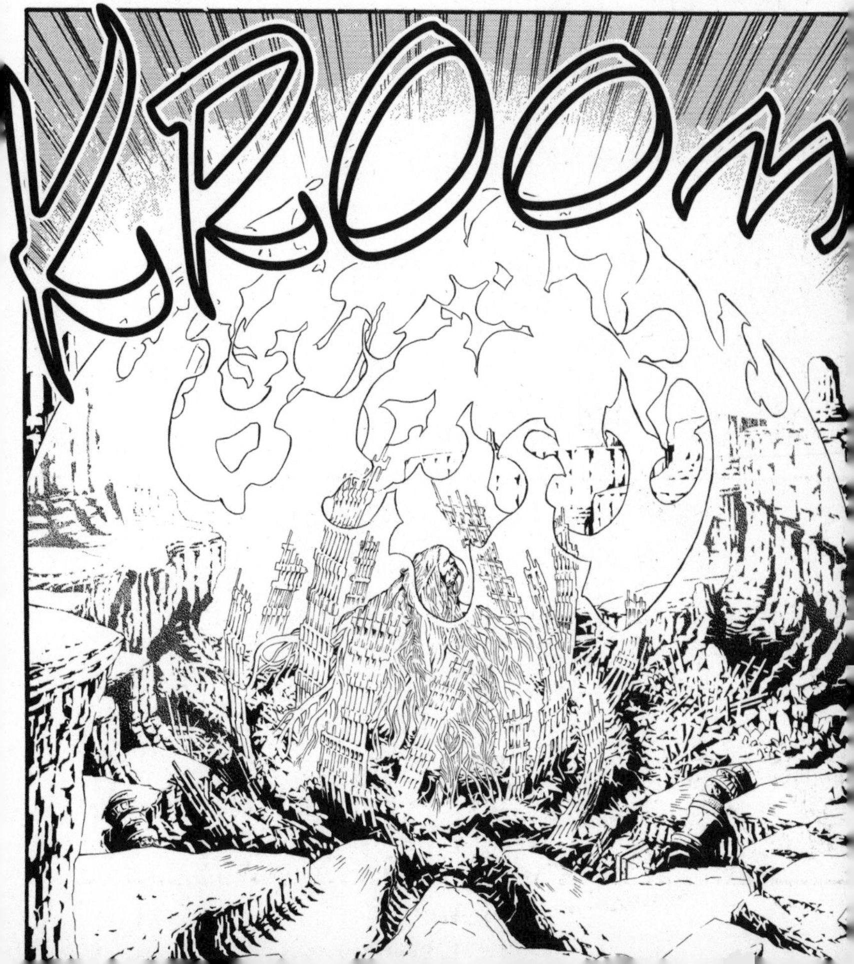
KROOM

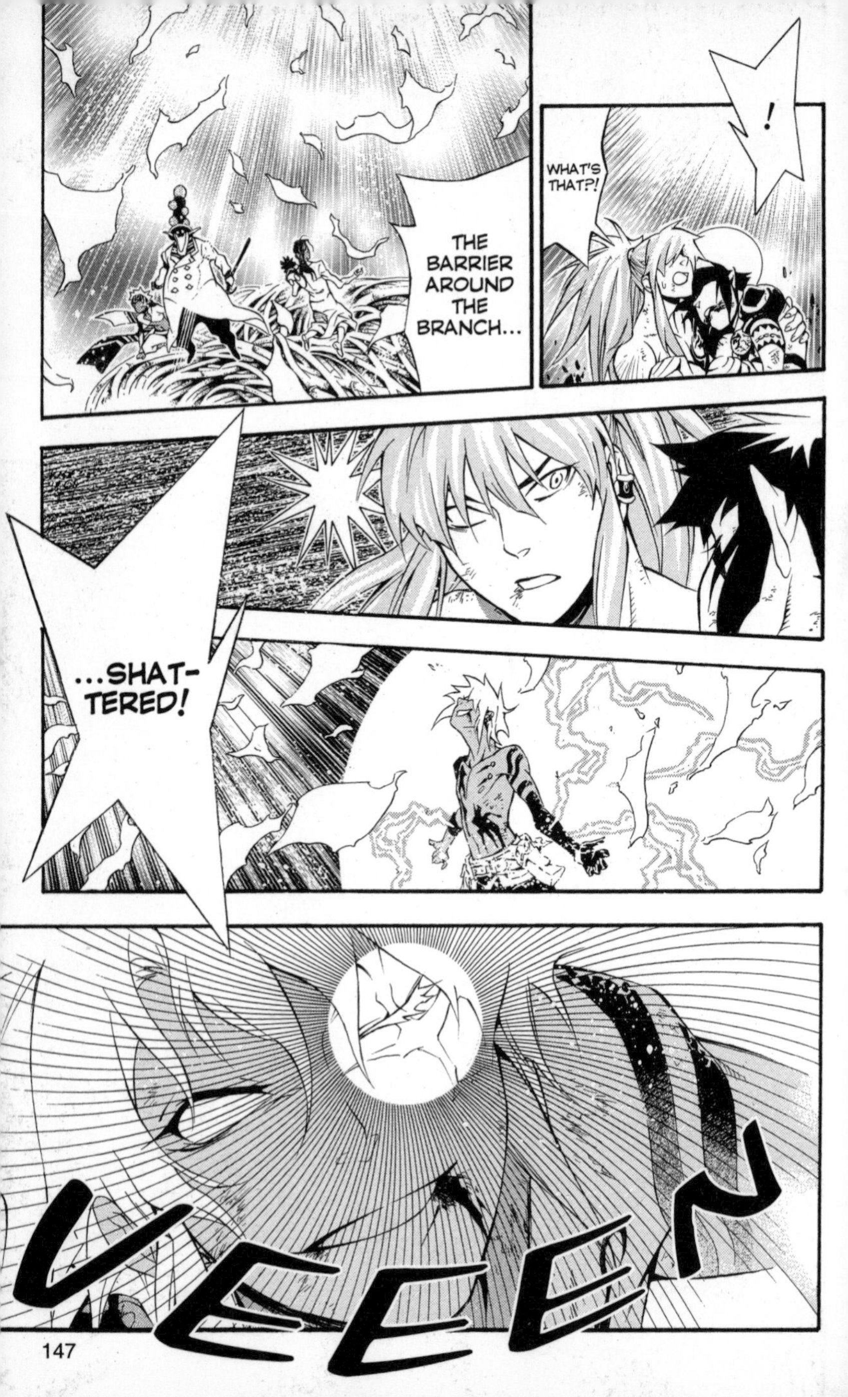
!
WHAT'S THAT?!
THE BARRIER AROUND THE BRANCH...
...SHAT-TERED!
VEEEN

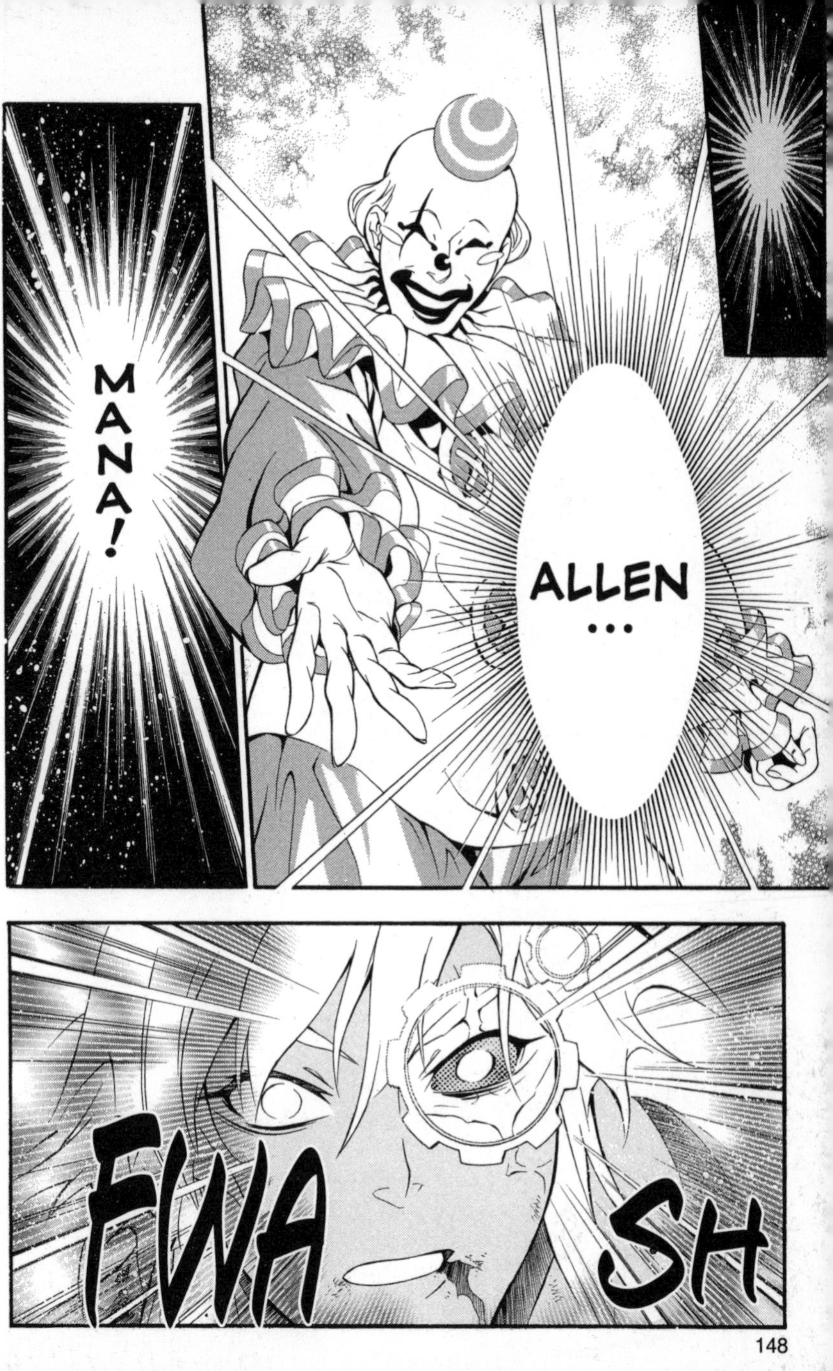
ALLEN ...
MANA!
FWASH

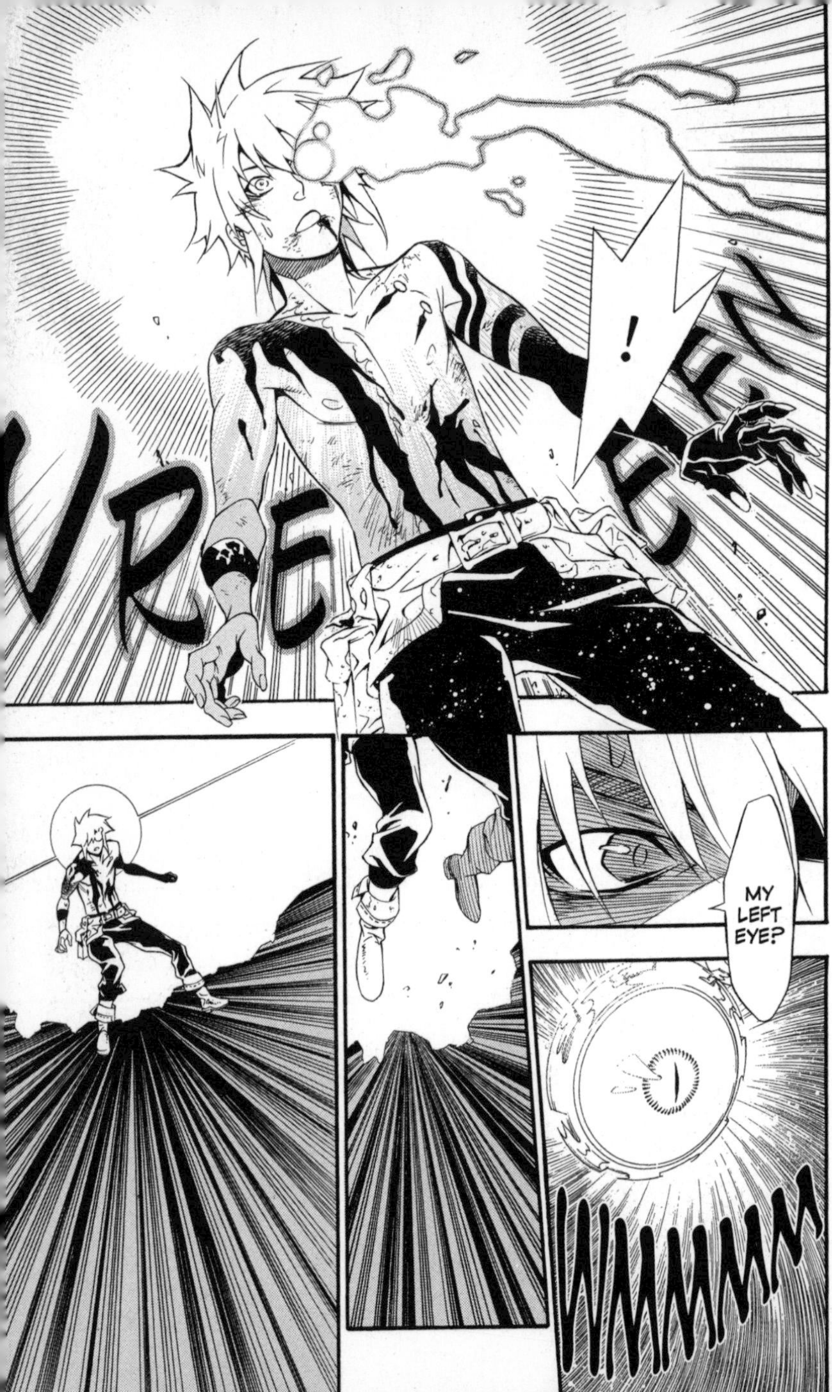
VREEEN
!
MY LEFT EYE?
WMMMM

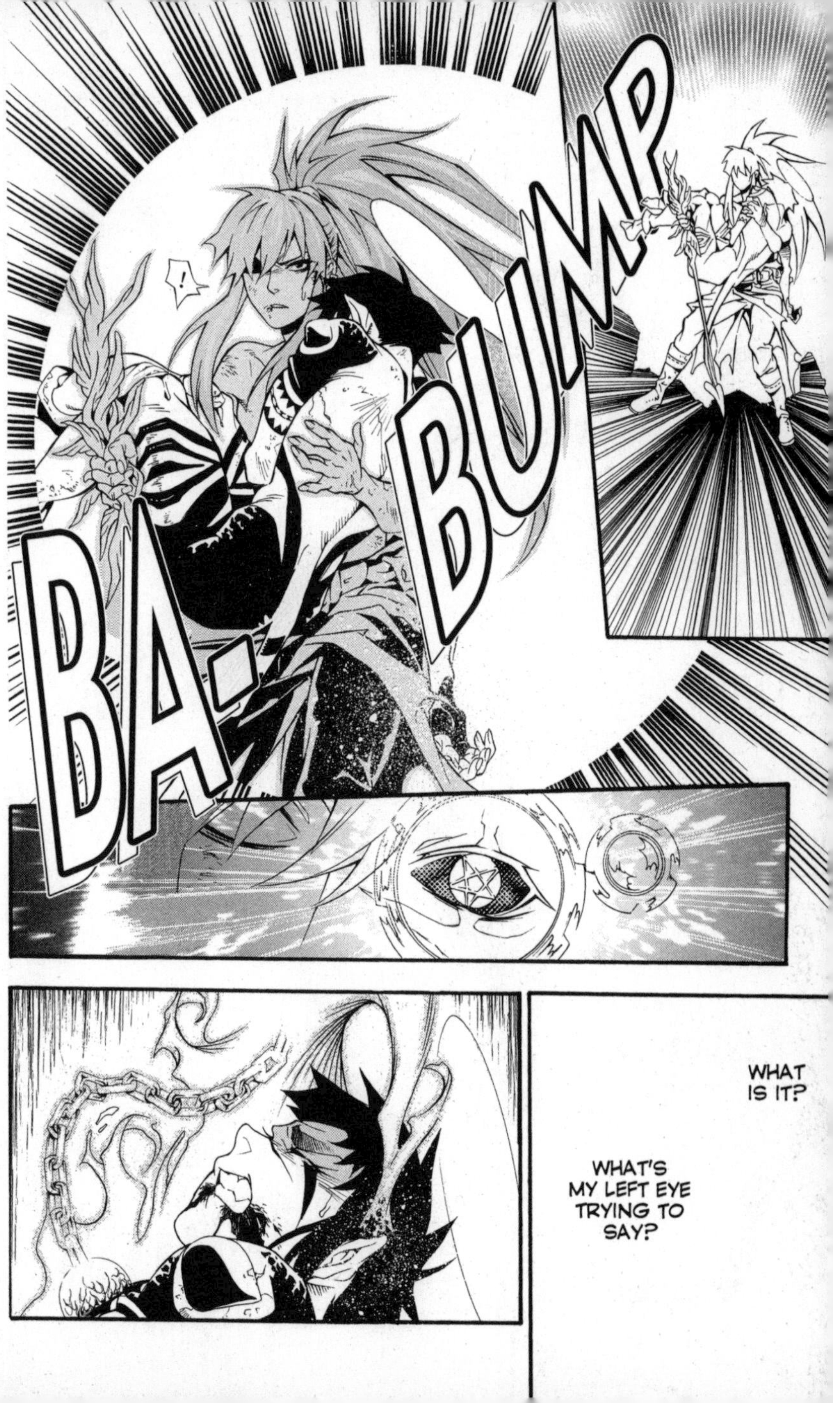
BA-BUMP
!
WHAT IS IT?
WHAT'S MY LEFT EYE TRYING TO SAY?

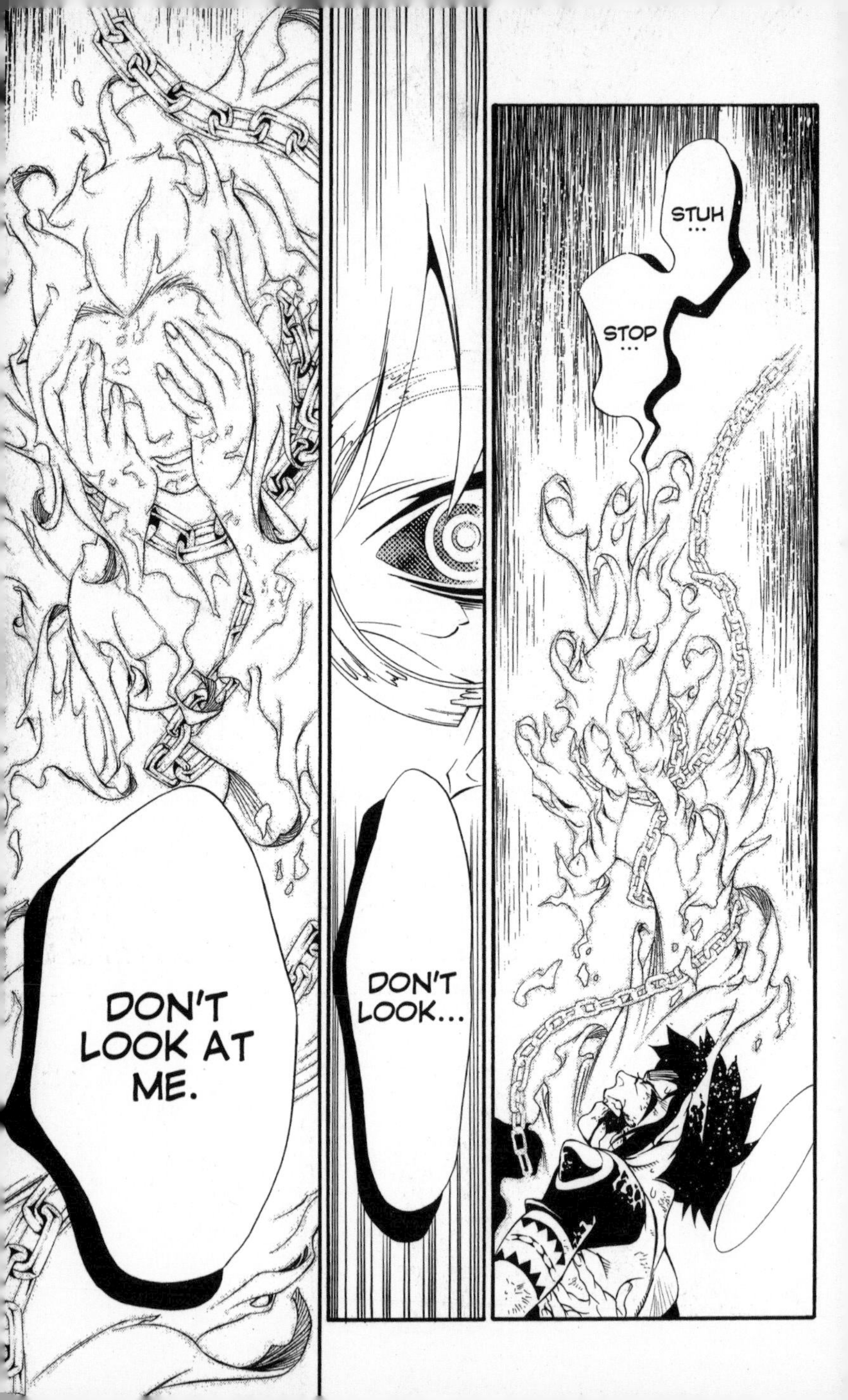
STUH...
STOP...
DON'T LOOK...
DON'T LOOK AT ME.

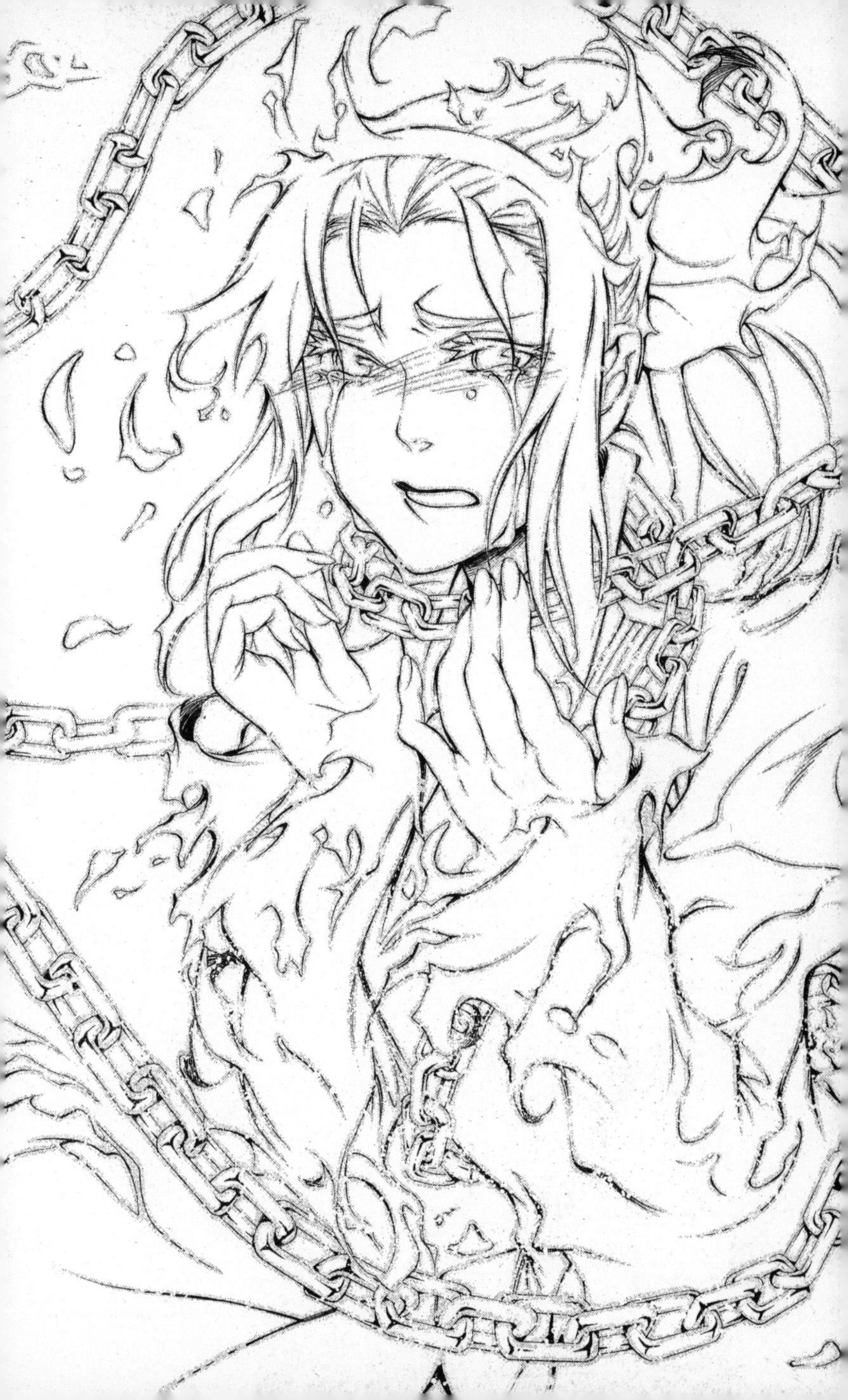

READ THIS WAY

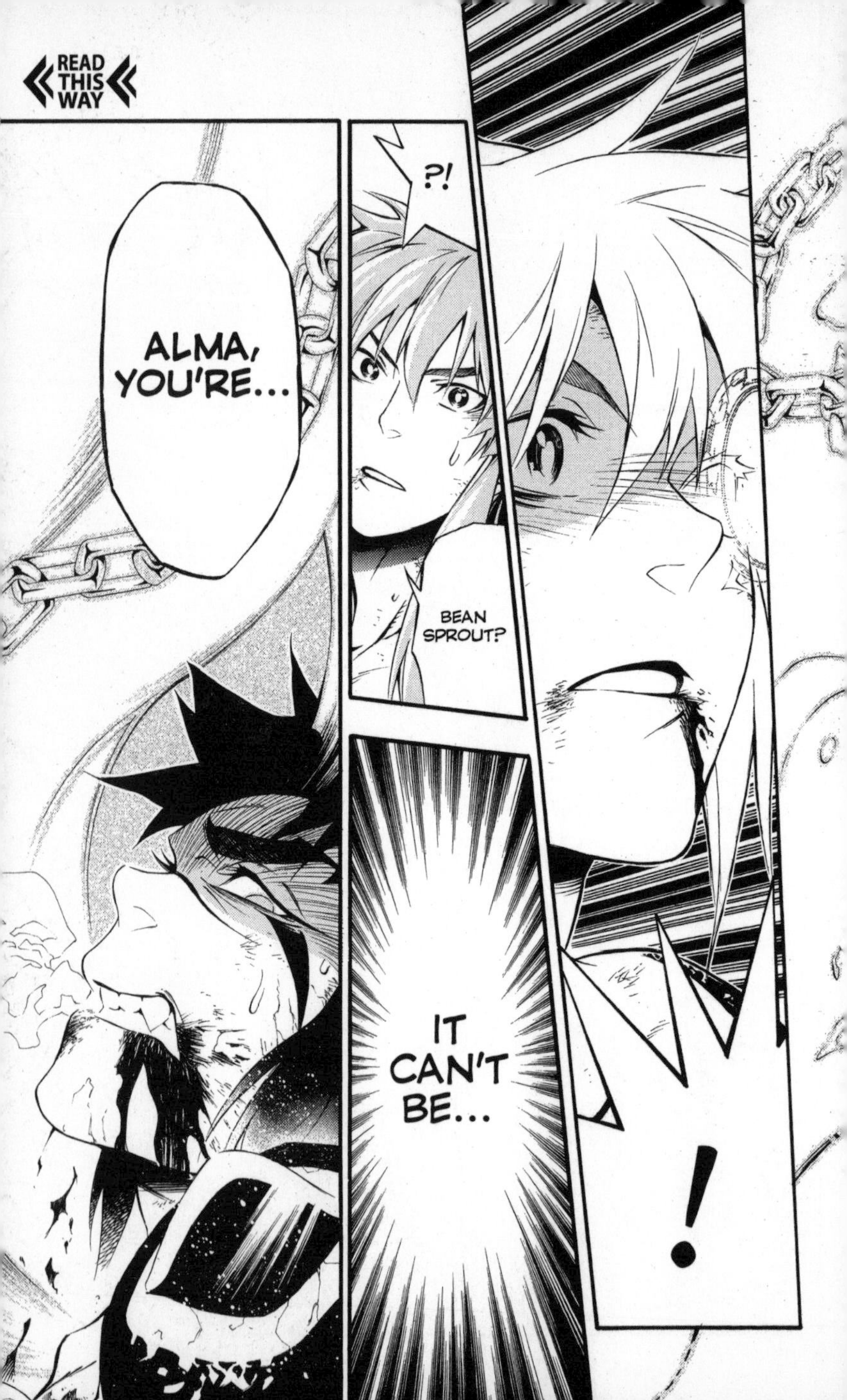
!
?!
BEAN SPROUT?
IT CAN'T BE...
ALMA, YOU'RE...

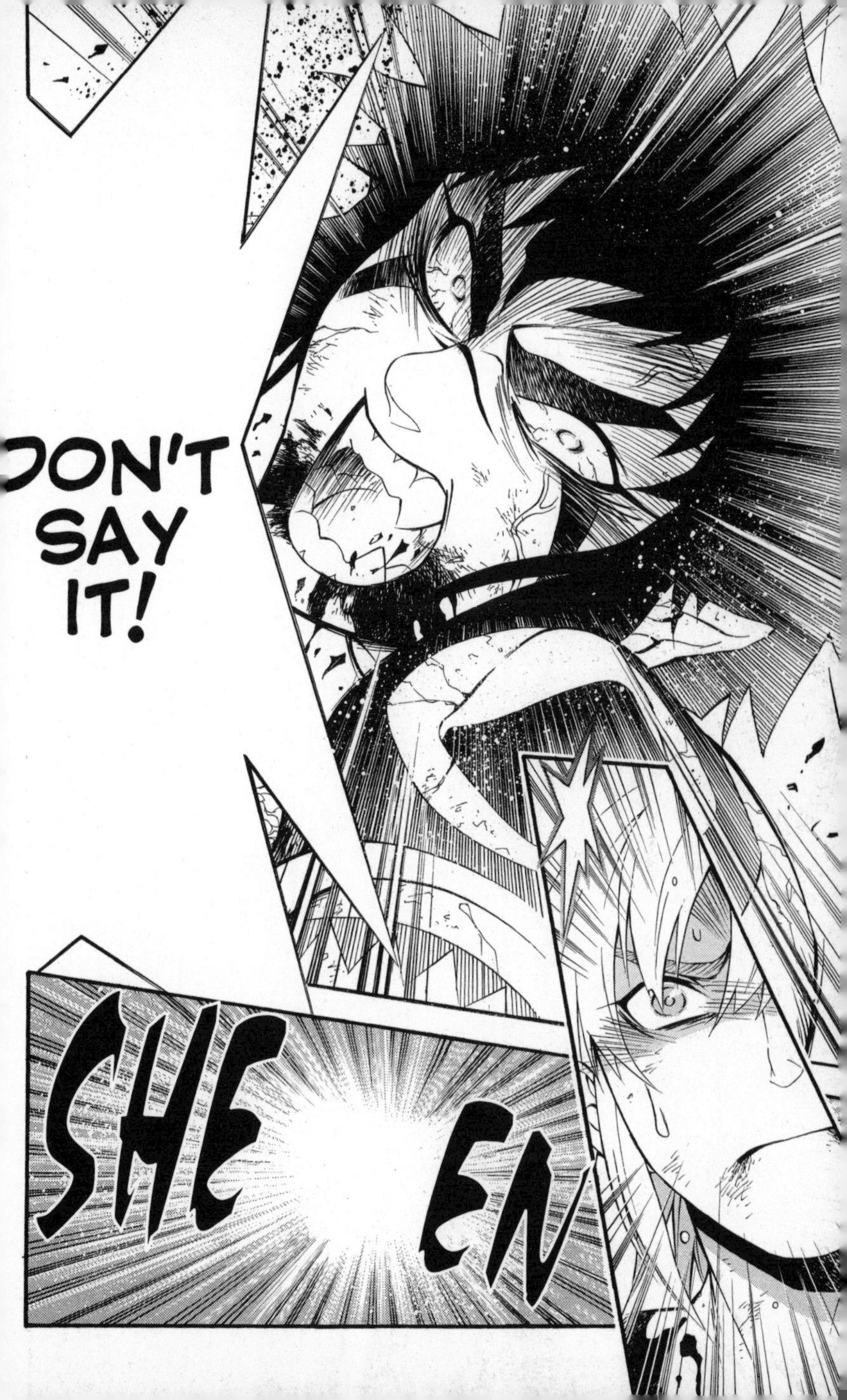
DON'T SAY IT!
SHE
EN

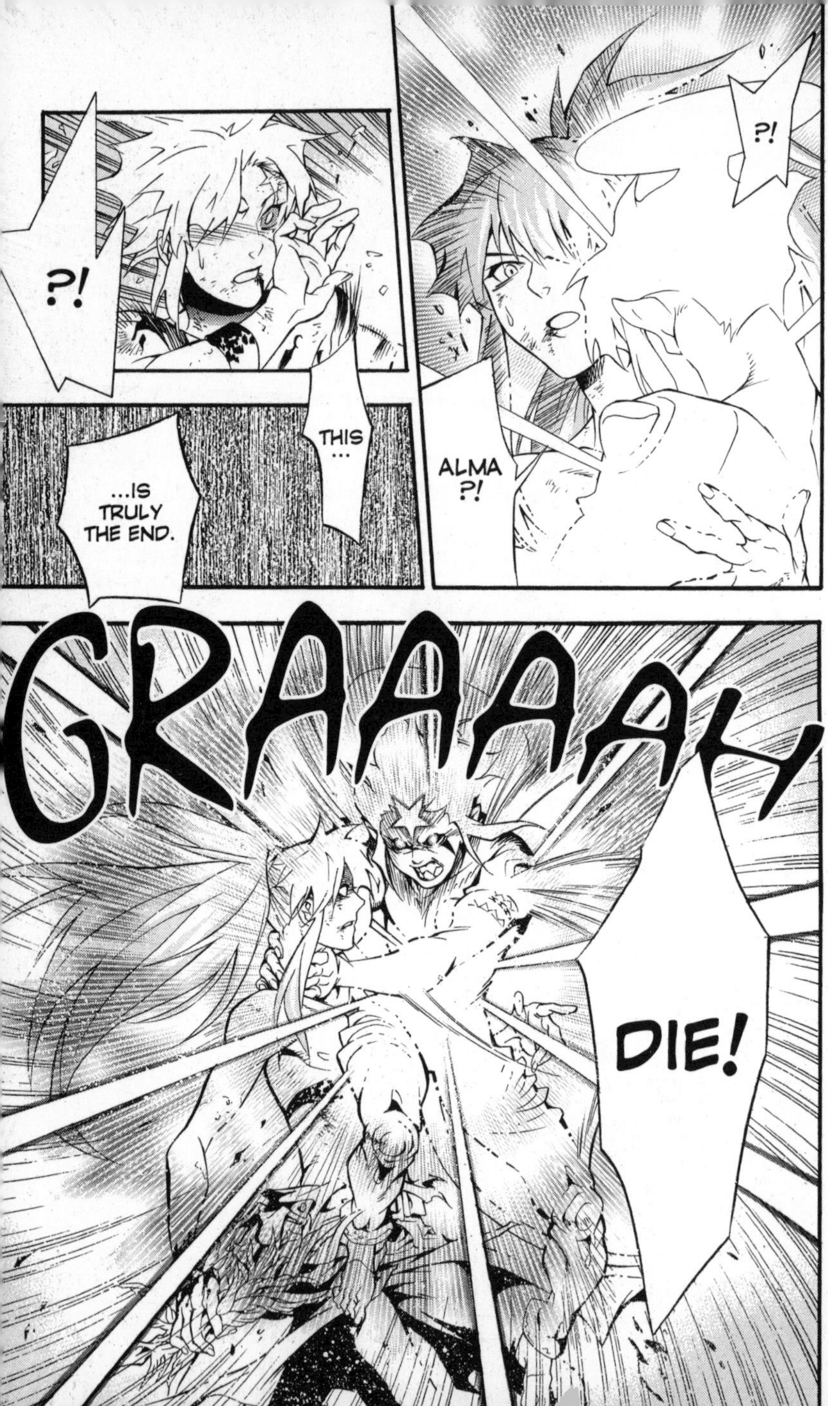
?!
ALMA ?!
?!
THIS …
…IS TRULY THE END.
GRAAAAH
DIE!

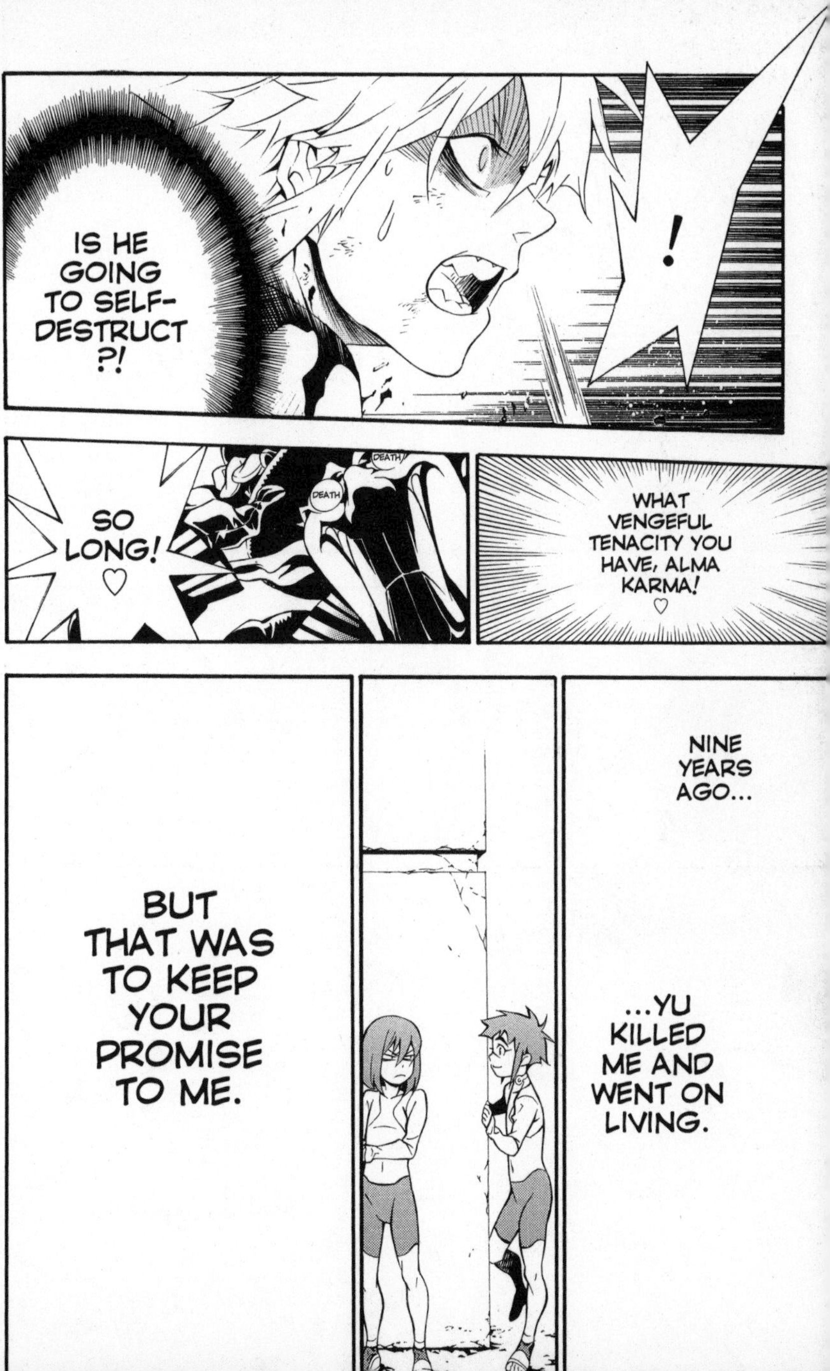
!
IS HE GOING TO SELF-DESTRUCT?!
WHAT VENGEFUL TENACITY YOU HAVE, ALMA KARMA! ♡
DEATH!
DEATH
SO LONG! ♡
NINE YEARS AGO...
...YU KILLED ME AND WENT ON LIVING.
BUT THAT WAS TO KEEP YOUR PROMISE TO ME.

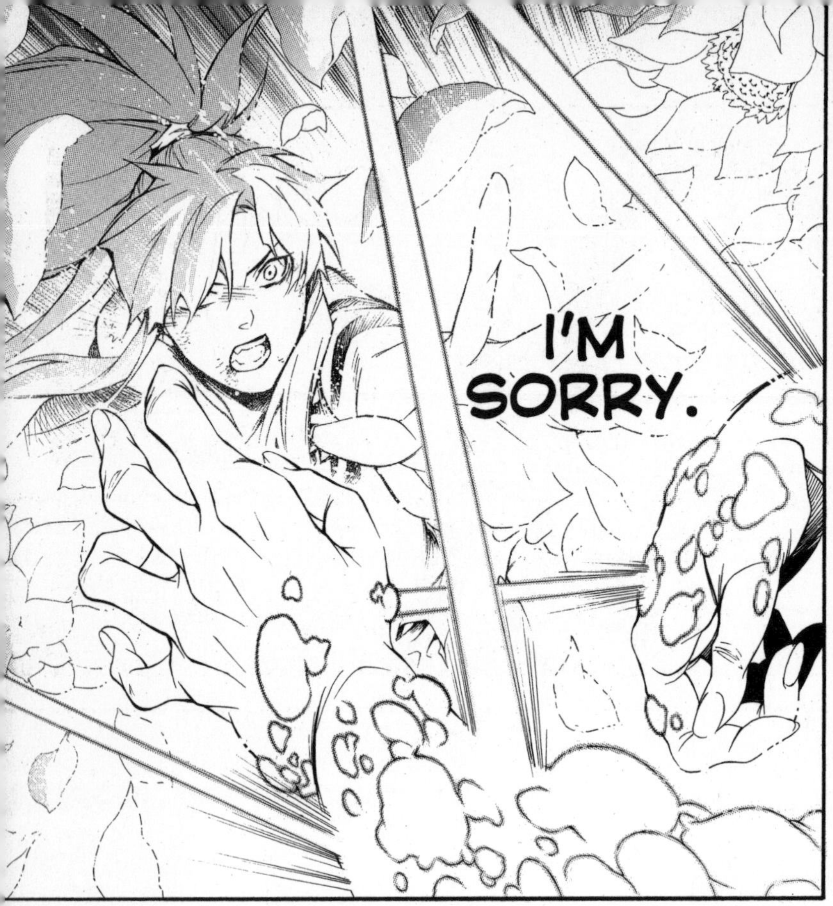
I'M SORRY.

AS LONG AS YOU WERE ALIVE, YOU WOULD SEARCH FOR ME.

AND EVENTUALLY YOU WOULD NOTICE THAT ALMA WAS ME.

I COULDN'T STAND THAT.

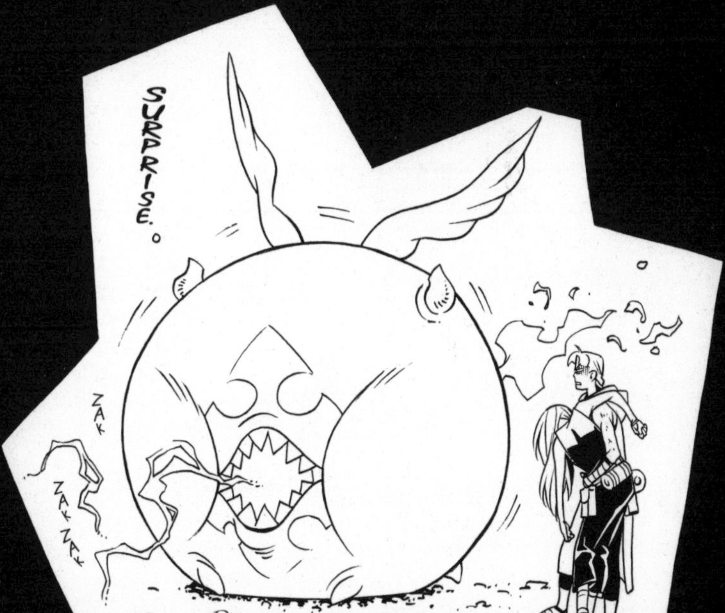
SURPRISE.
ZAK
ZAK
ZAK ZAK

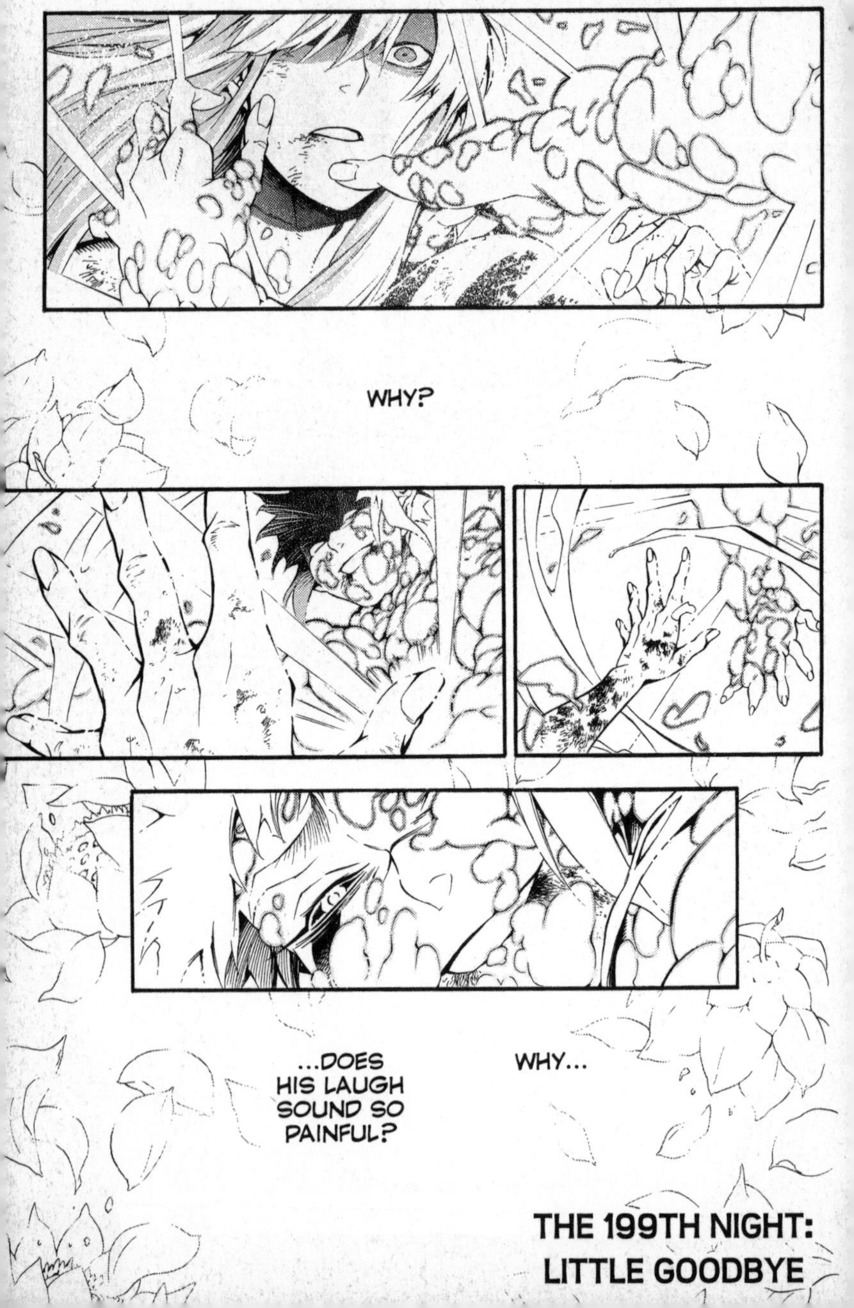
WHY?
WHY...
...DOES HIS LAUGH SOUND SO PAINFUL?
THE 199TH NIGHT: LITTLE GOODBYE

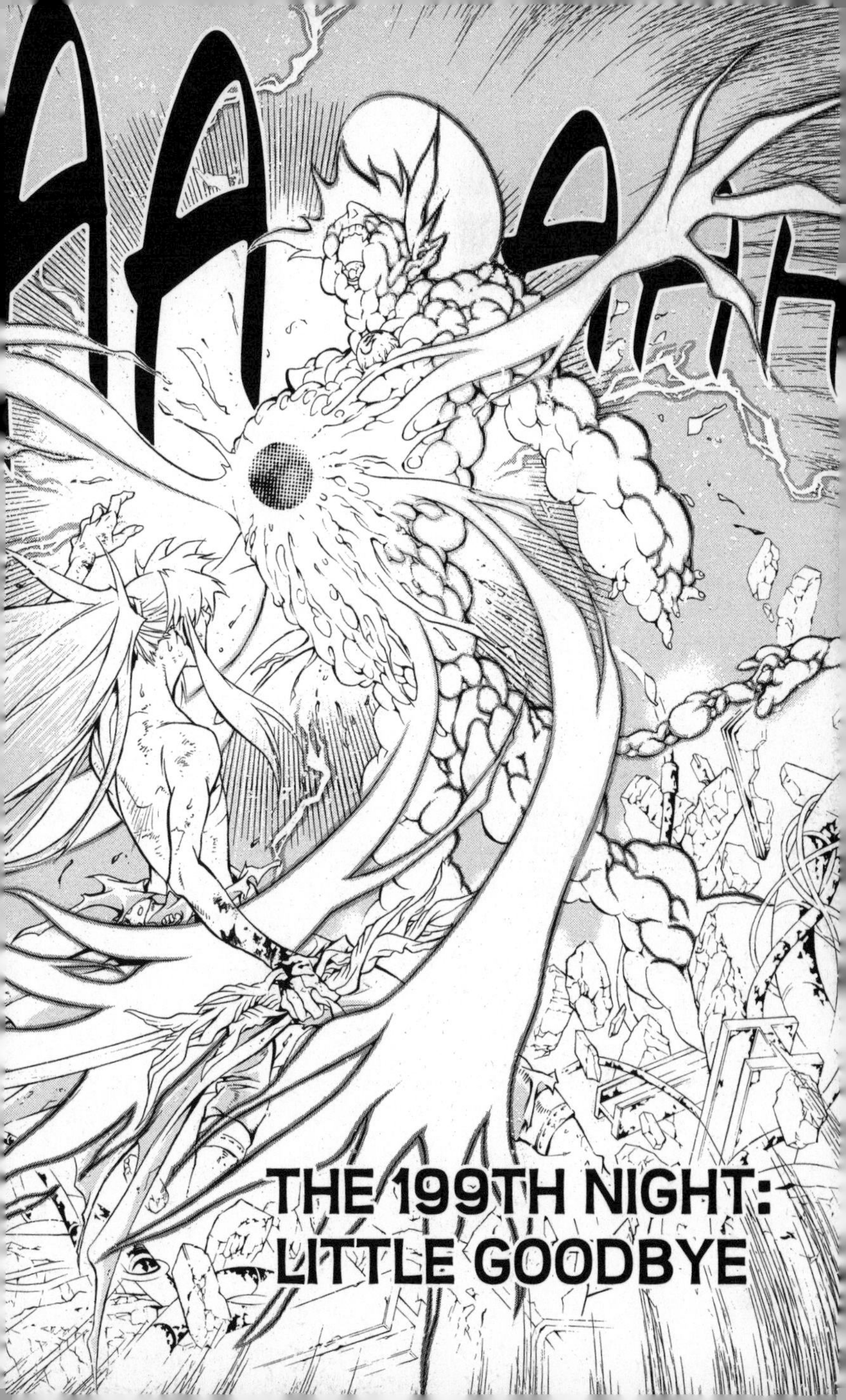
THE 199TH NIGHT:
LITTLE GOODBYE

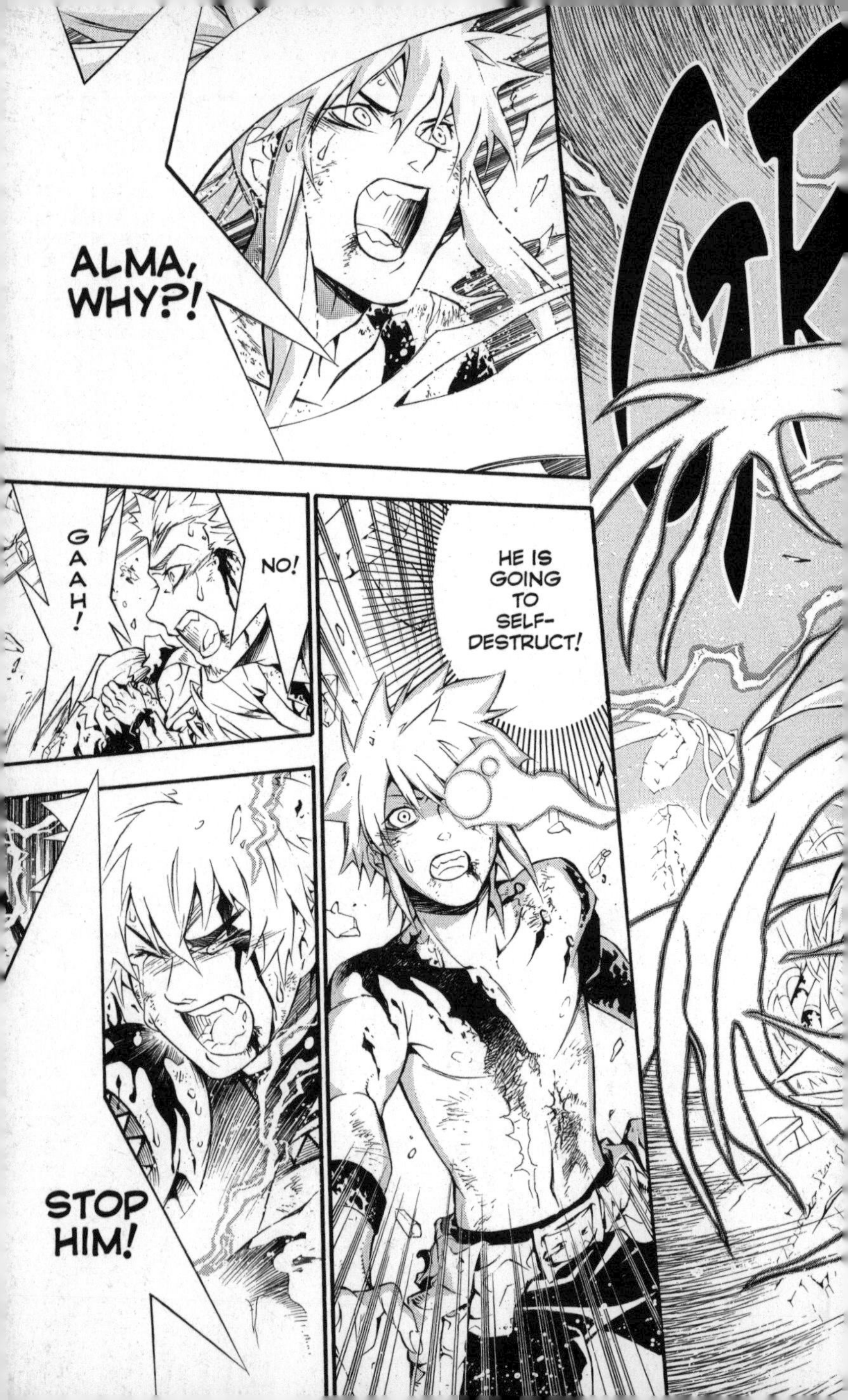

GK
ALMA, WHY?!
HE IS GOING TO SELF-DESTRUCT!
GAAH!
NO!
STOP HIM!

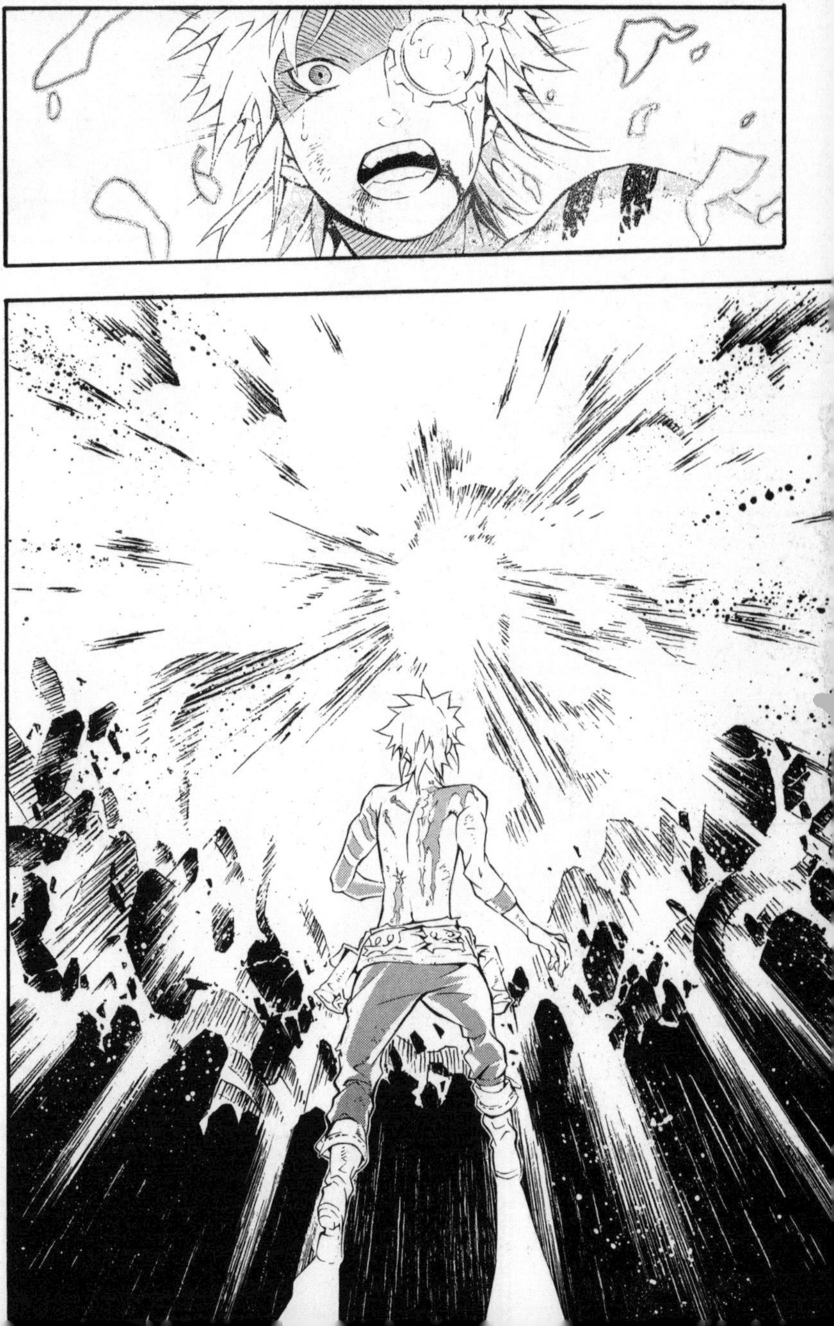

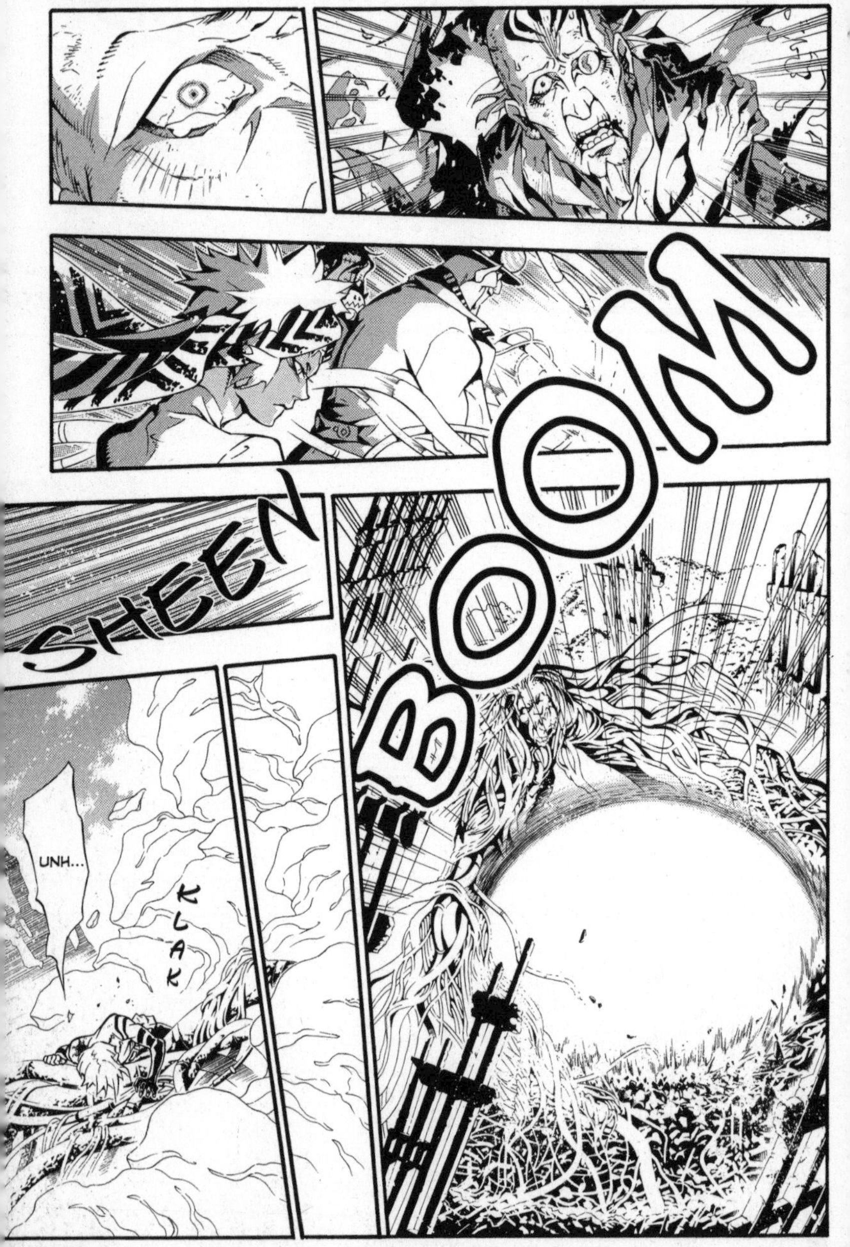
BOOM
SHEEN
UNH...
KLAK

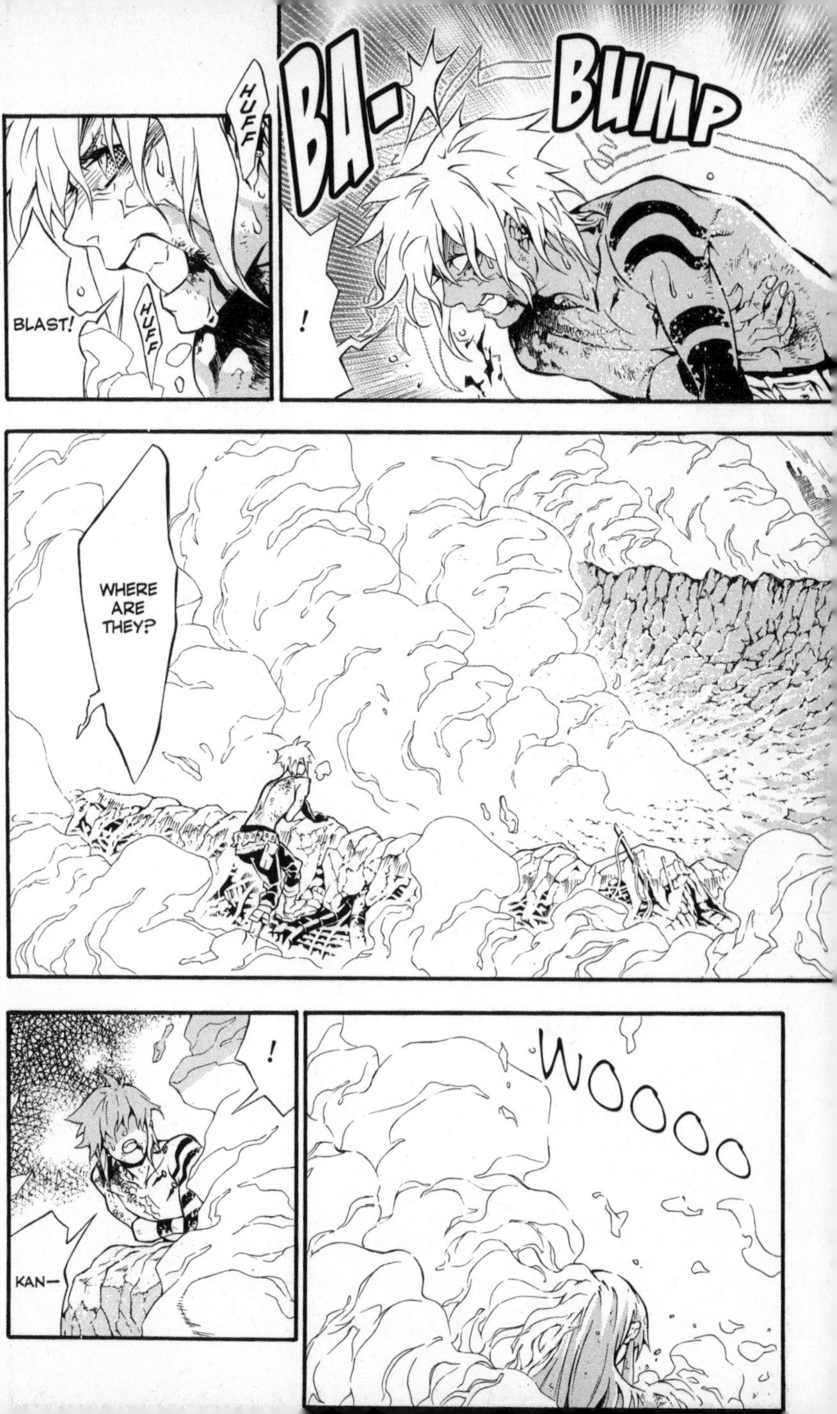
BA- BUMP
!
HUFF
HUFF
BLAST!
WHERE ARE THEY?
WOOOO
!
KAN—

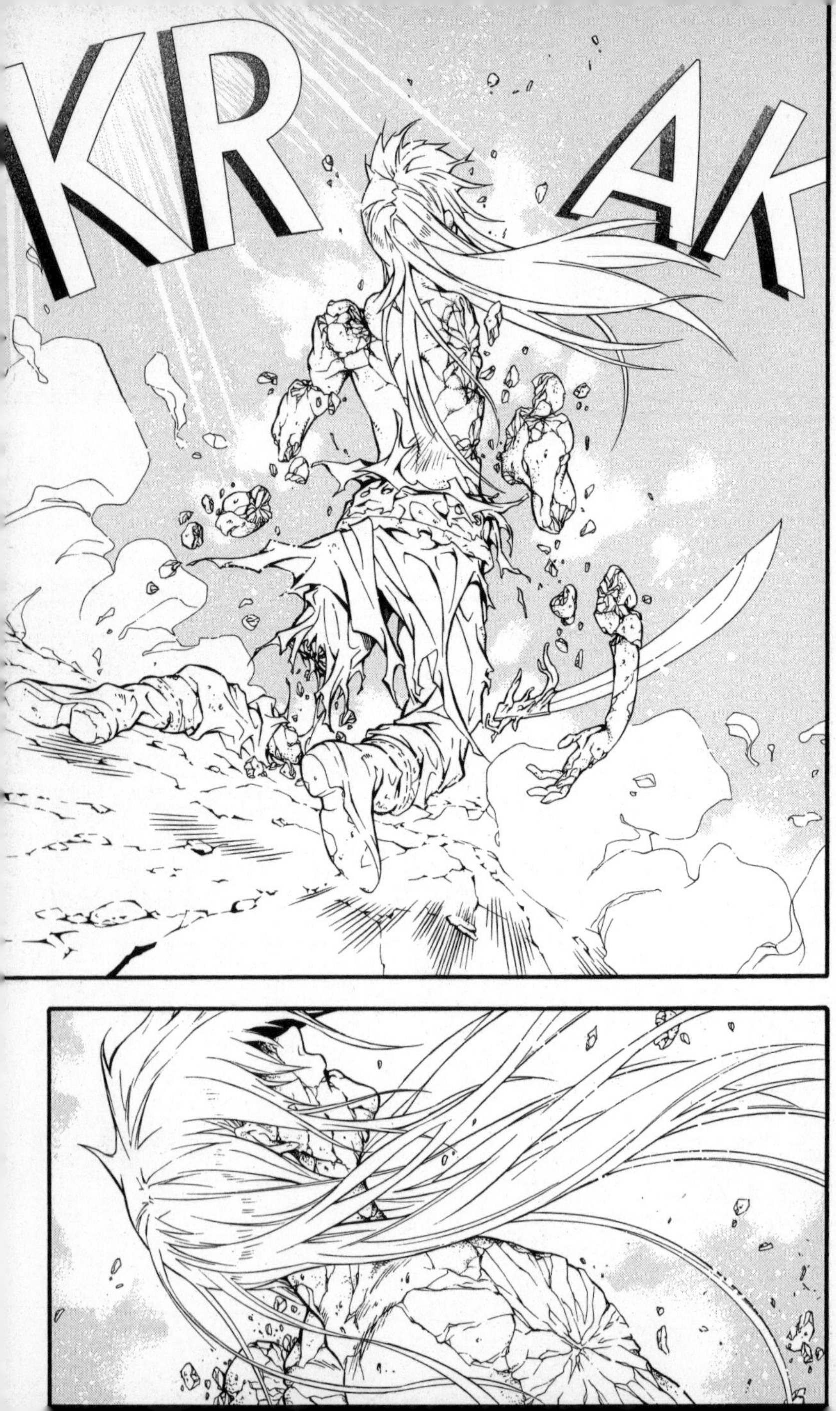
KRAK

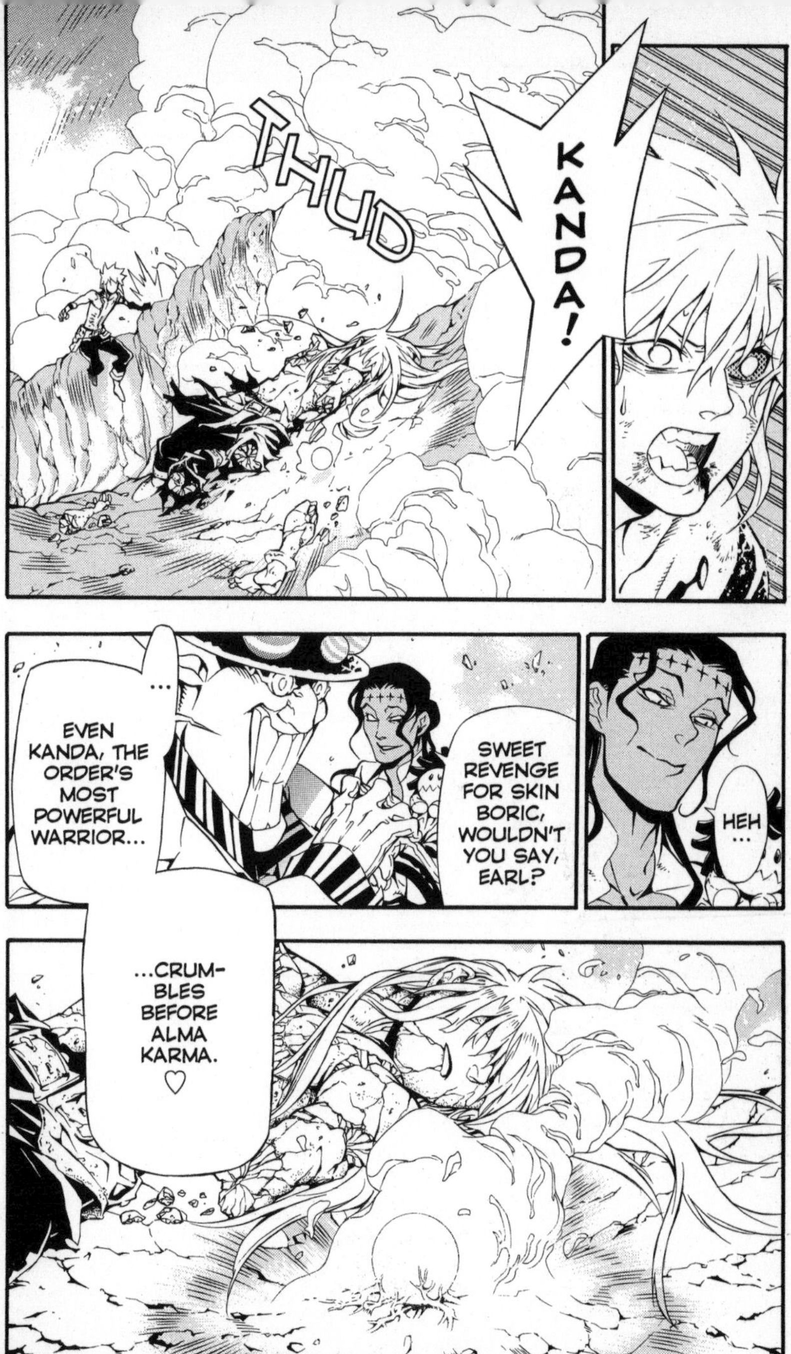
KANDA!
THUD
HEH...
SWEET REVENGE FOR SKIN BORIC, WOULDN'T YOU SAY, EARL?
...
EVEN KANDA, THE ORDER'S MOST POWERFUL WARRIOR...
...CRUMBLES BEFORE ALMA KARMA. ♡

HE DIDN'T
BECOME AN
AKUMA FOR
VENGEANCE.

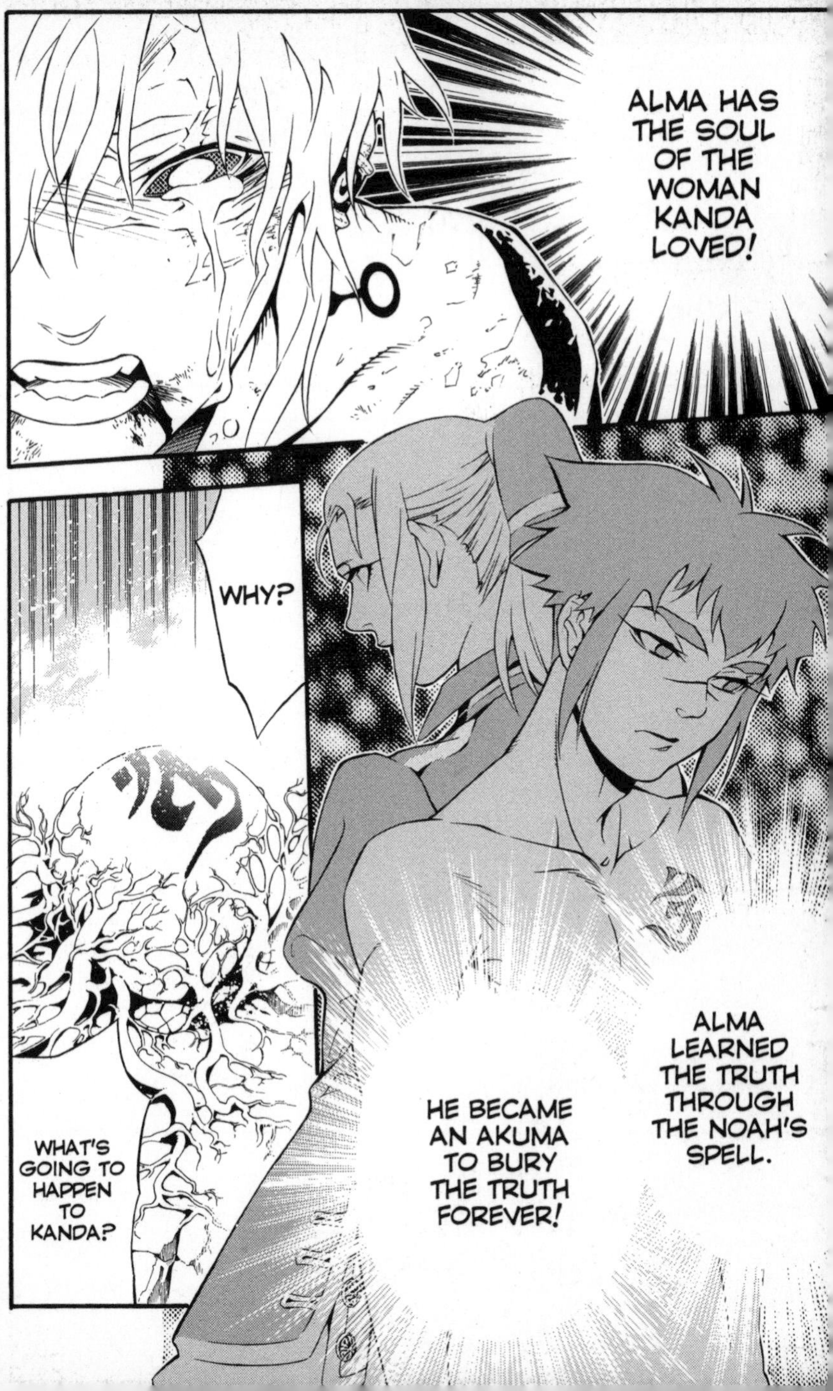
ALMA HAS THE SOUL OF THE WOMAN KANDA LOVED!
ALMA LEARNED THE TRUTH THROUGH THE NOAH'S SPELL.
HE BECAME AN AKUMA TO BURY THE TRUTH FOREVER!
WHY?
WHAT'S GOING TO HAPPEN TO KANDA?

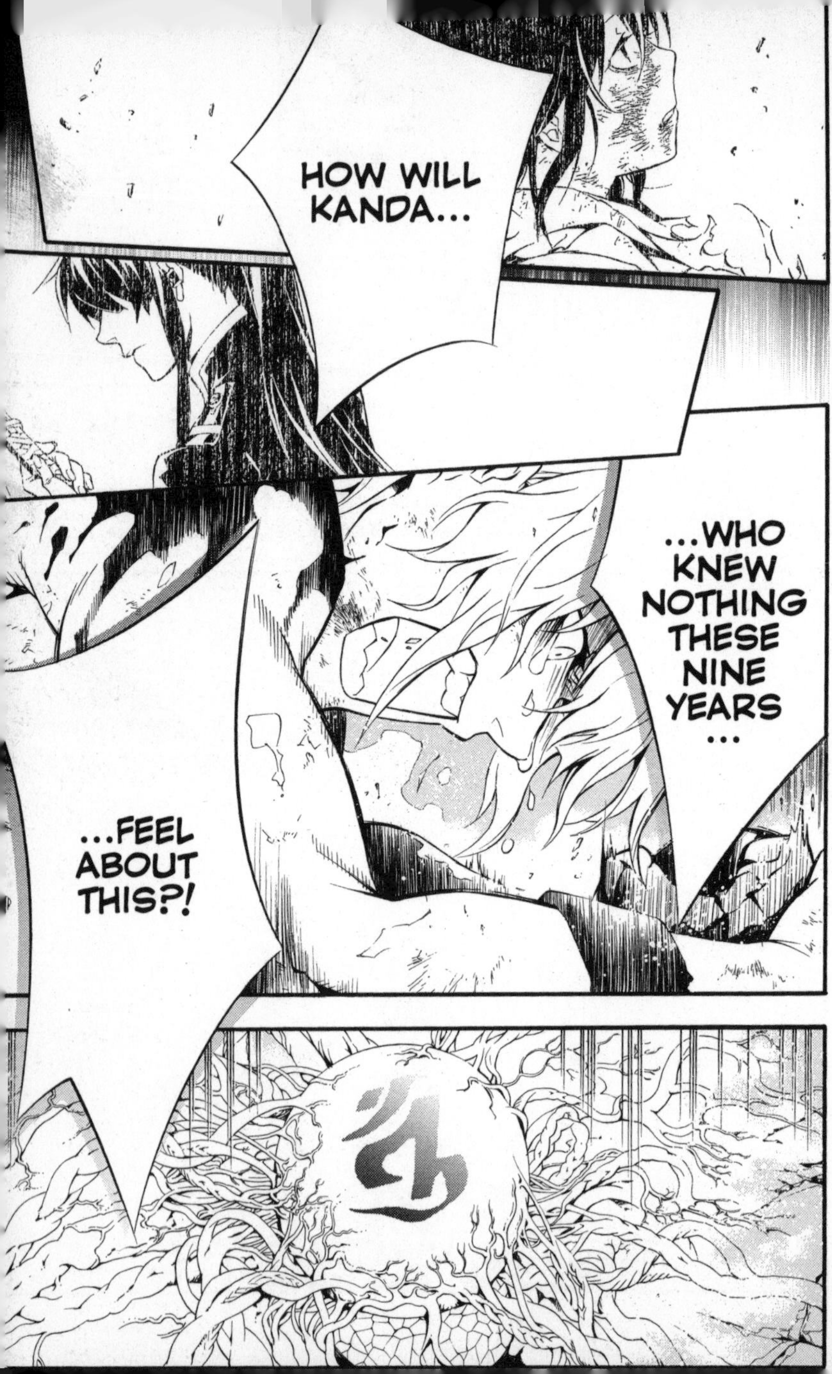
HOW WILL KANDA...
...WHO KNEW NOTHING THESE NINE YEARS...
...FEEL ABOUT THIS?!

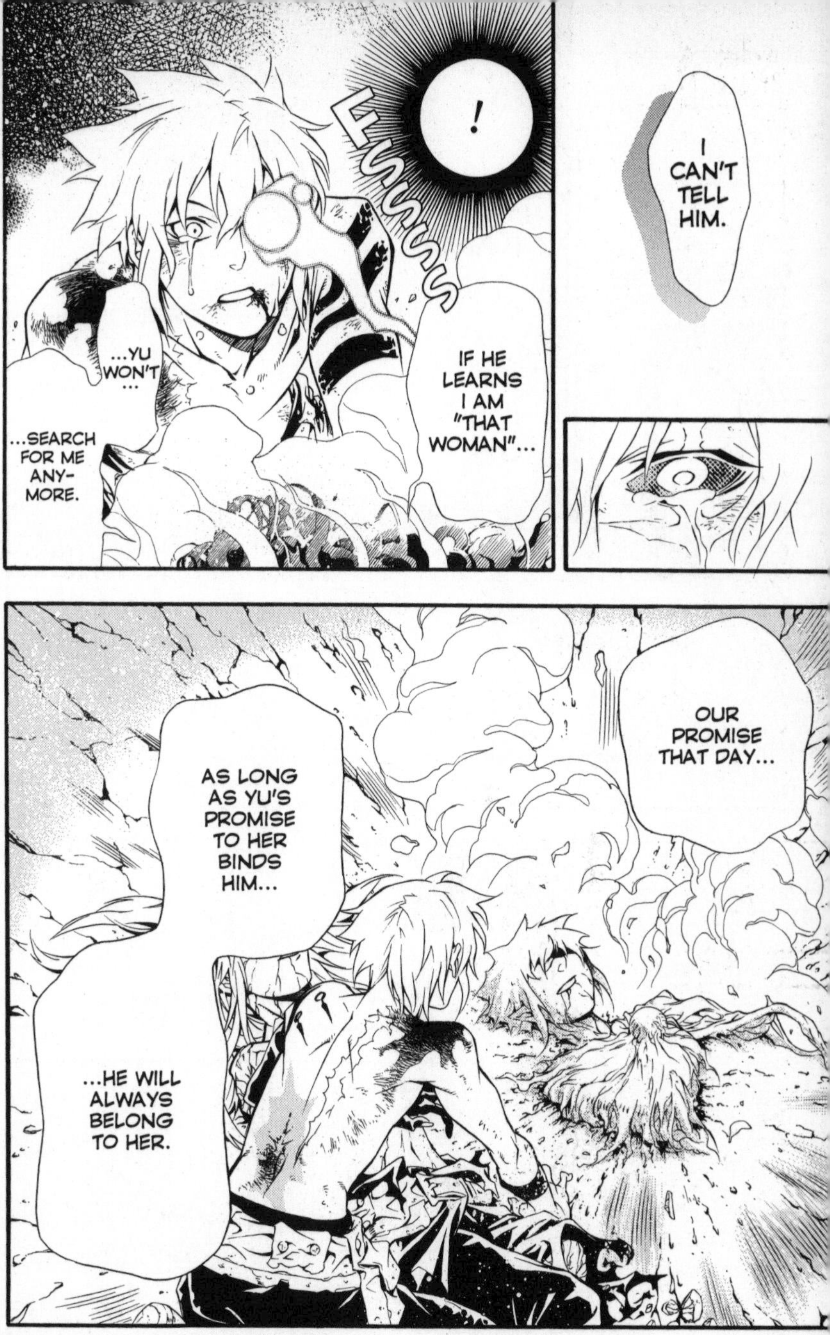
I CAN'T TELL HIM.
!
FSSSSS
IF HE LEARNS I AM "THAT WOMAN"...
...YU WON'T ...
...SEARCH FOR ME ANYMORE.
OUR PROMISE THAT DAY...
AS LONG AS YU'S PROMISE TO HER BINDS HIM...
...HE WILL ALWAYS BELONG TO HER.

READ THIS WAY

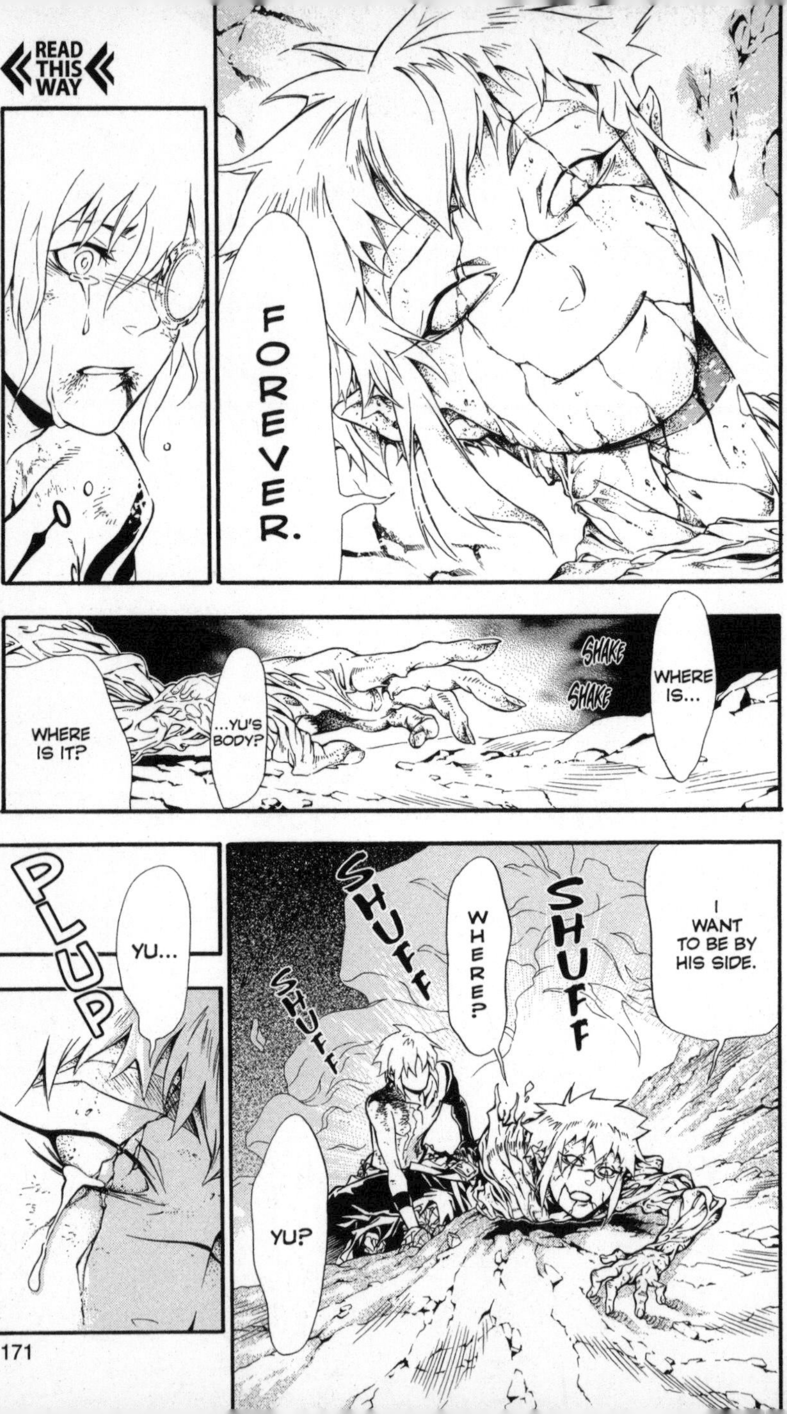

FOREVER.
WHERE IS...
SHAKE
SHAKE
...YU'S BODY?
WHERE IS IT?
I WANT TO BE BY HIS SIDE.
SHUFF
WHERE?
SHUFF
SHUFF
YU?
YU...
PLUP

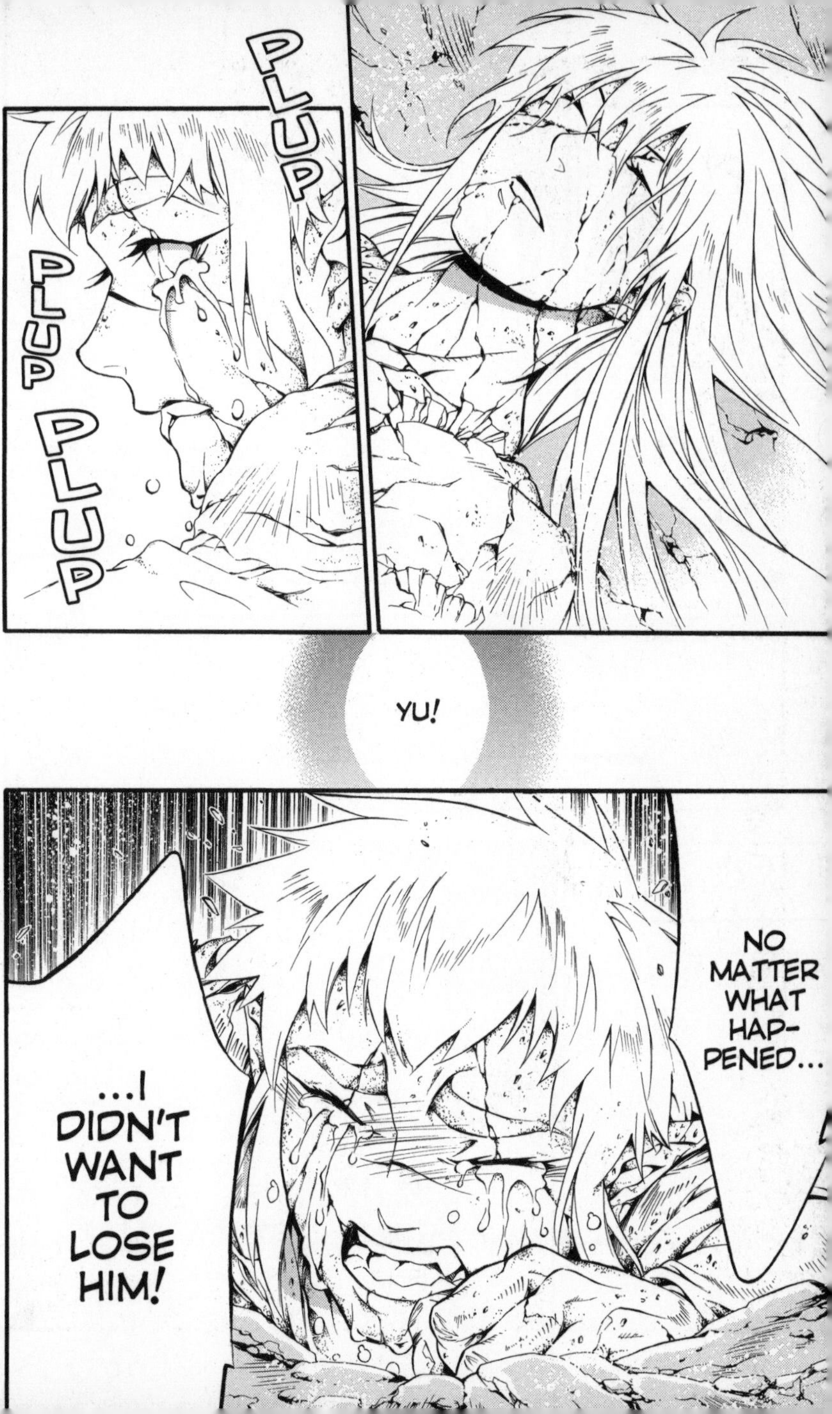
PLUP
PLUP
PLUP
YU!
NO MATTER WHAT HAP-PENED...
...I DIDN'T WANT TO LOSE HIM!

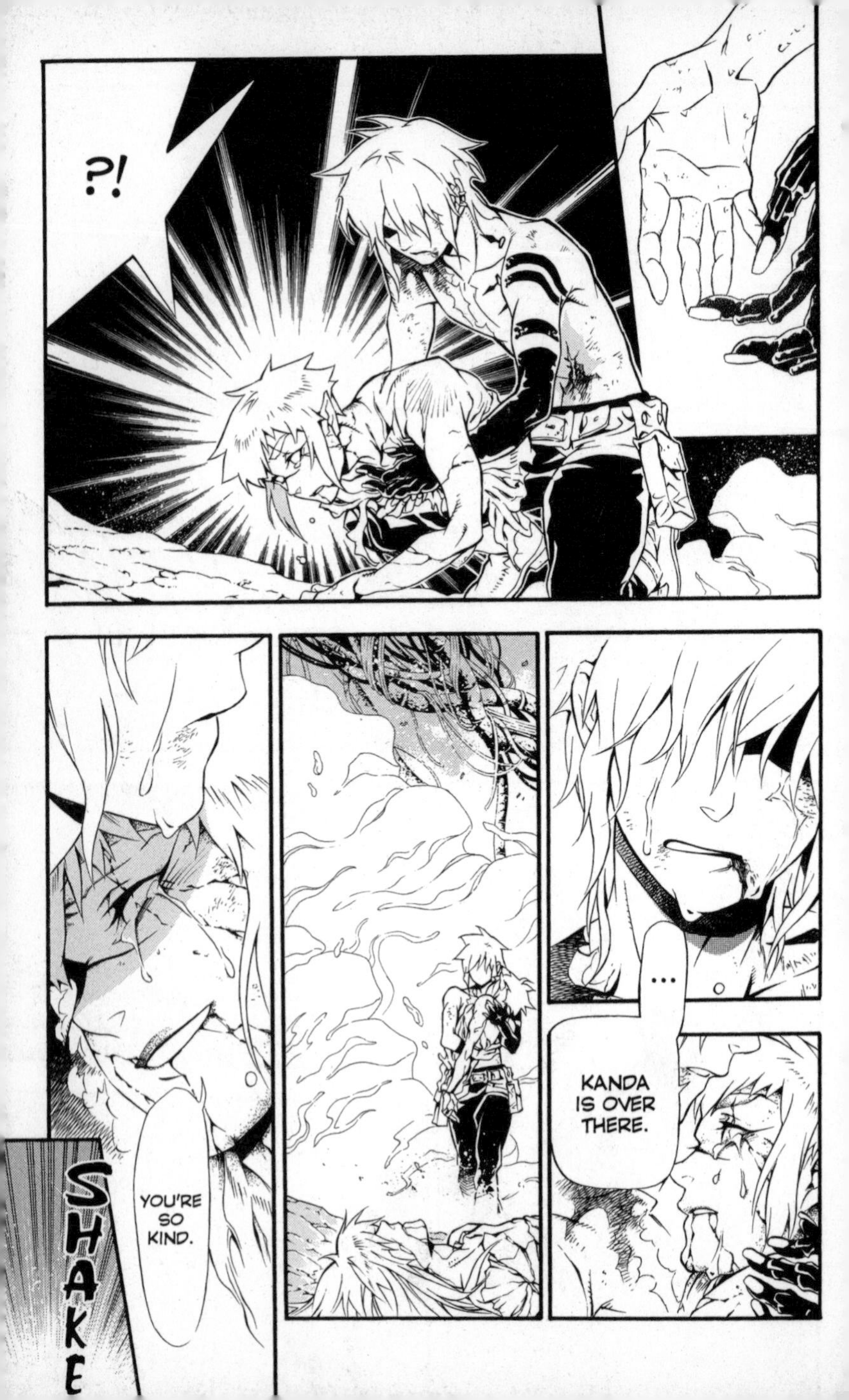
?!
...
KANDA IS OVER THERE.
YOU'RE SO KIND.
SHAKE

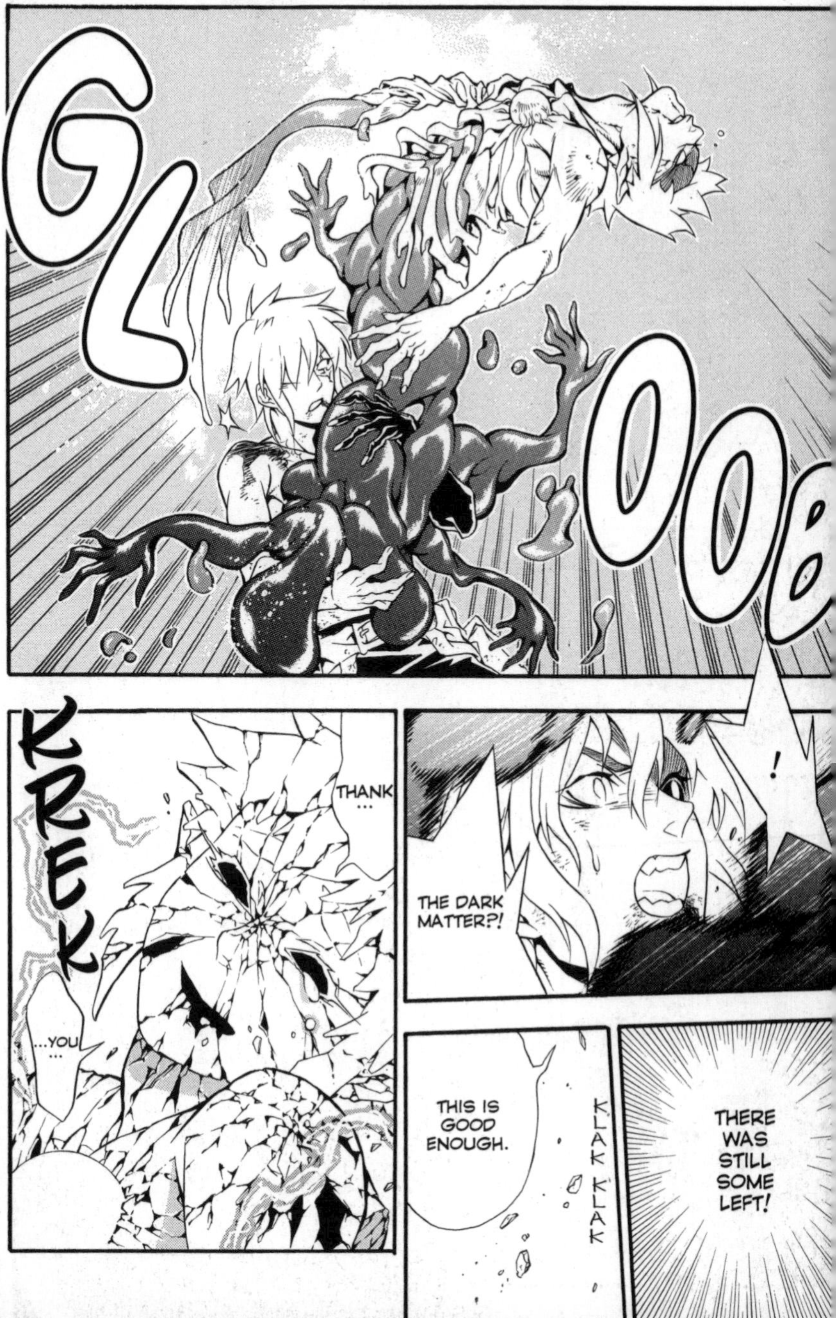
GLOOO
!
THE DARK MATTER?!
KREK
THANK...
...YOU...
THERE WAS STILL SOME LEFT!
THIS IS GOOD ENOUGH.
KLAK KLAK

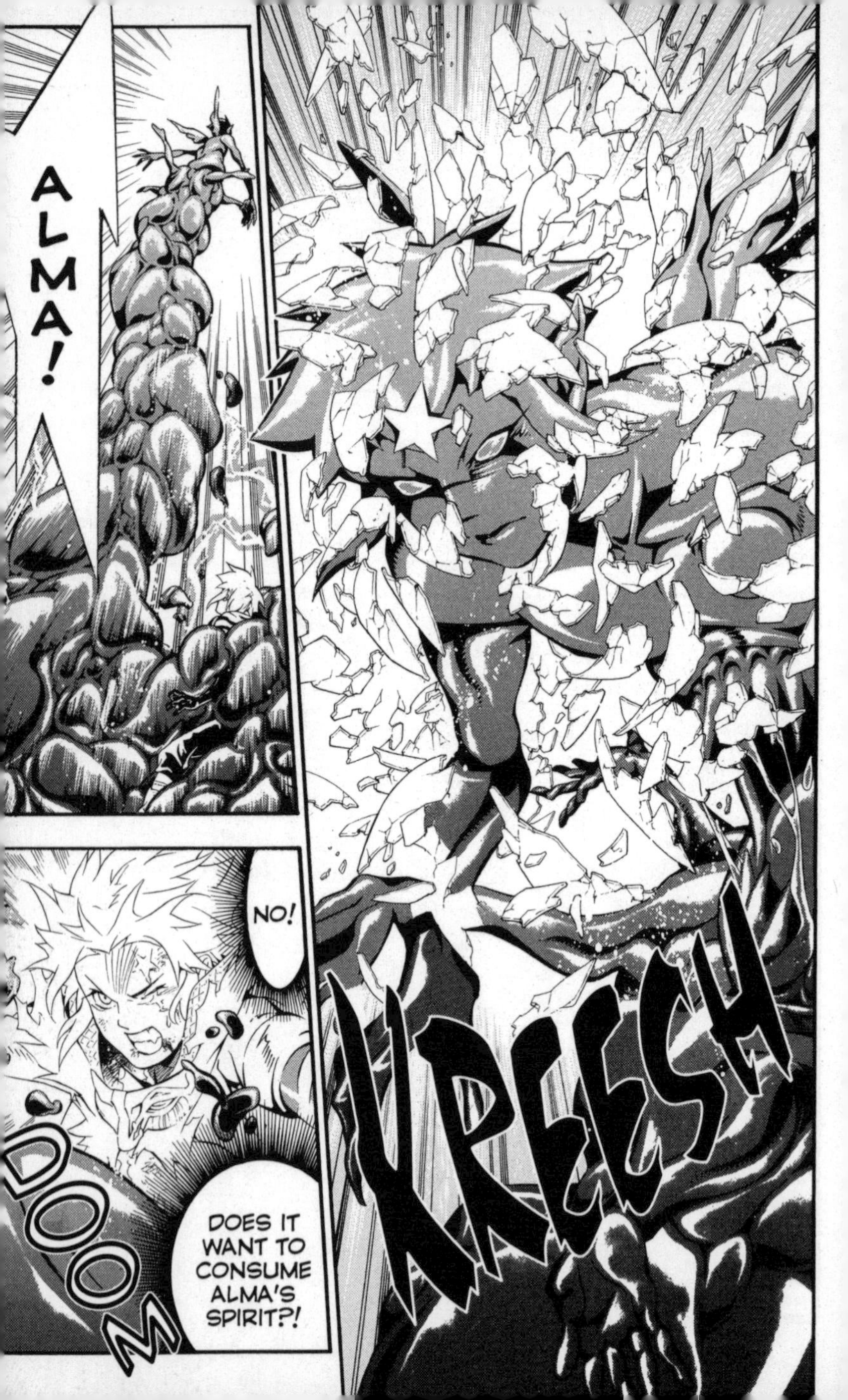
KREESH
ALMA!
NO!
DOES IT WANT TO CONSUME ALMA'S SPIRIT?!
DOOM

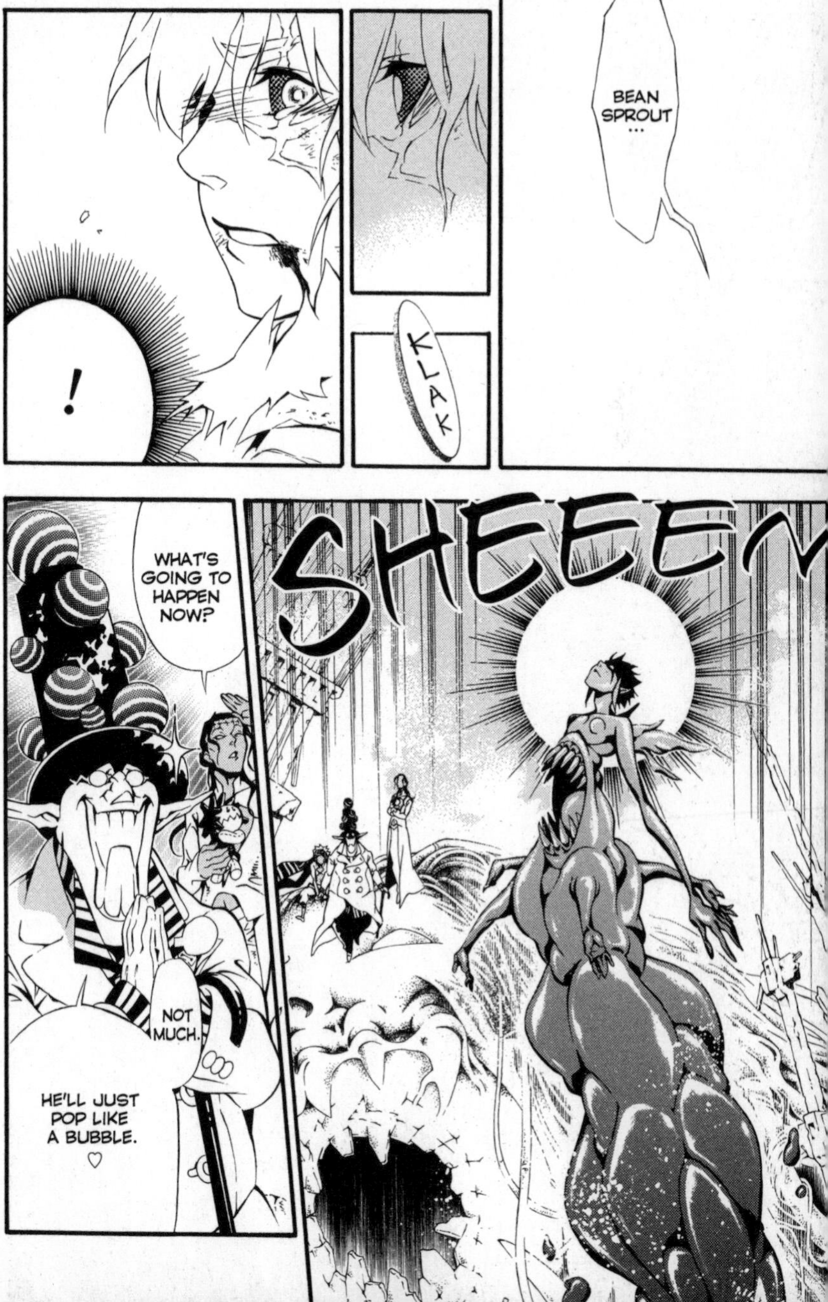
BEAN SPROUT ...
KLAK
!
SHEEEN
WHAT'S GOING TO HAPPEN NOW?
NOT MUCH.
HE'LL JUST POP LIKE A BUBBLE. ♡

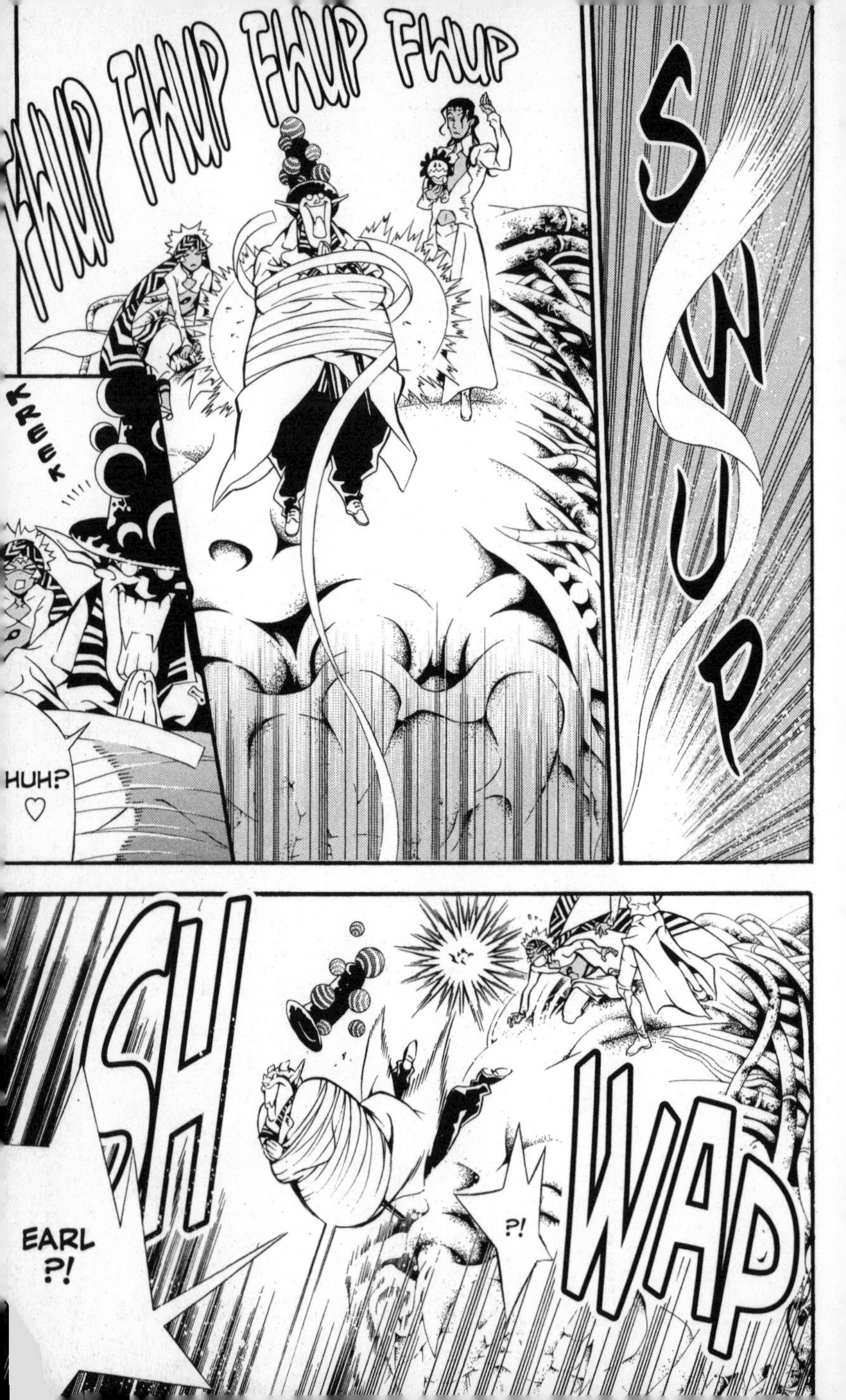

SWUP
FWUP FWUP FWUP FWUP
KREEK
HUH? ♡
SH
WAP
?!
EARL ?!

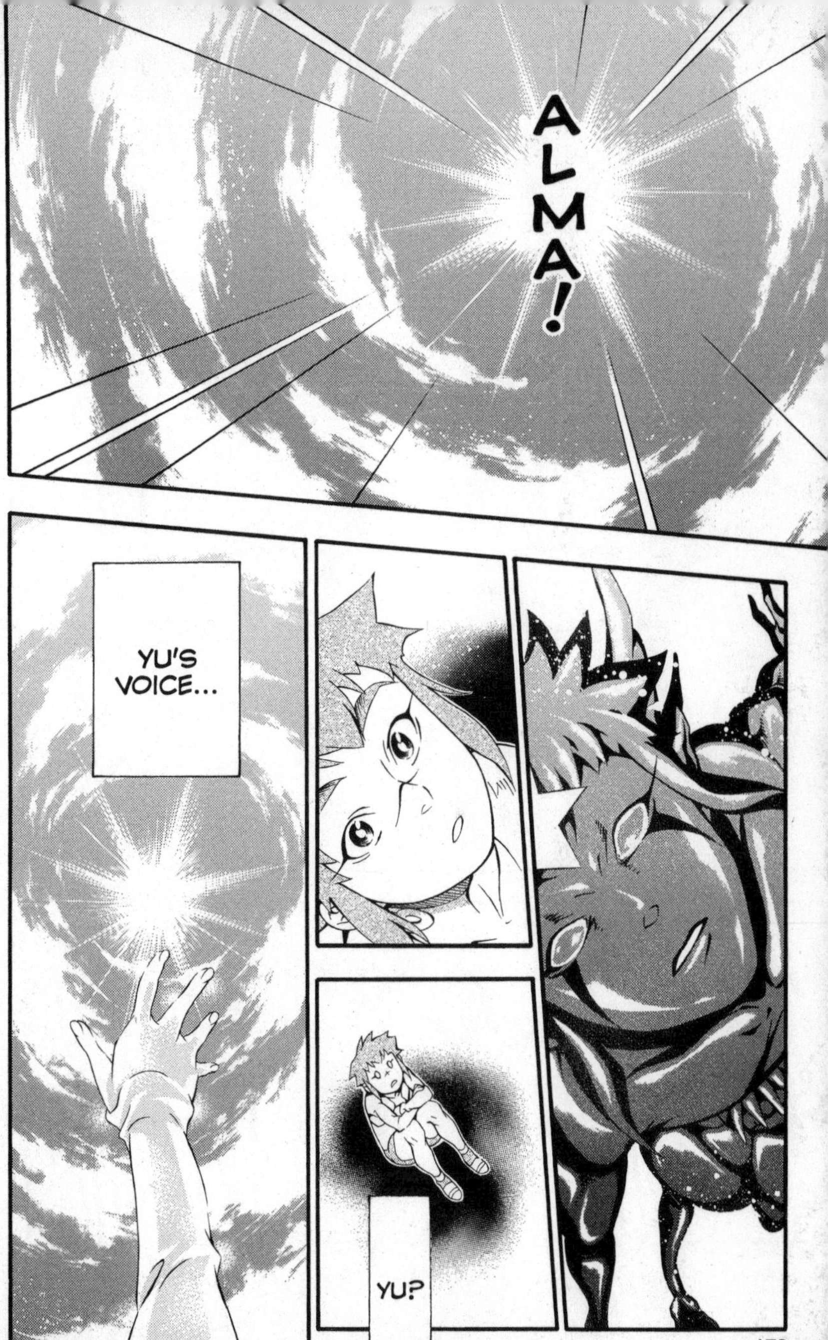
ALMA!
YU?
YU'S VOICE...

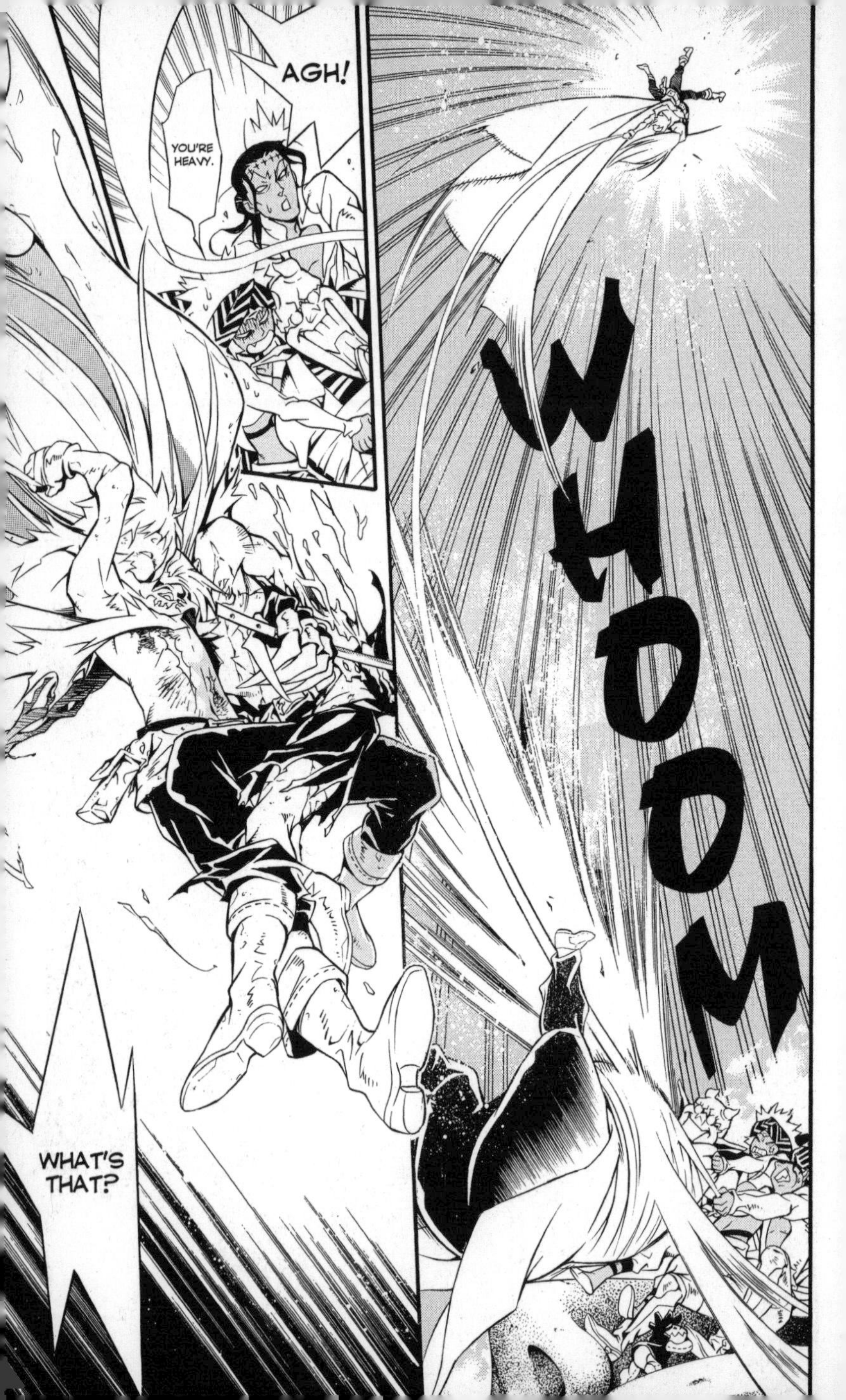
WHOOM
AGH!
YOU'RE HEAVY.
WHAT'S THAT?

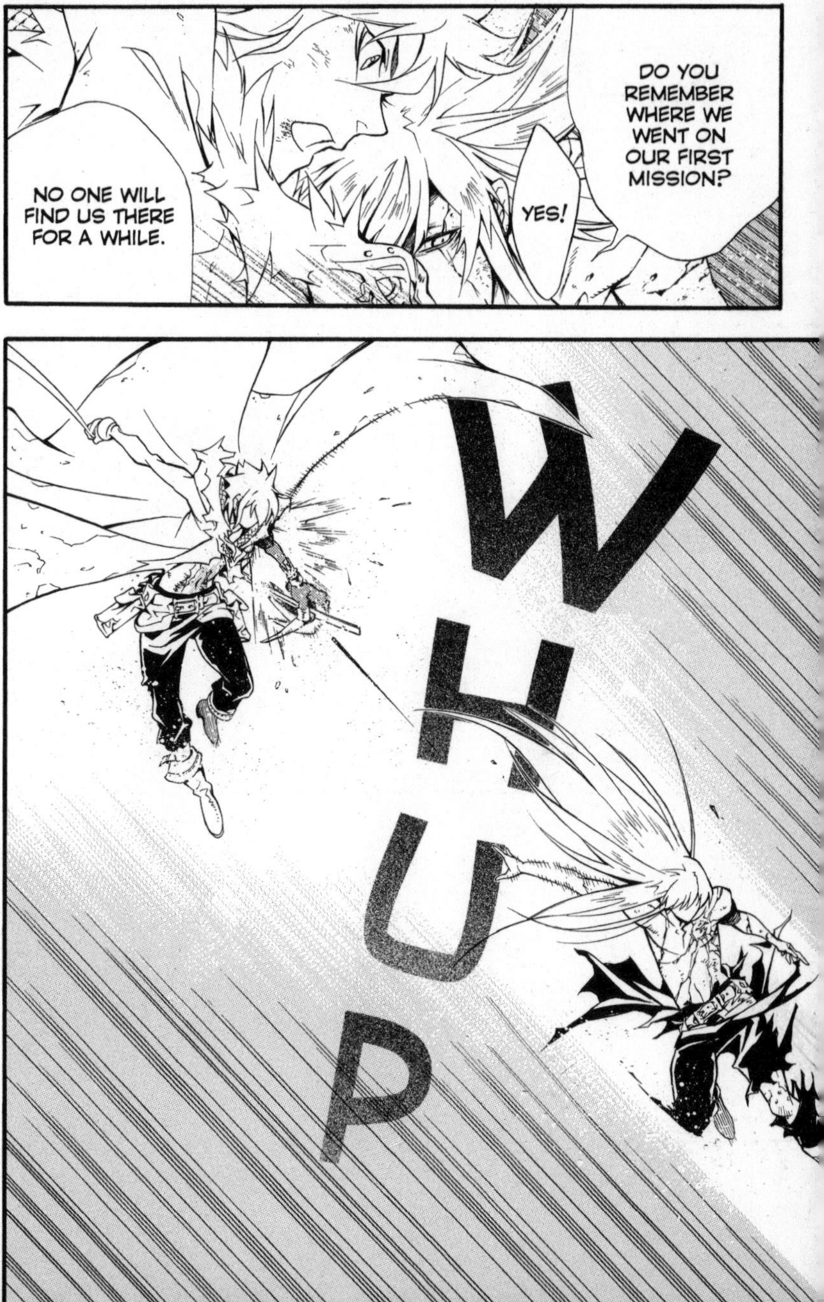
DO YOU REMEMBER WHERE WE WENT ON OUR FIRST MISSION?
YES!
NO ONE WILL FIND US THERE FOR A WHILE.
WHUP

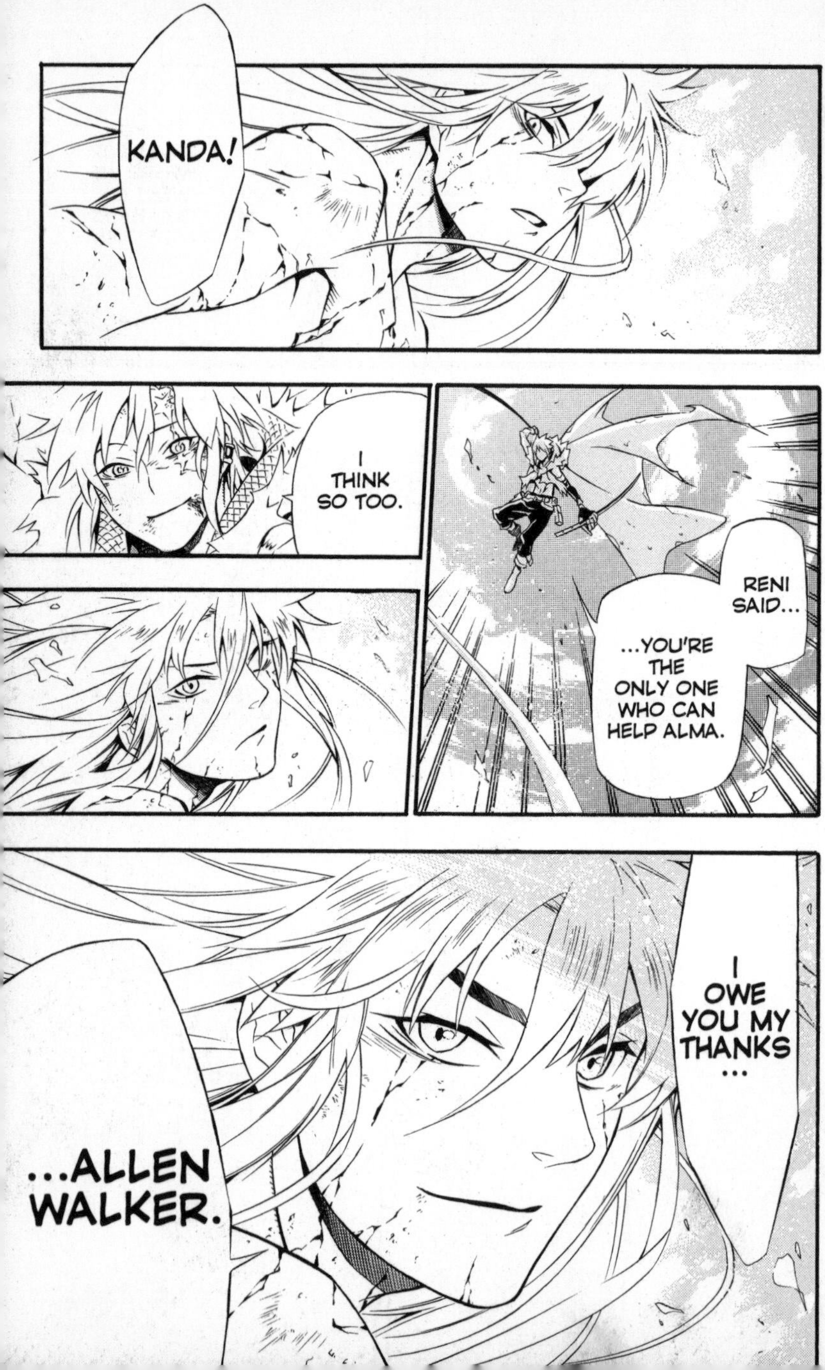
KANDA!
RENI SAID...
...YOU'RE THE ONLY ONE WHO CAN HELP ALMA.
I THINK SO TOO.
I OWE YOU MY THANKS...
...ALLEN WALKER.

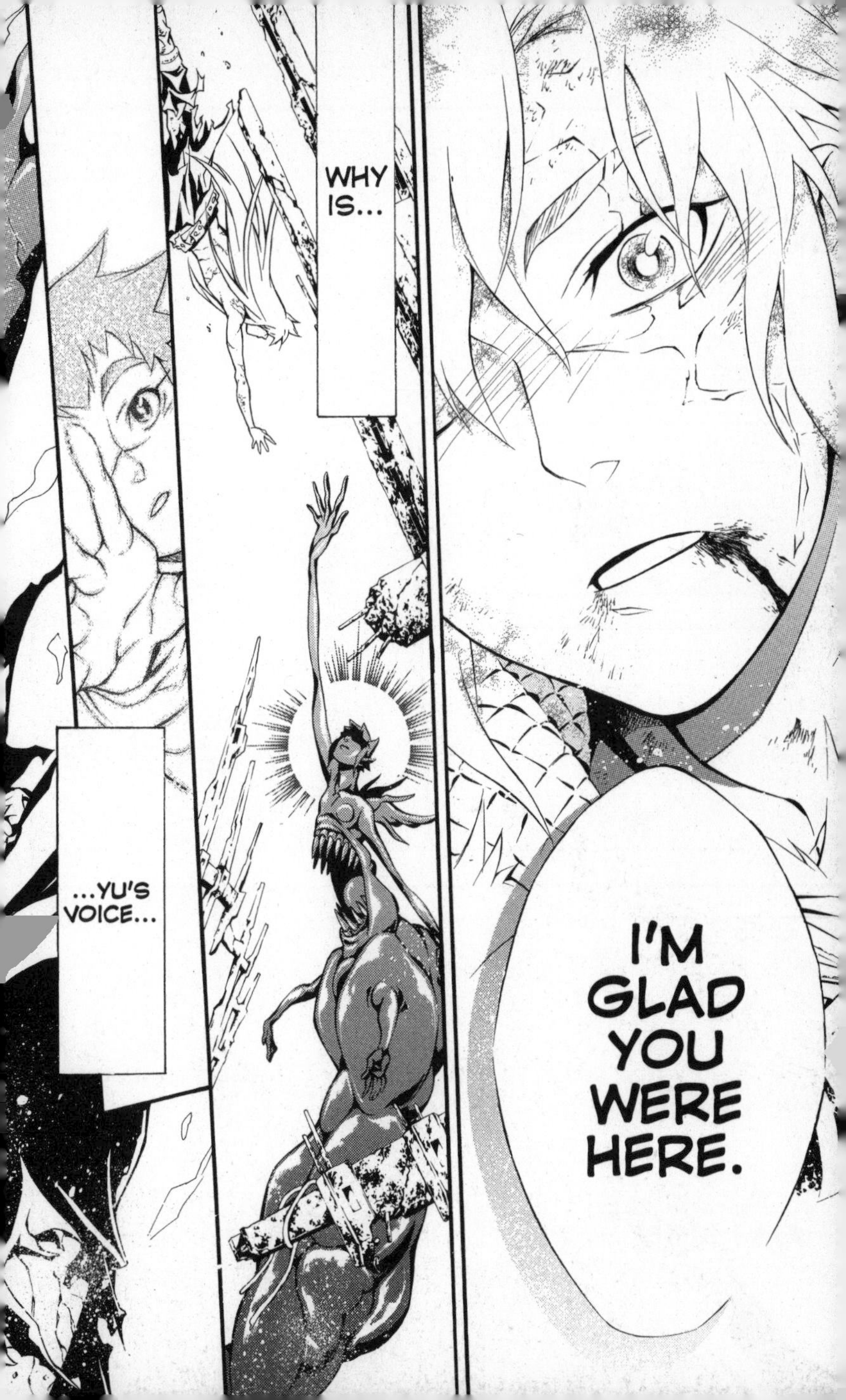
I'M GLAD YOU WERE HERE.
WHY IS...
...YU'S VOICE...

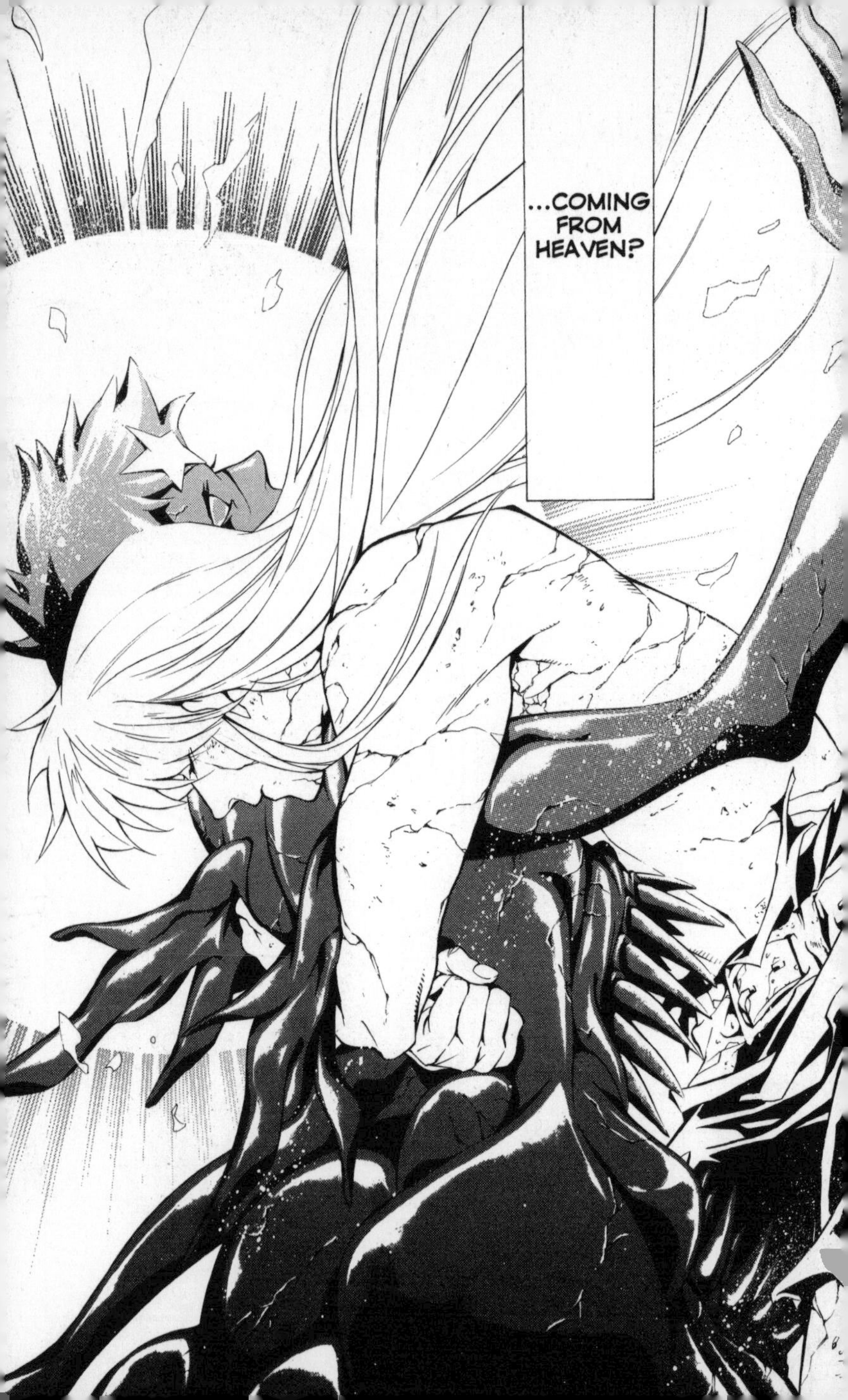
...COMING FROM HEAVEN?

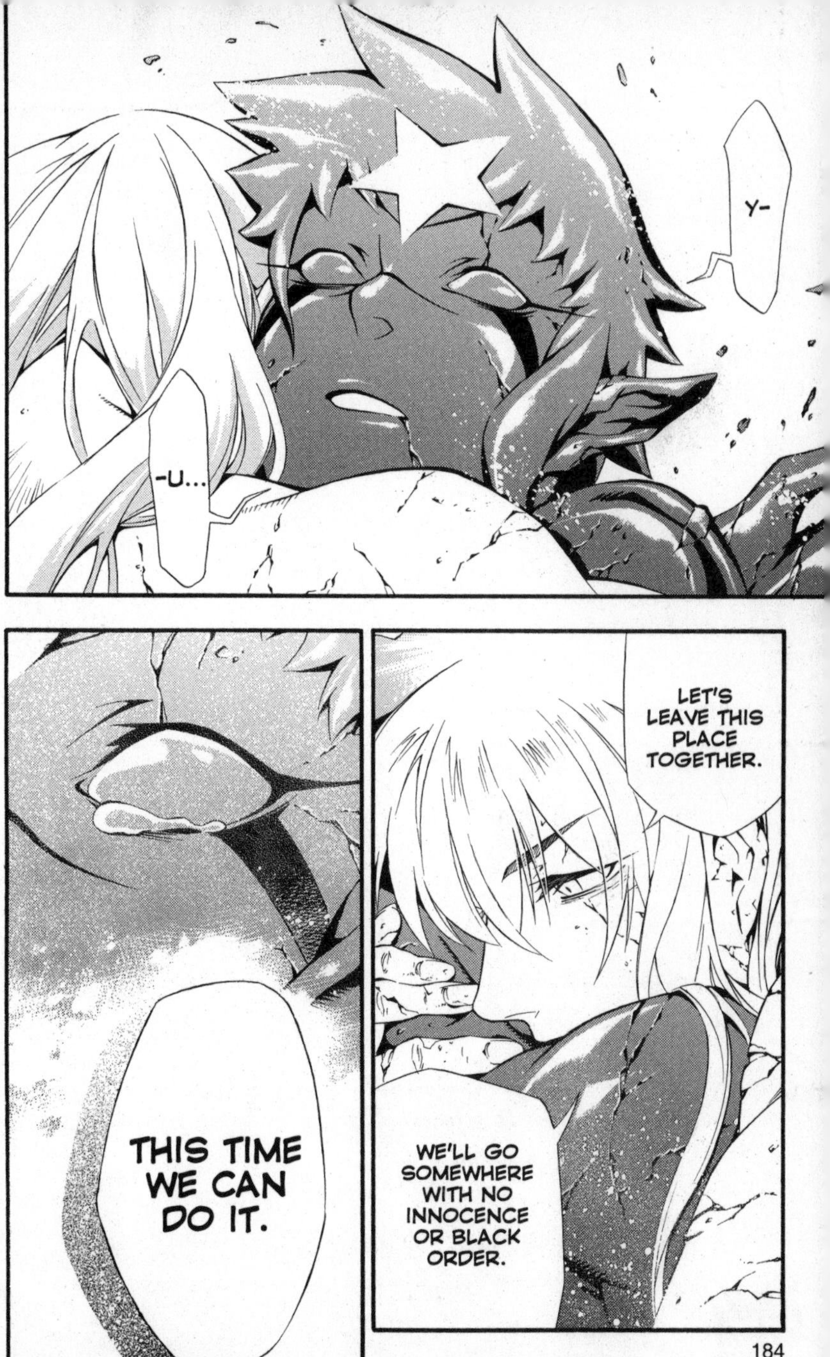
Y-
-U...
LET'S LEAVE THIS PLACE TOGETHER.
WE'LL GO SOMEWHERE WITH NO INNOCENCE OR BLACK ORDER.
THIS TIME WE CAN DO IT.

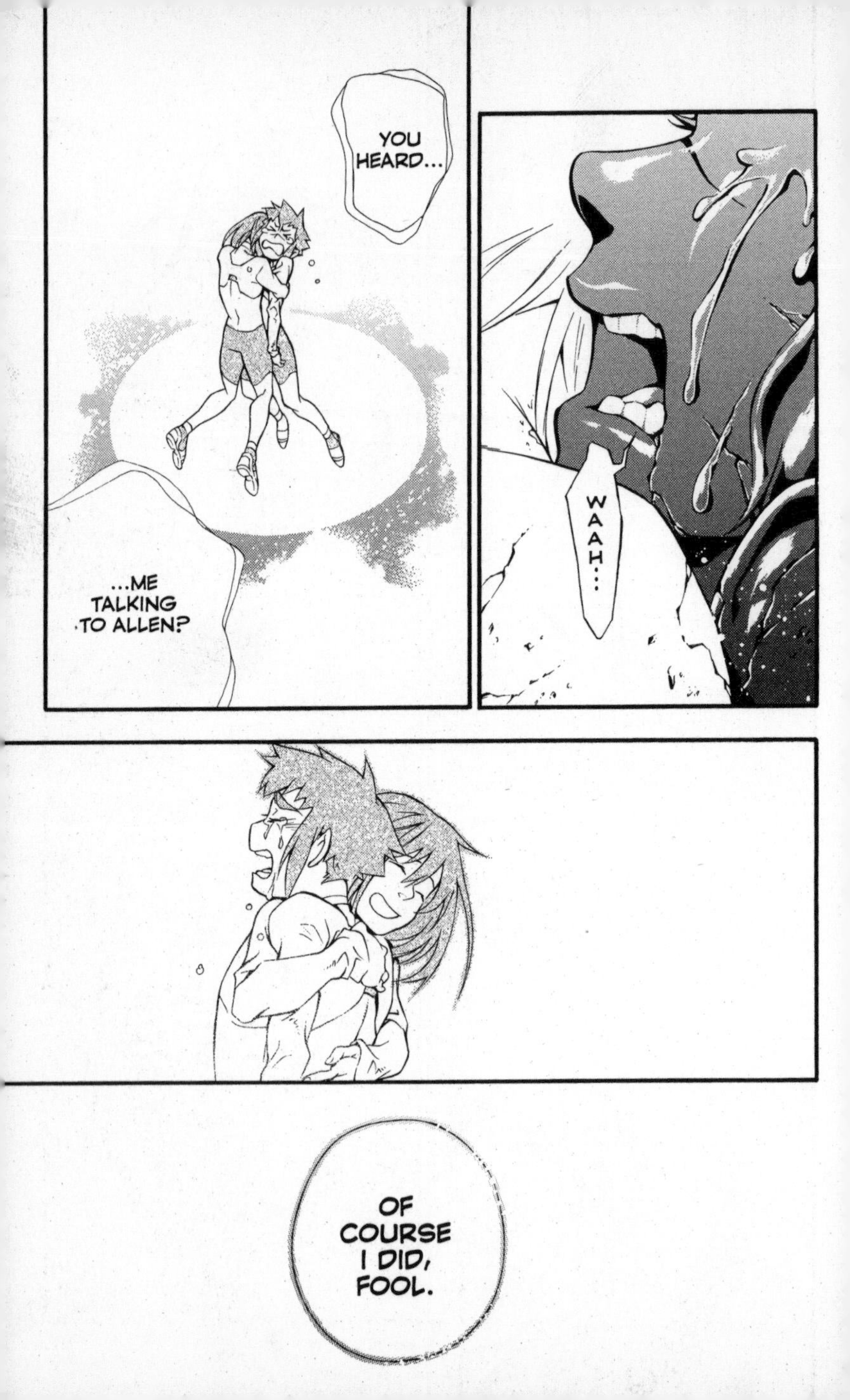
WAAH...
YOU HEARD...
...ME TALKING TO ALLEN?
OF COURSE I DID, FOOL.

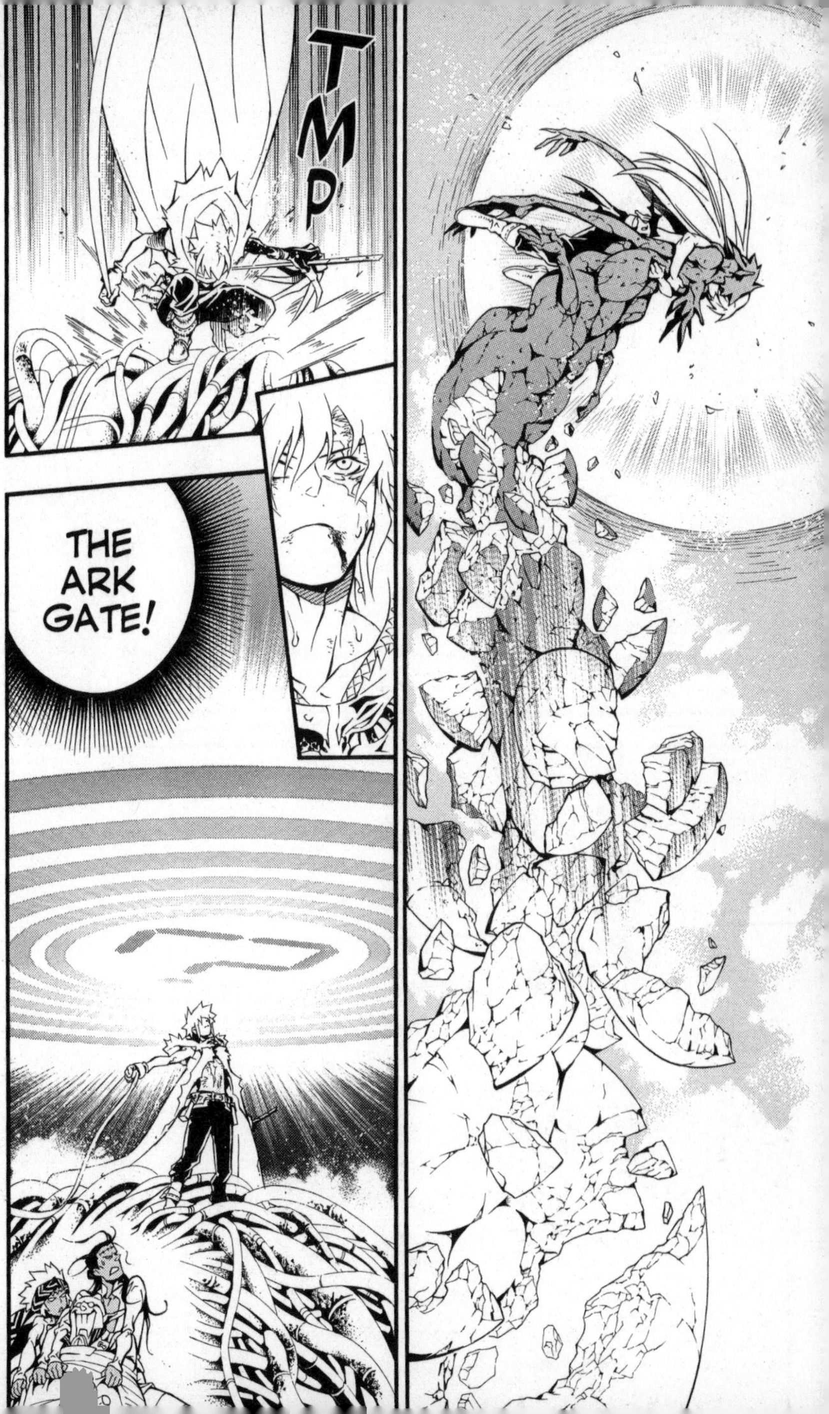
TMP
THE ARK GATE!

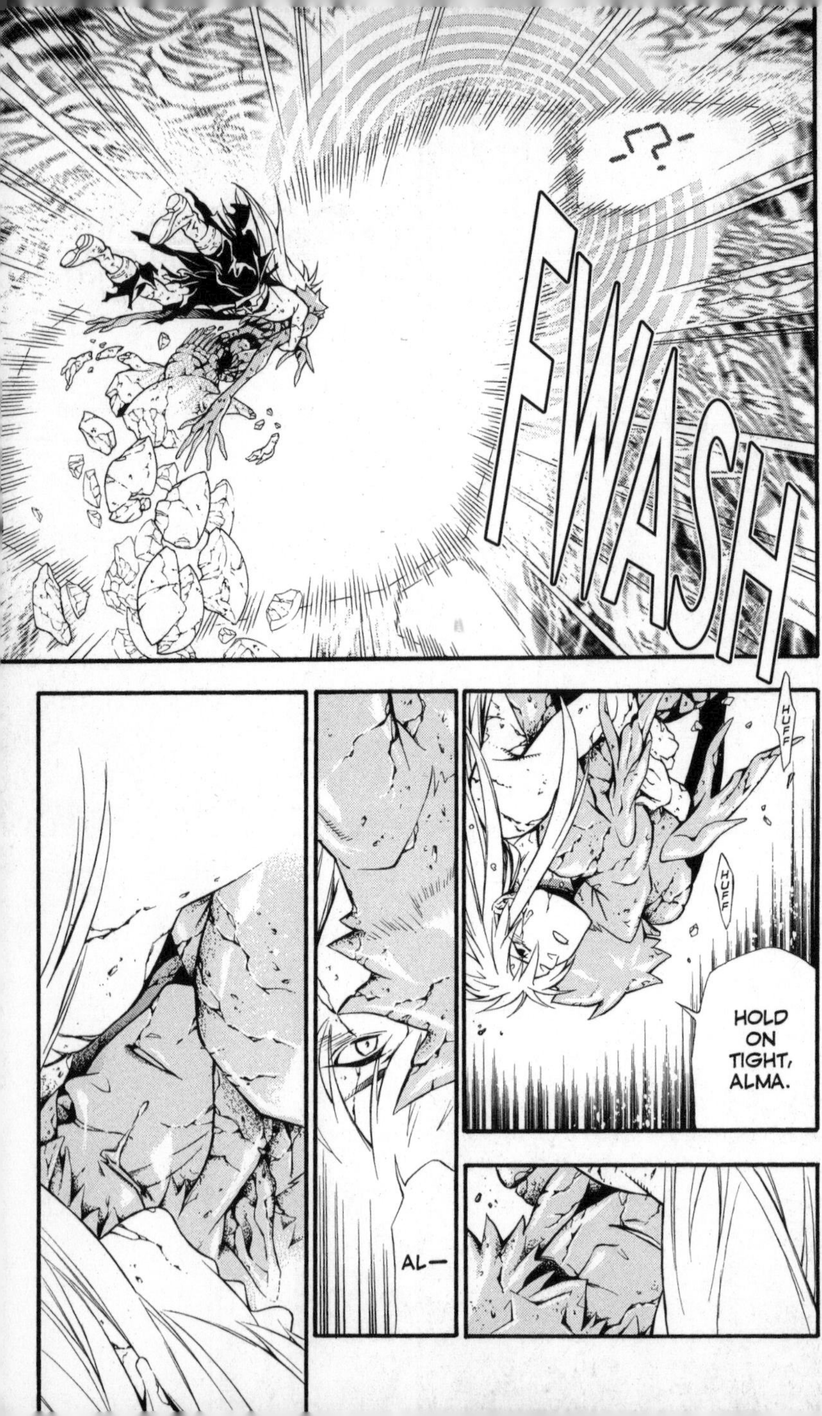
-?-
FWASH
HUFF
HUFF
HOLD ON TIGHT, ALMA.
AL—

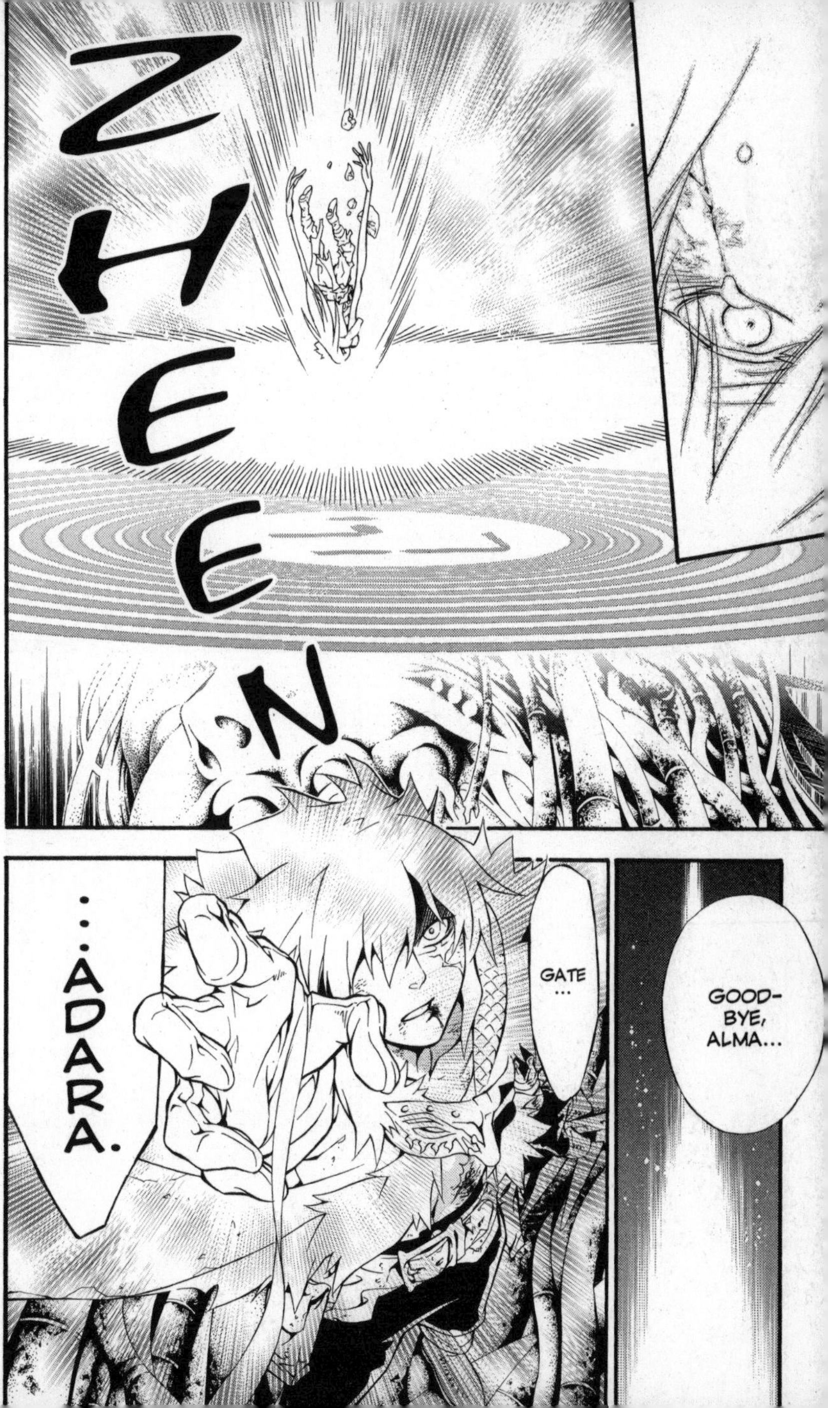
ZHEEEN
GOOD-BYE, ALMA...
GATE ...
...ADARA.

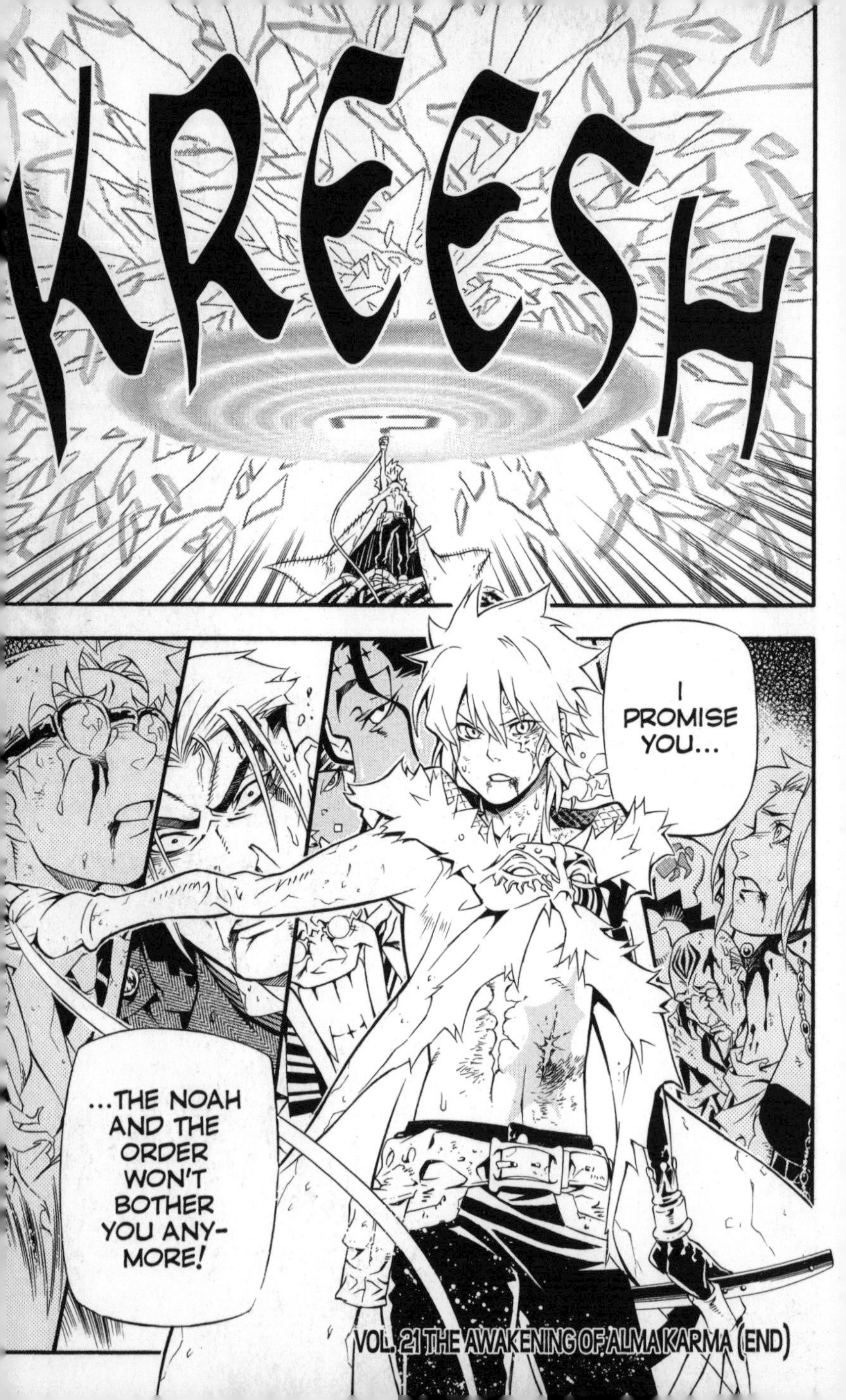
KREESH
I PROMISE YOU...
...THE NOAH AND THE ORDER WON'T BOTHER YOU ANY-MORE!
VOL. 21 THE AWAKENING OF ALMA KARMA (END)

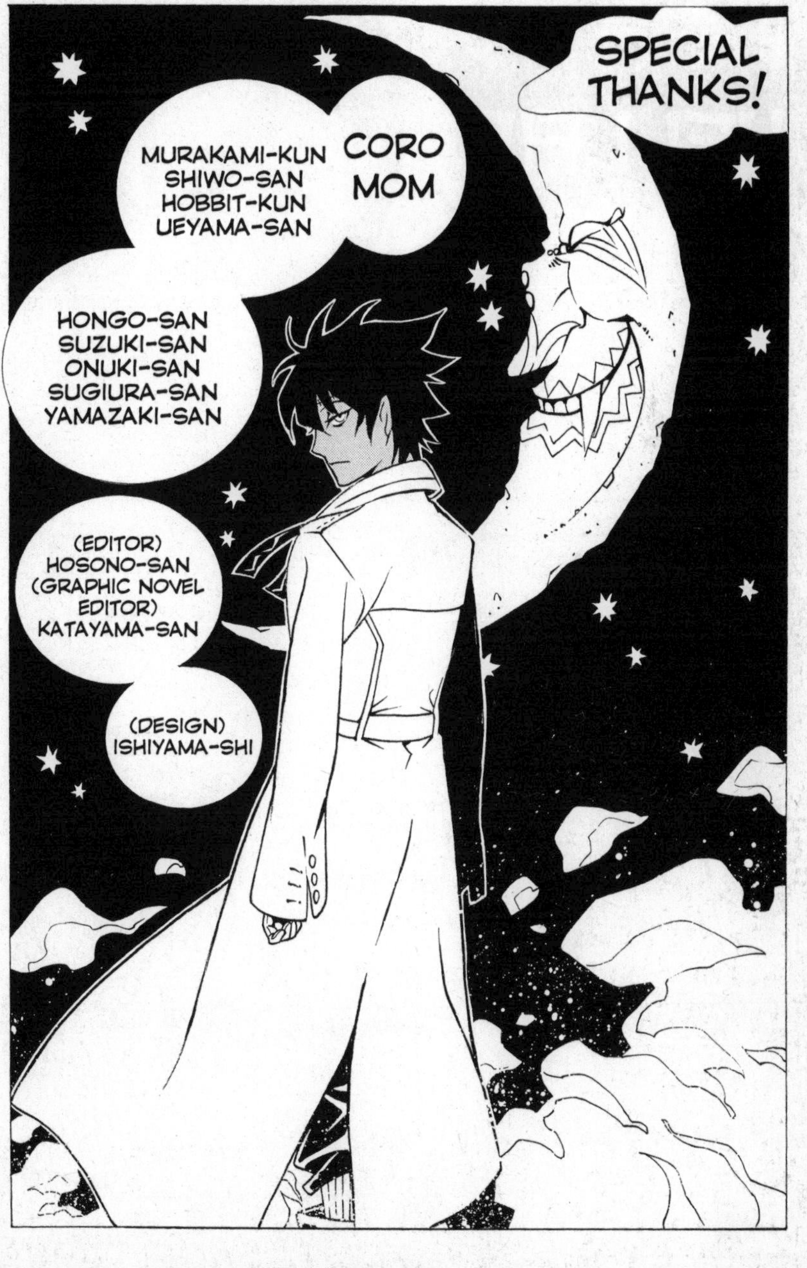
SPECIAL THANKS!
CORO MOM
MURAKAMI-KUN SHIWO-SAN HOBBIT-KUN UEYAMA-SAN
HONGO-SAN SUZUKI-SAN ONUKI-SAN SUGIURA-SAN YAMAZAKI-SAN
(EDITOR) HOSONO-SAN (GRAPHIC NOVEL EDITOR) KATAYAMA-SAN
(DESIGN) ISHIYAMA-SHI

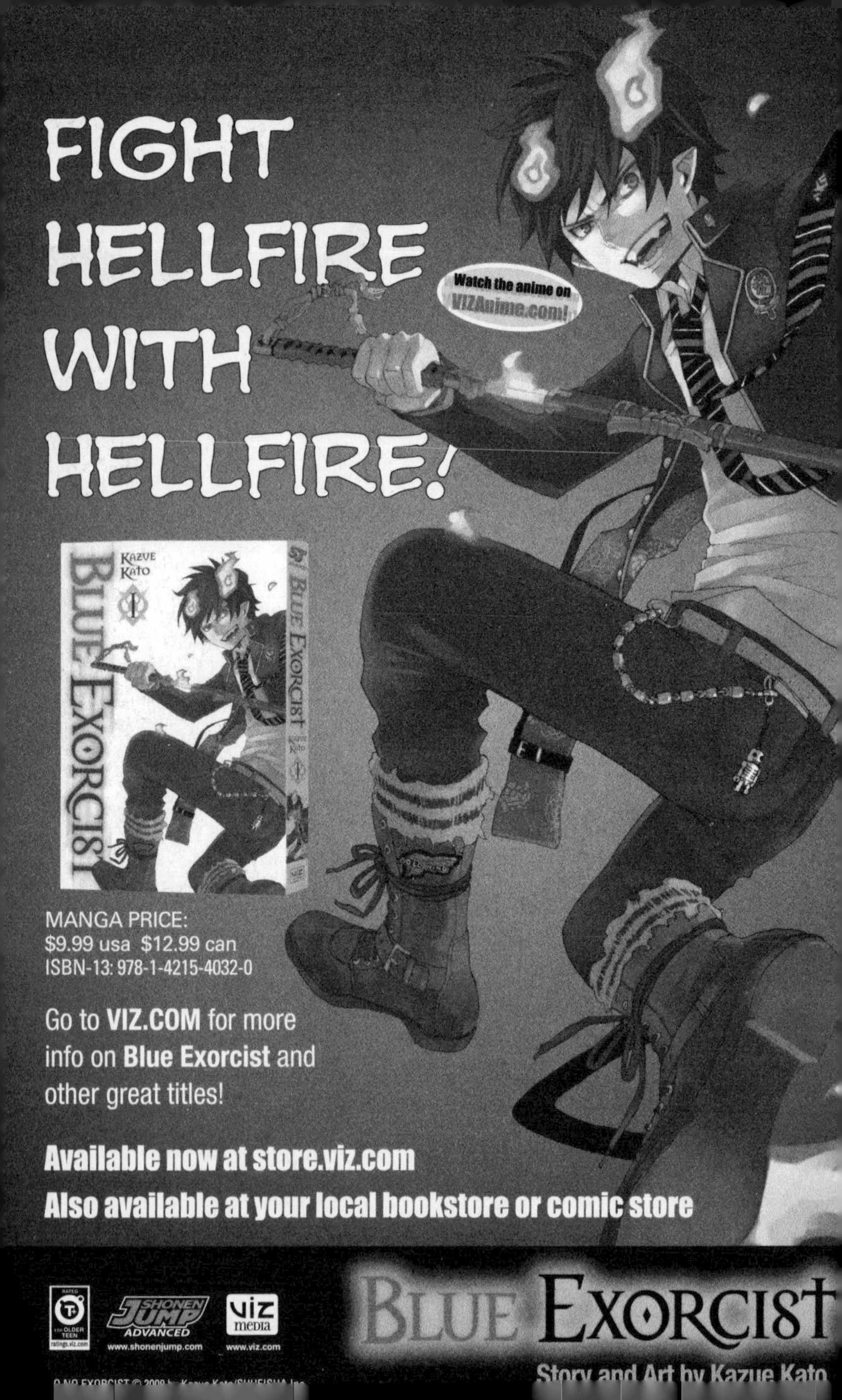

FIGHT HELLFIRE WITH HELLFIRE!
Watch the anime on VIZAnime.com!
Kazue Kato
Blue Exorcist
MANGA PRICE:
$9.99 usa $12.99 can
ISBN-13: 978-1-4215-4032-0
Go to VIZ.COM for more info on Blue Exorcist and other great titles!
Available now at store.viz.com
Also available at your local bookstore or comic store
RATED T+ FOR OLDER TEEN ratings.viz.com
SHONEN JUMP ADVANCED
www.shonenjump.com
viz media
www.viz.com
Blue Exorcist
Story and Art by Kazue Kato

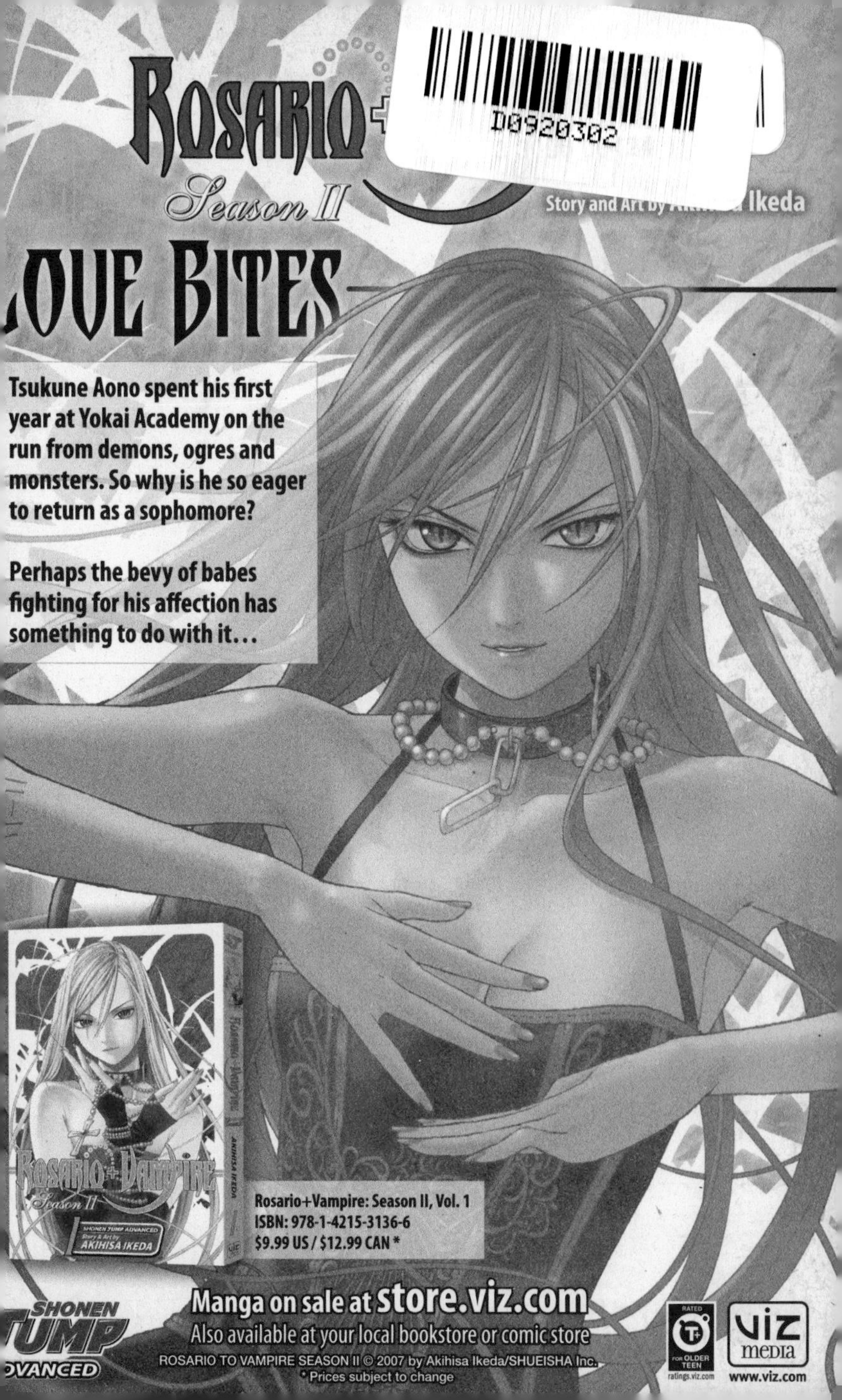
ROSARIO+
Season II
Story and Art by ... Ikeda
OVE BITES
Tsukune Aono spent his first year at Yokai Academy on the run from demons, ogres and monsters. So why is he so eager to return as a sophomore?
Perhaps the bevy of babes fighting for his affection has something to do with it...
Rosario+Vampire: Season II, Vol. 1
ISBN: 978-1-4215-3136-6
$9.99 US / $12.99 CAN *
SHONEN JUMP ADVANCED
Manga on sale at store.viz.com
Also available at your local bookstore or comic store
ROSARIO TO VAMPIRE SEASON II © 2007 by Akihisa Ikeda/SHUEISHA Inc.
* Prices subject to change
RATED T+ FOR OLDER TEEN
ratings.viz.com
VIZ media
www.viz.com